Contents

List of Maps

ACKNOWLEDGMENTS

We are truly grateful to everyone who gave us recommendations, anecdotes, and encouragement in this endeavor. We'd name them all but the list would be nearly as long as this book. We would especially like to thank our agent Lew Grimes; Lois Gerber at the Canadian Consulate in New York; Dick Griffith of Richard C. Griffith Associates in Chicago; Heather Chapman at Tourism Vancouver; Heather-Elayne Day at Tourism Victoria; Stephen Darling, former president of the Vancouver Hotel Association for his unfettered opinions; and Erica Spaberg and the editorial department at Macmillan Travel for all their efforts.

AN INVITATION TO THE READER

In researching this book, we discovered many wonderful places—hotels, restaurants, shops, and more. We're sure you'll find others. Please tell us about them, so we can share the information with your fellow travelers in upcoming editions. If you were disappointed with a recommendation, we'd love to know that, too. Please write to:

Anistatia R. Miller & Jared M. Brown
Frommer's Vancouver & Victoria, 3rd Edition
Macmillan Travel
1633 Broadway
New York, NY 10019

AN ADDITIONAL NOTE

Please be advised that travel information is subject to change at any time—and this is especially true of prices. We therefore suggest that you write or call ahead for confirmation when making your travel plans. The authors, editors, and publisher cannot be held responsible for the experiences of readers while traveling. Your safety is important to us, however, so we encourage you to stay alert and be aware of your surroundings. Keep a close eye on cameras, purses, and wallets, all favorite targets of thieves and pickpockets.

A WORD ABOUT PRICES

Unless stated otherwise, the prices in this guide are given in Canadian dollars, which is good news for U.S. travelers because the Canadian dollar is worth 25% less than the American dollar, but buys nearly as much. As we go to press, $1 Canadian is worth 75¢ U.S., which means that your $100-a-night hotel room will cost only U.S. $75 and your $6 breakfast will cost only U.S. $4.50 (plus taxes, which are substantial).

WHAT THE SYMBOLS MEAN

✪ Frommer's Favorites

Hotels, restaurants, attractions, and entertainment you should not miss.

⑤ Super-Special Values

Hotels and restaurants that offer great value for your money.

The following abbreviations are used for credit cards:

AE	American Express	EU	Eurocard
CB	Carte Blanche	JCB	Japan Credit Bank
DC	Diners Club	MC	MasterCard
DISC	Discover	V	Visa
ER	enRoute		

Introducing Vancouver & Victoria

1

Surrounded by snow-capped mountains to the north and east and nearly enveloped by placid tidal waters, Vancouver rests at the gateway to the majestically beautiful Canadian Pacific Northwest. Twenty years ago, Vancouverites considered themselves separate from the rest of Canada. As perennial beneficiaries of some of the finest, most temperate weather in the world (yes, it rains, but as they say, that's what makes it all so green), they pitied the residents of other provinces for having to put up with harsh winters, sweltering summers, and comparatively less natural beauty. The recent westward migration across Canada, however, has changed Vancouver's notions of exclusivity. Vancouverites nowadays *are* the rest of Canada—and a good part of the rest of the world as well.

While it is known as Canada's youngest major city, Vancouver has actually been inhabited for more than 5,000 years since nomads crossed over the land bridge from Asia. According to Coast Salish legend, the peaceful valley is guarded by twin mountain peaks that the Coast Salish people named the Two Sisters. The peaks are now called the Lions, after the lion statues guarding London's Trafalgar Square.

Ask a native-born Vancouverite about the city. He or she will tell you that it's kind of small (only a half million people live in the metropolitan area) and that not a lot goes on here. And, oh yeah, it rains a lot. (One local, afraid everyone would want to move here, asked us not to mention all the sunny days.)

But where else can you ski a world-class mountain, sailboard, rock climb, mountain bike, and kayak—all in the same day? (Not to mention find a Jacuzzi, a masseuse, and an all-night pharmacy to help you recover afterward.) It's impossible not to miss something when you're trying to list all of the sports Vancouverites enjoy: hiking, golf, tennis, swimming, in-line skating, fishing, sailing, horseback riding, curling, and cricket—to name just a few. If spectator sports are more your speed, Vancouver is home to the Canucks (NHL hockey), the Grizzlies (NBA basketball), the B. C. Lions (CFL football), and the

Vancouver: City of Lights

Looking at environmentally friendly Vancouver today, it's difficult to picture it covered with neon. But in the 1950s, Vancouver had the distinction of sporting more neon lights than any other city in the world. Brighter than Las Vegas, the city once used more power than Hong Kong. You can still see remnants of those bygone days around town: the neon waterfall that marks the downtown Hotel Niagara, the Ovaltine Café in Chinatown, and many other neon lights along suburban commercial strips such as Kingsway.

Vancouver Canadians (AAA Pacific League Baseball at a stadium that's right out of *Field of Dreams*). If you love the outdoors, shopping, fine dining, dancing, art, theater, or even beaches, Vancouver won't disappoint.

Victoria-born artist Emily Carr has been terribly misquoted by people who use the phrase "more British than the British" to describe Victoria, British Columbia's capital. Carr, a world-renowned painter of coastal First Nations life, was actually referring to her father's personality and gardening habits—not to the city. In fact, the Hudson's Bay Company, which helped to establish the city, was Scottish-owned. Writer Rudyard Kipling gave a better description. He instructed his readers to visualize Victoria by taking the best parts of Bournemouth, Torquay, the Isle of Wight, Hong Kong's Happy Valley, the Doon, Sorrento, and Camp's Bay; adding reminiscences of the Thousand Islands; and arranging it all around the Bay of Naples with some Himalayan peaks in the background.

Victoria is a small, quiet, seaport city on the southeastern tip of 300-mile-long Vancouver Island. Rich in a history filled with tales of whaling ships and fur traders, Victoria retains visible signs of its heritage in its buildings—from the landmark Empress Hotel and Parliament Buildings to Fan Tan Alley and the Chinese Settlement House.

Accessed only by ferry from Horseshoe Bay, Tsawwassen, or from nearby Seattle and Port Angeles or via its international airport, Victoria is also the step-off point to encounters with orcas (killer whales) and bald eagles; to deep-sea dives onto artificial reefs created by more than 2,000 hundred-year-old shipwrecks; and to rivers that run bright red in the early summer with salmon returning to spawn after their long journey from the sea.

1 Frommer's Favorite Vancouver & Victoria Experiences

- **Kayaking on False Creek:** Take a miniferry ride on the Aquabus to Granville Island and rent a sea kayak for a couple of hours. (See Chapter 6 for details.)
- **Traversing the Stanley Park Seawall:** Walk, bike, or in-line skate the six-mile seawall around Stanley Park promontory in Vancouver. (See Chapter 6 for details.)
- **Savoring Dim Sum:** Go for dim sum in Chinatown; eat amid the clatter at Park Lock, one of Vancouver's best Chinese restaurants. (See Chapter 5 for details.)
- **Sauntering Through Queen Elizabeth Park:** Stroll the sunken flower garden, formerly a quarry—an exquisitely beautiful testament to Vancouver's urban recovery. (See Chapter 6 for details.)

Southwestern British Columbia

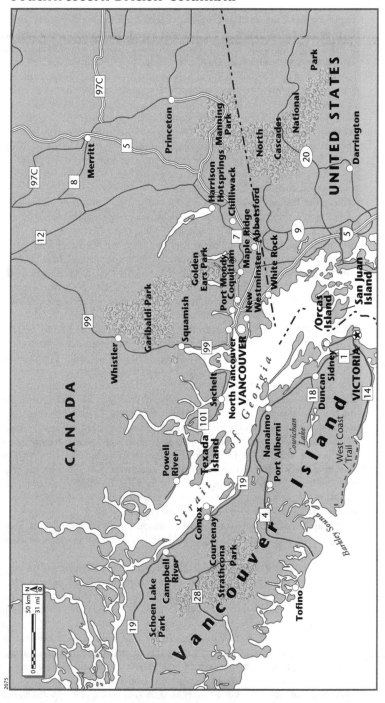

- **Exploring the Museum of Anthropology:** Admire the totem poles and other First Nations art at UBC's Museum of Anthropology in Vancouver; then hike down the cliff trail to the Point Grey beaches below. (See Chapter 6 for details.)

- **Fitting Six Sports into One Day:** Take advantage of the opportunity to do six sports. Few people have figured out how to load a car with skis, bikes, climbing gear, kayaks, in-line skates, and sailboards. If you can manage that, you've overcome the toughest obstacle. (Don't worry, the equipment is available for rent in both cities; you don't have to bring your own.) (See Chapters 6 and 13 for details.)

- **Kicking Back in Robson Square:** Relax for a moment by the three-tiered waterfall emanating from the provincial law courts in Robson Square in Vancouver. Watch out for the low-flying residents coming in for a landing, though. They're not pigeons but a pair of brant geese (Canada geese) that nest in this modern glass-and-steel structure. (See Chapter 6 for details.)

- **Hiking the Baden-Powell Trail:** Get out your hiking boots, map, and compass and tackle a segment of the famous 26-mile Baden-Powell trail that winds through North and West Vancouver. (See Chapter 6 for details.)

- **Star-gazing in Hollywood North:** Audition for a bit part in a production in Vancouver, nicknamed "Hollywood North." Check with the B.C. Film Commission for details, and who knows? Michael J. Fox, Richard Dean Anderson, and Raymond Burr all got their start here. Yvonne DeCarlo (TV's Mrs. Herman Munster) began as a Vancouver usher. You might turn out to be the city's next big discovery. (See Chapter 6 for details.)

- **Diving Amid Underwater Interpretive Trails:** To the delight of divers, there are 2,000 (no, that's not a misprint) shipwrecks in the waters around Vancouver and Victoria. Interpretive trails guide you along the underwater path. The Cousteau Society rates it as one of the best dive sites in the world (second only to the Red Sea). (See Chapters 6 and 13 for details.)

- **Biking to Butchart Gardens:** Rent a couple of bikes and take a scenic drive up the beach-lined coast from Victoria to Butchart Gardens. There are easy side roads so you don't have to go near the highway. If it's raining, head to Crystal Garden in Victoria; it's a jungle in there, with a menagerie that includes flamingos and bush babies. (See Chapter 13 for details.)

- **Posing at the World's Narrowest Building and Street:** Have your picture taken next to the world's narrowest building—the Sam Kee Building—in Vancouver's Chinatown or walk through one of the world's narrowest streets—Fan Tan Alley—in Victoria's Chinatown. (See Chapter 7 for details.)

- **Watching Orcas:** Sign up for a killer-whale watching expedition in Victoria. You'll also get the chance to see bald eagles and harbor seals along the way. (See Chapter 13 for details.)

- **Flying High Over Vancouver:** Take a floatplane tour of Vancouver and the north shore. Or, if you don't like flying, go to Cloud 9 at the top of the Landmark Hotel in Vancouver for a late-evening drink or coffee and for a terrific view of the city in lights; on a clear day, take the SkyRide up to the top of Grouse Mountain in West Vancouver. (See Chapter 6 for details.)

- **Discovering Wildlife in the City:** Get a bag of wild birdseed and some peanuts. Then head out to Stanley Park in Vancouver, where you'll meet ducks, swans, brant geese, squirrels, raccoons, beavers, and (very rarely) skunks along the lagoon and trails leading to Beaver Lake. (See Chapter 6 and 7 for details.)

- **Throwing Stones:** If it's wintertime, try your hand at curling. Pick-up matches are arranged throughout the city by Curl B.C., ☎ 604/737-3040. (See Chapter 6 for details.)

2 The Cities Today

In addition to having one of the most beautiful settings in the world amid mountains, parks, wildlife, marine life, and minimal pollution, Vancouver's greatest asset is its people. Canadians are known for their congeniality; Vancouverites doubly so. There's a uniquely relaxed feeling here—people are casual, outgoing, fun loving, and permissive (some might even say hedonistic). But when you're at the center of so many urban diversions and surrounded by so much natural beauty, there's no point in fighting the urge to have fun.

This city's inhabitants consume more wine than San Franciscans or residents of any other North American metropolis. And it's no wonder—therecent revitalization of the British Columbian wine industry has made regional wines into award-winning, world-class potables.

Where to dine in Vancouver can be a serious, thought-provoking dilemma. There are more than 2,000 restaurants serving every style of cuisine imaginable. Seafood and fare native to the Pacific Northwest are the most popular with locals, who demand fresh, locally grown produce, meat, and fish. Spotted prawns, Dungeness crabs, halibut, ling cod, and numerous varieties of salmon are just a few of the gifts from the sea served up at local restaurants. If you've never tasted lean, delicately spiced venison sausages, had a buffalo burger, or savored hearty caribou stew, then you're in for a few treats. On the other hand, if your taste buds crave classic French, Italian, or Chinese cuisine, don't fret. Great four-star spots and casual hideaways are ready to prepare the finest meal you've ever encountered and present it with impeccable service.

A First Nations legend says that life began here when the Raven flew down from the heavens thousands of years ago, when the earth was covered in snow. He made rivers, oceans, thick green forests, and many animals to roam through them. Then he found a clam shell on a sandy beach. He opened it and coaxed its inhabitants—five men—out of their dark prison into the land he created, promising them peace, harmony, and prosperity.

Despite a rich, and often overlooked, history, Vancouver is a young, rapidly expanding city. Growth is evident everywhere you turn. The influx of foreign money—especially from Hong Kong—has refueled Vancouver's perennial construction boom. New buildings are springing up all over town.

Dateline

- **3000 B.C.** Coast Salish people establish villages on the Burrard Inlet and Fraser River delta's shores.
- **A.D. 1790** The Songhees Coast Salish people find explorer Manual Quimper claiming their land as Spanish territory on Albert Head beach.
- **1791** Navigator José María Narvaez sails into the Burrard Inlet but doesn't explore the inner harbor.
- **1792** Capt. George Vancouver charts the Burrard Inlet after running into Spanish explorer Dionisio Alcala Galiano; Vancouver claims the land as British territory on his search for the Northwest Passage.
- **1808** North West Company fur trader Simon Fraser survives the Hell's Gate rapids and lands on the Fraser River delta's shores via what he thinks is the Columbia River. The waterway is later named after him.
- **1827** The Hudson's Bay Company establishes Fort Langley as a fur-trading post.
- **1842** Hudson's Bay Company Chief Factor James Douglas selects Camosack as the company's new depot site. He builds Fort Victoria there the next year.
- **1846** The Oregon Treaty sets the 49th parallel as the U.S.-Canadian boundary line.
- **1849** The British Crown grants the Hudson's Bay Company rights to Vancouver Island with

continues

the stipulation that it must establish colonial settlements within five years.

- **1858** Some 30,000 gold rushers flood in from the United States to mine the Fraser River valley and Vancouver Island. To prevent the southern invaders from claiming possession, the British Crown claims British Columbia as an official colony.
- **1859** Coal is discovered on Coal Harbour's shores by a British survey ship. The Fraser River town of New Westminster becomes the colonial capital.
- **1862** Three unsuccessful British gold rushers acquire 500 acres of land for $1 an acre to start a brickworks, which fails. This area is now known as the West End.
- Victoria is incorporated. Its first gas lights are installed over local pubs; the first "bride ship" carrying 61 young hopeful women arrives in the Inner Harbour met by hundreds of gold rushers, fur traders, and sailors.
- **1866** The colonies of British Columbia and Vancouver Island are united; New Westminster remains the capital.
- **1868** Victoria becomes the provincial capital.
- **1869** The town that grew up around Gassy Jack's Globe Saloon (affectionately called Gastown) is incorporated as the town of Granville.
- **1871** British Columbia enters the Confederation and becomes a Canadian province.

continues

One native returning after five years overseas was even more wide-eyed than the dozen tourists on the bus from the airport. "Amazing, amazing!" she kept repeating to herself. In 1995, Vancouver was ranked second only behind Geneva out of 118 worldwide cities for "quality of life." (Perhaps the surveyors were biased; they were from Geneva.)

This is where Hollywood glitter and Canadian natural beauty meet and coexist. Vancouver is Katherine Hepburn's favorite city, her escape from Hollywood life. Victoria was John Wayne's hideaway and the favorite vacation spot of budding actors Richard and Patricia Nixon. (The Nixons met on a Hollywood film set and honeymooned in Victoria.)

Vancouver is often referred to as "Hollywood North." What Hollywood is to the U.S. film production industry, Vancouver is to both U.S. and Canadian TV and movie producers—only without the smog and crime. *The X-Files, Highlander, The Commish,* and *The Outer Limits* are all in regular production here. In the past three years, Vancouver, Victoria, and their surroundings have served as backdrops for several films. On any given day, you'll find telltale signs of activity—dressing room trailers lined up along the street and catering tables surrounded by actors and extras taking a quick break from the action.

After a few days of wandering along city streets, sandy beaches, and thickly forested paths and exploring the cities' natural and human-made wonders, you'll know why Vancouver and Victoria locals tell outsiders that their cities are kind of small and that it rains a lot: They want to keep them all to themselves.

3   A Look at the Past

The Coast Salish people lived in this southwestern temperate rain forest region for more than 5,000 years. Their culture, steeped in tales about the world and the animals around them, evolved into a sophisticated society that used the *potlatch* ceremony as the centerpiece of social order. The village chief would invite an entire neighboring village for a feast that would last for a full moon cycle (about 28 days). Daily banquets, ceremonial myth dances, and generous gift giving were planned for weeks, even months, before the guests' arrival, and no guest left hungry or empty handed. The potlatch settled disputes and quelled any desire to seize possessions amongst the people, thereby creating a harmonious existence along the coast.

It wasn't until the 1790s that Spanish explorers in search of new trade routes and gold arrived on these temperate shores, claiming the land in the name of the king of Spain. Their explorations ceased when, in 1792, Capt. George Vancouver, after encountering Spanish explorer Dionisio Alcala Galiano, charted the Burrard Inlet and claimed the land as British territory on his search for the Northwest Passage.

A decade later, hearing stories about the abundance of whales, seals, otters, beavers, salmon, and lumber in this "new territory," such trading companies as the North West Company and the Hudson's Bay Company established fur-trading posts along the Fraser River and on Vancouver Island with the blessing of the British Crown. White settlers began building towns around these centers of commerce. By 1846, an agreement between the United States and Canada—the Oregon Treaty—set the 49th parallel as the boundary line between the two countries.

Just as the California Gold Rush fizzled out, gold was discovered in British Columbia's lower Fraser River valley and later in the Cariboo country. By 1865, this rush was over, but the thousands of settlers who came in search of riches in the region remained and built homes. To prevent more southern invaders from claiming possession, the British Crown officially colonized British Columbia with Victoria as its capital.

Some attribute the birth of Vancouver as we know it to a retired Yorkshire steamboat pilot named "Gassy" Jack Deighton. In 1867, Gassy Jack (so nicknamed for his loquaciousness) offered the locals all the whiskey they could drink if they helped him build a saloon near Hastings Mill. (Legend has it they built the Globe Saloon in one day.) Two years later, the lumber and coal town that grew up around Gassy Jack's saloon (affectionately called Gastown) was incorporated as the town of Granville. Much to the horror of officials in the neighboring town of Port Moody, 16 miles to the east, the Canadian-Pacific Railway decided to build its transcontinental terminus in the 1880s at Granville (which they renamed Vancouver).

- **1885** Much to the horror of Port Moody officials, the Canadian Pacific Railway decides to build its transcontinental terminus at Granville (which they rename Vancouver).
- **1886** The city of Granville is consumed by fire on June 13 in less than one hour. Meeting in a camp tent, the first Vancouver city council draws up the city charter.
- **1887** A Canadian-Pacific Railway steam train completes its maiden coast-to-coast voyage when it arrives in Vancouver.
- Victoria's first interchange telephone switchboard is installed.
- **1893** The Hudson's Bay Company replaces its fur trading post with its first department store, located at the corner of Granville and Georgia streets in Vancouver.
- **1903** The Victoria Terminal Railway and Ferry Company begin ferry service between Sidney and Tsawwassen, that is linked to its Sidney-Victoria rail service.
- **1905** The Canadian-Pacific Railway begins construction of Victoria's Empress Hotel.
- **1908** The University of British Columbia is founded and a campus is established on Point Grey.
- **1912** Vancouver's first reinforced concrete structure, the Hotel Europe, opens as a luxury, fire-proof hotel.
- **1932** The *City of Angels* ferry completes its maiden voyage from Sidney to Anacortes, Washington.
- **1936** Vancouver's permanent City Hall is completed, and

continues

offices are moved from their East Hastings street location.

- **1938** Built on land owned by the Guinness Brewing Company, Lions Gate Bridge opens, linking Vancouver to the north shore.
- **1939** A decade after construction is suspended during the Great Depression, the Canadian-Pacific's third Hotel Vancouver opens its doors.
- **1963** Victoria College becomes the University of Victoria.
- **1965** Designed by Arthur Erikson with the best southern view of metropolitan Vancouver, Simon Fraser University opens its academic doors.
- **1970** The Vancouver Canucks play their first National Hockey League game.
- **1977** The SeaBus commuter catamaran-ferry service begins regular shuttle runs between North Vancouver's Lonsdale Quay and downtown Vancouver.
- **1986** Vancouver celebrates its centennial by hosting Expo '86.
- **1992** Vancouver celebrates the bicentennial of Captain Vancouver's arrival at the Burrard Inlet.
- **1994** Victoria hosts the 15th Commonwealth Games, featuring an international array of athletes.
- **1995** Vancouver adds the new Vancouver Grizzlies basketball team to its roster of professional sports teams.

Fire consumed Granville in less than one hour the year before the railway was completed. The next day, the first Vancouver city council held a meeting and drew up the city charter in a camp tent that served as city hall, and hopeful citizens rebuilt their town.

The influence of the Hudson's Bay Company and the Canadian-Pacific Railway continued as the region grew. They built hotels and department stores and convinced other investors to bring in telephones and ferry services to link British Columbia to the rest of the world. The completion of the Panama Canal in 1915 made British Columbia a giant in grain and lumber exportation, with Vancouver and Victoria as its principal ports. Two sandbars in False Creek were joined by landfill to create an industrial park named Granville Island. Cheap rents and access to railway and shipping facilities attracted more new business. The province's population doubled, as did its share of coal and cement millionaires.

There was a lull between the two World Wars, when the area succumbed to the ravages of the Great Depression; work halted on the construction of new buildings, and industry fell into a severe decline. But development moved forward again when the need for raw materials to support the war effort brought the area back to life as an industrial center and critical military operations base.

The demand for wood pulp products kept the region going for decades after the Second World War, but despite its natural beauty, only a few travelers made their way to Vancouver and Victoria to bask in the temperate climate. Eventually, word got out, and tourism caught on.

Vancouver celebrated its 100th birthday in 1986 by hosting the five-month-long Expo '86 (a world's fair whose main theme was transportation). In honor of the event, the SkyTrain light-rail rapid-transit system and Canada Place cruise-ship terminal were constructed to welcome the millions of visitors who now flock to the city annually. The region continues to grow as a large influx of eastern Canadians escaping cold winters and unbearably hot summers and wealthy Hong Kong investors develop new business in this naturally rich setting.

4 The Arts

True British Columbian art is that of the indigenous coastal peoples. Today, contemporary Native and non-Native artists have adapted their totemic designs to silver jewelry, wood and jade carvings, paintings and drawings, ceramics and more traditional basketry. Galleries specializing in First Nations art are found throughout the province, including Water Street in Vancouver's Gastown and Government Street in downtown Victoria. Don't miss Haida artist Bill Reid's classic cedar sculpture *Raven and the First Men* in the University of British Columbia's Museum of Anthropology.

Emily Carr, a native of Victoria, is B.C.'s single most famous artist. Especially well-known for her sketches and almost mystical paintings of coastal rainforests and First Nations culture, Carr turned to writing later in life. By the time of her death in 1945 at the age of 74, she had produced six incisive autobiographical books. The Emily Carr Room in the Vancouver Art Gallery houses 157 paintings and drawings she bequeathed to the people of British Columbia. The Emily Carr College of Art and Design on Vancouver's Granville Island carries on the work she began as a teacher. More of her art is on display at her longtime home in Victoria and at the Emily Carr Gallery.

Today's B.C. artists are as likely to be working in fabrics or ceramics as on canvas. A large number of artists have studios on Granville Island; many more are scattered widely through both communities. Notable are Robert Davidson and his wife, Dorothy Grant, who draw upon Haida life and culture in their paper and print work. Of particular interest are their silk-screened prints and stylish clothing.

A large writers' community is also thriving in British Columbia. Perhaps the province's most successful commercial writer is W.P. Kinsella, a resident of White Rock on the U.S. border. Author of 18 books, Kinsella gained recognition so slowly that at first he had to support himself by managing a pizza joint and driving a taxi in Victoria. It wasn't until 1988 that his luck changed. In that year, his baseball novel *Shoeless Joe* (Ballantine) was turned into the successful movie *Field of Dreams* starring Kevin Costner. But science fiction writer and Vancouver area resident William Gibson, whose *Neuromancer* (Berkley Books) and *Mona Lisa Overdrive* (Bantam Doubleday Dell) have carved out the new subgenre of cyberpunk fiction, may now be just as successful. One of his recent novels, *Johnny Mnemonic* (Berkley Books), was recently made into a major motion picture and his controversial media pieces, including *Agrippa*, are drawing notice. Douglas Copeland, author of *Generation X* (St. Martin's Press), also lives nearby as does Nick Bantock, creator of the much-loved *Griffin and Sabine* trilogy (Chronicle Books).

2 Planning a Trip to Vancouver & Victoria

It's a good idea to prepare for any trip—whether it's a quick weekend away or a two-week expedition. Here are some tips to help you plan a safe, easy-going trip to the Pacific Northwest no matter how you travel.

1 Visitor Information & Entry Requirements

VISITOR INFORMATION

You can get Canadian tourism information at the Canadian consulate office in most major American cities. The provincial and municipal Canadian tourism boards are also great sources of travel information. They publish numerous booklets outlining marine, wilderness, riding, and other types of vacation adventures. Contact **Tourism British Columbia,** 865 Hornby St., 8th Floor, Vancouver (☎ 604/685-0032 or 800/663-6000) for information about travel throughout the province.

Tourism Vancouver's Vancouver Travel InfoCentre, 200 Burrard St., Vancouver (☎ 604/683-2000) and **Tourism Victoria,** 710-1175 Douglas St., Victoria (☎ 604/382-2160 or 800/663-3883), can help you with everything from booking accommodations to making suggestions for what to see and do.

If you're planning to spend time outside the cities, you should also check with the **Tourism Association of Southwestern British Columbia,** 204-1755 W. Broadway, Vancouver (☎ 604/739-9011) and the **Tourism Association of Vancouver Island,** 302-45 Bastion Sq., Victoria (☎ 604/382-3551).

Surfing the internet for British Columbian travel information is also a good way to access an up-to-date source. We found numerous postings with recommendations and information about what conditions are really like for mountain biking and skiing and what the locals do to get tickets for special events, for example. Just log on and search the keyword *travel.* You'll also find a lot of background information in the same forum if you would really like to delve into your destination. You can also surf through the gophers in the internet forum. UBC and the University of Manitoba have "ftp" sites with travel information (but these are not as comprehensive). **CompuServe** also has a travel forum that lists travel updates and background material. On the **World Wide Web** you can also find valuable Whistler/Blackcomb snow reports during the ski season.

ENTRY REQUIREMENTS

If you are driving from Seattle, you'll being clearing U.S. Customs at the Peace Arch Station (open 24 hours a day). You'll be passing through both U.S. and Canadian checkpoints here, a few hundred yards apart. If you are flying directly into Vancouver International Airport from another country, you will be clearing Customs on Level 2. Once you get through passport control, you and your luggage will go through Customs before you leave the terminal. (Customs officials will randomly select a few arriving people and search their luggage. Cooperating with them ensures that it's a quick process.)

DOCUMENTS FOR U.S. CITIZENS   Citizens or permanent U.S. residents do not require visas to enter Canada, but they do need to show proof of citizenship and residence; a passport or birth certificate plus a driver's license is sufficient in this regard. Naturalized citizens should carry their naturalization certificate.

Permanent U.S. residents should carry their passport and Resident Alien Card (U.S. form I-151 or I-551); foreign students and other U.S. residents should carry their passport or Temporary Resident Card (form 1688) or Employment Authorization Card (1688A or 1688B); a visitor's visa; I-94 Arrival-Departure Record; a current I-20 copy of IAP-66 indicating student status; proof of sufficient funds for a temporary stay; and evidence of return transportation. In either case, you should check with the Canadian Consulate before departure to see if you will also need a visitor's visa.

If you are bringing children into Canada, you must have proof of legal guardianship. This can cause long delays at the border if you forget. If you are under 18 years old and not accompanied by a parent or guardian, you should bring a permission letter signed by your parent or legal guardian allowing you to travel to Canada.

DOCUMENTS FOR COMMONWEALTH CITIZENS   British, Australian, New Zealand, and Northern Irish citizens do not require visas to enter into Canada, but they do need to show proof of commonwealth citizenship and residence—a passport plus a driver's license. Naturalized citizens should carry their naturalization certificate. Permanent residents should carry their passport and resident status card; foreign students and other residents should carry their passport or temporary resident card or employment authorization card; a visitor's visa; arrival-departure record; a current copy of student status; proof of sufficient funds for a temporary stay; and evidence of return transportation. You should check with the Canadian Consulate before departure to see if you will also need a visitor's visa.

CUSTOMS REGULATIONS   Your personal baggage can include the following: boats, motors, snowmobiles, camping and sports equipment, appliances, TV sets, musical instruments, personal computers, cameras, and other items of a personal or household nature (ours did!). But be sure to bring a detailed inventory list with you that includes the date acquired, serial number, and cost or replacement value of each item. It sounds tedious, but it can really speed things up at the border. Customs will help you fill in the forms that allow you to temporarily bring in your effects. This list will also be used to check off what you bring out. You will be charged customs duties for anything left in Canada.

Here are a few other things to keep in mind:

• Don't bring in any more than $10,000 in U.S. cash. If you do, you will have to file a transaction report with U.S. Customs.

- Don't joke about carrying explosives, drugs, or other contraband unless you want to have your bags and person searched in detail plus face arrest for conspiracy. Besides, they'll kick you out on your ear. Customs does regularly refuse entry to undesirable Americans. Remember, Canada is a foreign country. They don't have to let you in.
- Some prescription medicines may be considered contraband across the border. If you are bringing any, it's best to check with your doctor and bring a copy of your prescription.
- If you are over the age of 18, you are allowed to bring in 40 ounces of liquor and wine or 24 12-ounce cans or bottles of beer and ale; and 50 cigars, 400 cigarettes, or 14 ounces of manufactured tobacco per person.
- Gifts not exceeding $60 (Canadian) and not containing tobacco products, alcoholic beverages, or advertising material can be brought in duty free. Meats, plants, and vegetables are subject to inspection on entry. There are restrictions, so contact the Canadian Consulate for more details if you want to bring produce.
- If you plan to bring your dog or cat, you must bring proof of rabies inoculation during the preceding 36-month period. Horses, birds, or other types of animals need special clearance and health certification. (Many birds, for instance, require eight weeks in quarantine.)
- If you need more information concerning items you wish to bring in and out of the country, contact the **Customs Office,** Pacific Region, 333 Dunsmuir St. (☎ 604/666-0545).

2 Money

CURRENCY   The Canadian currency system is decimal based and resembles both British and U.S. denominations. Canadian monetary units are **dollars** and **cents.** Canadian dollars come in different colors, just like British currency. The standard denominations are $2, $5, $10, $20, $50, $100. The "Loonie" (so named because of the loon on one side)—the $1 coin—has replaced the $1 bill, just as the British pound was replaced by a coin a few years ago. There are plans to mint a $2 coin in the near future.

Banks and other financial institutions offer a standard rate of exchange based on the daily world monetary rate. Hotels will also gladly exchange your notes but sometimes pay a slightly lower exchange rate as a service fee. Some stores and shops post their exchange rate. If you buy something in U.S. dollars (many stores accept them) you might be paying for the privilege.

Unless stated otherwise, the prices in this guide are given in Canadian dollars, which is good news for U.S. travelers because the Canadian dollar is worth 25% less than the American dollar, but buys nearly as much. As we go to press, $1 Canadian is worth 74¢ U.S., which means that your $100-a-night hotel room will cost only U.S. $74 and your $6 breakfast costs only U.S. $4.44 (plus tax).

TRAVELER'S CHECKS   Traveler's checks in Canadian funds are the safest way to carry money and are universally accepted by banks (which may charge a small fee to cash them), larger stores, and hotels. If you are carrying American Express or Thomas Cook Traveler's Cheques, you can cash them at the local offices of those companies free of charge.

ATM NETWORKS   The 24-hour Plus and CIRRUS ATM systems work in Canada, but you have to check around with the banks. The systems convert Canadian withdrawals to your account's currency within 24 hours, so don't panic if you call your bank and hear a one-to-one balance. CIRRUS network cards work at the

The Canadian Dollar & the U.S. Dollar

Unless stated otherwise, **the prices cited in this guide are given in Canadian dollars,** which is good news for U.S. travelers because the Canadian dollar is worth 25% less than the American dollar, but buys nearly as much. As we go to press, $1 Canadian is worth 75¢ U.S., which means that your $100-a-night hotel room will cost only U.S. $75, and your $6 breakfast costs only U.S. $4.50.

Here's a quick table of equivalents:

Canadian $	U.S. $
1	0.75
5	3.75
10	7.50
20	15.00
50	37.50
80	60.00
100	75.00

What Things Cost in Vancouver & Victoria	C $	U.S. $
Taxi from the airport to downtown Vancouver	35.00	25.93
SeaBus to Lonsdale Quay (off-peak)	1.50	1.11
Local telephone call	0.25	0.19
Double at The Empress Hotel, Victoria (very expensive)	235.00	173.90
Double at Pacific Palisades Hotel, Vancouver (moderate)	145.00	107.41
Double at The Hotel at the YWCA, Vancouver (inexpensive)	76.00	56.30
Lunch for one at Reebar, Victoria (moderate)	11.00	8.14
Lunch for one at Benny's Bagels, Vancouver (inexpensive)	7.50	5.55
Dinner for one, without wine, at The Five Sails, Vancouver (deluxe)	42.00	31.08
Dinner for one, without wine, at Met Bistro, Victoria (moderate)	18.00	13.32
Dinner for one, without wine, at Stephos, (inexpensive)	9.50	7.03
Pint of beer	3.50	2.59
Cup of coffee	1.25	0.93
Admission to the Vancouver Art Gallery	6.00	4.44
Movie ticket	8.00	5.93

Bank of Montreal and the Hong Kong Bank of Canada ATMs but not at Royal Scot or CIBC machines. Neither system will show your current balance, so know how much you've got in your account before you go.

CREDIT & DEBIT CARDS Major U.S. credit cards are widely accepted in British Columbia, especially American Express, MasterCard, and VISA. British debit cards like Barclay's VISA debit card are also accepted here. Diners Club, Carte Blanche, and EnRoute are taken by a few establishments but not many. The amount spent in Canadian dollars will automatically be converted by your issuing company to your currency when you are billed.

3 When to Go

Vancouver's tourist season starts in June and ends around mid-September. This is when the weather is at its best. There are all kinds of festivals, beautiful beaches, and blooming gardens. This is also the priciest time of year to go, and hotel rates soar. Tourists from around the world are filtering through both Vancouver and Victoria around this time, so accommodations are scarce and restaurants are crowded.

There are a lot of package specials offered during the fall, winter, and spring, which make ski trips to Vancouver exceptionally good deals. It's easier to get reservations for both hotels and restaurants. The one catch is that it rains often during the winter. But as the locals will tell you, if it's raining in town, it's snowing up in the north shore mountains where the nearest skiing is. Besides, it's just a misty, intermittent rain—like those in Seattle or London.

CLIMATE Both Vancouver and Victoria enjoy moderately warm, sunny summers and mild, rainy winters. Above the 49th parallel, you get more sun per summer day than you do down south. You get about 16 hours of daylight in mid-June, which means you have more hours at the beach, shopping, or in the mountains here than you will in other parts of the world. Victoria gets half the rain, thanks to its surrounding protection: the Olympic Peninsula to the south and its own southeasterly position on huge Vancouver Island. The average annual rainfall in Vancouver is 57 inches, while in Victoria, it's just 26 inches.

Vancouver's Average Temperatures & Days of Rain

	Jan	Feb	Mar	Apr	May	Jun	July	Aug	Sept	Oct	Nov	Dec
(°F)	36	39	43	49	55	60	64	63	57	50	43	39
(°C)	3	4	7	9	13	16	18	18	14	11	7	4
Days of Rain	20	17	17	14	12	11	7	8	9	16	19	22

Victoria's Average Temperatures & Days of Rain

	Jan	Feb	Mar	Apr	May	Jun	July	Aug	Sept	Oct	Nov	Dec
(°F)	38	40	43	47	54	57	62	61	57	50	43	40
(°C)	3	5	6	9	12	14	17	16	14	10	6	4
Days of Rain	16	14	13	10	8	7	5	6	8	13	16	18

HOLIDAYS The official British Columbian public holidays are as follows: New Year's Day (January 1); Good Friday, Easter, Easter Monday (April 5 through 8, 1996); Victoria Day (May 20, 1996); Canada Day (July 1); B.C. Day (August 5, 1996); Labor Day (September 2, 1996); Thanksgiving (October 14, 1996); Remembrance Day (November 11); Christmas (December 25); and Boxing Day (December 26).

VANCOUVER & VICTORIA CALENDAR OF EVENTS

Vancouver and Victoria festivals are an important part of local cultural and social life. New and emerging artists, as well as established creators, perform for audiences totaling over three-quarters of a million annually. If no contact number is listed below, Discover B.C. (☎ 800/663-6000) should be able to give you details on most of these events.

January

- **Polar Bear Swim,** English Bay Beach, Vancouver. Thousands of hardy citizens show up in their bathing suits to take their first annual dip in the icy waters of English Bay. January 1.
- **Chinese New Year,** Chinatowns in Vancouver, Richmond, and Victoria. This is when the Chinese traditionally clear up their debts and forgive old grievances to start the new lunar year right. It's also when Chinese communities launch a two-week celebration to bring in the new year with firecrackers, dancing dragon parades, and other festivities. Late January or early February.
- ✪ **Annual Bald Eagle Count,** Brackendale and Goldstream Regional Park. In January 1994, 3,700 bald eagles were counted near Brackendale by rafters observing the eagles gathered to feed on salmon. In Brackendale, the count generally takes place the second Sunday in January and starts at Brackendale Art Gallery. In Goldstream Regional Park, it usually takes place in mid to late January. Call 604/478-9414 for exact dates.

February

- **Indoor Highland Games & Dancing,** Saanich. Piping, drumming, dancing, and Scottish field sports are the attractions. Contact the Highland Games Association (☎ 604/479-7804 or 604/477-8674) for exact dates. Mid-February.

March

- **New Play Festival,** Vancouver. Emerging playwrights show off their latest works at different venues. Call 604/685-6228 for more information. March.
- **Pacific Rim Whale Festival,** Tofino, Ucluelet, and Pacific Rim National Park. Every spring, 19,000 whales migrate past this coastline, attracting visitors from all over the world to the West Coast's beaches. In celebration of the orca, beluga, and other whales in the area, this event includes live crab races, Gumboot Golf Tournament, and Whales in the Park guided whale-spotting hikes. March 16–April 8. Call 604/726-4641 for more information.
- **Storytelling Festival,** Vancouver. Storytellers relate their best tales for both children and adults. Call 604/253-6292 for more information. March 22 through 24.

April

- **Brant Festival,** Parksville. The brant geese return from their winter sojourn. First week in April.
- ✪ **International Wine Festival,** Vancouver. A major wine-tasting event featuring the latest international vintages. You are handed a glass at the door. Cheese and pâté are laid out on strategically placed tables. Early April.
- **Vancouver Sun Run,** Vancouver. This is Canada's biggest race, with 17,000 runners, joggers, and walkers racing through six scenic miles. Second week in April.
- **Baisakhi Day Parade,** Vancouver. The Sikh Indian new year is celebrated with a colorful parade around Ross Street near Marine Drive and ends with a

vegetarian feast at the temple. Contact Khalsa Diwan Gurudwara Temple (☎ 604/ 324-2010) for more information. April.

May
- **Outdoor Highland Games,** Saanich. Authentic Scottish competitive sports, piping, drumming, and flinging take place on the fairgrounds. Contact the Highland Games Association (☎ 604/479-7804 or 604/477-8674) for exact dates. Mid-May.
- **International Vancouver Marathon,** Vancouver. Racers from all over the world compete in the streets. May.

June
- **International Children's Festival,** Vancouver. Activities, plays, music, and crafts all geared to children are featured at this annual event. First week in June.
- ✪ **Canadian International Dragon Boat Festival,** Vancouver. Traditional dragon-boat racing is a part of the city's cultural scene. Watch the races from False Creek's north shore, where 120 local and international teams compete. Four stages of music, dance, and Chinese acrobatics also take place as part of the events at the Plaza of Nations. Third week in June.
- ✪ **duMaurier International Jazz Festival,** Vancouver. More than 800 international jazz and blues players perform at venues from the Orpheum Theatre and the Yaletown Hotel to the Plaza of Nations. Contact Jazz Hotline (☎ 604/682-0706) for more information. June 28 through July 7.
- **Italian Days,** Vancouver. The Italian district sponsors a feasting and merry-making weekend. Contact Italian Cultural Centre, 3075 Slocan St. (☎ 604/ 430-3337) for more information. Late June or early July.

July
- ✪ **Canada Day,** Vancouver. Canada Place Pier hosts an all-day celebration which begins with the swearing-in of new citizens. Music and dance acts perform outdoors throughout the day, and a fireworks display on the harbor tops off the entertainment. July 1.
- **Steveston Salmon Festival,** Steveston. A parade, salmon barbecue, and other forms of entertainment all take place in this heritage fishing village. July 1.
- **Dancing on the Edge,** Vancouver. Canadian and international dance groups perform controversial and classic works at the Firehall Arts Centre. Contact Donna Spencer (☎ 604/689-0691) for more information. July 6 through 14.
- **Harrison Festival of the Arts,** Harrison Hot Springs, Lower Mainland. This arts festival in the Fraser River valley east of Vancouver attracts fine performing artists from around the world. Early July.
- **Vancouver Folk Music Festival,** Vancouver. International folk music is played outdoors on Jericho Beach Park. Contact Vancouver Folk Music Society (☎ 604/ 879-2931). Second or third weekend in July.
- **Powell Street Festival,** Vancouver. An annual festival of Japanese culture includes music, dance, food, and more. Contact Ilene Kage (☎ 604/682-4335) for more information. Last weekend of July.
- **Obon Festival,** Vancouver. The Japanese full moon festival takes place in Oppenheimer Park with kimonoed classical dancers and heart-quaking koto drummers. Contact the Vancouver Buddhist Church (☎ 604/253-7033) for exact dates. July.
- **Bathtub Race,** Nanaimo to Vancouver. Competitors design and attempt to sail or row all sorts of bathtub craft. Contact the Nanaimo Tourism Association (☎ 800/663-7337) for more information. July.

August

☀ **Benson & Hedges Symphony of Fire,** Vancouver. Three international fireworks companies compete for a coveted title and put up their best displays with accompanying music over English Bay Beach. Don't miss the big finale on the fourth evening. End of July through first week in August.

• **International Comedy Festival,** Vancouver. Comedians from all over Canada and the United States perform at a variety of venues around town. Contact Alan Scales (☎ 604/683-0883) for more information. First week in August.

• **Pacific National Exhibition,** Vancouver. The 10th largest fair in North America has everything from big-name entertainment to a demolition derby; livestock demonstrations and logger sports competitions; plus fashion shows and a midway. Contact Pacific National Exhibition (☎ 604/253-2311) for more details. Mid-August to Labor Day.

☀ **Abbotsford International Air Show,** Abbotsford. Barnstorming stuntmen and precision military pilots fly everything from Sopwith camels to VTOLs. This is one of the biggest air shows in the world. Mid-August.

• **Canadian International Dragon Boat Festival,** Victoria. Traditional dragon boat races in which 120 local and international teams compete. Mid-August.

September

☀ **Molson Indy,** Vancouver. The CART Indy Series features its biggest annual event, which roars through Vancouver's streets attracting more than 350,000 spectators. Contact Molson Indy at 604/684-4639 for information or 604/280-4639 for tickets. Labor Day.

• **Dixieland Jazz Festival and Vintage Car Rally,** Nanaimo. Competitors race from Victoria to Nanaimo in an amazing array of classic chaises. To entertain both racers and spectators, an end-of-summer jazz festival takes place in Nanaimo. Contact the Nanaimo Tourism Association (☎ 800/663-7337) for more information. Early September.

October

☀ **Vancouver International Film Festival,** Vancouver. This highly respected film festival features 250 new works, revivals, and retrospectives from 40 countries. Attendance reaches more than 110,000, not including the stars and celebrities who appear annually. Contact Vancouver International Film Festival (☎ 604/685-0260) for details. October 4 through 20.

• **Vancouver Writers Festival,** Vancouver. Readings from great works by Canadian and international authors are presented. Contact Alma Lee at 604/681-6330 for details. Mid-October.

• **Oktoberfest.** During the festivities, celebrated throughout the province, German food is served at a variety of restaurants. Early October.

November

• **Remembrance Day.** Celebrated throughout Canada, it commemorates Canadian soldiers who gave their lives in war. November 11.

December

• **First Night,** Vancouver's New Year's Eve performing arts festival and alcohol-free party. The city closes up the downtown streets for revelers. Admission to participating nightclubs and other sites is a $5 button. There's also a party held in Victoria. December 31.

4 Health & Insurance

STAYING HEALTHY   The region's clean environment and abundance of outdoor activities are a major part of life here. Locals and visitors alike enjoy a healthy lifestyle. But there are some risks involved. Know your limitations—physical exertion can lead to strains, sprains, and other injuries. Your worst enemies out here are heat, sun, and cold exposure.

When the sun's out at the beach or on the ski slopes, remember that water and snow reflect, increasing the potential for sunburns and skin damage. Bring your sun screen. If you're going hiking up on the north shore, or deep into Stanley Park, remember to bring a flashlight, maps, a compass, sunglasses, and extra clothing in case what you're wearing gets wet.

INSURANCE   U.S. travelers should review their health-insurance coverage for travel outside the United States. If you are not adequately covered, then you should take advantage of one of the many health and accident plans that charge a daily rate for the term of your trip, such as Thomas Cook or Mutual of Omaha's plan. These run about $3 per day for up to 90 days.

Auto insurance is compulsory in British Columbia. Basic coverage consists of "no-fault" accident and $200,000 third-party legal liability coverage. If you plan to drive in Canada, check with your insurance company to make sure that your policy meets this requirement. Always carry your insurance card, your vehicle registration, and your driver's license in case you have an accident.

SAFETY   Even though Vancouver has never had a major shake, you are in an earthquake zone. Check the exit and emergency information in your hotel's guest services book. It will advise you where to go and how to exit after the shaking has stopped.

5 Tips for Travelers with Special Needs

FOR TRAVELERS WITH DISABILITIES   You'll find that Vancouver is very wheelchair conscious; motorized wheelchairs are a common sight in the downtown area. The stairs along Robson Square have built-in ramps. Most of the major attractions have ramps or level walkways for easy access. Many Vancouver hotels have at least partial wheelchair accessibility, if not rooms built completely to suit. Most SkyTrain stations and the SeaBus are accessible to wheelchairs. Most of the bus routes are lift-equipped. For more information about accessible public transportation, contact **B.C. Transit** (☎ 604/264-5000) and ask for its brochure *Rider's Guide to Accessible Transit*.

Many downtown hotels are also equipping rooms with visual smoke alarms and other facilities for hearing-impaired guests. The Ridge Theatre (see Chapter 6, "What to See and Do in Vancouver") has special hearing devices. You'll also notice that downtown crosswalks have beeping alert signs to guide visually impaired pedestrians.

FOR GAY & LESBIAN TRAVELERS   Vancouver has a large, sophisticated gay and lesbian community similar to San Francisco's. Much of the activity centers around the West End and downtown, where many singles and couples live. The best way to get in the groove is to pick up a copy of *Xtra! West*, the biweekly tabloid, available throughout the West End. This will link you into metropolitan services, entertainment, and even the political scene.

To meet gays and lesbians, book a room at the West End Guest House or the Sylvia Hotel; have dinner at Delilah's or Lola's; and then head over to the numerous West End clubs, including Celebrities and Odyssey, or have a coffee at The Edge on Davie Street.

FOR SENIORS   Vancouver and Victoria may seem very youth oriented with all their outdoor sports, but these cities are also very kind to mature travelers. This part of the country is hospitable and courteous. You'll find many of your peers strolling down Denman or Robson streets along with the younger crowd. There is little discrimination here on either side, just an amiable respect.

Older travelers may qualify for discounts at hotels, attractions, and on public transit throughout Vancouver and Victoria. Get in the habit of asking for your discount. If you are over 55 and are not already a member of the **American Association of Retired Persons,** 3200 E. Carson, Lakewood CA 90712 (☎ 800/424-3410), consider joining. The AARP card is valuable throughout North America for additional restaurant and travel bargains.

FOR FAMILIES   Vancouver and Victoria are two of the most child-friendly, cosmopolitan cities around. Where else would you find a Kids Only market, filled with children's stores, located next to a free Water Park complete with water guns and changing rooms? In addition to the standard attractions and sights, you'll find there's a lot of adventurous, outdoor, and free stuff that both you and your kids will enjoy (see "Especially for Kids" in Chapters 6 and 13). Entertaining eateries that aren't cafeteria style or fast-food establishments but are kid-friendly also exist here (see "Family-Friendly Restaurants" in Chapter 5 and Chapter 12). Some hotels even offer milk and cookies to the younger set for evening snacks, plus special menus and their own terry robes (see "Family-Friendly Hotels" in Chapter 4 and Chapter 11).

FOR STUDENTS   This is definitely a student-oriented area. The University of British Columbia, located in the Point Grey and Kitsilano areas, and Burnaby's Simon Fraser University gather an enormous student population here. That means student travelers have a lot of free and inexpensive entertainment possibilities both day and night. (Many attractions and theaters offer student discounts if you have your student ID card with you.) The nightlife here is active, centering around Yaletown, Granville Street, the West End, and the UBC campus. Pick up a copy of *The Georgia Straight* to find out what's happening.

6 Getting to Vancouver

BY PLANE

THE MAJOR AIRLINES   The Open Skies agreement between the United States and Canada has made flying to Vancouver easier than ever. Daily direct flights between major U.S. cities and Vancouver are flown by **Air Canada** (☎ 800/776-3000); **United Airlines** (☎ 800/241-6522); **American Airlines** (☎ 800/433-7300); **Continental** (☎ 800/231-0856); and **Northwest Airlines** (☎ 800/225-2525). And if you haven't tried it yet, the service on **Air Canada** is exceptional, both on and off the ground. It is opening new U.S. destinations every month, so check if your city is on its route. Other new direct flights with major carriers have recently opened in Phoenix, Dallas, New York, Houston, Minneapolis, Reno, and San Francisco.

FINDING THE BEST AIRFARE   The best advice we can give you on shopping for an airfare bargain is to call the major airlines 30 days or more before your departure. That's when you'll find the best discounted seats on flights. Most airlines offer restricted ticketing on these deals: You cannot change dates without paying extra and the tickets are usually nonrefundable.

If you've got a computer, log on to **CompuServe** and check the prices via the OAG forum. You'll find a complete listing of flights and prices available. You can also book yourself a ticket if you don't feel like dealing with travel agents.

Non-U.S. and non-Canadian travelers should take advantage of the **airpasses** offered by **Continental** (☎ 800/231-0856) and **Air Canada** (☎ 800/776-3000). They must be purchased outside of North America in conjunction with an international fare. For an additional US$389, you can get three flight coupons, which allow you to fly anywhere on the continent in July and August. You can buy up to a maximum of eight coupons for US$679. They also offer low-season discounts. **Canadian Airlines** (☎ 800/426-7000) offers a similar deal to every destination on its flight schedule, including Hawaii.

VANCOUVER INTERNATIONAL AIRPORT   The airport is located eight miles south of downtown Vancouver on Sea Island across from Richmond and the Fraser delta. There are a lot of changes being made. Both the domestic and international terminals are getting overhauled and extended. More than 10 million air passengers pass through here annually on Canadian, U.S., and international carriers, including Air New Zealand, British Airways, Canadian Airlines, Cathay Pacific, Continental, Japan Air Lines, KLM Royal Dutch, Lufthansa, Qantas, and Singapore Airlines.

Existing airport services include restaurants, cocktail lounges, bookstores, newsstands, florists, duty-free shops, food specialty shops, bank ATMs, currency exchange, a post office, a barbershop, hotel reservation telephones, and public phones. **Tourist Information Centres** located on Levels 1 and 3 (☎ 604/276-6101) are open to assist you daily from 6:30am to 11:30pm.

Parking is available at the airport for both loading and long-term (☎ 604/276-6106). **Courtesy buses** to the airport hotels are available, and a **shuttle bus** links the Main and South terminals.

The airport is easily accessible via three bridges. Travelers heading into Vancouver will take the Arthur Laing Bridge, which leads directly into Granville Street (Highway 99)—the most direct route to downtown.

DEPARTURE TAX   Because of all of the airport expansion, you have to pay an international departure surcharge of $10 per person when you leave the country. Domestic flights are charged $5 per person.

LEAVING THE AIRPORT   **Airport bus service** to downtown Vancouver's major hotels, the **YVR Airporter** (☎ 604/244-9888), leaves from Level 2 every 15 minutes daily from 6:30am to 10:30pm and every 30 minutes from 10:30pm until 12:15am. The 30-minute ride whisks you up the Delta through central Vancouver, where it makes a few called-out stops before taking the Granville Street Bridge into downtown Vancouver. You can buy a one-way fare for $9 adults, $7 seniors, and $5 children or save a little money on your return by purchasing a round-trip ticket for $15 adults, $14 seniors, and $10 children. Bus service back to the airport leaves from selected downtown hotels every half hour between 5:35am and 10:55pm. There are pickups scheduled for the Four Seasons, Hotel Vancouver, Waterfront Centre Hotel, Georgian Court, Sutton Place, and others. Check with your hotel concierge about the nearest pickup stop.

If you don't mind transferring from one bus to another with your luggage and have spare time, you can take public transit. **B.C. transit bus no. 100** stops at both terminals. At the Marine Drive stop, get off and transfer to **bus no. 20** or **no. 17,** which take you into downtown Vancouver. B.C. transit fares are $1.50 during off-peak hours and $2.50 during rush hours.

The average **taxi** fare from the airport to a downtown Vancouver hotel is $35 plus tip. There are nearly 400 taxis serving the airport.

AirLimo (☎ 604/273-1331) is the city's only flat-rate limousine service. It operates 24 hours a day. The ride from the airport to downtown Vancouver is $26 per trip, not per person. During the rush hour, this can be more economical than taking a cab; they accept all major credit cards.

Most of the **car-rental firms** here have airport counters and shuttles. Make advance reservations for fast check-in and guaranteed vehicle availability—especially if you want a 4-wheel drive or a compact (see "Car Rentals," in Chapter 3).

FLYING WITH FILM, CAMCORDERS, AND LAPTOPS Film under 400 ASA is less likely to be damaged by exposure to X rays, but repeated trips through the airport X-ray machine can cause clouding. If you're carrying film, keep it in a small bag that can be hand inspected at customs. X rays don't affect camcorder tapes, but metal detectors might.

Though it's never been proven conclusively that X-ray machines affect floppy or hard disks, you should request they be hand checked. You may be asked to turn on your laptop and your camcorder to prove they're real. Be sure their batteries are charged before you get to the airport.

BY TRAIN

VIA Rail Canada, 1150 Station St. (☎ 604/669-3050), connects with Amtrak at Winnipeg. From there, you travel on a spectacular route that runs between Calgary and Vancouver. Lake Louise's beautiful alpine scenery is just part of this enjoyable journey. **Amtrak** (☎ 800/872-7245) also has a direct route from San Diego to Vancouver, stopping at all major U.S. west coast cities. Non-U.S. and non-Canadian travelers can buy a 15- to 30-day **USA Railpass** for US$229 to US$339 off-peak (US$340 to US$425 peak).

B.C. Rail, 1311 W. First St., North Vancouver (☎ 604/631-3500), also connects Vancouver to other cities throughout the province, including Whistler.

The main **Vancouver railway station** is at 1150 Station St., near Main Street and Terminal Avenue south of Chinatown (☎ 604/669-3050). You can reach downtown Vancouver from there by cab for about $5. There are plenty of taxis at the station entrance. One block from the station is the SkyTrain's Main Station. Within minutes, you're downtown. (Granville and Waterfront stations are two and four stops away, respectively.)

BY BUS

The **Greyhound Bus Lines** (☎ 604/662-3222) and **Pacific Coach Lines** (☎ 604/662-8074) also have their terminals at the 1150 Station St. train station. Greyhound's **Ameripass** offers 7 to 30 days of unlimited travel for US$259 to US$559. **Quick Coach Lines** (☎ 604/526-2836) connects Vancouver to the Seattle-Tacoma International Airport. The bus stops at Richmond's Delta Pacific Inn and the Sandman Inn, 180 W. Georgia St. The three-hour ride costs US$32 one way, US$60 round-trip.

BY CAR

You'll probably be driving into Vancouver along one of two routes: **U.S. Interstate 5** from Seattle intersects **Highway 99** when you cross the border at the Peace Arch. You pass under the Fraser River through the George Massey Tunnel, drive through Richmond, and cross the Oak Street Bridge. The highway ends right here and becomes Oak Street, a busy urban thoroughfare. Turn left onto 70th Avenue, then six blocks later turn right onto Granville Street. This is the business extension of Highway 99, which heads directly downtown via the Granville Street Bridge.

Trans-Canada Highway 1 is a limited-access freeway running all the way to Vancouver's eastern boundary. To enter through central Vancouver, exit at Cassiar

Street and turn left at the first light onto Hastings Street (Highway 7A), which is adjacent to the Exhibition Park. Follow Hastings Street four miles into downtown.

To enter through North Vancouver, stay on Highway 1 and cross the Second Narrows Bridge.

BY SHIP/FERRY

The Canada Place **cruise-ship terminal** (☎ 604/666-4452) is a multisailed landmark pier extending into the harbor from downtown's central business district. During the summer and fall, nearly 200 passenger ships dock and launch on cruises heading south to Seattle or north to Alaska. The **Cunard, Princess, Royal Viking,** and **Sitmar** lines sail from San Francisco to Alaska with stopovers in Vancouver to load new passengers. Public-transit buses and taxis greet new arrivals, but you can also easily walk to many major hotels like the Pan-Pacific, Waterfront Centre, and Hotel Vancouver.

B.C. Ferries (☎ 604/669-1211) arriving from Victoria dock at Tsawwassen, which is a few miles south of the city. Highway 17 joins Highway 99 just before the George Massey Tunnel, so you can follow the driving directions to Vancouver given above. **Nanaimo ferries** dock at Horseshoe Bay in West Vancouver (which is west of North Vancouver). The Trans-Canada Highway (Highways 1 and 99) heads south to North Vancouver. The south exit for Taylor Way leads into Lion's Gate Bridge and downtown Vancouver's West End.

PACKAGE TOURS　**Air Canada** (☎ 800/663-3721) offers a number of fly-drive packages. **Super Natural Adventures,** 626 W. Pender St., Vancouver (☎ 604/683-5101), specializes in vacation packages to Vancouver and Victoria.

7　Getting to Victoria

BY PLANE

THE MAJOR AIRLINES　**Air Canada** (☎ 800/776-3000), **Canadian Airlines** (☎ 800/363-7530), and **Horizon Air** (☎ 800/547-9308) service direct connections from Seattle, Vancouver, Calgary, Edmonton, Saskatoon, Winnipeg, and Toronto.

Provincial commuter airlines, including floatplanes that land in Victoria's Inner Harbour and helicopters, service Victoria as well. They include the following: **Air B.C.** (☎ 604/663-9826); **Harbour Air** (☎ 604/688-1277); **Kenmore Air** (☎ 800/543-9595); and **Helijet Airways** (☎ 604/382-6222 in Victoria or 604/273-1414 in Vancouver).

VICTORIA INTERNATIONAL AIRPORT　The Victoria International Airport is near the Sidney ferry terminal. Both are located 16 miles north of Victoria. For airport information, call 604/363-6600.

LEAVING THE AIRPORT　The Patricia Bay Highway (Highway 17) heads south straight into downtown Victoria. The **P.B.M. Transport** (☎ 604/475-2010) covers the distance in about 30 minutes; buses leave every half hour from 5:25am to 11:55pm. The one-way fare is $12. A limited number of hotel courtesy buses also serve the airport.

The average **taxi** fare from Victoria International to downtown is about $40 plus tip.

Several **car-rental firms** have desks at the airport with vehicles ready for drivers who've made advance reservations. They include **Avis** (☎ 604/656-6033); **Budget** (☎ 604/656-3731); **Hertz** (☎ 604/656-2312); and **Tilden** (☎ 604/656-2541).

BY TRAIN

Victoria's **E&N Station** is at 450 Pandora Ave., at the Johnson Street Bridge (☎ 800/561-8630 in Canada). The **VIA Rail/Esquimalt and Nanaimo Railway** leaves Courtenay, about 130 miles northwest of Victoria, at 1:15pm daily. It arrives in Nanaimo about two hours later and completes the final half of the journey through the beautiful Goldstream Regional Park at 5:45pm. Trains leave Victoria daily at 8:15am, arriving in Nanaimo at 10:40am and in Courtenay at 12:50pm. One-way fare from Victoria to Nanaimo is $19.26 for adults, $17.12 for seniors and students, and $9.53 for children 3 to 11. There are discounts on these fares if you purchase your tickets a week in advance of departure.

BY BUS

Victoria Depot (☎ 604/385-4411) is at 710 Douglas St., at the corner of Belleville Street, directly behind the Empress Hotel.

Pacific Coach Lines (☎ 604/385-4411) operates between here and Vancouver— a five-hour trip, including the ferry portion (see "By Ship/Ferry," below). Service runs daily from 6am to 9pm (until 8pm during the winter); times vary depending on the B.C. Ferries schedule.

BY SHIP/FERRY

B.C. Ferries (☎ 604/386-3431 or 604/656-0757) has three routes from the mainland. The most direct route for Vancouver-Victoria travelers is the Tsawwassen-Swartz Bay 95-minute trip through the Gulf Islands; this route operates daily between 7am and 9pm. The trip takes a minimum of five hours if you include the commute to and from both ferry terminals.

The Horseshoe Bay–Nanaimo ferry is a 95-minute run that operates on a similar schedule. You then have the option of taking the E&N Railway trip down to Victoria, or you can drive approximately one hour south on Highway 1. The Mid-Island Express ferry crosses from Tsawwassen to Nanaimo; it takes two hours and operates six times daily, from 5:30am to 11pm. The fare on all three routes is the same— $6.50 per driver or adult passenger, $3.50 for children 5 to 11, and $27 for a car.

B.C. Ferries provides year-round service on 24 routes throughout the province, including the Gulf Islands and the Inside Passage. There is a restaurant, snack bar, gift shop, play area, game arcade, and executive center on board every ship.

Several daily year-round services connect Washington state cities directly with Victoria and Vancouver Island. **Black Ball Transport** (☎ 604/386-2202) runs between Port Angeles, Washington, and Victoria. The fares are the same as B.C. Ferries.

Clipper Navigation, 1000A Wharf St., Victoria (☎ 604/382-8100), operates the *Victoria Clipper,* a first-class, 300-passenger, 130-foot water-jet–propelled catamaran that spoils you during your crossing from Seattle to Victoria with meals, refreshments, and duty-free shopping services. The *Clipper* leaves Seattle at 8am and returns from Victoria at 9:30pm. There are additional summertime sailings at 8:40am, 9:30am, and 3pm, and additional departures from Victoria at 11:15am, 2:30pm, and 5:30pm. Adult summer fares are US$89 round-trip.

Victoria–San Juan Cruises runs the *MV Victoria Star* from Bellingham, Washington, via the San Juan Islands to Victoria from June through October (☎ 206/738-8099 or 800/443-4552). The ship departs Bellingham at 9:30am and arrives in Victoria at 2pm, with a stopover in Friday Harbor, San Juan Island.

PACKAGE TOURS   See "Package Tours" under "Getting to Vancouver," earlier in this chapter.

3 Getting to Know Vancouver

Once you're here, you'll discover that Vancouver hotels, attractions, and restaurants all lie in relatively close proximity to each other. The north shore and delta regions are less than an hour away. You can leave your car in the hotel parking lot and stroll or take public transit—SkyTrain, SeaBus, or regular bus service—to the downtown area.

1 Orientation

VISITOR INFORMATION

The **Vancouver Travel InfoCentre,** 200 Burrard St. (☎ 604/683-2000), is your single best travel information source about Vancouver and the north shore. If you've ever been to London, you'll be happy to know that **Tourism Vancouver** runs an operation similar to the British Tourist Authority. This means you can also buy your bus passes and sports and entertainment tickets in the same place. If you're having trouble finding accommodations, they have catalogues of registered hotels and bed and breakfasts; they will even make reservations for you. The InfoCentre is open daily from May through Labor Day from 8am to 6pm; during the rest of the year it's open Monday through Saturday from 8:30am to 5:30pm.

Two smaller InfoCentres operate only during the summer. One is a **kiosk outside of Eaton's department store** at the corner of Georgia and Granville streets, which is open Tuesday to Friday from 10am to 5pm. The other, which is in **Stanley Park,** is open daily from 9am to 5pm.

If you plan to see more of this beautiful province, **Tourism B.C.,** 1130 W. Pender St. (☎ 604/685-0032), can help you. **Tourism Richmond,** George Massey Tunnel (☎ 604/278-9333), has information about this delta area, including the heritage village of Steveston.

Check out *Vancouver Magazine,* a monthly city-scene magazine that's a good, hip source on what's new in restaurants, products, and places. *The Georgia Straight,* a weekly tabloid newspaper, has the most comprehensive live music and events listings covering the city and surrounds.

CITY LAYOUT

MAIN ARTERIES & STREETS   Downtown Vancouver and Stanley Park are on the upraised thumb of the mitten-shaped Vancouver peninsula. Pointing northward, this main business district is bordered on the west by English Bay; on the north and east by the Burrard Inlet; and on the south by False Creek.

Two main downtown thoroughfares run westward from Chinatown and B.C. Place to the West End and Stanley Park. **Robson Street** starts at B.C. Place on Beatty Street, flows through the West End's more touristed shopping district, and ends at Stanley Park's Lost Lagoon on Lagoon Drive. Four streets running parallel to Robson Street are important to know; one block north of Robson is **Georgia Street,** which leads directly to Lion's Gate Bridge and the North Shore. Two blocks north of Georgia is **West Pender Street,** which runs eastward through Chinatown. One block north of West Pender is **West Hastings Street,** which skirts Gastown's southern border as it flows eastward to the Trans-Canada Highway.

The fourth important east-west artery is **Davie Street,** which starts at Pacific Boulevard near the Cambie Street Bridge, runs through the hip Yaletown district and the West End's more residential shopping district, and ends at English Bay Beach where Denman Street meets Beach Avenue—the western access route to Stanley Park.

Three **north-south downtown streets** will get you to everywhere you want to go both in and out of downtown. **Denman Street,** two blocks east of Stanley Park, stretches from West Georgia Street to Beach Avenue at English Bay Beach. This main West End thoroughfare is where the locals go to dine out. It's also the shortest north-south route to Third, Second, and English Bay beaches.

Eight blocks east of Denman is **Burrard Street**, which starts at Canada Place, crosses the Burrard Street Bridge to Vanier Park, where it becomes **Cornwall Avenue**. As it heads due west through Kitsilano, it changes its name to **Point Grey Road** and **NW Marine Drive** before entering the University of British Columbia campus. It eventually turns southward when it becomes **SW Marine Drive** before ending at Granville Street and the Oak Street Bridge.

Granville Street, which starts near Canada Place to the west and the SeaBus terminal to the east, runs the entire length of central Vancouver south to Richmond, where it officially becomes Highway 99. Central Vancouver's main east-west cross streets are successively numbered from First Avenue at the downtown bridges to 70th Avenue at the Oak Street Bridge. Granville intersects **Broadway (10th Avenue)**, which goes westward to Greektown and the University of British Columbia campus and runs eastward all the way to Burnaby, where it becomes the Lougheed Highway. It also intersects **Marine Way (70th Avenue)**, which heads eastward to New Westminster.

FINDING AN ADDRESS   One thing you should note about Vancouver addresses is that in many cases, the suite or room number precedes the building number. For instance, 100-1250 Robson St. is actually suite 100 at 1250 Robson.

In downtown Vancouver, Chinatown's **Carrall Street** is the axis from which east-west streets are numbered and designated. Numbers increase as they progress west toward Stanley Park and increase east as they head toward Burnaby Street. The low numbers on north-south streets start on the Canada Place side and increase they head toward False Creek.

Central Vancouver uses **Ontario Street** as its east-west axis, and as mentioned before, all north-south avenues from False Creek to the Fraser River have numerical names.

Greater Vancouver

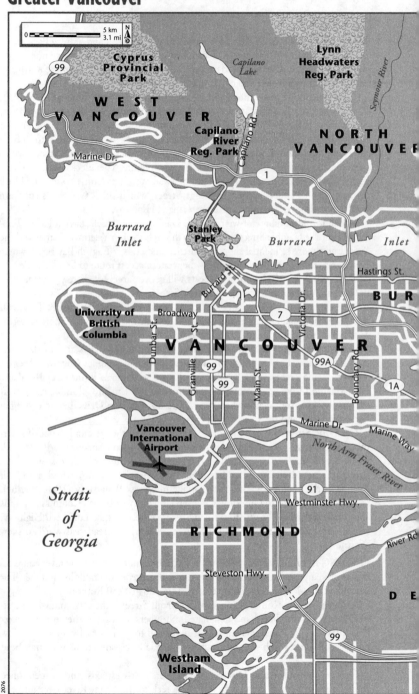

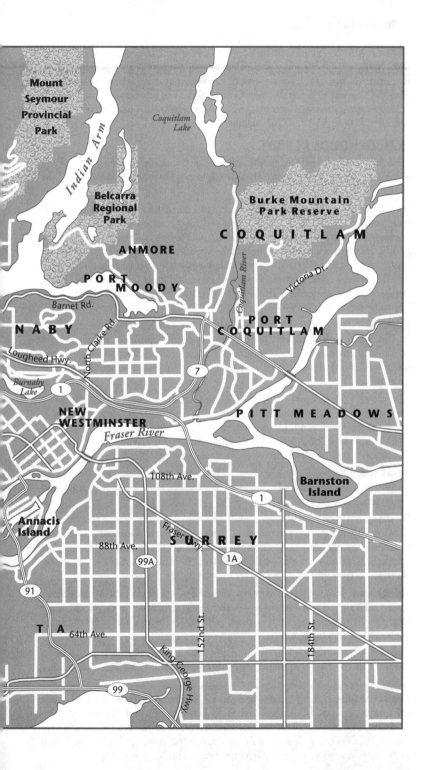

STREET MAPS   The Travel InfoCentres (see "Visitor Information," above) and many hotels can provide you with detailed downtown maps. A good all-around metropolitan area map is the *Rand McNally Vancouver* city map, which is available for $3 at the Vancouver Airport Tourism Centre booth. The best map we found is available from the Canadian Automobile Association (CAA). It is not for sale, but it is given free to both AAA and CAA members.

NEIGHBORHOODS IN BRIEF

Vancouverites love their neighborhoods and will proudly tell you which of the 22 communities is their favorite. There are eight neighborhoods you shouldn't miss strolling.

West End   The West End was once home to Vancouver's Edwardian rich and is now North America's most densely populated neighborhood. A few old Victorian homes—such as the Roedde House Museum on Barclay Street—still remain nestled among the high-rises along its tree-lined streets. The residents are young adults, seniors, and Western Canada's largest gay and lesbian population. This area is hospitable, safe, tolerant, obviously livable, and lively. Lined with 50 restaurants, as well as coffee bars and dessert cafes, Denman is at the center of the city's action.

Yaletown   This area used to be a seedy stretch of warehouses, but now they're being converted to loft apartments for architects, designers, filmmakers, art galleries, and boutiques. Looking a bit like Manhattan's TriBeca or SoHo, this is the hip district where billiard parlor/coffee bars and cybercafes have replaced the old saloons and street walkers.

Chinatown   Vancouver's Chinatown is the third-largest Sino–North American community next to San Francisco and New York. Even though the newest wave of immigrants are well-heeled Hong Kong families who live in Richmond, this is still a viable, historic cultural center worth visiting for its classic Ming Dynasty garden (the first ever built in North America), restaurants, and shops.

False Creek   False Creek grew up from an industrial wasteland into a residential area surrounding **Granville Island's** public market, marina, artists' studios, theaters, and restaurants.

Kitsilano   Affectionately known as "Kits," Kitsilano and **Point Grey** stretch west from Vanier Park at the mouth of False Creek to the **University of British Columbia**. Sandy beaches—Jericho, Kitsilano, Point Grey, and Wreck—edge its coastline. **Greektown** is also part of this formerly Haight-Ashbury–style district, which has been gentrified in most other respects during the last decade.

Shaughnessy   The mansions between 16th and 41st avenues near Arbutus Street are the main attractions in the city's most elite residential district, Shaughnessy, where they proudly stand among lush gardens, golf courses, blossoming trees, and three public Elizabethan hedge mazes.

Grandview-Woodland   This area is traditionally known as **Little Italy**, where on Commercial Drive you can find the best espresso in town, along with myriad other Italian delicacies.

Punjabi Market   The cultural focal point for Vancouver's large East Indian population is the Punjabi Market on Main Street between 49th and 51st avenues. The local Sikh Temple and school sponsor a number of exciting, colorful parades and festivals, but you don't have to wait for a special occasion to visit; the rich silks, sparkling gold jewelry, and exotic spice shops are tempting year-round.

2 Getting Around

BY PUBLIC TRANSPORTATION

The **Vancouver Regional Transit System (B.C. Transit),** 1100-1200 W. 73rd Ave. (☎ 604/521-0400), includes electrically powered buses, the SeaBus catamaran ferries, and the magnetic-rail SkyTrain. It's an ecologically conscious, highly reliable, and inexpensive system that allows you to get everywhere, including the ski slopes. Regular service on the main routes runs from 5am to 2am, and less frequent "Owl" service operates on several downtown/suburban routes until 4:20am.

Schedules and routes are available at the Travel InfoCentres, many major hotels, and on buses. Pick up a copy of *Discover Vancouver on Transit* at one of the Travel InfoCentres (see "Visitor Information," above). This publication provides you with the transit routes for many city neighborhoods, landmarks, and attractions, including numerous Victoria sites.

FARES   Fares are the same for the bus, ferry, and SkyTrain. One-way, all-zone, nonpeak fares are $1.50 for adults and 75¢ for seniors and children 5 to 13. Peak fares (one zone: $1.50 adults, 75¢ seniors and children 5 to 13; two zones: $2.25 adults, $1.10 seniors and children 5 to 13; three zones: $3 adults, $1.50 seniors and children 5 to 13) apply Monday through Friday before 9:30am and from 3pm to 6:30pm. Free transfers are available upon boarding. They're good for any direction as well as transfers to the SkyTrain and SeaBus but have a 90-minute travel limit.

A **DayPass** ($4.50 adults, $2.50 seniors and children 5 to 13) gives you unlimited travel after 9:30am Monday through Friday or all day on Saturday, Sunday, and holidays. You can buy tickets and passes at Travel InfoCentres, both SeaBus terminals, convenience stores, drugstores, credit unions, and other outlets displaying the "FareDealer" symbol.

BY SKYTRAIN   The SkyTrain is a fully computerized, magnetic-rail, rapid transit train that services 20 stations in its 35-minute ride from downtown Vancouver east to Surrey via Burnaby and New Westminster.

BY SEABUS   The SS *Beaver* and SS *Otter* catamaran ferries annually take more than 400,000 passengers—including cyclists and wheelchair riders—year-round on a scenic, 12-minute commute between downtown's Waterfront Station and North Vancouver's Lonsdale Quay. On weekdays, the SeaBus fleet leaves every 15 minutes from 6:15am to 6:30pm, then every 30 minutes until 1am. The fleet departs on Saturdays every half hour from 6:30am until 12:30pm, then every 15 minutes until 7:15pm, then every half hour until 1am. Sundays and holidays, their schedule is limited to every half hour from 8:30am until 11pm.

BY BUS   There are some key routes to keep in mind if you're touring the city by bus: **no. 8** (Robson Street), **no. 51** (Granville Island), **no. 246** (North Vancouver), **no. 250** (West Vancouver–Horseshoe Bay), and buses **no. 4** and **10** (UBC-Exhibition Park via Granville Street downtown). One of the most popular summertime-only bus routes is the hourly **no. 52** "Around the Park" service through Stanley Park.

BY TAXI

Taxi fares are reasonable unless you're traveling late at night, when you'll have to pay double. In the downtown area, you can expect to travel for less than $6 plus tip. During rush hour, the fares can be slightly higher. The typical fare for the 8-mile drive from downtown to the airport is $35. We usually tip a minimum of 15% to the driver.

Taxis are easy to catch on downtown streets and at major hotels. If you need one in outlying areas, call for a pickup from **Black Top** (☎ 604/731-1111), **Yellow Cab** (☎ 604/681-1111), or **MacLure's** (☎ 604/731-9211).

BY CAR

If you're planning a lot of out-of-town activities, then by all means, rent a car or bring your own. But if you have a city-bound agenda, be aware that cars really aren't welcome here, especially if they aren't alternatively fueled. (Most taxis and government cars as well as many private vehicles are powered by propane.) Vancouver prides itself on providing an efficient public transit system, and its residents enjoy breathing fresh air. Popular alternative modes of transportation are cycling, in-line skating, and walking. If you are a die-hard driver, then be forewarned that gas prices are high and sold by the liter. Also remember that speeds and distances are posted in kilometers.

RENTALS You can rent a vehicle from the following: **ABC,** 1133 W. Hastings St. (☎ 604/681-8555 or 800/464-6422); **Avis,** 757 Hornby St. (☎ 604/682-1621 or 800/879-2847); **Budget,** 450 W. Georgia St. (☎ 604/668-7000 or 800/527-0700 or 800/268-8900); **Hertz Canada,** 1128 Seymour St. (☎ 604/688-2411, 800/654-3131, or 800/263-0600); **Rent-a-Wreck,** 180 W. Georgia St. (☎ 604/688-0001); **Thrifty,** 1055 W. Georgia St. (☎ 604/688-2207 or 800/367-2277); or **Tilden International,** 1140 Alberni St. (☎ 604/685-6111 or 800/387-4747). **C.C. Canada Camper R.V. Rentals,** 1080 Millcarch St., Richmond (☎ 604/327-3003) specializes in recreational vehicles.

PARKING Metered **street parking** is hard to come by in the downtown area, and rules are strictly enforced. If you park in a designated rush-hour lane, expect to have your car towed away. Unmetered parking on side streets is equally rough. To give you an indication how tight parking is, West End residents purchase neighborhood permits to park in both streets and alleys.

All major downtown hotels have guest parking with rates varying from free to $20. There's public parking at **Robson Square** (enter at Smythe and Howe streets), the **Pacific Centre** (Howe and Dunsmuir streets), and **The Bay** (Richards near Dunsmuir Street). You'll also find **parking lots** at Thurlow and Georgia streets, Thurlow and Alberni streets, and Robson and Seymour streets.

SPECIAL DRIVING RULES Canadian driving rules are similar to California regulations; stopping for crossing pedestrians is the most notable law. Seat belts and daytime headlights are mandatory. Children under five must be in child restraints. Motorcyclists must wear helmets. It's legal to turn right on a red light after you've come to a full stop.

AUTO CLUB Members of the American Automobile Association (AAA) can get assistance from the **Canadian Automobile Association (CAA)**, 999 W. Broadway, Vancouver (☎ 604/268-5600 or for road service 604/293-2222).

BY BICYCLE

Cycling is the hottest mode of transportation in town. There are bike lanes throughout the city and paved paths along parks and beaches (see Chapter 6). Helmets are mandatory, and riding on sidewalks is illegal, except where bike paths are indicated.

B.C. Transit's Cycling B.C. (☎ 604/737-3034) accommodates cyclists commuting by bus or SkyTrain by providing "Bike & Ride" lockers at all "Park & Ride" parking lots; in addition, they provide loads of information about events, bike touring, and cycle insurance. Many downtown parking lots and garages also have free bike racks.

If you're North Vancouver–bound, you can take your bike on the SeaBus any time except rush hours (no extra charge). Bicycles are not allowed in the George Massey Tunnel, but a tunnel shuttle operates from mid-May to September, four times daily—at 8am, 11am, 3pm, and 7pm southbound and 30 minutes later northbound. From May 1 to Victoria Day (the third weekend of May), the service operates on weekends only.

ON FOOT

Walking is the best way to discover this city. Vancouverites are all inveterate walkers. Once you start walking, it's hard to stop. Downtown is about one square mile in area, so there's little reason to hail a cab.

BY FERRY

Crossing False Creek to Vanier Park or Granville Island by one of the blue miniferries is cheap and fun. The **Aquabus** docks at the foot of Howe Street and takes you to Granville Island's public market and Yaletown. The **Granville Island Ferry** docks at Sunset Beach below the Burrard Street Bridge and the Aquatic Centre. It goes to both Vanier Park and Granville Island. Costing only $1.50 for adults (75¢ for seniors and children), it's the scenic, as well as the cheap, way to go. Ferries to Granville Island leave every five minutes from 7am to 10pm. Ferries to Vanier Park leave every 15 minutes from 10am to 8pm.

FAST FACTS: Vancouver

Airport   See "Getting to Vancouver" in Chapter 2.

American Express   1040 W. Georgia St. (☎ 604/669-2813). It's open Monday through Friday 8:30am to 5:30pm, Saturday 10am to 4pm.

Area Code   The telephone area code for all of British Columbia is 604.

Babysitters   Most major hotels can arrange baby-sitting service and have cribs available; consult the guest services directory in your room for the phone number or hotel extension. If you need cribs, car seats, or other baby accessories, Cribs and Carriages (☎ 604/988-2742) delivers them right to your hotel.

Business Hours   Vancouver banks are open Monday through Thursday from 10am to 3pm, Friday until 6pm. Some banks, like Canadian Trust, are also open on Saturday. Office business hours are 9am to 5pm Monday through Friday (lunch time is from noon to 1pm). Stores are generally open Monday through Saturday from 10am to 6pm. Last call at the city's restaurant bars and cocktail lounges is 2am.

Camera Repair   Camtex Camera, 201-1855 Burrard St. (☎ 604/734-0242), is a good repair shop for new and old cameras.

Car Rentals   See "Getting Around," earlier in this chapter.

Climate   See "When to Go" in Chapter 2.

Currency   See "Money" in Chapter 2.

Currency Exchange   The best exchange rates are at Remo Exchange, 789 Burrard St., near Robson Street (☎ 604/685-4921). Banks also have a better exchange rate than most foreign exchanges (since the latter charges transaction and service fees).

Dentist   Most major hotels have a dentist on call. Denta Centre, Bentall Centre, 1055 Dunsmuir St. (☎ 604/669-6700), is an option. You must make an appointment. They are open Monday through Thursday from 8am to 5pm.

Doctor   Hotels usually have a doctor on call. Vancouver Medical Clinics, Bentall Centre, 1055 Dunsmuir St. (☎ 604/683-8138), is a drop-in clinic that is open Monday through Friday 8am to 4:30pm.

Documents Required   See "Visitor Information and Entry Requirements" in Chapter 2.

Driving Rules   See "Getting Around," earlier in this chapter.

Drugstores   See "Pharmacies," below.

Electricity   As in the United States, 110 volts, alternating current.

Embassies/Consulates   The U.S. Consulate is at 1095 W. Pender St. (☎ 604/685-4311). The British Consulate is at 1111 Melville St. (☎ 604/683-4421). The Australian Consulate is at 604-999 Canada Place (☎ 604/684-1177). Check the *Yellow Pages* for other countries.

Emergencies   Dial **911** for fire, police, ambulance, and poison control.

Etiquette   Canadians are a little more formal than U.S. citizens. They often don't use first names in direct conversation until they've gotten to know you for a while. Handshakes are a normal part of an introduction. Canadian English is in many respects similar to that spoken by the British, especially with regard to spelling words like "cheque," "centre," or "theatre." And, like the British, Canadians write out dates with the day preceding the month (for example, 15 January).

Eyeglass Repair   Eyeglass repair and replacement can be done at London Optical, 557 Granville St. (☎ 604/681-7202). If you wear contact lenses, you can get help at Image Contact Lens Centre, 815 W. Hastings St. (☎ 604/681-9488).

Holidays   See "When to Go" in Chapter 2.

Hospitals   St. Paul's Hospital is downtown at 1081 Burrard St. (☎ 604/682-2344). Central Vancouver hospitals include the following: Vancouver Hospital Health and Sciences Centre, 855 W. 12th Ave. (☎ 604/875-4111); British Columbia's Children's Hospital, 4480 Oak St. (☎ 604/875-2345); and Grace Hospital (limited to obstetrics), 4490 Oak St. (☎ 604/875-2424). In North Vancouver, there is Lions Gate Hospital, 231 E. 15th St. (☎ 604/988-3131).

Hotlines   Royal Canadian Mounted Police Tourist Alert is open for urgent messages only (☎ 604/264-2466 May through August). Messages for tourists are communicated in newspapers, radio, TV broadcasts, and postings at the InfoCentres. Other useful numbers include the following: Crisis Centre (☎ 604/872-3311); Rape Crisis Centre (☎ 604/255-6344); Victims of Violence (☎ 800/563-0808); Poison Control Centre (☎ 604/682-5050); Crime Stoppers (☎ 604/669-8477); SPCA animal emergency (☎ 604/879-7343); and B.C. Highway Conditions (☎ 604/525-4997).

Information   See "Visitor Information," earlier in this chapter.

Language   English and French are Canada's official languages. In British Columbia, however, English is the predominant language.

Libraries   The Central Library (Library Square) is located at 350 W. Georgia St., at the corner of Homer Street (☎ 604/331-3601). A visitor's lending card costs $20 (nonrefundable); residents borrow books for free. They are open Monday through Wednesday from 10am to 9pm (until 6pm Thursday through Saturday); and from October through April also Sunday 1pm to 5pm.

Liquor Laws   The legal drinking age in British Columbia is 19 years old. Spirits are sold only in government liquor stores, but beer and wine can be purchased from specially licensed, privately owned stores and pubs.

Lost Property   The Vancouver Police lost property room (☎ 604/665-2232) is the place to call; if you think you may have lost something on public transportation, call B.C. Transit (☎ 604/682-7887).

Luggage Storage/Lockers   Most downtown hotels will gladly hold your luggage before or after your stay. Just ask the bell captain. This service is usually free for guests. Lockers are available at the main Vancouver railway station, Pacific Central Station, 1150 Station St., near Main Street and Terminal Avenue south of Chinatown (☎ 604/669-3050). (This is also the main bus depot.) You can store your belongings for about $1.50 per day.

Mail   Both letters and postcards cost 50¢ to mail outside of Canada. The Canadian mail system is very quick; a letter mailed on Monday might actually arrive in New York by Wednesday. If you want to have mail sent to an address other than a hotel and you're an American Express cardmember, you can have mail forwarded to its office (see "American Express," above). You can buy stamps at the main post office (see "Post Office," above) or outlets displaying a "Postal Services" sign such as London Drugs in the Denman Plaza Centre. Once you've got your postcards and letters stamped, you can post them at any of the tall, red, rectangular mailboxes you see every few blocks on the street.

Maps   See "City Layout" earlier in this chapter.

Newspapers   The two local papers are the *Vancouver Sun*, which comes out Monday through Saturday, and *The Province*, which appears on the stands Sunday through Friday mornings. Other newsworthy papers are *The Financial Times of Canada*, the national *Globe and Mail*, the Chinese *Oriental Star*, the southeast Asian *Indo-Canadian Voice*, and the *Jewish Western Daily*. The weekly entertainment paper *The Georgia Straight* comes out on Thursday.

Pharmacies (Late-Night)   Shopper's Drug Mart, 1125 Davie St. (☎ 604/685-6445), is open 24 hours a day. Several Safeway supermarkets have late-night pharmacies, including the one at the corner of Robson and Denman Street, which is open until midnight.

Police   Dial **911.** The Vancouver City Police can be reached at ☎ 604/665-3321. The Royal Canadian Mounted Police handle most cases for tourists. They can be reached at ☎ 604/264-3111.

Post Office   The main post office is at West Georgia and Homer streets. It's open Monday through Friday from 8am to 5:30pm.

Radio   FM stations include 93.9 CJSF-SFU (new and alternative music); 99.7 THE FOX (album-oriented rock); 102.9 CFRO (community radio); 106.1 QM (soft favorites); and 107.1 CBU (classical, news, and drama). AM radio stations include 600 CHRX (classic rock); 690 CBU (classical, no commercials); 730 CKLG (top 40); 980 CKNW (talk and sports); 1040 CKST (alternate rock); 1130 CKWX (country); and 1320 CHQM (easy listening).

Restrooms   Hotel lobbies are your best bet for downtown facilities. The shopping centers have them as well.

Safety   Crime rates are relatively low in Vancouver, but it's best not to let your guard down. Crimes of opportunity, such as items being stolen from unlocked cars, are most common. Granville Street between Robson Street and False Creek is iffy at night. There are a lot of transient types milling around amid panhandlers and the homeless. Likewise, the areas surrounding the bus terminal, Chinatown, and Gastown are technically skid rows that should be avoided late at night.

Taxes   Hotel rooms are subject to a 10% tax. The provincial sales tax is 6% (excluding food, restaurant meals, and children's clothing). For specific questions, call the B.C. Consumer Taxation Branch (☎ 604/660-4500).

Most goods and services are subject to a 7% Canadian federal goods and services tax (GST). You can get a refund on short stay accommodations and all of your shopping purchases so long as they total at least $100. (This refund doesn't apply to car rentals, parking, restaurant meals, room service, tobacco, or alcohol.) Hotels and the InfoCentres can give you application forms. Save your receipts. For details on the GST, call 800/561-6990.

Taxis   See "Getting Around" earlier in this chapter.

Telephone/Fax   Phones in British Columbia are identical to U.S. phones. Local calls normally cost 25¢. Your calling cards are good in Vancouver, so take advantage of them. Many hotels charge up to $1 per local call and considerably more for long-distance charges. You can also buy phone cards at grocery and convenience stores; these cards enable you to use Touch-Tone pay phones without fiddling for coins. Many of the cards offer a substantial discount on long distance as well. They come in $10, $20, $30, and $50 denominations.

Television   Among Vancouver's television stations are CBUT (channel 2, cable 3) and BCTV (channel 8, cable 11), which are Canadian network affiliates, and KCTS (channel 9, cable 9), a PBS station. All three major U.S. networks are received from Seattle.

Time Zone   Vancouver is in the Pacific time zone, as are Seattle and San Francisco. Daylight saving time applies here, too, beginning April 7, 1996 and ending October 27, 1996 (beginning April 6, and ending October 26 in 1997).

Tipping   The tipping etiquette here is similar to that in the United States, so tip your waitperson 15%. Tip 50¢ per bag for bellboys and porters and $1 per day for the hotel housekeeper. Taxi drivers get a sliding-scale tip—fares under $4 deserve a $1 tip while fares over $5 should be tipped at 15%.

Transit Information   The B.C. Transit phone number is 604/521-0400.

Water   Vancouver's tap water comes from a pristine mountain reservoir on the outskirts of North Vancouver and is safe to drink.

Weather   Call 604/664-9010 or 604/664-9032 for weather updates; you can get marine forecasts by dialing 604/270-7411; each local ski resort has its own snow report line (see Chapter 6).

Vancouver Accommodations

Vancouver has a wide variety of fine accommodations in all price ranges. Expect the same high standards as in any Western city. In the past year, five new hotels have opened, others have renovated to keep up, and good-natured competition thrives among them. So no matter what your budget, there's no reason to settle for second best.

The lodgings listed in this chapter are located in the following city neighborhoods: **Downtown Vancouver,** which runs north-south from Canada Place and the Burrard Inlet to False Creek and east-west from Beatty Street to Thurlow Street; the **West End and English Bay,** which encompasses the area just west of downtown from Thurlow Street to Stanley Park; **Central Vancouver,** the area south of False Creek to the Fraser River; and the **University of British Columbia and Kitsilano** (including Granville Island), which lies due west of Central Vancouver from Granville Street to Point Grey. Other areas in which we list accommodations are **North Vancouver and West Vancouver,** on the north shore across the Burrard Inlet from downtown Vancouver and Stanley Park; and the city of **Richmond and the airport area**, south of the Fraser River and central Vancouver.

Room rates given in this guide are sorted into the following categories: **Very Expensive** ($200 and up a night); **Expensive** ($150 to $200); **Moderate** ($100 to $150); and **Inexpensive** (under $100) per summer double occupancy. All rates listed are in Canadian dollars. They are not inclusive of the 10% provincial accommodations tax nor the 7% goods and services tax (GST). Non-Canadian residents can get a GST rebate on short-stay accommodations by filling out the Tax Refund Application (see "Taxes" under "Fast Facts: Vancouver" in Chapter 3).

Weekend special rates are often 50% lower than midweek business travelers' rates, especially in the off-season. Many hotels also offer special packages that include dinners, theater tickets, or day excursions along with your accommodations. Ask about any specials a given hotel might be running when you make your reservations.

RESERVATIONS Reservations are highly recommended from June through September and, of course, over the holidays. If you arrive without a reservation or have trouble finding a room, call **Tourism Vancouver's** hotline **Discover British Columbia** (☎ 800/663-6000). Specializing in last-minute bookings, they can make arrangements for you through their large daily listing of hotels, hostels, and bed-and-breakfasts.

BED-AND-BREAKFAST REGISTRIES   If you prefer to stay in a bed-and-breakfast, the following agencies specialize in matching guests to establishments that best suit their needs:

- **Beachside Bed and Breakfast Registry,** 4208 Evergreen Ave., West Vancouver B.C., Canada VTV 1H1 (☎ 604/922-7773 or 800/563-3311). Coordinators Gordon and Joan Gibbs arrange accommodations in Vancouver, the North Shore, Parksville, the Whistler Mountain Area, Victoria, Chemainus, and Nanaimo—to name just a few places. Rates average from $40 to $80 for a double and $75 to $180 for a luxury suite that might include a private hot tub or fireplace. Joan is president of the Western Canada Bed and Breakfast Innkeepers Association and one of two bed-and-breakfast registry operators we found who personally inspects every one of the properties she represents. Hosts offer a range of accommodations, from popular romantic getaways and secluded retreats to cozy homes; quality is the common denominator. Gordon and Joan have also run the Beachside Bed and Breakfast for 10 years (see "North Vancouver & West Vancouver," below).
- **Born Free Bed and Breakfast of B.C.,** 4390 Frances St., Burnaby V5C ZR3 (☎ 604/298-8815 or 800/488-1941). Norma McCurrach, president of the B.C. Bed and Breakfast Association, regularly represents about 100 properties across the province and specializes in arranging bed-and-breakfast tours across British Columbia. Her registry covers budget travel as well. Norma is usually available from 6am to 11pm.
- **Canada-West Accommodations Bed and Breakfast Registry,** P.O. Box 86607, North Vancouver V7L 4LZ (☎ 604/929-1424 or 800/561-3223). Ellison Massey covers Vancouver, Victoria, Kelowna, and Whistler. Rates average from $65 to $85 per double. This registry has more than 100 bed-and-breakfast accommodations. All serve a full breakfast, and most have a privat e guest bath.
- **Town and Country Bed and Breakfast,** P.O. Box 74542, 2803 W. Fourth Ave. V6K IK2 (☎ 604/731-5942). Helen Burich arranges stays in Vancouver, Vancouver Island, and Victoria. Rates average from $45 to $160 per night for a minimum two-night stay. Hers is the oldest reservation service in British Columbia; dozens of host homes, many of which have been accommodating guests for 10 years, range from modest houses to lovely heritage homes. There are also a couple of cottages and self-contained suites. There is a $5 surcharge for Victoria and Vancouver Island reservations. In addition to normal business hours, Helen is often available evenings and weekends.

1 Best Bets

- **Best Historic Hotel: Hotel Vancouver,** 900 W. Georgia St. (☎ 604/684-3131 or 800/441-1414), was built by the Canadian-Pacific Railway in 1929 as Vancouver's grandest hotel. The chateau-style exterior, the lobby, and even the rooms—though thoroughly renovated—are built in a style and scale reminiscent of the great European railway hotels.
- **Best for Business Travelers:** The majority of guests at the **Delta Place Hotel,** 645 Howe St. (☎ 604/687-1122, or 800/877-1133 in the U.S.), are repeat customers, thanks to this hotel's Business Zone rooms. Each has a cordless phone, a halogen desk lamp, a real office chair, and even a stapler, paper clips, and other

small essentials. Printers, fax machines, laptops, and cellular phones are available through the business center (which also has work stations, a meeting room, secretarial services, and even equipment to bind reports).

- **Best for a Romantic Getaway:** The **Wedgewood Hotel,** 845 Hornby St. (☎ 604/689-7777), is an elegant, opulent European-style hotel. Balconies decorated with small flower beds overlook Robson Square. The intimate atmosphere of the rooms, restaurant, and cocktail lounge will keep you from straying too far from this wonderful hideaway.

- **Best Trendy Hotel:** The **Sylvia Hotel,** 1154 Gilford St. (☎ 604/681-9321), which opened in 1912, is the hottest place for hip thirty-something people. With a down-at-the heels beat generation atmosphere it's like Los Angeles' Chateau Marmont—with a perfect view of English Bay. Wealthier travelers may find their crowd at the sleek, posh, **Wall Centre Garden Hotel,** 1088 Burrard St. (☎ 604/331-1000 or 800/223-5652).

- **Best for Families:** The **Four Seasons,** 791 W. Georgia St. (☎ 604/689-9333, 800/332-3442 in the U.S.), provides kids with milk and cookies in the evening, along with their own menus and terry robes. The **Quality Hotel Downtown/Inn at False Creek,** 1335 Howe St. (☎ 604/682-0229 or 800/663-8479), offers families spacious accommodations and kitchens at reasonable prices.

- **Best Moderately Priced Hotel:** The **Pacific Palisades Hotel,** 1277 Robson St. (☎ 604/688-0461 or 800/663-1815), has the finest accommodations and facilities in this price range. With spacious rooms, an outstanding staff, and full amenities, the only thing that's moderate about this hotel is the price.

- **Best Inexpensive Hotel:** The accommodations at the **University of British Columbia,** 5961 Student Union Blvd. (☎ 604/822-1010), win hands down. You have ready access to the campus restaurants and pub, three Olympic-class swimming pools, tennis courts, Wreck Beach, a golf course, Pacific Spirit Park, and numerous other amenities right at your fingertips for less than $45 per night.

- **Best B&B:** Built in 1905 by one of early Vancouver's few photographers, the **West End Guest House,** 1362 Haro St. (☎ 604/681-2889), is filled with his work as well as an impressive collection of Victorian antiques. Fresh-baked brownies or cookies appear in your room with the turn-down service every evening, and the staff is truly professional.

- **Best Alternative Accommodation:** The **Rosellen Suites,** 2030 Barclay St. (☎ 604/689-4807), has truly spacious, furnished apartments with full kitchens and dining and living rooms for the same price as many standard hotel rooms.

- **Best Service:** Invisible when you don't need them but instantly attentive, professional, and cheerful when you do, the staff at the **Pacific Palisades Hotel,** 1277 Robson St. (☎ 604/688-0461 or 800/663-1815), is its best asset.

- **Best Location:** Finding the best located Vancouver hotel depends on what you plan to do while you're here. Beachcombers can stay steps from the sand at the **West Vancouver Beachside Bed and Breakfast,** 4208 Evergreen Ave., West Vancouver (☎ 604/922-7773 or 800/563-3111). The **Waterfront Centre Hotel,** 900 Canada Place Way (☎ 604/691-1991 or 800/828-7447 in the U.S.), is the perfect spot for business travelers. Professional sports fans can't get any closer to the stadium than the **Georgian Court Hotel** (☎ 604/682-5555 or 800/663-1155). The **Rosedale on Robson** (☎ 604/689-8033 or 800/661-8870) places theatergoers near both major theater complexes.

- **Best Health Club:** The indoor/outdoor pool, fitness center, weight/exercise room, aerobics classes, whirlpool, and saunas at **The Four Seasons,** 791 W. Georgia St. (☎ 604/689-9333), are without a doubt the best in town.

- **Best Hotel Pool:** The **Westin Bayshore,** 160 W. Georgia St. (☎ 604/682-3377), has a huge circular outdoor pool surrounded by lush greenery in a patio garden facing the harbor.
- **Best Views:** So many Vancouver hotels have outstanding views of the surrounding waterways, forested hills, and snow-capped mountains that it is difficult to choose the best. The unimpeded view from the **Pan-Pacific Hotel,** 300–999 Canada Pl. (☎ 604/662-8111, or 800/663–1515 in the U.S.) of floatplanes landing and taking off in the busy harbor, Stanley Park with the Lions Gate Bridge, North Vancouver, Grouse Mountain, and Mount Seymour in the background is our favorite.

2 Downtown Vancouver

Because downtown Vancouver is limited to a small peninsula resembling an upraised thumb pointing northwest from central Vancouver's outstretched hand, all downtown hotels are within reasonable walking distance of shopping, dining, and attractions. Most of the area is safe, though as one Vancouverite put it, "Whatever you do, don't reserve anything on Granville Street or Hastings Street unless you enjoy a wide, interesting, and exciting series of encounters with the weird and dangerous."

If you're traveling on the **SkyTrain,** you can get to the downtown hotels from the Granville or Burrard stops, which are just a few blocks apart. The Waterfront Station will leave you close to the Pan-Pacific and Waterfront Centre Hotels. Get off at Stadium for the Georgian Court Hotel, Rosedale on Robson, and the YWCA. On the **bus,** the **no. 8** will take you to the West End hotels, and the **no. 4** or **10** will get you to many hotels near False Creek.

VERY EXPENSIVE

Metropolitan Hotel

645 Howe St., Vancouver, B.C., Canada V6C 2Y9. ☎ **604/687-1122,** 800/268-1133 in Canada, or 800/877-1133 in the U.S. Fax 604/643-7267. 197 rms, 18 suites. 4 nonsmoking floors. Wheelchair-accessible rooms. Small pets allowed. A/C MINIBAR TV TEL. May–Sept, $260 double; $189 double on weekends. Oct–Apr, $220 double; $149 double on weekends. Suites to $1,500. AE, DC, ER, JCB, MC, V. Valet parking $16; underground parking.

When Delta Hotels took over this elegant 18-story hotel from the Mandarin hotel chain, they were careful not to disturb the building's original *feng shui* (an ancient Chinese system that claims buildings can be constructed to bring prosperity and good health to their inhabitants). Now owned by Liverton Hotels, it is still as elegant and intimate as ever. Decor in the soundproof guest rooms is tastefully subdued and designed to be functional. Most rooms have small balconies. Studio suites are recommended—they're much roomier and only slightly more expensive. Business Zone rooms and suites, which are well worth the additional $15, are equipped with cordless phones, modem hook-ups, power strips, printers, halogen desk lamps, real office chairs, and even staplers, tape, and paper clips. Children stay free in parents' room, and those under six eat free in the restaurant when accompanied by a paying adult.

Dining/Entertainment: Gates Restaurant is a fine dining room serving West Coast cuisine at breakfast, lunch, and dinner (entreés from $11.50 to $22.50). The Clipper Lounge has daily buffet and lunch entrées. There's also an evening piano bar.

Services: 24-hour room service; concierge (one of the best in Vancouver); valet; in-room coffee; morning newspaper; shoeshine service; umbrellas; cellular phone rental.

Facilities: Three lane, glass-enclosed lap pool and Jacuzzi; steam room; massage; squash and racquetball courts; weight/exercise room; saunas with TV; sundeck; business center; meeting/banquet facilities.

Four Seasons Hotel

791 W. Georgia St., Vancouver B.C., Canada V6C 2T4. ☎ **604/689-9333,** 800/332-3442 in the U.S., or 800/268-6282 in Canada. Fax 604/684-4555. 330 rms, 55 suites. Wheelchair-accessible rooms. A/C MINIBAR TV TEL. Year-round, $285–$385 double; $335–$900 suite. AE, CB, DC, ER, JCB, MC, V. Parking $16 .

This modern 28-story palace lies so discreetly atop the Pacific Centre shopping complex that you could walk right past it without noticing. Once inside, however, you are instantly immersed in the Four Seasons's signature understated luxury. Built in 1978, the hotel has an Asian-influenced decor; a seated Buddha statue serenely commands the lobby. Standard rooms are average sized. For more space, try a corner deluxe or deluxe Four Seasons room. All have thick terry robes, fluffy bath towels, marble vanities, and top-quality amenities. The service is outstanding.

Dining/Entertainment: The Four Seasons boasts one of Vancouver's three four-star restaurants—Chartwells (which has hosted the queen herself)—and possibly Canada's most gorgeous cocktail bar. The Garden Terrace offers dining in a less formal atmosphere.

Services: 24-hour room service; concierge; laundry and valet service; complimentary shoeshine; twice-daily housekeeping. Children get cookies and milk in the evening as well as their own special room service menus and robes.

Facilities: Indoor/outdoor pool; fitness center; weight/exercise room; aerobics classes; whirlpool; saunas; banquet/meeting space for 800 people.

Hotel Vancouver

900 W. Georgia St., Vancouver B.C., Canada V6C 2W6. ☎ **604/684-3131** or 800/ 441-1414. Fax 604/662-1929. 466 rooms, 42 suites. Nonsmoking rooms. Wheelchair-accessible rooms. Small pets allowed. A/C MINIBAR TV TEL. From $245 double; from $260 suite. AE, CB, DC, DISC, ER, MC, V. Parking $13.

A massive, stately stone landmark, this is the grand dame of Vancouver hotels. Its green copper château-style roof decorated with looming gargoyles once dominated the skyline. Artisans from 10 countries spent 12 months carving the facades, and 166 tons of marble were used for the interior. Designed on a generous scale, the Vancouver has big everything—bathtubs, hallways, elevators, and chandeliers—giving it a feeling of wonderful spaciousness. The hotel exudes old-style comfort, starting with the mighty armchairs and svelte showcases in the brown-russet lobby and piano bar. The bedrooms, offering city, harbor, and mountain views, are reasonably large. But the best rooms are on the Entrée Gold floors, with French doors and upgraded furniture.

Dining/Entertainment: The Panorama Roof is one of Vancouver's plushest dining and dance spots. The ground-floor informal restaurant serves three meals a day.

Services: 24-hour room service; complimentary morning coffee and newspaper; twice-daily housekeeping; overnight pressing and shoeshine; valet laundry; babysitting; business center and business amenities available including secretarial service. The Entrée Gold executive floor has direct check-in with a concierge on the floor; private lounge and boardroom; free local phone calls; and includes continental breakfast with stay.

Facilities: Indoor pool; wading pool; Jacuzzi; health club with weight room; sauna; tanning; massage; kinesiology; banquet/meeting space; car rental; beauty salon;

Downtown Vancouver Accommodations

Barclay Hotel 9
Best Western Listel
  O'Doul's Hotel 11
Blue Horizon 3
Buchan Hotel 4
Days Inn Downtown 18
Metropolitan Hotel 20
Four Seasons Hotel 25
Georgian Court Hotel 24
Hotel Georgia 21
Hotel Vancouver 15
Hyatt Regency
  Vancouver 16
Landmark Hotel 5
Pacific Palisades Hotel 10
Pan-Pacific Hotel
  Vancouver 26
Quality Hotel Downtown/
  Inn at False Creek 23
Rosedale on Robson 2
Rosellen Suites 8
Sunset Inn 17
Sutton Place Hotel 14
Sylvia Hotel 1
The Hotel at the YWCA 19
Waterfront Centre Hotel 27
Wedgewood Hotel 22
West End Guest House 7
Westin Bayshore 12
YMCA 13
The Wall Centre Garden
  Hotel 28

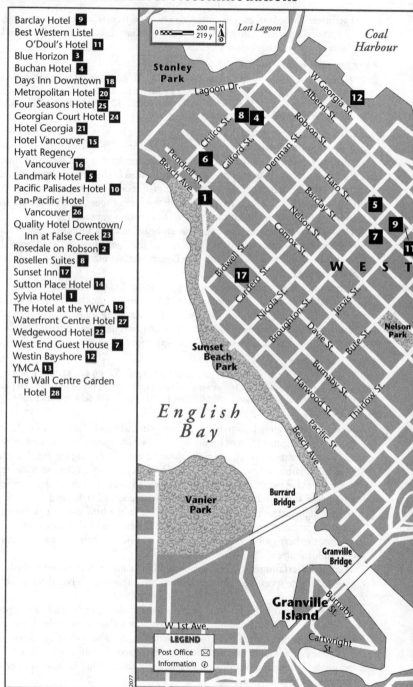

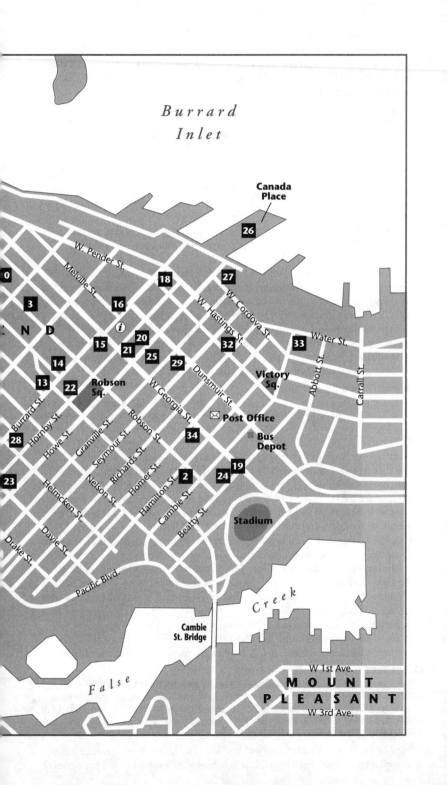

barbershop; shoeshine; shopping arcade including tobacconist that carries an excellent humidor of Cuban hand-rolled cigars.

Hyatt Regency Vancouver

655 Burrard St., Vancouver B.C., Canada V6C 2R7. ☎ **604/683-1234** or 800/233-1234. Reservations fax 604/682-3118. Guest fax 604/689-3707. 644 rms, 34 suites. Wheelchair-accessible rooms. A/C MINIBAR TV TEL. Apr 16–Oct, $210–$230 double; $330–$650 suite; Nov–Apr 15, $165–$195 double; $280–$650 suite. Weekend discounts available. AE, CB, DC, ER, MC, V. Parking $16.50.

The Hyatt is a 34-story white tower built over the huge Royal Centre Mall with scores of shops. The rooms are very large, and the furnishings are new. Corner rooms on the north and west sides have balconies with lovely views. For an additional $25, rooms on the Regency Club floors offer access by keyed elevator, concierge, continental breakfast, 5pm hors d'oeuvres service, evening pastries, coffee, tea, and soda in a private lounge with a stereo and large-screen TV. Rooms come with terry robes and an assortment of amenities.

Dining/Entertainment: Fish and Co. offers upscale seafood and continental cuisine for lunch, dinner, and Sunday brunch buffet. The Café serves casual breakfast and lunch, including salad bar and pasta bar daily. The Peacock Club Lounge also serves a weekday lunch buffet. The Gallery Bar features big-screen sports.

Services: Room service; concierge; laundry; valet service; doctor and dentist on call; summer programs for children; in-room coffeemaker; iron and ironing board.

Facilities: Heated outdoor pool; health club; saunas; access to squash and racquetball courts; business center; 26 meeting rooms.

Pan-Pacific Hotel Vancouver

300-999 Canada Place, Vancouver, B.C., Canada V6C 3B5. ☎ **604/662-8111**, 800/937-1515 in the U.S., or 800/663-1515 in Canada. 467 rms, 39 suites. Nonsmoking rooms. A/C MINIBAR TV TEL. Mid-Apr–Nov, $250–$270 double. Dec–mid-Apr, $210–$235 double; $200–$900 suite. Children under 18 stay free in parents' room. AE, DC, ER, MC, V. Valet parking $18.

Canada Place, with its five soaring white-Teflon sails, houses the Vancouver Trade and Convention Centre and the Cruise Ship Terminal. It dominates the harbor as Vancouver's signature structure. Rising 23 stories above it is the Pan-Pacific Hotel. Opened for Expo '86 at a cost of $100 million, it is the most expensive hotel ever built in Vancouver. The lobby, reached by a five-story escalator, has a three-story atrium with a sprawling Pacific Rim fountain that flows in from the terrace. The Cascades Lounge is enclosed by a huge expanse of glass exposing dramatic harbor and mountain views. Rooms are large and elegant. Try to get a room with a harbor view.

Dining/Entertainment: The Five Sails Restaurant is one of the city's best eateries. Café Pacifica serves Canadian specialties; it also has a Chinese dim sum bar and a Friday night Italian buffet by chef Enrico Balestra, a former opera tenor who serenades diners with his repertoire.

Services: 24-hour room service, massage, shiatsu.

Facilities: The health club is well worth the $15 fee; it offers state-of-the-art aerobics equipment, weights, squash, racquetball, paddle-tennis courts, and pool.

✪ The Sutton Place Hotel (formerly Le Meridien)

845 Burrard St., Vancouver, B.C., Canada V6Z 2K6. ☎ **604/682-5511** or 800/543-4300. Fax 604/682-5513. 397 rms, 47 suites. Nonsmoking floors. 4 wheelchair-accessible rooms. A/C MINIBAR TV TEL. May–Sept, $215–$295 double; $350–$450 suite. Oct–Apr, $190–$220 double; $350–$450 suite. Children under 18 stay free in parents' room. AE, CB, DC, DISC, JCB, MC, V. Underground parking $14.95; valet parking available.

Fans of the former Le Meridien will be pleased to know that the service has not slipped a bit at this hotel, though it is now under the ownership and management of the Grand Group. The modern 21-story luxury property maintains the feel of a small, elegant European-style hotel in both its short-stay and long-stay towers. A marble-floored, stately entry welcomes you into comfortable rooms tastefully furnished in subdued creams and dusky pastels. Single female business travelers will appreciate both the feeling of security and special touches like the full in-house salon. Personable service, fine amenities, and the excellent location off Robson Street make your stay a grand experience.

Dining/Entertainment: Le Club is the hotel's fine dining establishment. Café Fleuri serves breakfast and lunch daily, a Sunday jazz brunch, and a seafood buffet on Friday and Saturday evenings. On Thursday through Saturday evenings, the cafe also presents a 20-item "chocolaholic" dessert bar. La Promenade Lounge and the Gerard Lounge both offer light snacks and a piano bar.

Services: 24-hour room service; concierge; limo service; complimentary newspaper; twice-daily housekeeping; laundry/valet service with 24-hour pressing; shoeshine; babysitting; multilingual staff; in-room movies.

Facilities: Glass-covered indoor pool; outdoor deck; weight/exercise room; whirlpool; women's sauna; men's steam room. Full salon services from Le Spa, including massage, manicurist, tanning, body treatments, and hairstylist. Business center, meeting/banquet space, gift shop, and florist.

The Wall Centre Garden Hotel

1088 Burrard St., Vancouver BC, Canada V6Z 2R9. ☎ **604/331-1000** or 800/223-5652. Fax 604/331-1001. 249 rooms, 142 suites. Nonsmoking rooms. Wheelchair-accessible rooms. A/C MINIBAR TV TEL. $210–$380 double. AE, DC, ER, MC, V. SkyTrain: Granville. Valet parking $14.

The newly constructed Wall Centre is hard to miss. Its two distinctive blue-gray glass towers are among the tallest in the central downtown area (a third tower, yet to be built, will expand the hotel to a total of 1,500 rooms). There is a neat lineup of guests' and managers' cars out front: Jaguars, Rolls Royces, Mercedes, and the occasional Lambourghini. Owner Peter Wall is the quintessential maverick millionaire, and the Wall Centre is his personal tribute to everything he's ever liked in the world's finest hotels.

The decor was carefully chosen, from the gold-leaf covered staircase, custom-designed furniture, and hand-blown glass chandeliers in the lobby to the half-dozen peepholes on each guest room door. The rooms are elegant: blond-wood furniture, down comforters, video checkout in five languages, a safe, three two-line phones, and all the amenities.

Dining/Entertainment: There are three restaurants ranging from fine dining spots to a lounge/cafe with live music five nights a week.

Services: 24-hour room service, concierge, massage, and beauty center.

Facilities: Business center, full gym, aerobics, indoor pool, sauna, Jacuzzi.

Waterfront Centre Hotel

900 Canada Place Way, Vancouver B.C., Canada V6C 3L5. ☎ **604/691-1991,** 800/828-7447 in the U.S., or 800/268-9411 in Canada. Fax 604/691-1999. 489 rms, 29 suites. Nonsmoking floors. Wheelchair-accessible rooms. Small pets allowed. A/C MINIBAR TV TEL. Nov–late Apr, $220–$260 double. Late Apr–Oct, $225–$275 double. Weekend packages from $115 double. Suites $350–$1,700. AE, CB, DC, ER, MC, V. Parking $12.

With 23 stories of reflective blue glass, this Canadian-Pacific hotel (opened in 1991) takes great advantage of its location on the harbor—70% of the rooms have spectacular harbor and mountain views. The spacious glass, brass, and fossilized-limestone lobby is dominated by a huge mixed-media tapestry *Voyage of Discovery*, depicting Captain Vancouver's final Pacific Northwest journey. This is just one of many works by emerging Canadian artists that decorates both the public spaces and the sprawling guest rooms. Showing true concern for the environment, this hotel is a leader in recycling and reducing environmental impact. A concourse links the hotel to the rest of Waterfront Centre, Canada Place, and the Cruise Ship Terminal.

Dining/Entertainment: The Heron Lounge/dining room just off the lobby offers Mediterranean cuisine from an open kitchen. It serves light meals and snacks, as well as full breakfast, lunch, and dinner. The lounge has nightly piano entertainment and has seating on the outdoor terrace during the summer.

Services: 24-hour room service; newspapers; coffee and tea service in the guest foyer on each floor beginning at 5:30am; modem access lines; in-room movies.

Facilities: Full service health club; heated outdoor pool; business center.

EXPENSIVE

Georgian Court Hotel

773 Beatty St., Vancouver B.C., Canada V6B 2M4. ☎ **604/682-5555** or 800/663-1155. Fax 604/682-8830. 160 rms, 20 suites. Two nonsmoking floors. Wheelchair-accessible rooms. A/C MINIBAR TV TEL. May–Sept, $150–$170 double. Oct–Apr, $115–$135 double. AE, DC, ER, MC, V. Parking $6.

This hotel lies in a nondescript, 10-year-old, 14-story brick building located directly across the street from B.C. Place and the new General Motors Plaza on the less populated side of downtown. While it may never be considered trendy or stately, this small business/luxury hotel is a class act. It is ideal for sports fans and people attending the various trade shows at the stadiums. The recently renovated rooms are large and clean; the decor is dark and masculine. The best views are from the front rooms, dominated by the stadium's white dome.

Dining/Entertainment: The William Tell Restaurant serves classic Swiss cuisine prepared by 1995 Restauranteur of the Year Erwin Doebeli (see Chapter 5). If you don't have tickets to a local game, you can always catch the action in Rigney's Bar and Grill, named for a former B.C. Lions football player. It's good, casual, cheap, and packed when there's a game on TV.

Services: Room service, turndown service, morning newspaper, in-room coffeemaker, in-room movies.

Facilities: Health club with weights, lifecycle, stairmaster, whirlpool, sauna, indoor lap pool; sundry shop (open morning and evenings); banquet/meeting rooms.

✪ Wedgewood Hotel

845 Hornby St., Vancouver B.C., Canada V6Z 1V1. ☎ **604/689-7777** or 800/663-0666. Fax 604/688-3074. 59 rms, 34 suites. Nonsmoking rooms. A/C MINIBAR TV TEL. $190–$260 double; $340–$360 suite; $440–$460 penthouse. AE, CB, DC, ER, JCB, MC, V. Underground parking $10; valet parking available.

The romance, elegance, and opulence of this truly European-style hotel are the personal touches of owner/general manager Ileni Skalbania. In 1984, she acquired the failing 13-story Mayfair Hotel and completely gutted and rebuilt the interior, furnishing the public spaces with many pieces from her own art and antique collection. The result is an eclectic decor that blends French provincial, Italianate, and Edwardian styles. On weekdays, the hotel is frequented by a corporate crowd (and is notable as a hotel where single female business travelers feel secure), but on weekends it becomes a romantic getaway. All guest rooms have landscaped balconies overlooking Robson Square. Terry robes, dark-out drapes, a morning paper, and a box of chocolates upon arrival are just a few of the hotel's special touches.

Dining/Entertainment: Bacchus Ristorante serves outstanding northern Italian cuisine (see Chapter 5). The Bacchus Piano Lounge features Wes Mackey playing blues guitar nightly except Sunday (see Chapter 9). They also serve breakfast, lunch, afternoon tea (daily from 2 to 4pm), cocktails, and snacks.

Services: 24-hour room service; twice-daily housekeeping; babysitting; limousine service; a box of chocolates for every new guest; business services, overnight laundry service; modem access; in-room movies.

Facilities: Hairstylist; dedicated fax lines; access to adjacent Chancery Squash Club, with weight room, aerobics, sauna, massage.

MODERATE

Days Inn Downtown

921 W. Pender St., Vancouver B.C., Canada V6C 1M2. ☎ **604/681-4335**, 800/325-2525 or 800/329-7466. Fax 604/681-7808. 80 rms, 5 suites. TV TEL. Nonsmoking rooms. May–Sept, $120 double; $140 twin; $160 suite. Oct–Apr, $89–$99 double; $109 twin; $119 suite. Children under 12 stay free in parents' room. AE, DC, DISC, ER, JCB, MC, V. Free parking.

The only moderately priced hotel in the downtown business center, this well-maintained seven-story hotel is more than 70 years old. Standard rooms are rather small. While there is no room service and only basic amenities, the rooms are quiet and clean (if without views). In addition, the satellite TVs have remotes, and in-room movies are free. Casablancalike ceiling fans replace air-conditioning, which is rarely necessary in Vancouver. In your room, you'll also find a safe in the closet, voice-mail message service, coffeemaker, and hairdryer. They also have guest laundry facilities, refrigerators available on request, and photocopying/faxing/secretarial services for a nominal charge.

The Chelsea Restaurant serves three meals daily. The Bombay Bicycle Club, an English-pub style lounge, and the Bull and Bear Sports Lounge, with a large-screen TV, are popular spots with local businesspeople.

Hotel Georgia

801 W. Georgia St., Vancouver B.C., Canada V6C 1P7. ☎ **604/682-5566** or 800/663-1111. Fax 604/682-8192. 310 rms, 2 suites. A/C TV TEL. May–mid-Oct, $140–$170 double. Mid-Oct–Apr, $130–$140 double. Suites $350–$500. Children under 16 stay free in parents' room. AE, CB, DC, ER, MC, V. Parking $12.

The Hotel Georgia stands squarely in the heart of downtown Vancouver across the street from the Four Seasons Hotel. A massive, tan-brick corner building, the Georgia has an impressive wood-paneled lobby with a genuine fireplace, beautiful chandeliers, heavy carpeting, and ornate brass elevators. In addition to a vast array of facilities, the hotel has an exceptionally friendly, helpful staff. Bedrooms are medium sized. The bathrooms are tiny but well equipped. Each executive room has an almost separate sitting area. The best views are from the rooms facing the Vancouver Art Gallery.

There are no health club facilities; room service is available. There is a candlelit restaurant for serious dining, an Olde English pub filled with good cheer and folksy entertainment, and a street-side patio lounge devoted to business luncheons.

Quality Hotel Downtown/The Inn at False Creek

1335 Howe St., Vancouver B.C., Canada V6Z 1R7. ☎ **604/682-0229**, 800/663-8474, or Quality Hotels International at 800/221-2222. Fax 604/662-7566. 157 rms, 20 one-bedroom and junior suites. A/C TV TEL. May–Oct 12, $130 double; $140–$160 suite. Oct 13–Apr 30, $89 double; $99–$109 suite. Children under 18 stay free in parents' room. AE, CB, DC, ER, MC, V. Parking $5 per day.

This newly renovated, seven-story hotel blends relaxed southwestern elegance with Mexican art, pottery, and rugs. The room decor, which features a deep-blue, gray, and russet color scheme and decorative brick, captures the same easy feeling. The hotel is ideal for families. The one-bedroom suites have fully equipped kitchens. Rooms on the back side might be preferable because the front, though it has a view of False Creek, is right on top of the Granville Bridge on-ramp. Noise is not a problem, however, thanks to double-pane windows and dark-out curtains. Rooms for the hearing impaired are equipped with strobe light fire alarms.

In the off-season, the "Adventure Passport" offer entitles guests to discounts of up to 50% at many major local attractions, restaurants, and theaters. Laundry, valet, and room service are available, along with an outdoor pool as well as complimentary fitness facilities at Fitness World, just a block away. The Creekside Café serves well-prepared basics at reasonable prices throughout the day, while the Sports Lounge offers a relaxed atmosphere, friendly service, and a full bar.

Ⓢ Rosedale on Robson Suite Hotel

838 Hamilton (at Robson Street), Vancouver B.C., Canada V6B 5W4. ☎ **604/689-8033** or 800/661-8870. Fax 604/689-4426. 275 one- and two-bedroom suites with kitchens. Nonsmoking rooms. Wheelchair-accessible rooms. A/C MINIBAR TV TEL. May–Oct, studio suite: $145–$180 double; one-bedroom suite: $185–$270 double; two-bedroom suite: $240–$470 double. Nov–Apr, studio suite: $100–$125 double; one-bedroom suite: $145–$210 double; two-bedroom suite: $210–$470 double. AE, DC, ER, MC, V. Parking $7.50.

Vancouver's newest hotel as of this writing, the Rosedale is capped by a 15-foot-tall rose emblem. Guests arrive through a covered driveway and are welcomed in a grand marble lobby. The suites feature separate living rooms (except the 12 studio suites); two TVs; and full kitchenettes with a microwave, stove, oven, sink, and half refrigerator. Dishes and cooking utensils are available on request. Rooms are not huge, but ample bay windows and light wood furnishings scaled to the rooms give them a feeling of spaciousness. Corner suites have more windows. Upper-floor suites have furnished terraces and great city views. This end of Robson is not crowded with little shops and restaurants, but you'll find the Pacific Centre Mall, Library Square, the Queen Elizabeth Theatre, the stadiums, and the Ford Centre for the Performing Arts within a few blocks.

Dining/Entertainment: The restaurant is a New York–style deli (without the attitude, of course)—a rarity in this city filled with West Coast cuisine.

Services: Room service; concierge; computer and fax connections. Executive floors include bathrobes, free local calls, daily newspaper, nightly turndown service, in-room movies, Nintendo games, modem access lines.

Facilities: Indoor pool; Jacuzzi; sauna; weight/exercise room; gift shop.

INEXPENSIVE

Ⓢ The Hotel at the YWCA

733 Beatty St., Vancouver B.C., Canada V6B 2M4. ☎ **604/662-8188** or 800/663-1424. Fax 604/681-2550. 155 rms with hall, shared and private baths. TV TEL. $76–$86 twin; $55–$76 double; $73 family. Student, senior, group, and weekly rates. Off-season discounts as well as weekly and monthly rates available. MC, V. Parking available.

Opened in the fall of 1995, this attractive, newly constructed 12-story residence provides an excellent alternative for female travelers or families with limited budgets. The YWCA is next door to the Georgian Court Hotel and across the street from B.C. Place Stadium. Bedrooms are simply furnished. Some have TVs, and all have telephones. Although there are no restaurants in the building, there are quite a few reasonably priced places nearby, and three communal kitchens are open to guests with

🏛 Family-Friendly Hotels

Vancouver hotels offer a wide range of choices if you're bringing the kids—and you don't have to sacrifice service or quality. To add to their appeal, a lot of the downtown hotels offer babysitting.

Four Seasons Hotel *(see p. 39)*   They give your kids cookies and milk in the evening as well as their own special room-service menus and robes.

Westin Bayshore *(see p. 47)*   Its location in Coal Harbor marina makes it a great family hotel. Your kids can walk to Stanley Park, the Vancouver Aquarium, Nature House, and other park attractions without ever crossing a street.

Quality Hotel Downtown/The Inn at False Creek *(see p. 45)*   Family suites in this hotel are spacious and well designed. There's even an enclosed balcony area in some of the upper-floor suites where your kids can play without leaving the suite. The full kitchen facilities, casual restaurant, and off-season Adventure Passport discounts also make this an excellent deal for families.

Rosellen Suites *(see p. 48)*   This is the perfect place for you and your family if you are looking for a homelike atmosphere in full apartment accommodations. Its location—a block away from Stanley park, the beaches, and Denman Street—makes it easy to do grocery shopping as well as to play.

their own utensils. There are also three TV lounges; a coin-operated laundry; and free access to the coed YWCA Fitness Centre (a 15-minute walk from the hotel), which has 25-meter pool, steam room, whirlpool, aerobic studios, and conditioning gym.

YMCA

955 Burrard St., Vancouver B.C., Canada V6C 2K6. ☎ **604/681-0221.** Fax 604/688-0220. 111 men's and women's rms (none with bath), 120 beds. May–Sept, $170 per week; $48 twin. Oct–Apr, $160 per week; $42 twin. Additional cot in room $7. MC, V. Parking $3.75.

The guests here are mostly a mixture of new arrivals, business people with tight budgets, and travelers seeking an alternative to youth hostels. The building is not nearly as new as the YWCA (see above), but it is a little more centrally located. Rooms for both men and women are small and simply furnished but spotlessly clean. Some rooms include a private TV for $2 extra. The bathrooms are shared, as are the pay phones. Guests have full use of the facilities, including two swimming pools, lifecycles, nautilus and universal gyms, a rooftop running track, racquetball courts, and a coin-op laundry. Jonathan T's, the restaurant, is open Monday through Saturday for breakfast and lunch. No alcoholic beverages are permitted in building, and there is a midnight curfew.

3 The West End & English Bay

VERY EXPENSIVE

Westin Bayshore

1601 W. Georgia St., Vancouver B.C., Canada V6G 2V4. ☎ **604/682-3377** or 800/228-3000. Fax 604/691-6959. 484 rms, 33 suites. Nonsmoking rooms. 2 floors handicapped accessible. A/C MINIBAR TV TEL. Mid-Apr–Oct, $215–$230 double; $310 junior suite; $450–$1,375 full suite. Nov–mid-Apr, $139–$169 double; $255–$750 suite. Children 18 or under stay free in parents' room. AE, CB, DC, ER, MC, V. Parking $7.

Perched on Coal Harbor at the eastern edge of Stanley Park, the Bayshore has a wonderfully relaxing resort atmosphere, yet it's almost right downtown; the main shopping streets are only a few minutes away. Built in the 1960s and renovated in 1994, the rooms in the original building are comfortable and well furnished. The rooms in the 20-story tower (a 1970 addition) are larger and have balconies and bigger windows. The unimpeded view below is a dazzling array of luxury yachts (many for charter) docked in the marina, with the park and the mountains in the background. Also available are 75 new environmentally friendly guest rooms.

Dining/Entertainment: The Garden Restaurant offers delicious continental fare for breakfast, lunch, dinner, and Sunday brunch in an informal atmosphere. Trader Vic's nautical theme and seafood menu are world renowned.

Services: The hotel's "Service Express" department coordinates all guest needs such as room service, concierge, laundry, valet service, boat charters, bicycle and car rentals, as well as free shuttle service to the downtown area.

Facilities: Outdoor swimming pool surrounded by a sundeck, rock gardens, and lush greenery; indoor pool; complete health club with juice bar; nine retail shops; barber shop and beauty salon.

EXPENSIVE

Best Western Listel O'Doul's Hotel

1300 Robson St., Vancouver B.C., Canada V6E 1C5. ☎ **604/684-8461** or 800/663-5491. Fax 604/684-8326. 119 rms, 11 suites. Nonsmoking rooms. Wheelchair-accessible rooms. A/C MINIBAR TV TEL. May–Sept, $180–$200 double; $275–$350 suite. Oct–Apr, $135–$165 double; $150–$250 suite. AE, DC, DISC, ER, JCB, MC, V. Parking $10.

Located on Vancouver's liveliest strolling, shopping, and dining strip, O'Doul's has ascended from its humble beginnings in the late 1960s as a four-story motor inn. Bay windows were added to the original facade along with a 1986 two-story addition. O'Doul's has been renovated and improved; it is now regarded as one of Vancouver's better hotels. Its bright contemporary California style is complemented by potted plants, brass accents, and original artworks commissioned by the hotel. Deluxe rooms facing Robson Street are worth the price. Soundproof windows eliminate traffic noise.

Dining/Entertainment: O'Doul's Restaurant serves breakfast, lunch, and dinner in a street-side dining room that is whimsically decorated in a jungle motif complete with ceramic panthers and painted papier-mâché parrots.

Services: 24-room service; concierge; valet; laundry; and secretarial services.

Facilities: Indoor pool; exercise room; whirlpool; meeting/banquet space.

✪ Rosellen Suites

2030 Barclay St., Vancouver B.C., Canada V6G 1L5. ☎ **604/689-4807.** Fax 604/684-3327. 30 one- and two-bedroom private apartments with full kitchens and dining rooms. A/C TV TEL. $129–$130 one-bedroom; $170–$230 two-bedroom; $365 penthouse. Minimum 3-night stay. Additional person $15 per night. AE, DC, ER, MC, V. Free, limited parking.

Located on a quiet residential street right beside Stanley Park and near lots of restaurants, this unpretentious low-rise apartment building was converted in the 1960s into an apartment hotel. There is no lobby; the manager's office is only open from 9am to 5pm, but each guest gets a front door key. Upstairs, white stucco hallways are lined by the artistically designed copper doors to the suites. Modern and extremely comfortable, each suite features a spacious living room, separate dining area, full-sized kitchen with all necessary utensils, and other homey touches. This is a haven for film industry people as well as corporate travelers and families who wish to avoid the inconveniences of hotel living. (The penthouse is named after Katherine Hepburn, who stays there when she's in town.)

Services: Full maid service twice a week; laundry facilities; dry cleaning; two phones with a direct-line private phone number; 24-hour answering service; and free local calls.

Facilities: Cots and cribs available; business center; access to West End Community Weight Room and Vancouver Aquatic Centre nearby; fireplaces in some suites; dishwashers in medium and large suites; 28-inch Sony stereo TVs in large suites.

MODERATE

Barclay Hotel

1348 Robson St., Vancouver B.C., Canada V6E 1C5. ☎ **604/688-8850.** Fax 604/688-2534. 79 rms, 10 suites. A/C MINIBAR TV TEL. June–Sept, $85–$95 double; $119 suite. Oct–May, $69–$79 double; $99 suite. Senior discounts. AE, DC, MC, V. Limited parking $5 per day.

The Barclay is a small older hotel housed in a white, 1920's style three-story building surrounded by small shops and good restaurants; it's not far from Stanley Park. Chairs in the white-tiled lobby are rococo style, and there's an adjacent bistro lounge with a glassed-in patio facing Robson Street. Bedrooms are not large, but the space is expertly used. The rooms come with modern bathrooms. Some have minibars as well. Barkley's, the house restaurant, serves passable French cuisine at reasonable prices.

Blue Horizon

1225 Robson St., Vancouver B.C., Canada V6E 1C5. ☎ 604/688-1411 or 800-663-1333. Fax 604/688-4461. 214 rms. Nonsmoking rooms. Wheelchair-accessible rooms. A/C FRIDGE/MINIBAR TV TEL. $125–$135 double; $135–$145 twin; $159 studio; $225 suite. Off-season and senior discounts. Children under 16 sharing parents' room stay free. Additional person charge $15 per night. AE, DC, DISC, ER, JCB, MC, V. Parking $5.

Despite the appearance of its recently renovated lobby, which is decorated in blue tones and frosted, etched glass with an abstract glacial motif, this is not a luxury hotel. The hotel does, however, boast a great location, large rooms with balconies, and terrific views (the best views are high on the north side). The TVs have remotes, and in-room coffeemakers are standard. Superior rooms include minibars, duvets, and hairdryers. The service is inconsistent, and there is no room service or concierge; there is, however, the option of having refrigerators or minibars. There is a one-lane lap pool, sauna, whirlpool, and global gym available to guests. The restaurant and lounge offer three meals daily in a casual atmosphere.

Landmark Hotel & Conference Centre

1400 Robson St., Vancouver B.C., Canada V6G 1B9. ☎ 604/687-0511 or 800/830-6144. Fax 604/687-2801. 353 rms, 5 suites. Nonsmoking rooms. Wheelchair-accessible rooms. A/C TV TEL (MINIBARS in superior rooms). May–Oct 15, $125–$195 double; $225–$450 suite. Winter discounts from $85 double. AE, DC, ER, DISC, MC, V. Parking $6.

The Landmark—Vancouver's tallest hotel at 42 floors—stands at the west end of the Robson shopping strip. The small lobby was recently completely renovated and now includes an attractive coffee bar overlooking Robson Street. Many of the rooms have also been refurbished. Bedrooms are medium sized; all have private balconies, and some boast refrigerators as well. The hotel offers room service; laundry; valet; gift shop; concierge; exercise facilities; and sauna.

Crowning the hotel is Cloud Nine, a revolving restaurant with spectacular views at night. The food is a mix of continental and West Coast cuisines; prices are steep. If you prefer to dine at lower elevations, it's still great for drinks or an evening cappuccino.

✪ Pacific Palisades Hotel

1277 Robson St., Vancouver B.C., Canada V6E 1C4. ☎ 604/688-0461 or 800/663-1815. Fax 604/688-4374. 233 suites. Children under 18 stay free in parents' room. Full kitchens available

($10 extra). A/C MINIBAR MICROWAVE TV TEL. Mid-Apr–Oct, $145–$230 suite. Nov–mid-Apr, $99–$175 suite. Penthouses from $425. AE, CB, DC, ER, MC, V. Parking $10.50.

Although its two towers lack glamorous exteriors and the small lobby is hardly the place to make a grand entrance, the Pacific Palisades has all the facilities of a luxury hotel in addition to an outstanding staff. The hotel is popular with visiting film and TV production companies that frequently shoot in Vancouver. The North American flagship of the renowned Asian Shangri-La chain, it was converted from luxury apartments in 1991.

Suites are divided into studio, executive, and penthouse. All are spacious, well appointed, and have panoramic views (for the most part). Most suites have terraces. The kitchenettes have microwave ovens, coffeemakers, and minibars. Full kitchens are also available.

The Monterey Lounge and Grill, a laid-back, elegant street-side café, features surprisingly good, innovative West Coast cuisine. It serves three meals daily as well as Sunday brunch. The lounge offers cocktails accompanied by live entertainment in the evenings.

Services: 24-hour room service; concierge; limousine service; valet; laundry; complimentary shoeshine; business center with full secretarial services; voice-mail message service; and doctor on call.

Facilities: Tea/coffeemaker; daily newspaper; baby cribs; modem access; in-room movies; complete fitness center with health bar, sauna, indoor Olympic lap pool, tanning room; bicycle rentals (mountain bikes available); gift shop; and meeting/ banquet rooms.

Sunset Inn

1111 Burnaby St., Vancouver B.C., Canada V6E 1P4. ☎ **604/684-8763.** Fax 604/ 669-3340. 50 studios and one-bedroom suites. TV TEL. $78–$118 studios; $88–$128 one-bedroom suites; $528–$768 per week. 5 nonsmoking floors. Weekly rates and off-season discounts. AE, DC, ER, MC, V. Free parking.

Located on a quiet side street in the busy West End, this tall, gray concrete structure offers completely self-contained apartments that are nicely furnished in striking contemporary color schemes, each with a little balcony. Kitchens are completely equipped and include a toaster, coffeemaker, can opener, and utensils. The living rooms are spacious, the beds are comfortable, and the closets are reasonably large. There are leather armchairs and settees as well as a dining table. There's a fitness room on the main floor.

West End Guest House

1362 Haro St., Vancouver B.C., Canada V6E 1G2. ☎ **604/681-2889.** Fax 604/688-8812. 7 rms, all with private baths and nonsmoking. No pets allowed. TV TEL. $104–$195 double. AE, DC, MC, V. Free off-street parking.

Set back from a quiet residential street just a block from Robson Street and a short walk from Denman Street and Stanley Park, this lavender Victorian heritage house is easy to mistake for a private residence. Antiques and framed photographs of Vancouver abound in the front parlor as well as the bedrooms. Brass beds are covered with exquisite linens and goose-down duvets. Each room has its own TV, telephone, and private bath. Most rooms have an opening skylight or Casablanca-style ceiling fan. The basement rooms have the same charm, but no view. The veranda is discreetly labeled "smoking area," while the rest of the house is nonsmoking.

There is a guest lounge with a fireplace and a private garden for relaxing. A sundeck in the south-facing backyard invites sunbathing. An outstanding full breakfast is served in the salon, sherry is complimentary at tea time, and the pantry is stocked with tea and snacks. Guests can help themselves. You also have bicycles and fax service here.

INEXPENSIVE

Buchan Hotel

1906 Haro St., Vancouver B.C., Canada V6G 1H7. ☎ **604/685-5354.** Fax 604/685-5367. 60 rms (30 with private bath). All rooms nonsmoking. TV. May–Sept, $70 double. Oct–Apr, $75 double. Children under 12 stay free in parents' room. Weekly rates and off-season specials. AE, DC, MC, V. Street parking.

Built in the 1930s, this three-story building overlooks a minipark on a quiet, tree-lined, residential street. It's a two-minute walk to Stanley Park and Denman Street and 10 minutes to the business district. The rooms are small and the bathrooms smaller, but the rates are low and the staff is friendly. Rooms overlooking the park are brighter; front corner rooms are the largest. They also have in-house bike and ski storage and a guest laundry.

⊛ Sylvia Hotel

1154 Gilford St., Vancouver B.C., Canada V6G 2P6. ☎ **604/681-9321.** 97 doubles, 18 suites. TV TEL. Pets allowed. $55–$85 double; $85–$95 triple; $85–$95 suite. Additional charge for extra person $10. Additional charge for baby crib $5. Children under 18 sharing parents' room stay for free. AE, DC, MC, V. Parking $3.

Built in 1912—soon after the city streets reached its gorgeous location—the Sylvia is set on English Bay a few blocks from Stanley Park overlooking the beach. It's one of the oldest hotels in Vancouver. Only eight stories high, it was the tallest building in the West End for years. In recent years, it has become deservedly trendy.

Gray-stoned and ivy-wreathed, the Sylvia resembles a city mansion. The lobby sets the tone—it's small, restful, dark and has red carpets, ivory drapes, and overstuffed chairs. The same atmosphere prevails in the adjoining restaurant and crowded cocktail lounge (which was Vancouver's first when it opened in 1954). The restaurant serves three meals daily and has the same fabulous view as the historical cocktail lounge (see Chapter 9).

In the guest rooms, the furnishings are appropriately mismatched, in a manner similar to those in Los Angeles' Chateau Marmont. The views from the upper floors are unparalleled. Suites—all with full kitchens—are large enough for families. Sixteen rooms in a 1986 low-rise annex offer individual heating, but they're less interesting. There is valet and room service available in both sections. During the summer make reservations a few months ahead.

4 Central Vancouver

EXPENSIVE

Granville Island Hotel

1253 Johnston St., Vancouver B.C., Canada V6H 3R9. ☎ **604/683-7373** or 800/663-1840. Fax 604/683-3061. 49 rms, 5 suites. A/C TV TEL. June–Sept, $190 double; $205–$225 suite. Oct–May, $170 double; $185–$205 suite. Winter specials. AE, DC, ER, MC, V. Parking $7.

This small, modern hotel lies near the Granville Island public market and other attractions. Along with close-up views of False Creek, rooms have balconies, skylights, wooden venetian blinds, and bidets. There's also a marina; the staff will happily arrange boat charters. If you like to go to sleep before two in the morning, ask for a room as far away from the hotel's Pelican Bar as possible; from Thursday through

Saturday, it turns into a popular disco. Downtown and English Bay are a 10-minute drive or a two-minute ferry ride ($1.50) away.

MODERATE

⊛ Kenya Court Guest House

2230 Cornwall Ave., Vancouver B.C., Canada V6K 1B5. ☎ **604/738-7085.** 4 suites. All nonsmoking rooms with private bath. TV TEL. $85–$105 double. Rates include full breakfast. Additional charge for up to six guests. No credit cards. Free, limited on-street parking.

Every room in this heritage building has an unobstructed waterfront view of the park, ocean, mountains, and downtown Vancouver. Its Kitsilano location is ideal for strolling around Granville Island, Vanier Park, and other central Vancouver locales. There are also a nearby outdoor pool, tennis courts, and jogging trails. All of the rooms are large and tastefully furnished. A full breakfast (including eggs and bacon) is served in a glass solarium with a spectacular view of English Bay. There is also a piano in the guest lounge. Your hosts, the Williamses, speak French, German, and Italian as well as English.

Pillow 'n Porridge Guest House

2859 Manitoba St., Vancouver B.C., Canada V5Y 3B3. ☎ **604/879-8977.** 4 rms, 2 with private baths, 1 with kitchen. $95 double; $125 suite. Rates include full breakfast.

The Pillow 'n Porridge offers you the warm atmosphere of a 1908 coach house filled with antique furnishings and fireplaces. Situated in the city hall heritage area, this bed-and-breakfast is within walking distance of fine dining, ethnic restaurants, shops, Granville Island, and Queen Elizabeth Park. At no extra cost, enjoy a hearty breakfast of wild oat porridge topped with fruit, nuts, seeds, and brown sugar.

Johnson House Bed & Breakfast

2278 W. 34th Ave., Vancouver B.C., Canada V6M 1G6. ☎ **604/266-4175.** 3 rms, one with private bath. $55–$90 double. Discounts for long stays and off-season rates.

Sandy and Ron invite guests into their charming Kerrisdale district home. Outside, the rock garden and sculpture will catch your eye, as will the wooden carousel animals inside. After a good night's sleep in a big brass bed, you'll be treated to homemade muffins, breads, and jams.

Penny Farthing Inn

2855 W. 6th Ave., Vancouver B.C., Canada V6K 1X2. ☎ **604/739-9002.** Fax 604/739-9004. 4 rms, all nonsmoking. $75 double; $135–$155 suites. Rates include full breakfast.

This 1912 heritage house, located on a quiet residential street is filled with antiques and stained glass. A full breakfast is served on the brick patio of the English country-style garden. There are bikes available for trips to the surrounding beaches or nearby parks. To accommodate smokers (and the resident cats), wicker chairs are placed on the front porch of this nonsmoking establishment.

5 The University of British Columbia & Kitsilano

INEXPENSIVE

⊛ University of British Columbia Conference Centre

5961 Student Union Blvd., Vancouver B.C., Canada V6T 2C9. ☎ **604/822-1010.** Fax 604/822-1001. 3,600 rms, all with private bath and kitchenette or kitchen, including 48 triple suites available any time. A/C TV TEL. Walter Gage Residence: $74 double; $96 triple suite May–Aug; $69 triple suite Sept–May 1. Family rates available. Totem Park Residence bed-and-breakfast packages available May–August: $48 double. MC, V. Free parking May 4–Aug 26, $3 per day the rest of year. Bus: 4 or 10.

The University of British Columbia has a gorgeous setting overlooking English Bay, about 45 minutes from downtown via the no. 10 bus. The Walter Gage Residence is a convenient place to stay if you plan to spend a lot of time in Kitsilano and central Vancouver. These suites are comfortable, clean, and quiet (except for the occasional marauding raccoon rustling through the garbage cans). The Totem Park Residences have adequately sized dormitory rooms with shared baths. Local calls are free, and a full breakfast is included with the room rate. The campus has restaurants, a pub, and banking services. Nearby attractions include Wreck Beach, Pacific Spirit Park, Nitobe Memorial Gardens, the Museum of Anthropology, and a golf course.

Vancouver International Youth Hostel

1515 Discovery St., Vancouver B.C., Canada V6R 4K5. ☎ **604/224-3208.** Fax 604/224-4852. 285 beds. Wheelchair-accessible rooms. $12.50 IYHA members, $17.50 Canadian nonmembers, $10 foreign nonmembers. Linen/blanket rental extra. Annual adult Canadian membership $26.75. Family and group memberships available. Maximum stay is 3 nights during busy periods. Family rooms by advance booking. No credit cards. Free, limited parking.

This hostel is located right on the beach in Jericho Park. Individuals, families, or groups are welcome, but there are no facilities for children under five or pets. Wholesome, inexpensive food is served here or you have the option of cooking your own. Bring your sleeping bag or rent linen.

6 North Vancouver & West Vancouver

EXPENSIVE

Park Royal Hotel

540 Clyde Ave., West Vancouver B.C., Canada V7T 2J7. ☎ **604/926-5511.** Fax 604/926-6082. 30 rms. TV TEL. $121–$162 twin; $121–$191 double; $214–$260 suite. AE, DC, ER, MC, V. Free parking. Bus: 250, 251, 252, 253.

Make reservations months in advance if you want to stay in this Tudor, British-style country inn with exposed beams, stone fireplace, and a pub. The hotel sits on the banks of the Capilano River—a great place for salmon and steelhead fly fishing. The brass beds in the rooms afford a good night's sleep. You will be treated to complimentary coffee or tea and a morning newspaper before you venture out onto the river. The Tudor Room Restaurant offers three meals daily plus Sunday brunch. The only tricky part of this hideaway is finding it: Go over Lions Gate Bridge, head into West Vancouver, and take the first right onto Taylor Way. Then turn right immediately at Clyde Avenue.

MODERATE

✪ Beachside Bed & Breakfast

4208 Evergeen Ave., West Vancouver B.C., Canada VTV 1H1. ☎ **604/922-7773** or 800/563-3111. Fax 604/926-8073. 3 rms with private bath. $100 double. Rates include full breakfast. Additional person charge $20. Bus: 250, 251, 252, 253.

You are welcomed to your room in this beautiful waterfront home with a fruit basket and fresh flowers. The house, located at the end of a quiet cul-de-sac, is a Spanish-style structure with stained-glass windows. Its southern exposure affords a panoramic view of Vancouver. A sandy beach is just steps from the door. You can watch the waves from the patio or spend the afternoon fishing and sailing. The hearty breakfast features homemade muffins, French toast, and Canadian maple syrup.

Hosts Gordon and Joan are knowledgeable about local history and can gladly direct you to Stanley Park, hiking, skiing, and much more.

Deep Cove Bed & Breakfast

2590 Shelley Rd., North Vancouver B.C., Canada V7H 1V9. ☎ **604/929-3932.** Fax 604/929-9330. 2 units with bath in a private guest cottage. Nonsmoking rooms. TV VCR. $75 double. Rates include breakfast. Parking on the street. Bus: 211 or 212.

Only 15 minutes from downtown Vancouver, Deep Cove Bed and Breakfast, hosted by Diane and Wayne Moore, provides the privacy of a large, secluded property within easy access of city attractions. A separate guest cottage offers you a choice of a twin or queen bed in your room with a private bath. You are invited to relax in the red cedar hot tub on the terrace or in the lounge with billiard table, wood-burning fireplace, TV, and VCR. Hearty breakfasts—served either in the morning room or on the patio—feature French toast, freshly baked breads, and muffins topped with homemade jams and jellies or Quebec maple syrup. Diane will be happy to direct you to all the special places that make this area so exciting.

Lonsdale Quay Hotel

123 Carrie Cates Court, North Vancouver BC, Canada V6M 3K7. ☎ **604/986-6111** or 800/836-6111. Fax 604/986-8782. 57 rms, 13 suites. Nonsmoking rooms. A/C MINIBAR TV TEL. $135–$155 double or twin; $180–$200 harbor view or waterfront executive suite. Additional person $20 per night. Senior discount available. AE, DC, ER, MC, V. Parking $6. SeaBus: Lonsdale Quay.

This hotel is actually atop the Lonsdale Quay Market at the SeaBus terminal. An escalator rises from the market to the front desk on the third floor. Sporting fabulous views of the harbor, waterfront, and the city, it is also only 20 minutes by bus from Grouse Mountain Ski Resort and Capilano Regional Park. The Waterfront Bistro serves lunch, cocktails, and dinner and features dancing. The Q Café serves breakfast, lunch, and dinner in relaxed atmosphere. They also have a whirlpool, weight/exercise room, and in-room coffeemakers for early morning starts on the slopes.

Mountainside Manor

5909 Nancy Greene Way, North Vancouver B.C., Canada V7R 4W6. ☎ **604/985-8484.** 4 rms. TV. $75–$120 double. Rates include breakfast. Off-season discounts. Free parking.

This is the closest house to both the ski slopes on Grouse Mountain and the 26-mile-long Baden-Powell hiking trail. It's a spectacular, modern home that rests in a peaceful, rustic, alpine setting. High above the city and nestled in a tree-covered ridge, the Mountainside Manor treats you to a magnificent view of the Coast Mountains and the Burrard inlet from your room or from the outdoor hot tub.

7 Richmond & Near the Airport

EXPENSIVE

Delta Vancouver Airport Hotel

3500 Cessna Dr., Richmond B.C., Canada V7B 1C7. ☎ **604/278-1241,** 800/877-1133 in the U.S., or 800/268-1133 in Canada. Fax 604/267-1975. 410 rms, 5 suites. A/C MINIBAR TV TEL. Jan–May and Sept 7–Oct, $198 double. June–Sept 6, $220 double. Nov–Dec, $184 double. Year-round $175–$375 suite. Children under 18 stay free in parents' room. AE, CB, DC, DISC, ER, JCB, MC, V. Free parking; valet available. Bus: 404 or 405.

Set on the edge of the Fraser River, this hotel is a two-minute drive from the airport. The free airport shuttle is just the beginning of a long list of business-oriented services such as Delta's trademark Business Zone rooms, which include a cordless phone, in-room desk essentials, and computer hook-ups. Rooms on the south side have the

best view. The hotel's location appeals to Richmond-bound travelers who don't want
to waste 30 minutes commuting from Vancouver.

⑤ Delta Pacific Resort & Conference Centre

10251 St. Edwards Dr., Richmond B.C., Canada V6X 2M9. ☎ **604/278-9611** or 800/
268-1133. Fax 604/276-1121. 456 rms, 4 suites. A/C MINIBAR TV TEL. May–Sept, $140–$160
double. Oct–Apr, $120–$140 double. Year-round $150–$300 suite. Children 18 and under stay
free in parents' room. AE, CB, DC, ER, MC, V. Free parking. Bus: 401 or 403.

The facilities and location of its 12-acre site make up for the minimal view at this
hotel. Delta's executive services, offered by the entire chain, include free airport
shuttle service, two guest-room towers, and a few low-rise buildings allocated
for conventions. The rooms are standard, unlike at the downtown branch, but its
location five minutes from the airport makes it worthwhile. There are outdoor volleyball courts, golf practice nets, year-round tennis courts, squash courts, shopping
center, kids' summer camps, as well as a playground and play center. In spite of its
size, it's a casual and friendly place. The Japanese restaurant is expensive, showy, and
mediocre.

MODERATE

Best Western Abercorn Inn

9260 Bridgeport Rd., Richmond B.C., Canada V6X 1S1. ☎ **604/270-7576** or 800/
663-0085. Fax 604/270-0001. 98 rms. Nonsmoking floor. Wheelchair-accessible rooms. A/C TV
TEL. Oct–May, $105 double. June–Oct, $115–$135 double. Weekend specials, senior discounts,
group rates, and honeymoon packages. AE, DC, ER, MC, V. Free parking. Bus: 401 or 403.

From its modern version of a Tudor exterior to its Scottish decor (including a fireplace lounge), this hotel is less business-travel oriented than the neighboring establishments, but is still a convenient airport hotel. Some of the rooms have double
Jacuzzis or large tubs so you can shake off jet lag in style. The restaurant offers three
hearty meals daily. In synch with the ambience, you can order breakfast kippers or
dine on a rack of lamb. Complimentary airport shuttle service completes your stress-
free stay.

5 Vancouver Dining

It would be impossible to give a complete listing of Vancouver's restaurants. There are more than 2,000 of them. Vancouverites dine out more than residents of any other Canadian city, and with good reason—outstanding meals are available in all price ranges. There is an array of ethnic cuisine, including Chinese, Japanese, Greek, French, Italian, Mongolian, Ethiopian, and Vietnamese, often prepared by immigrant chefs who authentically re-create dishes from their native lands. Entrée prices here are arguably among the lowest of similarly sophisticated world cities. Wherever you go in greater Vancouver—into the midst of the downtown bustle, deep into Stanley Park, to any of the beaches, or to ethnic neighborhoods—a superb meal or snack is not far away.

As of this writing, there is a veritable renaissance of Pacific Northwest cooking taking place in Vancouver and Victoria. The North American passion for pasta seems to have ebbed here. Justified pride in local produce, game, and seafood, combined with innovation and creativity, has led to such reduced-fat Pacific Northwest dishes as grilled tuna steak in green peppercorn sauce served with buttermilk mashed potatoes and garden-fresh asparagus. More and more restaurants are shifting to seasonal, even monthly, menus to give their kitchen staffs greater freedom. West Coast cuisine (fresh ingredients prepared with a blend of Asian and Western influences) is popular among Vancouver's chefs. While there are as many variations on this regional fare as there are fine chefs here, the focus on freshness, flavor, and enjoyment, combined with local ingredients, makes this cuisine unique and unparalleled.

British Columbian wines, once less than palatable, have improved to the point that they are now winning international acclaim. The grapes are grown and the wine is produced mainly in the Okanagan Valley, 170 miles east of the city in southern B.C.'s dry plateau country. In the hills surrounding the 75-mile-long Lake Okanagan and the Okanagan River, there are more than 30 wineries, including Mission Hill, Grey Monk, Summerhill, Le Compte, Quail's Gate, Cedar Creek, Hanle, and Sumac Ridge. Fortunately, these wines have received far less publicity than they deserve, and some great bargains can still be had in well-balanced Chardonnays; rich, full-bodied Merlots and Cabernets; and dessert ice wines that stand up to the best Muscat d'or.

We have listed our restaurant recommendations first by **geographical area** and then by price category within the area. If you're staying in **Downtown Vancouver,** you can walk to **The West End and English Bay** (the area west of downtown from Thurlow Street to Stanley Park); **Gastown;** or **Chinatown.** If you're willing to travel farther, you can venture to **Central Vancouver**, the area south of False Creek to the Fraser River, from Gran-ville Street to Main Street, including Kitsilano, Granville Island, and the University of British Columbia.

The restaurants are grouped into four **price categories: Very Expensive** (with entrées averaging more than $20), **Expensive** (entrées $15 to $20), **Moderate** (entrées $10 to $15), and **Inexpensive** (entrées less than $10). Remember, *the prices quoted in this book are in Canadian dollars.* There's no provincial tax on restaurant meals in British Columbia—just the 7% federal goods and services tax.

Restaurant hours vary. Lunch is typically served from noon to 1pm; Vancouverites begin dining around 6:30pm—later in summer. **Reservations** are recommended at most restaurants and are essential at the popular places. Reservations may not be accepted at some of the inexpensive and moderately priced restaurants.

1 Best Bets

- **Best Spot for a Romantic Dinner:** The **Tea House Restaurant,** Ferguson Point in Stanley Park (☎ 604/669-3281), is nestled amid a romantic cedar forest behind a hedge. The English-style hunter's cottage is softly lit and decorated in muted florals. Book a table on the terrace and arrive in time to dine while the sun sets behind Vancouver Island, which, weather permitting, is visible in the distance.
- **Best Spot for a Business Lunch:** The **William Tell,** 765 Beatty St. in the Georgian Court Hotel (☎ 604/688-3504), has been one of Vancouver's three four-star favorites for nearly 30 years. It is *the* place for a business lunch. Try the fondue for two.
- **Best Spot for a Celebration:** If your party wardrobe consists only of black clothes, **Lola's,** 432 Richards St. at the Century House (☎ 604/684-5652), is ideal. If you're more inclined toward pastels, florals, Lacostes, and blazers, The **Five Sails,** 999 Canada Place Way in the Pan Pacific Hotel (☎ 604/878-9000), has a winning combination of fabulous views, impeccable service, romantic atmosphere, and an eclectic menu that highlights French, seafood, and continental dishes.
- **Best Decor: Lola's,** 432 Richards St. at the Century House (☎ 604/684-5652), has 20-foot ceilings painted midnight blue with gold trim, huge bouquets of flowers, dark wood and purple silk furnishings, and a gorgeous staff to match.
- **Best View:** The picture windows at **The Cannery,** 2205 Commissioner St., near Victoria Drive (☎ 604/254-9609), look out onto the busy harbor, with North Vancouver in the background. The view from **Cloud Nine,** 1400 Robson St. atop the Landmark Hotel (☎ 604/687-0511), presents a perfect panorama of the north shore and Burrad Inlet from its West End revolving perch.
- **Best Wine List:** The award-winning wine cellar at **The Cannery,** 2205 Commissioner St. near Victoria Drive (☎604/254-9606), contains Vancouver's finest collection of regional and international vintages.
- **Best Value: Stepho's,** 1124 Davie St. (☎ 604/683-2555), is the best value in town—even though there's a line outside and the other Greek restaurant on the block has tables available. Do you see any of the locals getting irritable and rushing down the street? They're happy to wait. The fare is a perennial contender

for the best Greek food in Vancouver, yet there's no entrée over $10 and the portions are huge.

- **Best for Kids:** At the **Old Spaghetti Factory,** 53 Water St. (☎ 604/684-1288), you can sit in a vintage trolley car while dining. The outgoing staff serves up simple, home-style pasta, which is always a favorite with kids.
- **Best Chinese Cuisine: Park Lock Seafood Restaurant,** 544 Main St. in Chinatown (☎ 604/688-1581), has the distinctive atmosphere of a Hong Kong dim sum parlor. The **Imperial Chinese Seafood Restaurant,** 355 Burrard St. (☎ 604/688-8191), offers the best Cantonese fare prepared by Hong Kong–trained chefs. It's a great spot to watch the Vancouver Stock Exchange wheelers and dealers carry on power lunches.
- **Best Continental Cuisine:** At **Bishop's,** 2183 W. 4th St. (☎ 604/738-2025), the owner personally greets you, escorts you to your table, and introduces you to a catalog of fine wines and what he describes as "contemporary home cooking." If there is a Vancouver cuisine, it's being created here: The best fresh local ingredients are combined to create culinary masterpieces like Dungeness crab ravioli.
- **Best French Cuisine: Chez Thierry,** 1674 Robson St. (☎ 604/688-0919), offers truly classic French cuisine. If you order champagne, the owner emerges from the kitchen dressed something like a flamboyant version of Napoleon, and marches to the center of the room holding the bottle aloft in one hand, with a saber in the other (which he uses to cut off the top). House specialties like bouillabaise or grilled duck breast in a peach and port wine sauce make a visit here warm and rewarding.
- **Best Italian Cuisine: Il Giardino di Umberto,** 1382 Hornby St. (☎ 604/669-2422), looks like a rustic Italian villa with a grapevine-covered garden terrace for dining alfresco, and a truly Tuscan menu emphasizes that pasta and game.
- **Best Seafood:** At **The Cannery,** 2205 Commissioner St. near Victoria Drive (☎ 604/254-9606), broad picture windows provide a spectacular harbor view, and you can watch your dinner arrive as the fleet rolls in with the day's catch. Dishes like Salmon Wellington (a sockeye salmon fillet topped with mushrooms duxelle and shrimp baked in flaky puff pastry) or delicately grilled halibut cheeks are simply prepared with an emphasis on quality and freshness.
- **Best Pacific Northwest Cuisine: The Fish House,** 2099 Beach Ave. in Stanley Park (☎ 604/681-7275), has the most inventive seafood menu in town, including wood-oven roasted calamari and a seafood hotpot. The dishes are an inspired blend of Pacific Rim cuisines and fresh local ingredients creatively combined by a talented chef.
- **Best West Coast Cuisine: Raincity Grill,** 1193 Denman St. (☎ 604/685-7337), has a crab salad, ravioli with sun-dried tomatoes in an oyster mushroom broth, and rare grilled Ahi tuna steak served with a Pinot Noir mint reduction sauce, and much more. The food rivals the best in Los Angeles, at a third of the price.
- **Best Coffee House:** There are more than 30 Starbucks here, plus other chains like Blenz, Roastmastirs, Breadgarden, Murchies, and more. They all brew a good cup of coffee. But at **Benny's Bagels,** 1095 Hamilton St. (☎ 604/688-8018) and 2505 W. Broadway (☎ 604/736-4686), you can also shoot some pool in cavernous postmodern surroundings.
- **Best Pizza:** Great pizza is something new to Vancouver. **Flying Wedge,** 1205 Davie St. (☎ 604/689-2805), produces an excellent standard pepperoni slice, but it's their specialties like Broken Hearts, topped with marinated artichokes, onions, mushrooms, and asagio that really soar.

- **Best Desserts: Yaletown Brewing Company,** 1110 Hamilton St. (☎ 604/681-2739), makes a white Belgian chocolate mousse cake that's pure ecstasy. Try it with a glass of light red wine such as a Gamay to balance the dessert's rich taste, which overpowers the sweetest of dessert wines.
- **Best Late-Night Dining: Bread Garden,** has a 24-hour restaurant on Denman and another one at 812 Bute St. just off Robson (☎ 604/688-3213). The food is wholesome, cheap, and fresh, and the coffee is excellent. So what if the staff looks a little dazed at three in the morning? We probably did, too.
- **Best Outdoor Dining:** The **Tea House Restaurant,** Ferguson Point in Stanley Park (☎ 604/669-3281) and **Monk McQueen's,** 601 Stamps Landing (☎ 604/877-1351), on False Creek, both have great patios. The Tea House is wonderfully romantic and secluded; Monk's lively terrace, with great city and mountain views, is a hub of activity on summer weekends.
- **Best People-Watching:** The **Cactus Club Café,** 1136 Robson St. (☎604/687-3278), has a few tables outside, and it's a prime spot to watch the young and beautiful stream past endlessly.
- **Best Afternoon Tea:** Tea in **The Bacchus Lounge,** 845 Hornby St. in the Wedgewood Hotel (☎ 604/689-7777), is presided over by British-born Chef Alan Groom. Both the atmosphere and the repast are authentic. Try the scones with Devonshire cream.
- **Best Brunch: The Teahouse,** Ferguson Point in Stanley Park (☎ 604/669-3281), is a romantic, scenic spot for brunch. It's the perfect start to an afternoon stroll along the Seawall.
- **Best Fish and Chips: Olympia Oyster & Fish Co. Ltd.,** 1094 Robson St. (☎ 604/685-0716), offers you a choice of fresh and flaky halibut, cod, salmon, prawns, and oysters, all prepared in a light batter and served with freshly cut french fries.
- **Best for Pre-Theater Dinner: Las Tapas,** 760 Cambie St. (☎ 604/669-1624), is in the heart of Vancouver's growing cultural and sporting district near the Queen Elizabeth and Ford Theatres as well as B.C. Stadium and G.M. Plaza. Tapas means "little dishes." At Las Tapas these include grilled calamari, roasted pork, and prawn scampi.

2 Restaurants by Cuisine

AMERICAN
Brothers Restaurant (Gastown/
  Chinatown, *I*)
Hard Rock Cafe (Downtown, *M*)

CAFETERIA
The Fresgo Inn (West End, *I*)

CAJUN
Mulvaney's (Central Vancouver, *E*)

CAMBODIAN
Phnom Penh Restaurant
  (Gastown/Chinatown, *I*)

CANADIAN
Rooster's Quarters (West End, *I*)

CHINESE
Park Lock Seafood Restaurant
  (Gastown/Chinatown, *M*)

CONTINENTAL
Delilah's (West End, *E*)
The Hart House (Outside
  Vancouver, *E*)
Monk McQueen's (Central
  Vancouver, *E*)

Key to abbreviations: *I*=Inexpensive; *M*=Moderate; *E*=Expensive; *VE*=Very Expensive

The Prow Restaurant
(Downtown, *E*)
The Tea House Restaurant in
Stanley Park (West End, *E*)
William Tell Restaurant
(Downtown, *VE*)

DIM SUM
Park Lock Seafood
Restaurant (Gastown/
Chinatown, *M*)

EAST AFRICAN
Kilimanjaro (Gastown/
Chinatown, *M*)

FISH & CHIPS
Olympia Oyster & Fish Co.
(Downtown, *I*)

FRENCH
Café de Paris (West End, *M*)
The Chef & the Carpenter
(West End, *M*)
Chez Thierry (West End, *M*)
Le Crocodile
(Downtown, *E*)

GREEK
Stepho's (West End, *I*)

HUNGARIAN
Bandi's (Downtown, *E*)

INDIAN
Kilimanjaro (Gastown/
Chinatown, *M*)

INTERNATIONAL
Lola's (Downtown, *E*)

ITALIAN
Azzurro (West End, *I*)
Old Spaghetti Factory (Chinatown/
Gastown, *I*)
Romano's Macaroni Grill at
the Mansion (West End, *M*)

JAPANESE
Hanada (West End, *I*)
Japanese Deli (Gastown/
Chinatown, *M*)

Naniwa-Ya Seafood Restaurant
(Downtown, *E*)
Tojo's Restaurant (Central
Vancouver, *E*)

MEDITERRANEAN
Bacchus Ristorante (Downtown, *E*)
North 49° Restaurant & Market
(Downtown, *M*)

MONGOLIAN
Great Wall Mongolian BBQ
Restaurant (West End, *I*)

PACIFIC NORTHWEST
Bishop's (Central Vancouver, *E*)
The Fish House in Stanley Park
(West End, *M*)
A Kettle of Fish (Downtown, *E*)
Raintree Restaurant at the Landing
(Gastown/Chinatown, *E*)
Liliget Feast House & Catering
(West End, *E*)

PASTA
Old Spaghetti Factory (Gastown/
Chinatown, *I*)

SEAFOOD
The Cannery (Gastown/
Chinatown, *M*)
The Fish House in Stanley Park
(West End, *M*)
Joe Fortes Seafood House
(Downtown, *M*)
A Kettle of Fish (Downtown, *E*)
Monk McQueen's (Central
Vancouver, *E*)
The Only (Fish & Oyster Café)
(Gastown/ Chinatown, *I*)
The Prow Restaurant
(Downtown, *E*)
Restaurant Starfish and Oyster Bar
(Downtown, *I*)

SOUTHWESTERN
Cactus Club Café
(West End, *M*)

SPANISH TAPAS
Las Tapas (Downtown, *I*)

SUSHI

Hanada (West End, *I*)

SWISS

William Tell Restaurant
(Downtown, *VE*)

THAI

Malinee's (Central Vancouver, *E*)

TUSCAN

Il Giardino di Umberto (Downtown, *E*)

VEGETARIAN

The Naam Restaurant (Central
Vancouver, *I*)

VIETNAMESE

Phnom Penh Restaurant (Gastown/
Chinatown, *I*)
Saigon (West End, *M*)

WEST COAST

Alma Street Café (Central
Vancouver, *M*)
The Five Sails (Downtown, *VE*)
The Hart House (Outside
Vancouver, *E*)
Isadora's Cooperative Restaurant
(Central Vancouver, *I*)
Picasso Café (Central Vancouver, *M*)
Raincity Grill (West End, *E*)
Yaletown Brewery (Downtown, *M*)

3 Downtown Vancouver

VERY EXPENSIVE

The Five Sails

999 Canada Place, in the Pan-Pacific Hotel. ☎ **604/662-8111.** Reservations recommended. Main courses $22–$38; table d'hôte: two courses, $29.50; three courses, $36; four courses $42. AE, DC, ER, JCB, MC, V. Sun–Fri 5pm–10pm; Sat 6pm–11pm. SkyTrain: Burrard. WEST COAST.

The harbor and north shore view from The Five Sails is spectacular. Although the room is elegant, the dress code is strictly casual. Dishes are an eclectic blend of Thai, Mongolian, Japanese, Vietnamese, and nouvelle ingredients. Grilled scallop napoleon, smoked Alaskan cod chowder, Tangiers crab ravioli perfumed with fresh tarragon, honey-glazed duck, and Alaskan king prawns with lobster wontons are just a few of their surprises. Request a table near the window when you make reservations.

☉ William Tell Restaurant

765 Beatty St., in the Georgian Court Hotel. ☎ **604/688-3504.** Reservations recommended at dinner. Lunch main courses $8–$12; dinner main courses $17–$28. AE, DC, ER, JCB, MC, V. Breakfast daily 7–10:30am; lunch Mon–Fri 11:30am–2pm; dinner Mon–Sat 6–9:30pm. SkyTrain: Stadium. SWISS/CONTINENTAL.

Erwin Doebeli, 1995 restauranteur of the year (as voted by the B.C. and Yukon Restaurant Association), has maintained the William Tell as one of Vancouver's three four-star favorites for nearly 30 years. His traditional cuisine is a sharp contrast to the current trend toward eclectic and innovative dishes you'll find in other downtown establishments. And that's exactly what keeps people coming back. Most dishes are loaded with cream and butter (a few lighter alternatives have crept onto the menu). Try the fondue for two. This is *the* place for a business lunch.

EXPENSIVE

✪ Bacchus Ristorante

845 Hornby St., in the Wedgewood Hotel. ☎ **604/689-7777.** Reservations recommended for the dining room. Main courses $13–$27. AE, DC, MC, V. Daily 6:30am–10:30pm; lounge menu until 1am; Sunday lounge menu until midnight. Afternoon tea daily 2–4pm. MEDITERRANEAN.

Downtown Vancouver Dining

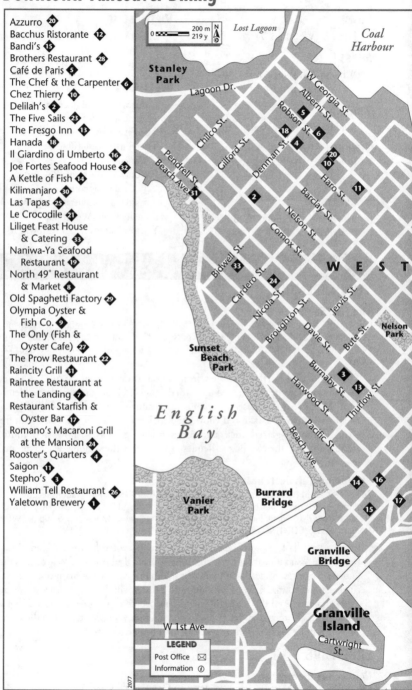

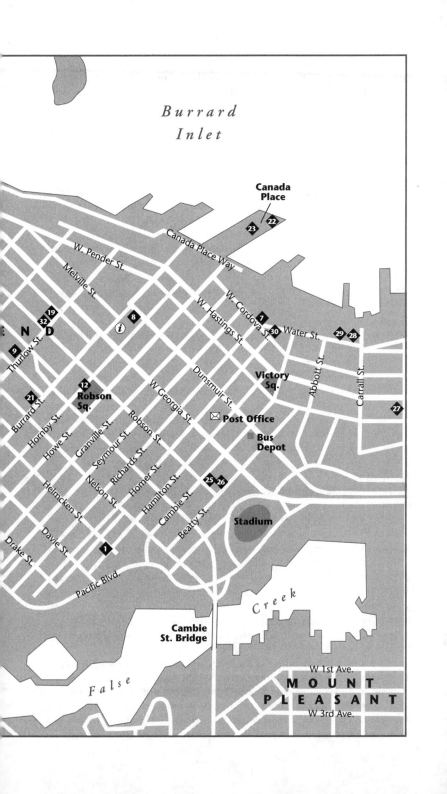

Set back behind the bar and wrapped around the open kitchen, the Bacchus is the centerpiece of Eleni Skalbania's Wedgewood Hotel. British Chef Alan Groom has created an eclectic menu for lunch and dinner that includes such diverse dishes as papardelle with smoked chicken and shiitake mushrooms in a ginger sauce, Washington rack of lamb in a black olive crust (highly recommended), and tiger prawns with risotto. For dessert, his tiramisu is absolutely luscious. Groom's love of his work shows in every dish. He also has an intimate knowledge of tea and has made the Bacchus lounge the afternoon destination for Vancouver tea lovers.

Bandi's

1427 Howe St. ☎ 604/685-3391. Reservations recommended. Main courses $15.50–$22.50. AE, MC, V. Lunch Mon–Fri 11:30am–2pm; dinner daily 6–11pm. Bus: 401, 403, or 406. HUNGARIAN.

Chef/owner Bandi Rinkhy's establishment has served upscale Hungarian cuisine in the same little house on Howe for years, with little change to the menu. This isn't food that inspires thoughts of gypsy caravans and is accompanied by bad violin music. The delicious, heavy dishes with unpronounceable names include reindeer filet, pan-fried trout, stuffed herring filets, and breaded mushrooms. Skip lunch if you're headed here for dinner.

Il Giardino di Umberto

1382 Hornby St. ☎ **604/669-2422.** Reservations required. Lunch $12–$15; dinner main courses $15–$29. AE, DC, ER, MC, V. Lunch Mon–Fri noon–2:30pm; dinner Mon–Sat 6–11pm. Bus: 22 or 401. TUSCAN.

If you changed nothing about the restaurant itself and moved it to Los Angeles, you would have to wait about six months for a table, the prices would triple, and the reindeer filet would disappear from the menu. Fortunately, Vancouver restaurant magnate Umberto Menghi has no intention of moving. His empire here also includes Umberto's, Umberto Al Porto, and Splendido. Il Giardino, with the ambience of seaside villa, has carved out its own niche. There's an enclosed garden terrace for dining alfresco. The truly Tuscan menu emphasizes pasta and game.

A Kettle of Fish

900 Pacific St. ☎ **604/682-6853.** Reservations recommended. Lunch $7.59–$9.95; dinner main courses $13.95–$29.95. AE, DC, MC, V. Lunch Mon–Fri 11:30am–2pm; dinner daily from 5:30pm. Bus: 22, 401, 403, or 406. PACIFIC NORTHWEST/SEAFOOD.

Find out the day's catch, then do like the sign at the entry says: Eat Lotsa Fish. The dishes, which include papaya and hand-peeled shrimp, are inventive and flavorful. Seafood on the barbecue is a house specialty; you can also order it grilled, pan fried, or blackened. The light, airy dining room occupies the main floor of a renovated, turn-of-the-century building.

Le Crocodile

100-909 Burrard St. ☎ **604/669-4298.** Reservations recommended. Lunch main courses $14.95–$18; dinner main courses $16–$22. AE, DC, MC, V. Lunch Mon–Fri 12pm–2pm; dinner Mon–Sat 5:30pm–10:30pm. Bus: 22. FRENCH.

Considered by critics and diners alike to be Vancouver's finest French restaurant (though there's some hot competition), Le Crocodile has received many top awards. The caliber of the cuisine surpasses the prices. It is difficult to get reservations on weekend evenings because managers Michael Jacob and John Blakeley refuse to rush their guests. The grilled venison medaillons with chantrelle sauce, the roast duck breast, and the prime rib with béarnaise sauce, however, are worth the effort.

⑤ Lola's

432 Richards St., at the Century House. ☎ **604/684-5652.** Reservations recommended. Main courses $15–$22. AE MC V. Open daily lunch 11:30am–2pm; dinner 5pm–1am. Bus: 8. INTERNATIONAL.

Lola's was born when a group of former employees of Delilah's (see above) decided they could do it better on their own. They can indeed! The restaurant is located in a restored 1911 stone building just a block southwest of Gastown. Inside, Victorian chandeliers are suspended from 20-foot vaulted ceilings painted midnight blue and trimmed with gold leaf. Dark wood, deep-purple silk, and fresh flowers are reflected in the beveled-glass mirror that stretches up to the ceiling behind the bar.

Opened in August 1995 with no fanfare, Lola's quickly earned rave reviews and caught on with the "in" crowd. Dining here is an experience. The cocktail list is divided between martinis and champagne cocktails. Start with segruva or seared fois gras with red currant and chive vinaigrette; follow with Moroccan-style marinated lamb or sea bass with mushrooms and lemongrass. The desserts, including crème brûlée, tiramisu, and chocolate saba cake, are fabulous. The staff, though terminally hip, are surprisingly friendly.

Naniwa-Ya Seafood Restaurant

745 Thurlow St. ☎ **604/681-7307.** Reservations recommended. Complete meals $17.50–$27.95; lunch $5.75–$13.95. AE, DC, JCB, MC, V. Lunch Mon–Fri 11:30am–2:30pm; dinner Mon–Thurs 5–10pm, Fri–Sat 5–11pm. Bus: 8. JAPANESE SEAFOOD.

This delightful country-style restaurant was the first in Canada to offer patrons the chance to select live seafood from tanks in the dining room. Crabs, lobsters, geoduck, and butter clams are prepared in a variety of ways, such as with ginger or soy sauce. The atmosphere is intimate, and the staff is attentive.

The Prow Restaurant

100-999 Canada Place. ☎ **604/684-1339.** Reservations recommended at dinner. Lunch $8.50–$11.75; dinner main courses $12.95–$21.50. AE, ER, MC, V. Lunch daily 11:30am–2:30pm; dinner daily 5:30–10:30pm. SkyTrain: Waterfront. CONTINENTAL/SEAFOOD.

Canada Place pier, home of both the Vancouver Convention Centre and the Alaska cruiseship terminal, looks like a ship with its five, tall, Teflon sails headed into the wind. The Prow Restaurant stands like a figurehead at its very tip. The view is of tugboats, ferries, fishing boats, and floatplanes crisscrossing the water below, surrounded by the city and north shore mountains. The spiced corn and seafood chowder is creamy and delicious. The seafood is primarily fresh and local, but there are a variety of land-based dishes, like beef, pork, and chicken as . If you come for lunch, leave time for a leisurely stroll around Canada Place afterwards.

MODERATE

Hard Rock Café

686 West Hastings St. ☎ **604/687-ROCK.** Reservations recommended. Main courses $5.95–$14.95. AE, DC, MC, V. Mon–Sat 11am–1am; Sun 11am–midnight. Skytrain: Waterfront. AMERICAN.

Housed in an old downtown bank building, this branch of the internationally famous theme restaurant offers you dishes that are otherwise hard to find in Vancouver: a juicy hamburger or a real reuben sandwich. A host of Junior Rocker specials on their huge menu can be somewhat wacky, like the Elvis sandwich (grilled peanut butter and banana). The superfriendly staff provides better service in this cavernous duplex stuffed with rock memorabilia than in the New York, Chicago, London, or Toronto branches.

Joe Fortes Seafood House

777 Thurlow St. ☎ **604/669-1940.** Reservations recommended. Lunch $6.95–$11.95; dinner main courses $11.95–$19.95. AE, DC, DISC, ER, MC, V. Lunch daily 11:30am–4pm; light meals daily 4–5:30pm; dinner Sun–Thurs 5:30–11pm, Fri–Sat 5:30pm–midnight. Bus: 8. SEAFOOD.

Named after the burly Caribbean seaman who became English Bay's first lifeguard and swimming instructor and a popular local hero, this cavernous, dark-wood restaurant with an immensely popular bar is continually filled with Vancouver's young and successful. The single-malt list scotch is the best in town. The decor and atmosphere recall a New York oyster bar, but the roof garden is pure Vancouver. Pan-roasted oysters are a staple on the menu, and there are a half-dozen varieties of them and twice as many varieties of fish; selections change daily. The set menu includes one or two nonseafood entrées, but fish is the best of the offerings, save the gold medal–winning dark and white chocolate mousse cake. It can get a bit loud here, but it's always upbeat.

North 49° Restaurant & Market

1055 Dunsmuir St., Plaza level, Bentall Four. ☎ **604/669-0360,** ext. 160. Reservations recommended. Lunch $10.50–$16.50; dinner main courses $10.50–$22.50. AE, DC, ER, JCB, MC, V. Daily 11:30am–11pm. MEDITERRANEAN.

The cuisine from every country in the Mediterranean, mingled with fresh local ingredients and a minimum of pasta, have made North 49° into a rapidly rising star. This isn't too surprising when you consider the same owners have also enjoyed success with Starfish Restaurant & Oyster Bar; Raintree Restaurant (see listing below); and Victoria's Harvest Moon Café. The atmosphere is casual, and sharing is encouraged. After all, it's the only way you'll be able to sample a fraction of the 100-plus items on the regular and specials menus.

The highlights of the fare are definitely the spit-roasted meats, cooked on open rotisseries in the dining room. The pork is our favorite. The sampler plate will also give you a taste of the lamb and chicken prepared in the same manner.

⊗ Yaletown Brewery

1110 Hamilton St. ☎ **604/681-2739.** Reservations recommended. Lunch $6.95–$13.50; dinner main courses $9–$15. Sun–Wed 11:30am–12am; Thurs–Sat 11:30am–1am. Bus: 8. WEST COAST.

If you opt to eat at the dining room bar (which is impossible on Thursday, Friday, and Saturday nights when a meat-market crowd throngs three-deep to the bar) instead of sitting at one of the tables that line the windows, you will get a front-row seat to watch your dinner being prepared in the open kitchen.

The pizzas—baked in a wood-fired oven—are whimsical; hoisin and chipotle sauces replace tomato on some. If your taste buds are more conventional, move straight to the hearty entreés, including rosemary chicken stew and baked salmon with vermouth herb butter, which are prepared with surprising delicacy. The desserts are quite good; the white Belgian chocolate mousse cake is excellent. Brew master Frank Appleton has created a range of six brews—a light lager, two light ales, a robust red bitter, a truly creamy stout, and a nut brown ale.

INEXPENSIVE

Las Tapas

760 Cambie St. ☎ **604/669-1624.** Tapas $3.45–$12.95. MC, V. Mon–Fri 11:30am–2pm, Sun–Thurs 5–11pm, Fri–Sat 5–12pm, Sun 5–9:30pm (later if concert schedules warrant). Bus: 15 or 242. SPANISH TAPAS.

This place has been serving tapas, or "little dishes," for 19 years. You can sample marinated lamb chops, spicy chorizo, calamari, garlic prawns, and much more; all tapas are available in three sizes. The tasty sandwiches served at lunch include roast pork, chicken breast, and chorizo on fresh-baked foccacia; skip the fish sandwich. The decor is distinctly Mediterranean—whitewashed walls, exposed beams, fireplaces, and niches that give diners a bit of privacy.

Olympia Oyster & Fish Co.

1094 Robson St. ☎ **604/685-0716.** Main courses $3.95–$7.95. Mon–Sat 11am–8pm. Sun Noon–8pm. Bus: 8. FISH & CHIPS.

This tiny shop, where you can only sit on bar stools at a narrow counter on each wall, makes outstanding fish and chips. A lot of locals get takeout in neat boxes, not in the customary old newspapers. The seafood platter ($7.95) is enough for two. You can shop for smoked salmon or caviar to be shipped home while you wait.

✪ Restaurant Starfish & Oyster Bar

1600 Howe St. (off Pacific Street near the Aquabus landing). ☎ **604/681-8581.** Reservations recommended for dinner. Main courses $7.95–$11.95. Mon–Sat 11:30am–11pm; Sun 10:30am–11pm. Bus: 7. SEAFOOD.

Starfish is designed to attract a younger crowd, which it does. It may get a little loud at times, but it's supposed to. Sounds echo amid the whitewashed walls, ceramic tile floors, bare-wood tables, and the huge expanse of glass that exposes a close-up view of False Creek, Granville Island, and the Granville Street Bridge.

This new bistro serves up very inventive variations on an eclectic collection of dishes, including a steamed mussel hot pot with black beans and ginger or grilled Ahi tuna with a burned orange and wasabi soy glaze. The menu changes often, but the cuisine remains basically the same. While the portions wouldn't have satisfied one of the lumberjacks who once cleared the area of trees, they definitely find favor with in-line skaters on their way to peruse the Granville Island art galleries.

4 The West End & English Bay

EXPENSIVE

Delilah's

1739 Comox St. in the Denman Place Mall. ☎ **604/687-3424.** Reservations accepted for parties of 6 or more. Fixed-price dinner $18.50–$29. MC, V. Daily 5–mignight. Bus: 8 to Denman Street. PACIFIC NORTHWEST.

Delilah's just relocated from the Buchan Hotel, where its excellent reputation was established. Oscar Wilde and Sarah Bernhardt would have praised Delilah's decadently opulent, sensuous and intimate decor as well as its impressive martini menu and wine list. Have a Cosmopolitan Martini (made with vodka, cranberry and lime juices topped with fresh cranberries) and order from their delectable Pacific

Northwest menu which lists grand entrees like grilled swordfish with papaya lime butter sauce and grilled kiwi fruit; fresh Australian rack of lamb with a balsamic demi-glaze; or penne with an eggplant, zucchini, tomato sauce and feta cheese. If you have a light appetite, Delilah's two-course prix-fixe dinner is a perfect option to the full five-course gourmet version. Delilah's brownie sandwich—espresso ice cream between two thin, chocolate brownies, drizzled with hot fudge sauce— is positively sinful!

Liliget Feast House & Catering

1724 Davie St. ☎ **604/681-7044.** Reservations recommended. Main courses $12.95–$19.95. Open daily 5pm–10:30pm. AE, MC, V. Bus: 8. PACIFIC NORTHWEST.

Its nondescript entrance gives no hint of this truly unique restaurant at the bottom of the stairs under a burger joint. The dining room is filled with natural cedar columns rising from the water-worn stone floor; the tables are sunken tatami style into stone platforms around a central cedar-and-stone walkway. Recorded song-stories about potlatch ceremonies play in the background.

The food is traditional First Nations fare. Appetizers include grilled oysters, clam fritters, grilled prawns, salmon or venison soup, and bannock (delicious fried bread). Entrées include sweet alder-smoked salmon, lightly smoked duck breast, and grilled venison steak. For people curious about First Nations culture, this is one experience that should not be missed.

Ⓢ Raincity Grill

1193 Denman St. ☎ **604/685-7337.** Reservations recommended. Lunch $8.75–$15; main courses $12–$21. AE, DC, MC, V, ER. Mon–Thurs 11:30am–11pm, Fri 11:30am–midnight, Fri–Sat 10:30am–midnight, Sun 10:30am–11pm. Bus: 8. WEST COAST.

With an outdoor patio that catches the afternoon sun and an extensive wine list with 128 West Coast wines available by the glass, you might feel like you've been transported 1,000 or so miles south of Vancouver. The menu varies seasonally and depends on what's exceptional at the Granville Island produce market. Start out with a crab salad or ravioli with sun-dried tomatoes in an oyster mushroom broth. Also try the rare grilled Ahi tuna steak served with a Pinot Noir mint reduction.

The Tea House Restaurant in Stanley Park

Ferguson Point, Stanley Park. ☎ **604/669-3281.** Reservations required. Lunch $11.95–$16.95; dinner main courses $13.95–$22.75. AE, MC, V. Lunch Mon–Fri 11:30am–2:30pm; dinner daily 5:30–10pm; brunch Sat–Sun 10:30am–2:30pm. Bus: 19. CONTINENTAL.

Nestled into a secluded spot on the far side of Stanley Park are the low main building and greenhouse that make up the Teahouse Restaurant. The original structure was built in 1928 as a troop barracks, but time and careful decorating have transformed it into something resembling an English hunter's cottage. Soft light and muted florals create what is regarded as Vancouver's most romantic atmosphere. Book a table on the terrace and arrive in time to dine while the sun slowly sets behind Vancouver Island, which is visible in the distance (weather permitting).

The emphasis here is on game; a tender, delicious rack of lamb is the signature dish. We, however, thought the venison medaillons, served with a slightly sweet dried cranberry and port-wine sauce, were even better. Salmon, more common on Van-couver menus than pasta, is also special here; it comes topped with crab meat, shrimp, and a delicate dill hollandaise. But even if the food weren't good, the romance here is so infectious that you could eat your tie and still enjoy yourself.

MODERATE

Cactus Club Café

1136 Robson St. ☎ **604/687-3278**. Main courses $6.95–$13.95. Daily 11:30am-1:30am. AE MC V. SOUTHWESTERN.

Young staff and patrons pack this lively restaurant. Tables outside on Robson Street are great for people-watching (but be prepared to vie or wait for seating). Inside, papier-mâché cows and strings of jalapeño pepper lights hang over booths with cowhide-print seat covers. There's a great juke box. From the open kitchen at the back, you can watch the chef prepare sizzling fajitas; six variations on Caesar salad; slow-cooked jerked chicken; succulent ribs; and piles of hot wings, calamari, potato skins, nachos, and the like.

Café de Paris

751 Denman St. ☎ **604/687-1418**. Reservations recommended. Main courses $14–$17. AE, MC, V. Lunch Mon–Fri 11:30am–2pm; dinner daily 5:30–10pm. Bus: 8. FRENCH.

The new owners of this place, chef André Bernier from the Ritz Carlton in Montreal and maître d' Richard Toussaint from the William Tell, have made extensive changes to the decor and menu to recreate an authentic Parisian bistro. Dark wood, brass accents, wine racks, marble-topped tables, and such classic bistro items as duck confit, steak tartare, smoked rack of lamb roasted with fresh herbs (all served with *pommes frites*) complete the authentic bistro experience. For more elaborate dining, try the three-course table d'hôte menu ($24.95 at dinner or $13.95 at lunch). There's an extensive wine list with prices ranging from $16 to $400. After a long hike through nearby Stanley Park, it's an ideal destination.

The Chef & the Carpenter

1745 Robson St. ☎ **604/687-2700.** Reservations required. Main courses $12.95–$17.95. AE, DC, ER, MC, V. Lunch daily 11:30am–2pm; dinner daily 5:30–10pm; Sat–Sun dinner only. Bus: 8. FRENCH.

There hasn't been a carpenter in the business for years, but the chef still attracts a regular crowd. You might start with the rich cognac pâté or coquille St. Jacques, then devour a Caesar salad prepared at your table. In addition to the requisite rack of lamb and filet mignon, the entrées include scallops Bombay in a creamy curry and pear sauce and two choices of supreme of chicken (try the one marinated in maple syrup). Every plate is piled high with five vegetables, and there's always a tempting dessert selection, including homemade ice cream, parfaits, and an exquisite chocolate-hazelnut cake. The predominantly French wine list ranges from $15 to around $90.

⊖ Chez Thierry

1674 Robson St., near Bidwell Street. ☎ **604/688-0919.** Reservations recommended. Main courses $10–$16.95. AE, DC, ER, MC, V. Daily 5:30–10:30pm. Bus: 8. FRENCH.

This nice little place, as owner Thierry Damilano (former coach of the Canadian national women's windsurfing team) describes it, serves, in our opinion, Vancouver's best French country–style cuisine. Classic country fare such as prawns and artichokes in a light, velvety curry sauce; perfectly crisped boneless duck in a peach and port sauce (our favorite dish); and bouillabaisse (a house specialty) head up the menu. The dessert menu's highlight is the apple tart, flamed at your table with apple brandy. If you order champagne, Thierry will emerge from the kitchen dressed like a flamboyant Napoleon and open it with a cutlass.

✪ The Fish House in Stanley Park

2099 Beach Ave., in Stanley Park. ☎ **604-681-7275.** Reservations recommended Sundays and in summer. Lunch $6.95–$11.95; dinner main courses $9.95–$17.95; brunch $9.95–$15.95. AE, DC, ER, JCB, MC, V. Mon–Sat 11:30am–10pm; brunch Sun 11am–2:30pm. Bus: 19. PACIFIC NORTHWEST/SEAFOOD.

The Fish House has been completely renovated with a new kitchen and now features a menu designed by chef Karen Barnaby (formerly of the Harvest Moon Café in Victoria). Originally a clubhouse, the white wooden building harks back to a more genteel era. It's surrounded by public tennis courts, golf and lawn-bowling greens, and ancient cedar trees and sports a Ralph Lauren–style decor. The menu includes some very innovative dishes, including surprisingly tender wood-oven roasted calamari served with a piquant tomato oil; a seafood hot pot; and our favorite, Karen's grilled Ahi tuna steak served with creamy buttermilk mashed potatoes. The oyster bar serves at least a half dozen fresh varieties daily. The desserts—like coconut cream pie on a bed of passion fruit puree or chocolate brownie ice cream cake—are sumptuous and truly irresistible. And there's no way to adequately describe how the rich, melted Belgian chocolate erupts onto the creme anglais of their chocolate lava cake. The bar draws a mix of golfers, strollers, and local executives.

Romano's Macaroni Grill at the Mansion

1523 Davie St. ☎ **604/689-4334.** Dinner reservations recommended. Lunch $6.95–$10.95; dinner main courses $7.95–$14.95. AE, DC, MC, V. Daily 11:30am–10:30pm. Bus: 3 or 8. ITALIAN.

This fun, casual pasta and pizza restaurant is housed in a manor built just after the turn of the century by sugar baron B. T. Rogers. The extensive menu emphasizes southern Italian dishes; the hearty pastas in rich tomato-based sauces are definitely the most popular items. This is not nouvelle, high-concept, or cutting-edge food; it's just simple, understandable, and consistent fare like veal scalloppini, chicken parmesano, and pizzas piled high with pepperoni, sausages, and mushrooms. If you order the house wine, you're charged by how much you consume (measured on the side of the unlabeled bottles, not with a Breathalyzer). Your kids will love the children's menu, tasty pizzas, and the permissive staff.

Saigon

1500 Robson St. ☎ **604/682-8020.** Main courses $6.95–$16. AE, DC, MC, V. Sun–Thurs 11am–12am, Fri–Sat 11am–midnight. Bus: 8. VIETNAMESE.

This is downtown Vancouver's oldest Vietnamese restaurant, yet the food is still authentic. Lovers of Vietnamese food won't be disappointed by the crisp, moist *cha-gio* (spring rolls filled with roast pork, shrimp, and bean sprouts) or by the well-marinated, charcoal-grilled chicken or beef brochettes (shish kebabs) served over rice vermicelli. Big, steaming bowls of noodles in clear broth with a selection of meats are perfect for warming up on a rainy day. There's no bar, but the restaurant is fully licensed and has a good selection of beers.

INEXPENSIVE

Azzurro

1706 Robson St. ☎ **604/688-8294.** Main courses $3.25–$6.95. Mon–Sat 11:30am–7pm. ITALIAN.

Dario Fracca and his wife, Avelina, have been quietly serving up exquisite, simply prepared pastas, salads, and traditional Italian sandwiches on Robson for nine years. Penne with Italian sausage, rigatoni Bolognese, lasagne, Caesar salad, and hearty soups are prepared in the cleanest kitchen we've ever encountered. There's no menu— just a daily specials board. Regulars often don't have to order at all—Avelina remembers everyone's favorites. There are only a few tables covered with blue-and-white checkered tablecloths in the narrow storefront, which is easy to miss. Look hard for this place; the food is unforgettable.

The Fresgo Inn

1138 Davie St. ☎ **604/689-1332.** Dishes $3.50–$8. No credit cards. Mon–Sat 8am–3am, Sun 8am–midnight. Bus: 3 or 8. CAFETERIA.

Set back from Davie Street, the Fresgo has been quietly churning out big portions of diner-style basics for 23 years. The hot and cold buffet offerings range from sandwiches, salads, and burgers to huge breakfast platters. Though it's not the greatest spot for people-watching, it draws an eclectic crowd from businessmen to bikers and even tourists in search of a simple, filling meal.

Great Wall Mongolian BBQ Restaurant

717 Denman St. ☎ **604/739-4888.** Lunch buffet $5.95–$6.95; dinner buffet $9.95. Daily 11:30am–3pm; 4:30pm–10pm. MC V. MONGOLIAN.

This place has a casual atmosphere and no decor worthy of mention, but the food and service are surprisingly good. Instructions printed on the menu tell newcomers to pick up a bowl from the end of the buffet; fill it with a combination of four high-quality meats, 20 very fresh vegetables, noodles, tofu, and 16 flavorful sauces (careful with the hot pepper); then hand it to the chef, who spills everything out onto the sizzling hot grill. He spins it around the grill with a pair of oversized chopsticks then flips it back into the bowl. Everything is fully cooked in less than a minute. The final instruction is to sit back and enjoy. One more step might say repeat until stuffed, since this is an all-you-can-eat affair. Don't confuse this place with other Vancouver Mongolian restaurants; we found the food at Mongolie Grill, a local chain on Thurlow, as horrible as the fare at Great Wall is delicious.

Hanada

823 Denman St. ☎ **604/685-1136.** Lunch $3.95–$6.95; dinner main courses $.4.50–$9.75. Lunch Mon–Fri 11:45am–2:30pm; dinner Mon–Thurs 5–10pm, Fri 5–10:30pm; Sat noon–10:30pm. Bus: 8. JAPANESE/SUSHI.

What makes one inexpensive Japanese restaurant better than another? For us, it's the quality of the tuna in the sushi, the flavor of a perfectly char-grilled teriyaki chicken breast, and the artful presentation of a bento box. Imagine our surprise when we discovered this little corner restaurant dishing up all of our favorites for next to nothing. The service is great, too; hot moist towels are dispensed to clean your hands before eating, special requests are accommodated with a smile, and the wine is served in a chilled glass. These are just some of the reasons locals frequent Hanada. Crude hand-drawn signs with photos of the dishes posted in the front window seem to deter tourists. If you're looking for delicious, affordable Japanese, this is the best we've found in town.

⊕ Family-Friendly Restaurants

Old Spaghetti Factory (see p. 77) The entertaining decor and delicious home-style pasta appeal to kids.

Romano's Macaroni Grill at the Mansion (see p. 70) Kids can choose from the huge children's menu, and the friendly staff will even let them wander up the inviting mansion staircase to explore the upper rooms.

Brothers Restaurant (see p. 76) Here, your kids get balloons along with their own menu.

Rooster's Quarters

836 Denman St. ☎ **604/689-8023.** Dishes $6–$9. AE, MC, V. Mon–Fri 11:30am–11pm, Sat–Sun noon–11pm. Bus: 3 or 8. CANADIAN.

Rooster's Quarters offers the antidote to diet food: succulent Danish baby-back ribs are imported from Denmark and served in a Montreal-style, sweet, tangy maple barbecue sauce and Quebec-style fried chicken crisped on the outside and tender and dripping on the inside. If those don't hit the spot, try the *poutine* from Eastern Canada: french fries covered with melted cheese and gravy. It can get a little crowded, but just pick out a table and seat yourself. That's what the regulars do.

✪ Stepho's

1124 Davie St. ☎ **604/683-2555.** Reservations accepted for parties of 5–8. Main courses $4.25–$9.95. Daily 11:30am–11:30pm. Bus: 3 or 8. GREEK.

There's a reason this place is packed every day for lunch and dinner: The fare is simple Greek food at its finest. Customers line up outside and wait up to half an hour to be seated (usually the wait is around 10 minutes). Inside, a delicious meal awaits: generous portions of deliciously marinated lamb, chicken, pork, or beef over pilaf; tzatziki (yogurt dip) which is a garlic-lover's dream come true; and heaping platters of kalamari. Beware of ordering too much food; it's easy to do here. We never saved room for dessert, but the baklava looked good.

5 Central Vancouver

EXPENSIVE

⑤ Bishop's

2183 W. Fourth Ave. ☎ **604/738-2025.** Reservations required. Lunch $10.50–$13.95; dinner main courses $10.50–$13.95. AE, DC, MC, V. Lunch Mon–Fri 11:30am–2:30pm; dinner Mon–Sat 5:30–11pm, Sun 5:30–10pm. Bus: 4 or 7. PACIFIC NORTHWEST.

If you have only one evening to dine in Vancouver, spend it here. Many Vancouverites regard Bishop's as the city's best restaurant. Though we haven't yet tried every restaurant in town, we are willing to agree based on those we have tried. In addition, John Bishop is the ultimate host. He personally greets you with a warm and gracious welcome, escorts you to your table in his small but elegant restaurant, and introduces you to a catalog of fine wines and what he describes as "contemporary home cooking." Bright, stunning abstract art by Jack Shadbolt decorates the walls and menu covers. Taped light jazz provides the background sound, giving the establishment an arty feel. The decor features candlelight and white linen.

The menu, presided over by executive chef Michael Allemeier, changes three or four times a year, but the quality remains consistent. Recent favorites have included grilled baby calamari with a sesame, soy, tomato sauce; steamed clams served in an ale, leek, and pear broth; ravioli filled with Dungeness crab, eggplant, and mascarpone cheese; and roasted pork tenderloin stuffed with shiitake mushrooms and sun-dried plums.

Malinee's

2153 W. Fourth Ave. ☎ **604/737-0097.** Reservations recommended. Main courses $11.95–$14.75. AE, MC, V. Lunch Mon–Fri 11:30am–2:30pm; dinner Sun–Thurs 5:30–10pm, Fri–Sat 5:30–11pm. Bus: 4. THAI.

Two former *farang* (white foreigners) returned to North America from Bangkok and brought with them gourmet chef Kem Thong. Together they opened Malinee's, whose menu and service are truly a step above other Thai restaurants. Amid the greenery, neoclassical Thai paintings, and batik tablecloths are attentive waiters in handsome black-and-white outfits.

Lovers of spicy Thai food who are used to curries, lemongrass, coconut milk, and chili-peanut sauces will find their standard favorites and much more. A meal for four might start with stir-fried clams or steamed mussels, chicken satay, spring rolls, and fried cashews. Follow your appetizer with lemon-shrimp soup *(tom yum kung)*; tenderloin of beef marinated in soy and garlic with fresh coriander *(nua ga tiam)*; chicken cashew in red curry *(kai pad pangali)*; vegetables; and rice (to cool your palate). Don't miss the special house curry of squid, shrimp, and mussels stir-fried in coconut milk with green and red chilies. Try a tropical fruit—jackfruit or rambutan—with mango or coconut ice cream for dessert.

Monk McQueen's

601 Stamps Landing. ☎ **604/877-1351.** Reservations recommended. Fixed-price lunch $14–$18; dinner main courses $12–$24. AE, DC, ER, JCB, MC, V. Lunch daily 11:30am–2pm; dinner daily 5:30–11pm. Bus: 50. Ferry: Aquabus. SEAFOOD/CONTINENTAL.

One of the best ways to end a warm, sunny Vancouver summer afternoon is to hop on the diminutive Aquabus to Stamps Landing, find a table on either of Monk McQueen's two wooden decks built out over False Creek, and dig into a delicious seafood dinner while the sun fades. Downstairs at Monk's Oyster Bar, you can get a bucket of steamers and a locally brewed beer or heartier fare including spicy Szechwan seafood stir-fry or fantastic roasted prawns. You can find better bouillabaisse for less at Chez Thierry (see above), but the jambalaya here would be hard to beat if you went all the way to New Orleans.

McQueens Upstairs is a more formal (though still casual), less boisterous affair. Executive chef Robert Craig creates an enticing assortment of seafood dishes: baked oysters, prawn and scallop stew, steamed sea bass, clams marinara. Other entreés include venison with pears, rack of lamb roasted in Dijon mustard, and grilled filet mignon with roasted garlic. The wine list, divided by price ($21.75 to $45.00), has a truly international mixture of vintages.

Mulvaney's

1535 Johnston St., Granville Island. ☎ **604/685-6571.** Reservations recommended. Main courses $9.95–$19.95. AE, DC, ER, MC, V. Lunch (in the downstairs Créole Café only) Mon–Fri 11:30am–2pm; dinner daily 5:30–10:30pm; brunch Sun 11:30am–2pm. Bus: 51, Aquabus, or Granville Island Ferry to Granville Island. CAJUN.

This New Orleans–style restaurant was already flourishing when Granville Island was still an industrial wasteland. It's beautifully situated overlooking False Creek adjacent to Granville Island's theater complex.

The cuisine is straight from Bourbon Street. For an appetizer, try the apple-wood smoked duck, Oysters Bienville, or Acadian pepper prawns served in a cast-iron skillet. The spicy corn-and-chorizo gumbo is outstanding. Entrées include rack of lamb Lafayette topped with a Creole herb crust; jambalaya; Cajun cioppino; lime and tequila scallops and prawns; and mesquite-grilled halibut St. Charles. The Créole Café in Mulvaney's courtyard is open for lunch. Mulvaney's offers dinner-theater packages and dancing Thursday through Saturday nights.

✪ Tojo's Restaurant

777 W. Broadway. ☎ **604/872-8050.** Reservations recommended; required for the sushi bar. Full dinners $12.50–$99.50 per person. AE, DC, MC, V. Mon–Sat 5–11pm. Bus: 9. JAPANESE.

Hidekazu Tojo makes the best sushi in Vancouver. This nondescript restaurant and sushi bar attracts Japanese businessmen, Hollywood filmmakers, and others willing to pay for the best. The sushi menu changes with the chef's moods, and the seasons are reflected in Tojo's abstract, edible masterpieces (Dungeness crab and asparagus norimaki appeared one spring night). Nonsushi dishes are available from a seasonal menu that has included everything from tempura to teriyaki. Reserve seats at the bar for the true Tojo's experience.

MODERATE

Alma Street Café

2505 Alma St., at West 10th Avenue. ☎ **604/222-2244.** Reservations recommended. Main courses $9–$14. AE, MC, V. Mon 8am–2:30pm, Tues–Thurs 8am–11pm, Fri 8am–midnight, Sat 9am–midnight, Sun 9am–10pm. Bus: 10 or 22. WEST COAST.

This much-lauded neighborhood eatery and jazz haven can best be described as eclectic. The restaurant combines natural foods with what owner Dr. Kevin B. Leslie describes as a marriage of East and West with an emphasis on fresh herbs and Pacific seafood. The menu changes daily to include the best of the produce and seafood markets. One of the best is free-range chicken breast stuffed with corn and sweet potatoes topped with a cherry and port sauce. Try the vegetarian strudel or any of the fresh vegetable pastas.

There are changing exhibits of photography and fabric art on the walls and modern jazz performances Wednesday through Sunday from 8 to 11:30pm. Recent acts have included such big names as Herb Ellis, singers Dee Daniels and Nancy King, and Chuck Isreals. Leslie himself is a former musician.

✪ Picasso Café

1626 W. Broadway. ☎ **604/732-3290.** Reservations recommended. Main courses $5.25–$10.95 at lunch, $8.95–$15.95 at dinner. MC, V. Lunch Mon 8:30am–2:30pm, Tues–Fri 8:30am–9pm. Bus: 10. WEST COAST

If your arteries are shying away from French fare or wincing at deep-fried fish, stop by this smoke-free establishment. The food is surprisingly good and quite creative, and much of it lives up to the stringent HeartSmart guidelines established by Canada's Heart and Stroke Foundation. A tasty and filling dinner might start with the baked Moosewood Mushroom Walnut Pâté served with grilled sourdough pumpernickel bread, and continue with grilled salmon filet complemented with pink hibiscus-flower cream sauce on a bed of spinach. The diverse, tasty fare also features tofu chocolate cheesecake, fresh juices, and mocha shakes. Framed prints by many of Vancouver's finest artists hang on the walls of this garden-style cafe. The restaurant provides on-the-job training for youths through the auspices of the Option Youth Society.

INEXPENSIVE

⑤ Isadora's Cooperative Restaurant

1540 Old Bridge St., on Granville Island. ☎ **604/681-8816.** Reservations recommended for groups of six or more. Main courses $6.25–$12.95; kids' menu $4.75. MC, V. Mon–Fri 7:30am–9pm, Sat–Sun 9am–10pm. Closed Mon in winter. Bus: 50 or 51. Ferry: Granville Island Ferry or Aquabus. WEST COAST.

This is the only restaurant in Vancouver that will offer you part ownership (at $100 a share) along with your meal if you're inclined to invest in Isadora's vision of community support. Most patrons, however, are content to pay low prices for hearty, family style cuisine. Appetizers include vegetarian nutcakes and seafood Danika—a Scandinavian-style ceviche of fresh seafood marinated with fresh dill and juniper. Salads are imaginative and delicious, and the range of entrées is wide enough to suit any palate. Try the Khatsah'lano burger—a salmon fillet on bannock with cranberry chutney—or perhaps the Malaspina chicken stuffed with shrimp, crab, and cream cheese in a chili-cream sauce. The pear gingerbread and German double-chocolate cheesecake are excellent desserts. Isadora's is wheelchair accessible; there's also a small children's play area and a children's menu.

The Naam Restaurant

2724 W. Fourth Ave. ☎ **604/738-7151.** Main courses $3.95–$8.25. MC, V. Daily 24 hours. Bus: 4 or 22. VEGETARIAN.

Vancouver's oldest vegetarian and natural-food restaurant, the Naam has often been voted its best. This holdover from the days when Kitsilano was Vancouver's version of Haight-Ashbury has not changed much over time, but that seems to be its appeal. There's a certain integrity to the unapologetically healthy fare, served 24 hours a day, that ranges from open-face tofu melts, enchiladas, and burritos to tofu teriyaki, Thai noodles, and a variety of pita pizzas. No entrée is over $8.75. Breakfast (served from 6 to 11am, Saturday to 1pm, Sunday to 2:30pm) is a testament to the variety of delicious foods that can be prepared without meat; eggs and dairy products are, however, served. If you're a fan of vegetarian cuisine, the Naam is worth a visit.

6 Gastown & Chinatown

EXPENSIVE

Raintree Restaurant at the Landing

375 Water St. ☎ **604/688-5570.** Reservations recommended. Main courses $9.95–$33.95. AE, DC, JCB, MC, V. Daily lunch 11:30pm–2pm, dinner 5:30pm–11pm. Bus: 50. PACIFIC NORTHWEST.

Even before we paid our first visit here, we had heard a lot of whispers that Raintree wasn't what it used to be. Nothing could be farther from the truth. The restaurant has left the West End and relocated to Gastown. The exposed brick walls of its new space in a restored waterfront warehouse dramatically frame a fabulous panoramic harbor-side view of the north shore.

The service is attentive and professional, and the menu is filled with the creativity that made Raintree the first and best place for Pacific Northwest cuisine in town. Try the roast lamb with cracked wheat salad and yogurt dressing or the grilled rare marlin steaks with fresh steamed seasonal vegetables.

MODERATE

⑤ The Cannery

2205 Commissioner St., near Victoria Drive. ☎ **604/254-9606.** Reservations recommended. Main courses $12–$20. AE, DC, DISC, MC, V. Lunch Mon–Fri 11:30am–2:30pm; dinner daily 5:30–10pm. Bus: 7 to Victoria Drive. Directions: From downtown, head east on Hastings Street, turn left on Victoria Drive (two blocks past Commercial Drive), and then right on Commissioner Street. SEAFOOD.

A seven- or eight-minute drive from downtown, The Cannery, hidden among the Burrard Inlet wharves, is Vancouver's best place for seafood. Built over the water and filled with seafaring memorabilia (the bar was once a Steveston fishing shack and the fireplace is a converted ship's boiler), The Cannery is an upscale, thoroughly romantic dining spot. Picture windows facing the water provide sweeping views of the busy harbor, North Vancouver, and the mountains rising in the background. Harbor seals frolic in the waters below the windows.

The seafood is fresh and plentiful. Start out with a bowl of creamy clam chowder or rich lobster bisque, then scan the daily fresh sheet. Those in the know order from the mesquite-grilled section. Our personal favorites are the tender halibut cheeks with a fresh sweet pepper and tomato salsa and the seafood combo platter, which resembles a Rembrandt still-life painting: a silvery platter spilling over with perfectly prepared gifts from the sea. The Cannery's perennial gold-medal wine list has some good bargains, and the desserts, especially the famous desert soufflés, are exquisite.

Japanese Deli

381 E. Powell St. ☎ **604/681-6484.** Full meals $4.95–$35; fixed-price meal $8.95 at lunch, $11 at dinner. No credit cards. Mon 11:30am–3pm, Tues–Fri 11:30am–8pm, Sat–Sun 11:30am–6pm. Bus: 4 or 7. JAPANESE.

If you happen to be exploring the remnants of Vancouver's Japantown (which never quite recovered after the Japanese were interned during World War II) and you're in the mood for sushi, this is the place. The best time to get here is a little before noon, when the lunch-hour crowd rushes in. There's nothing fancy and no California rolls; this is a real Japanese worker's lunch counter. The prices are cheap, and the fresh fish is handled by experts. Many customers eat here every day.

Kilimanjaro

332 Water St. ☎ **604/681-9913.** Reservations recommended. Appetizers $3.95–$8.95; main courses $13.95–$23.95. AE, DC, DISC, ER, MC, V. Lunch Mon–Fri 11:30am–4pm; dinner daily 5:30–11pm. Bus: 1 or 50. EAST AFRICAN/INDIAN.

Transplanted to East Africa, Indian cooking underwent many changes. Amyn Sunderji's restaurant in Gastown's Le Magasin mall captures those unique tastes in a setting that looks like a scene from the film *Out of Africa,* complete with tribal masks and batiks on the walls. Start out with samosas, savory Indian-inspired pastries traditionally filled with beef or not-so-traditional salmon; mombasa mussels broiled on the half shell; or the *hasusa* (appetizer) platter for a sample of everything. In addition to lamb Serengetti, spicy goat curry, and trout tukutuku, Amyn has added a game menu offering alligator, wild boar, caribou, and surprisingly popular ostrich prepared in port and tamarind. For lunch, he's succumbed to pasta mania but with a twist: Sauces include coconut and chicken as well as Bolognese with Congo peppers. For more casual dining and lower prices, try out the Safari Club coffeehouse downstairs.

✪ Park Lock Seafood Restaurant

544 Main St. at East Pender Street. ☎ **604/688-1581.** Reservations recommended. Main courses $9.95–$35; dim sum dishes $2.50–$3.25. Daily 10am–3pm; Tues–Sun 5–10pm. Bus: 19 or 22. CHINESE/DIM SUM.

This second-floor Hong Kong–style restaurant has nondescript entrances on both Main and East Pender streets. Narrow staircases lead up to the large carpeted dining room. Though dinner is an experience in Chinese fine dining, the real attraction here is dim sum. For five hours every day (from 10am to 3pm), waitresses roll carts loaded with Chinese delicacies past the white linen–covered tables. There's rarely an empty seat, but the wait is usually less than 10 minutes.

Dishes include spring rolls; hargao; and shumei (steamed shrimp, beef, or pork dumplings); prawns wrapped in fresh white noodles; small steamed buns; sticky rice cooked in banana leaves; and curried squid. All the dishes are fresh from the kitchen, flavorful, and have the lowest MSG content of any food we've tried in Chinatown. The staff is surprisingly friendly.

INEXPENSIVE

⑤ Brothers Restaurant

1 Water St. ☎ **604/683-9124.** Reservations recommended, especially on weekends. Lunch $4.95–$7.95; dinner main courses $6.95–$12.95. AE, DC, JCB, MC, V. Mon–Thurs 11:30am–10pm, Fri–Sat 11:30am–midnight, Sun 11:30am–9pm. Bus: 1 or 50. AMERICAN.

Brothers is a standard restaurant thinly disguised as a Franciscan monastery complete with staff in friars' robes. The warm ambience here especially appeals to families and older folks. Main offerings include chowder, pastas, burgers, and prime rib. Children get balloons and their own menu. A bistro lounge featuring sushi and oyster bars caters primarily to young adults.

Old Spaghetti Factory

53 Water St. ☎ **604/684-1288.** Reservations accepted only for parties of six or more. Lunch $5.75–$7.45; dinner main courses $6.95–$11.85. AE, MC, V. Mon–Thurs 11:30am–10pm, Fri–Sat 11:30am–11pm, Sun 11:30am–9pm. Bus: 1 or 50. ITALIAN/PASTA.

Formerly a coffee- and tea-packing plant, the Old Spaghetti Factory is crammed with every imaginable kind of contraption—old street lamps; fine Tiffany glass; a penny farthing cycle mounted on a wall; and a B.C. electric trolley car, vintage 1904, that's now part of the restaurant's seating area. Needless to say, the place is a hit with kids. You can enjoy New York steak, veal à la parmigiana, green-and-gold fettuccine, or Mama Pulosi's secret lasagne; most folks come for the spaghetti, prepared in nine different ways.

The Only (Fish & Oyster Café)

20 E. Hastings St. ☎ **604/681-6546.** Main course $5.25–$11.95. No credit cards. Mon–Sat noon–7pm. Bus: 8, 14, 20, or 21. SEAFOOD.

This skid-row eatery is a Vancouver institution. Opened in 1912, it's reputed to be the city's oldest restaurant. Alcohol is not served and there are no public restrooms, but every day, lines form outside at mealtime with all sorts of people waiting for a taste of fresh pan-fried fish or rich clam chowder. Sit down at the meticulously scrubbed 1930s-style lunch counter and have a brimming hot bowl of creamy, New England clam chowder made fresh daily. Then try the fresh trout, lemon sole, or halibut which are all cooked to perfection: Never dry or greasy.

Phnom Penh Restaurant

244 E. Georgia St., near Main Street. ☎ **604/682-5777.** Dishes $4.50–$10.75. DC, MC. Wed–Mon 10am–9:30pm. Bus: 8 or 19. CAMBODIAN/VIETNAMESE.

This family run restaurant (which has a second location at 955 Broadway at Oak Street), serves a mixture of Vietnamese and slightly spicier Cambodian cuisine. Phnom Penh is a perennial contender for, and occasional winner of, *Vancouver Magazine's* award for the best Asian restaurant in town. The walls are adorned with artistic renderings of the ancient Cambodian capital of Angkor, Khmer dolls are suspended on glass cases, and the subdued lighting is a welcome departure from the harsh glare often found in inexpensive Chinatown restaurants. Try the outstanding hot and sour soup, loaded with prawns and lemon grass in a light, flavorful broth. The garlic squid, deep fried and served with rice, is also delicious. For dessert, the fruit and rice pudding is an exotic treat.

6

What to See & Do in Vancouver

Adventure travelers, mountain bikers, skiers, and people who love good living: Vancouver is your kind of place. This city has more natural attractions than you'll ever have time to see. Even if you stay here for a few months, you'll keep discovering more. Just wandering the beaches could take weeks alone. Vancouver's cultural attractions are also abundant. The museums and art galleries will astound you with rare collections you won't find anywhere else in Canada, North America, or the world.

SUGGESTED ITINERARIES

If You Have 1 Day

Get up early and take a stroll, put on your in-line skates, or rent a mountain bike. Start out at the Canada Place Pier, then head down Robson Street to Stanley Park. (Pick up a bite at the Bread Garden on Bute Street off Robson Street or in the street-side restaurant at the Pacific Palisades hotel. If it's winter, pick up a 90¢ cup of coffee at the Stanley Park Pavilion, which is open at 8am.) Take the path around Lost Lagoon or watch the rowing teams near Dead Man's Island. If you're feeling ambitious, follow the morning rush hour of joggers, skaters, and cyclists around the seawall (a 6.4-mile loop with magnificent views). Now that you've had a good morning stretch, spend the afternoon exploring the West End and downtown. Robson, Denman, and Davie are the main streets for shopping and dining. Relax at sunset by taking in the view from English Bay Beach. Savor such examples of Pacific Northwest cuisine as salmon or spotted prawns and take in a show.

If it's raining, have a leisurely breakfast in one of the West End's many sidewalk restaurants. Then browse the downtown museums and stores. You can go on a shopping spree from Robson Street to Canada Place through a maze of underground concourses and hardly get your Reeboks wet.

If You Have 2 Days

Take a miniferry over to Granville Island and spend your second morning exploring the public market, the artist studios, and outfitter stores. Stroll the Mariner's Promenade over to Vanier Park, where you can discover the Vancouver Museum, Pacific Space Center, or Maritime Museum. Have lunch along West Broadway before taking

What's Special About Vancouver

Beaches
- English Bay Beach at the edge of Stanley Park, a beautiful spot to enjoy the sun, sand, and view.
- Kitsilano Beach, where you can play volleyball in the sand or just relax.

Buildings
- Library Square, which looks more like the Roman Coliseum than a new seven-story public library; it's the largest public library in the world.

Museums
- UBC's Museum of Anthropology, which contains the country's most impressive collection of First Nations art.

Parks/Gardens
- Stanley Park, where beavers, raccoons, ducks, geese, eagles, and even skunks reside right in the downtown area.
- The Sunken Garden at Queen Elizabeth Park, which has the city's best view and is the best example of Vancouver land reclamation—it was once a quarry.

Events/Festivals
- The Wine Festival, where you can try the world's best wines, including British Columbia's award-winning vintages.
- The Benson and Hedges Symphony of Fire, four days of competitive fireworks displays on English Bay Beach.

For Kids
- Science World British Columbia, a hands-on romp through the mysteries of the universe that appeals to kids of all ages.
- The Grouse Mountain tram, which takes you on a memorable ride up past the treetops to an incredible view of the city (unless it's cloudy) and to a local ski area in the winter.

Attractions
- Vancouver Aquarium, where you can meet Canada's first baby Beluga whale born in captivity as well as orcas and sea otters.

Natural Spectacles
- Lighthouse Park in West Vancouver, where you may be lucky enough to see the orcas that live in the nearby coastal waters.

Literary Shrines
- Pauline Johnson's shrine, which overlooks English Bay in Stanley Park.
- The Malcolm Lowry Walk, which commemorates the Beat author's residence in North Vancouver's Cates Park.

Lazy Sundays
- Weekly cricket trial matches and rugby games, which take place near the totem poles in Stanley Park.
- Morning string quartet concerts, given at the Queen Elizabeth Theatre.

Offbeat Oddities
- The Vancouver Centennial Police Museum, which displays local crime and punishment at their best—or rather their worst.
- The Lynn Headwaters suspension bridge, a wood-and-wire pedestrian bridge that's not for the faint of heart.

in the extensive First Nations art collection at the University of British Columbia's Museum of Anthropology.

If You Have 3 Days

Spend your first two days as described above. On your third morning, take an excursion to North and West Vancouver via the SeaBus. Wander through the Lonsdale Quay Market, located right at the SeaBus terminal, then take the tram ride up Grouse Mountain. Travel a little further west by bus or car to Horseshoe Bay, a lovely seaport town that is home to the Nanaimo ferry.

If you're into skiing, you've got three great ski resorts from which to choose: Cypress Bowl, Mount Seymour, or Grouse Mountain Resort (in season, of course). In the warmer months, the Baden-Powell Trail as well as the trails in Lynn Canyon Park, Lynn Headwaters Regional Park, and Capilano River Regional Park are great places for an exhilarating hike.

If You Have 5 Days or More

Spend your first three days as suggested above. During your next two days, take a half- or full-day excursion to the Whistler and Squamish areas—only an hour's drive from downtown Vancouver. Or you can take a ferry from Horseshoe Bay to the relaxed atmosphere of nearby Bowen Island.

If you want to stay in the city, do a little stargazing. Pick up a copy of the B.C. Film Commission's *Hot Sheet* (at the commission's offices at the SeaBus Terminal) to find out which film or TV production companies are currently shooting in the city. There are usually three or four productions being filmed here monthly. You could watch your favorite stars in action out by False Creek or Stanley Park.

Or if you're up for more physical adventure, return to Granville Island and rent a sea kayak, sailboat, or jet ski for the day. Instructions and complete packages cost as little as $18 for a two-hour kayaking trip.

1 The Top Attractions

DOWNTOWN

Sri Lankan Gem Museum

150-925 W. Georgia St. ☎ **604/662-7768.** Admission $3.50 adults, $2.50 seniors, $2 children. Tickets available from Shelton Jewelers across the hall. Daily 10:30pm–5:30pm. SkyTrain: Burrard. Bus: 3.

From its 9,000-piece Brazilian-agate mosaic floor to its handpainted enamel, 24-carat gold-leaf walls and ceiling, this privately owned, hand-constructed grotto of precious and semiprecious gems is a truly unique sight. If the dazzle of the twin jewel-box rooms isn't enough, the glittering contents of the built-in glass displays will strike awe in the most jaded eyes: The beauty of a three-ton amethyst geode explodes in a rain-forest setting, a stream of sparkling raw emeralds pours out of an etched-brass cornucopia, and a 20,000-carat topaz radiates atop its pedestal.

Vancouver Art Gallery

750 Hornby St. ☎ **604/682-5621.** Admission $6 adults, $4 seniors, $3 students, children under 12 free, pay-what-you-can Thurs after 5pm. Mon–Sat 10am–5pm, Thurs 10am–9pm, Sun and holidays noon–5pm. Closed Mon–Tues Oct–May (gift shop and cafe stay open). SkyTrain: Granville. Bus: 3.

Originally, this 1906 building housed the provincial courthouse designed by Francis Rattenbury (the architect who designed Victoria's Empress Hotel and the Parliament buildings). The interior was renovated in 1983 by Arthur Erickson (see

"Architectural Highlights," under "More Attractions," below). There is an impressive collection of art by B.C. native Emily Carr as well as works by the Canadian Group of Seven; international and regional paintings, sculpture, graphics, photography, and video. The gallery's library contains a large collection of reference material, including periodicals, books, and files. The Annex Gallery, geared to younger audiences, features rotating visually exciting, educational exhibits.

The gift shop carries art books, multiples (original prints, jewelry, and objects produced and signed by artists in more than one copy), toys, and stationery, much of it created by regional artists. Patrons can contemplate what they've seen and refresh themselves in the Gallery Café, which overlooks the Sculpture Garden.

WEST END

✪ Vancouver Aquarium

Stanley Park, P.O. Box 3232. ☎ **604/682-1118.** Fax 604/631-2529. Admission $9.50 adults, $8.25 seniors and students, $6.25 children 5–12, children under 5 free, $27 families. Open 365 days a year. June 23–Sept 4 9:30am–8pm; Sept 5–June 22 daily 10am–5:30pm. Bus: 19; "Around the Park" bus Apr 15–Oct, weekends, and holidays only.

North America's third-largest aquarium, this site has more than 8,000 marine species in re-created environments. The Sandwell North Pacific Habitat houses a giant octopus, orca (killer) whales, sea otters, stellar sea lion pups, and anemones—all attended by staff scuba divers who feed hungry halibut and harvest the ever-growing kelp.

In the icy blue world of Arctic Canada, you can watch beluga whales peering at you or gracefully singing and dancing as they pass by the windows. Human-sized freshwater fish await you in the H. R. MacMillan Tropical Gallery's Amazonian rain forest. In the Graham Amazon Gallery, an hourly rain storm thunders over your head while you meet crocodiles, poison arrow tree frogs, sloths, and piranhas. Regal angelfish glide through a re-creation of Indonesia's Bunaken National Park coral reef, and blacktip reef sharks menacingly scour the waters of the Tropical Pacific Gallery (call for the shark tank feeding time, which is extremely popular with visitors).

Wildlife Crime Busters, a new exhibit, shows you how the Environment Canada Team uses forensic tools including DNA testing to identify products made from endangered species and to solve wildlife crimes such as poaching and smuggling.

This is also Canada's largest Marine Mammal Rescue and Rehabilitation Centre. Conservation techniques are on display in the Habitat Success Stories exhibit. The outdoor Max Bell Marine Mammal Centre features orca and beluga whales, sea otters, and harbor seals rescued from the *Exxon Valdez* oil spill. Marine mammal behavior is explained by aquarium staff in on-going narratives.

Clamshell, the Nature Gift Shop (☎ 604/685-5911), sells a great collection of marine-oriented mementos, crafts, souvenirs, and books.

CENTRAL VANCOUVER

Pacific Space Centre

1100 Chestnut St., in Vanier Park. ☎ **604/738-STAR.** Fax 604/736-5665. Admission to special shows $5.50–$7.75 adults, $3.75–$7.75 seniors and students. Seniors admitted Tues free to all regular shows. Fri–Sun noon–5pm, 7–11pm. Occasional unannounced closures; call ahead. Bus: 22.

The Pacific Space Centre (formerly the H. R. Macmillan Planetarium and Gordon Southam Observatory) shares space with the Vancouver Museum (see below). The building is hard to miss—its low, conical roof is modeled on a Coast Salish hat. Astronomy and space science programs are new additions to the displays and

Downtown Vancouver Attractions

0   400 m
       436 y

N

Stanley Park

Beaver Lake

2

1

Lost Lagoon

Coal

Lagoon Dr.

Chilco St.
Gilford St.
Pendrell St.
Beach Ave.
Denman St.
Comox St.
Nelson St.
Barclay St.
Haro St.
Robson St.
W. Georgia St.
Alberni St.

Bidwell St.
Cardero St.
Nicola St.
Broughton St.
Jervis St.
Burnaby St.
Harwood St.
Pacific St.
Beach Ave.

W E S

English Bay

Sunset Beach Park

7

Ogden Ave.

Vanier Park

Burrard Bridge

Whyte Ave.

9

Granville Bridge

Granville Island

11

Cornwall Ave.

Cartwright St.

W 1st Ave.

W 3rd Ave.

W 5th Ave.

LEGEND
Post Office ✉
Information ⓘ

W 7th Ave.

W. Broadway

2079

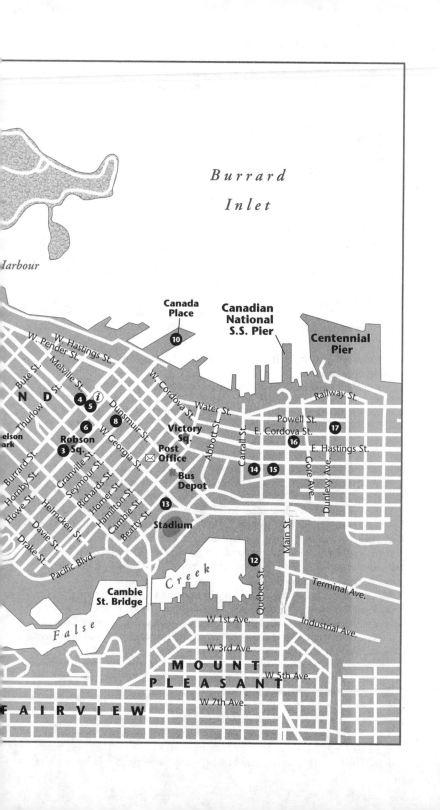

laser-light shows housed under the planetarium's 62-foot domed ceiling. You can journey into space in the Cosmic Simulator, explore Canadian inventions and pioneering endeavors in the Groundstation Canada theater, surf the Internet from the center's on-line site, or view the skies from the geosphere's satellite-image display. Photography buffs can shoot the moon through a half-meter telescope for $10 per camera (☎ 604/736-2655).

Vancouver Museum

1100 Chestnut St. ☎ **604/736-4431** or 604/736-7736 for 24-hour recorded information on programs and exhibits. Fax 604/736-5417. Admission and hours change seasonally; call ahead. Bus: 22, then walk 3 blocks south on Cornwall Avenue. Boat: Granville Island Ferry or Aquabus.

This museum houses displays about Vancouver's history from prehistoric times through the Coast Salish settlement and early pioneers to its early 20th-century maturation as a great urban center. The exhibits allow visitors to walk through the steerage deck of a 19th-century immigrant ship, peek into a Hudson's Bay Company trading post, or sit in an 1880s Canadian-Pacific passenger car. Re-creations of Victorian and Edwardian rooms show how early Vancouverites decorated their new homes. Rotating exhibits present additional items in the museum's vast artifact collection.

The museum's self-service vending-machine lunch area (☎ 604/738-6336) offers basic sandwiches and refreshments. The gift shop sells contemporary First Nations jewelry and crafts as well as publications and souvenirs.

✪ The University of the British Columbia & Kitsilano Museum of Anthropology

University of British Columbia, 6393 NW Marine Dr. ☎ **604/822-5087.** Recorded information 604/822-3825. Fax 604/822-2974. Admission $6 adults, $3.50 seniors and students, children under 6 free, $15 families, free all day Tues June–Sept. Daily 11am–5pm, Tues 11am–9pm. Closed Mon Sept–June and Dec 25–26. Bus: 4 or 10.

This isn't just any old museum. In 1976, architect Arthur Erickson (see "Architectural Highlights," below) re-created a classic Salish post-and-beam structure out of modern concrete and glass to house the world's finest Pacific Northwest First Nations art collection (which is incidentally prominently featured in the movie *Intersection*).

You enter through a huge, open, Ksan-carved, bent-cedar box. Bowls, canoes, funerary articles, and house posts from Coastal Salish potlatch feasts flank both sides of the ramp leading to the main exhibition spaces. Ancient monolithic totem poles in the Great Hall stand guard over works in progress being carved on-site by First Nations artisans. The space is naturally lit by floor-to-ceiling windows that face the museum's grassy background.

Master sculptor Bill Reid's touchable cedar bear and sea wolf sculptures sit at the Cross Roads, where source books rest on a reading-height display wall. The museum's bound photo archives include Edward S. Curtis's works. The Koerner Ceramics Gallery contains a rare international ceramic arts collection, including an intricately sculpted, German-glazed ceramic stove.

The Masterpiece Gallery's argillite sculptures, beaded jewelry, and carved ceremonial masks lead the way to Bill Reid's monumental sculpture *Raven and the First Men*, as well as some of his precious-metal creations. More than 15,000 artifacts arranged by culture are preserved in the Visible Storage Galleries. You can open the glass-topped drawers to view these small treasures, look at larger pieces in the tall glass cases, and refer to the conveniently placed reference books for more detailed information. The gift shop sells contemporary First Nations artwork as well as books and publications. The final—but no less breathtaking—stop is the grounds in back, where there are 2 Haida longhouses, positioned on the traditional north-south axis; 10 attending house posts; and contemporary carvings overlooking Point Grey.

NORTH VANCOUVER & WEST VANCOUVER

Grouse Mountain Resort

6400 Nancy Greene Way, North Vancouver. ☎ **604/984-0661.** Admission $14.50 adults, $12.50 seniors, $9.25 students, $5.95 children 6–12, children under 6 free. SkyRide free with advance restaurant reservation. Daily 10am–10pm. SeaBus to Lonsdale Quay, transfer to bus 236.

On a clear day, Grouse Mountain has one of the most impressive views of the Vancouver skyline, English Bay, Mount Baker, and the Strait of Georgia. The SkyRide tram's four cable cars lift visitors every 10 minutes from the ticket office and Valley Station Gift Shop to the 3,700-foot summit. Before you venture across for the eight-minute tram ride, you should look at the peaks from the city. If the mountains are hazy or cloudy, change your plans. On the wrong day, the SkyRide can be an exercise in sensory deprivation with the occasional Douglas fir tree top as the only excitement.

The resort also offers summertime hiking and wintertime day and night skiing. Major hang-gliding competitions take place up here as well (see "Outdoor Activities," below). There are interpretative trails, a picnic area, a snack bar, and a triple-screen presentation of Vancouver history and Haida folklore entitled *Our Spirit Soars.* If that isn't enough to keep you entertained, there are two helicopter tours for an additional charge (see "Air Tours," under "Organized Tours," below); the Peak chairlifts to the 4,100-foot-high peak; the Spirit Gallery and Inpost shops; and daily summertime logger-sport demonstrations and competitions.

Phone ahead for special events, including jazz concerts and Shakespeare on the Peak. For the kids, the resort's Adventure Playground, Log Cabin Players, and staff of face painters provide the day's thrills.

The Grouse Nest Restaurant serves lunch, Sunday brunch, and dinner, featuring a selection of continental and West Coast cuisine.

Capilano Canyon Suspension Bridge & Park

3735 Capilano Rd., North Vancouver. ☎ **604/985-7474.** Fax 604/985-7479. Admission summer: $7.45 adults, $6.25 seniors, $5 students, $2.50 children 6–12, children under 6 free; winter: $6.95 adults, $5.50 seniors, $4.50 students, $2.50 children 6–12, children under 6 free. Daily May–Sept 8am–dusk, Oct–Apr 9am–5pm. Closed Dec 25. Bus: 246 to Ridgewood/Capilano.

Marilyn Monroe did it. So did Walter Cronkite, Katherine Hepburn, and the Rolling Stones. Margaret Thatcher liked it so much she did it twice. Here, amid the towering Douglas firs and red cedars of a 20-acre park, lies the city's oldest tourist attraction, the Capilano Suspension Bridge. Stretching 450 feet across the roaring Capilano River as it races to the Burrard Inlet, this impressive cedar and steel-cable footbridge has wowed visitors to Vancouver since its construction in 1889. If you too want to walk 230 feet above the river floor, try to make yourself look down as you make your way across—only the most timid will want to miss the kayakers shooting the rapids below, shrouded by mist from a 200-foot waterfall. There are also breathtaking views from a newly constructed, canyon-hanging, cantilevered deck.

Courageous souls pay a fee to traverse the bridge, which is privately owned and operated. The 1911 trading post on the other end of the bridge houses the souvenir shop, the Bridge House Restaurant, and a barbecue snack bar. First Nations carvers demonstrate their skills at the Totem Park Carving Centre and The Longhouse. The Living Forest and Rock of Ages exhibits have been recently added to the attractions roster. For those who want a less commercial experience, the nearby Lynn Head-water Suspension Bridge stands 10 feet higher and is free of charge, but it has no gift shops. (See "The *Other* Suspension Bridge," below.)

2 More Attractions

ARCHITECTURAL HIGHLIGHTS

Vancouver was leveled by fire in 1886, so most of its architecture is less than a century old. Some notable examples include the following:

The 1912 **Hotel Europe** (see "Historic Buildings/Monuments," below) resembles Manhattan's Flatiron Building. This former luxury hotel, designed by Vancouver architects Parr and Fee, originally had bay windows covering the entire facade. Fortunately, subsequent changes stripped the building of only a few of its interesting features. It appeared in the film *Legends of the Fall.*

The Art Deco **Marine Building,** 355 Burrard St. at Thurlow Street, is a lovely mid-20th century office building; it was the tallest building in the British Commonwealth when it opened in 1930. Designed by McCarthy and Nairie, the building was meant to emulate a rocky promontory rising from the sea. Its facade is detailed with terra-cotta, brass, stone, and marble bas-reliefs depicting the local aquatic environment.

John S. Archibald and John Schofield designed Canadian-Pacific Railway's **Hotel Vancouver** (see Chapter 4 for hotel review). Construction of this dignified French-Renaissance structure, which replaced the smaller hotel edifice on the same site, took the workmen 10 years to complete. But when it finally opened in 1929, it was the Vancouver skyline's tallest building. Topped by a green-patina copper roof decorated with intricately carved stone gargoyles and statuesque Hermes, the grand hotel's exterior walls are made of Haddington Island stone; they're the same kind used in Victoria's Parliament buildings. Sweeping marble staircases and an Edwardian grand lobby elegantly grace the interior.

Arthur Erikson is Canada's most prominent 20th-century architect. His modernist genius is in evidence throughout Vancouver. This native Vancouverite was the master designer of UBC's **Museum of Anthropology** (see "The Top Attractions," above); the **Vancouver Art Gallery's** interiors (see "The Top Attractions," above); the **Robson Square provincial law courts, Khalsa Diwan Gurudwara Temple** (see "Neighborhoods," below); and **Simon Fraser University** (see "Universities/Colleges," below). Erikson's home is at the corner of Courtenay and 14th streets. It's a surprisingly unremarkable house with a remarkable garden screened by bamboo.

The **Vancouver Museum** (see "The Top Attractions," above) sits on a promontory near the Burrard Street Bridge. A little over a century ago, Vanier Park was the site of a Coast Salish village. During World War II, it became a military defense base. In the 1960s, it was dedicated as a park. The museum's roof resembles a cone-shaped woven-cedar-bark Salish hat. The metal crab fountain in front of the museum is possibly Vancouver's most-photographed object.

Resembling the Roman Coliseum, **Library Square** on Robson Street contains voluminous rooms of book stacks; restaurants; a day-care center; and a seven-story reading atrium where visitors can comfortably take in the view.

The **Kuan-Yin Buddhist Temple** (see "Churches/Temples," below) is a traditional Chinese building. Behind sheltered walls in Chinatown lies **Dr. Sun Yat-Sen Classical Garden** (see "Parks/Gardens," below), a painstakingly exact Ming Dynasty private courtyard garden.

CHURCHES/TEMPLES

With such a growing and diverse ethnic populace, it's no wonder that Vancouver has such a wide variety of churches and temples.

Holy Rosary Cathedral, 646 Richards St. (☎ 604/682-6774), is a Gothic-Revival style Roman Catholic cathedral built between 1899 and 1900. On Sunday mornings, the angelic carillon bells still call the congregation to worship.

Colorful late-morning Sikh wedding ceremonies take place at the Arthur Erickson-designed **Khalsa Diwan Gurudwara Temple,** 8000 Ross St. (☎ 604/324-2010). You are welcome to observe, provided you ask permission in advance.

The Byzantine iconography and architecture of **St. George's Orthodox Church,** West 31st Avenue and Arbutus Street, is as classic as the Sunday services, which are still held in Greek before the magnificently decorous sanctuary doors.

Golden porcelain roof tiles sweep upward to two glittering flying dragons high atop the International Buddhist Society's **Kuan-Yin Buddhist Temple,** 9160 Steveston Hwy., Richmond (☎ 604/274-2822). After ascending the bleached granite stairway, you are greeted by two marble lions before entering the burnt-red doorway of the Main Gracious Hall, where a treasury of Chinese sculpture, woodworking, painting, and embroidery is on display. The center courtyard is graced with a ceramic mural of Kuan-Yin resting in a bamboo grove and a magnificent bonsai collection. The society invites you to participate in Saturday morning prayers at 10:30am as well as in other religious and cultural events.

On your way to this beautiful temple, check out the **Buddha Supplies Centre,** 4158 Main St., where you can pick up incense or joss sticks and tiny paper replicas of earthy belongings such as CD players and cellular phones.

COLLEGES/UNIVERSITIES

During the academic year, more than 32,000 students attend the **University of British Columbia (UBC),** one of Canada's largest universities. UBC has many attractions open to the public, including the **Museum of Anthropology** (see "The Top Attractions," above); the **Botanical Garden** and **Nitobe Memorial Garden** (see "Parks and Gardens," below); **TRIUMF (Tri-University Meson Facility),** 4004 Wesbrook Mall (☎ 604/222-1047), where the world's largest subatomic cyclotron is housed; the **M. Y. Williams Geological Museum,** Geological Sciences Centre, Stores Road, Gate 6 (☎ 604/822-5586); the **UBC Astronomical Observatory** and the **UBC Geophysical Observatory,** Main Mall, Gate 1 (☎ 604/822-2802).

You can also use the university's sports facilities, including the **Aquatic Centre, Thunderbird Winter Sports Centre,** and nearby **tennis courts** (see "Outdoor Activities," below). Miles of trails wind through the **University Endowment Lands** and **Point Grey beaches,** overlooking the Strait of Georgia and English Bay (see "Outdoor Activities," below).

The **Fine Arts Gallery, Frederic Wood Theatre,** and **UBC School of Music** are venues that present student work (see Chapter 9). For more information, contact the **Public Affairs Office,** 207-632B Memorial Rd. (☎ 604/822-3131). To get to UBC, take bus no. 4 or 10.

The modern **Simon Fraser University** campus has an expansive view of metropolitan Vancouver, thanks to its 1,200-foot elevation atop Burnaby Mountain. Architect Arthur Erickson won immediate acclaim for his stunning design when it opened in 1965 (see "Architectural Highlights," above).

The **Museum of Archaeology and Ethnology/University Art Gallery** (☎ 604/291-3325) exhibit contemporary works and historic First Nations art and artifacts by Inuit, Kwakiutl, and other provincial aboriginal bands. Admission is free. For more information, call 604/291-3210. Take bus 135, 144, or 145 to the campus.

HISTORIC BUILDINGS/MONUMENTS

Vancouver's oldest surviving edifice is the **Hastings Sawmill Store Museum,** 1575 Alma St. (☎ 604/228-1213), housed in an 1865 structure that served as the city's first general store. It was moved to Jericho Beach from Gastown by barge in 1930. Once inside, you are surrounded by Victorian notions and dry goods—period clothing, furnishings, hardware, toiletries, woven First Nations basketry, and historical photographs. Admission is by donation. The museum is open from June to mid-September daily from 11am to 4pm and on weekends from mid-September until May from 1pm to 4pm. Take bus 4, 7, or 42.

The triangular **Hotel Europe,** 43 Powell St., was an architectural wonder when it first opened its doors in 1912. Designed by local architects Parr and Fee and built by Cincinnati contractors, it proudly stood as Vancouver's first reinforced-concrete structure and fire-proof hotel. The design consciously imitated New York's 1903 Flatiron building, and its lobby was famous for its marble and brass construction. When Gastown fell into decline, so did the hotel. The main entrance was blocked off to expand the lobby beer parlor, and someone stole the original entrance balcony lamps; recent renovations, however, have saved Maple Tree Square from the wrecking ball (see Chapter 7).

Topped by a patina-green copper cupola and mansard windows, the **Sun Tower,** West Pender and Cambie streets, stands amid a somewhat desolate landscape that is just beginning to be redeveloped. This heritage building was constructed by Vancouver mayor L. D. Taylor, who ran his *Vancouver World* newspaper enterprise here from 1912 until 1915. The *Vancouver Sun* took over in 1937 and stayed at this location until 1964 (see Chapter 7).

At the outbreak of World War I, **Point Grey** residents watched artillery carriages rumble through the streets toward the headlands to establish Point Grey Battery on the beach below UBC Museum of Anthropology's parking lot. It was one of Vancouver's three military defense sites. In 1939, the 58th Heavy Battery of the 15th Coast Brigade took over the point, which had remained unused since the Armistice. They poured concrete gun emplacements and built officers' quarters two weeks before war was officially declared. The installation was closed down nine years later and was finally abandoned in the 1960s. The searchlight tower, No. 1 gun emplacement, and quarters' foundations are the only remaining relics. They have been restored by the 15th Field Artillery Regiment Museum and Archives Society.

MUSEUMS/GALLERIES

✪ B.C. Sports Hall of Fame and Museum

B.C. Place Stadium, Gate A, Beatty and Robson streets (777 Pacific Blvd. South). ☎ **604/687-5520.** Recorded information 604/687-5523. Fax 604/687-5510. Admission $2 adults, seniors, and students; children under 5 free. Tues–Sun 10am–5pm. SkyTrain: Stadium. Bus: 15.

The Hall of Champions and Builders Hall document British Columbia's greatest athletes, referees, and coaches with photographs and videos. There are also galleries dedicated to early provincial sports history, as well as to the achievements of super-athletes Terry Fox and Rick Hansen. You get the chance to be an athlete yourself in the Participation Gallery, a huge playroom where running, climbing, throwing, riding, rowing, and racing are not only allowed, they're encouraged.

The Canadian Craft Museum

639 Hornby St. ☎ **604/687-8266.** Fax 604/684-7174. Admission $4 adults, $2 seniors and students, children under 12 free. Mon–Sat 10am–5pm, Sun and holidays noon–5pm. Closed Tues Sept–May. SkyTrain: Granville. Bus: 3.

The Canadian Craft Museum was founded in 1980 as the Cartwright Gallery; it was renamed in 1990. It is committed to displaying the central role craftsmanship plays in heritage and culture. The museum occupies a three-story pyramid-topped complex that houses both a gallery and a workspace. In addition to its vast permanent Canadian treasury, the museum exhibits rotating international shows. Recent examples have included an impressive display of carved Chinese signature seals and calligraphy, a spectacular exhibition of Bill Reid's precious metal works, and furnishings by Canada's best industrial designers. You can buy unique, creatively designed ceramics, sculptures, and other works in the museum's gift store.

✪ Science World British Columbia

1455 Quebec St. ☎ **604/268-6363.** Admission $8 adults, $5 seniors, students, and children, children under 3 free; extra for Omnimax film. Mon–Fri 10am–5pm, Sat & Sun 10am–6pm. SkyTrain: Science World–Main Street Station.

Science World moved into Expo '86's geodesic-domed Omnimax Theatre right after the exposition closed. It's a hands-on scientific discovery center where you can light up a plasma ball; walk through a 1,700-square-foot maze; create a cyclone; lose your shadow; blow square bubbles; walk through the interior of a camera; play music on a walk-on synthesizer; watch a zucchini explode as it's charged with 80,000 volts; stand in the interior of a beaver lodge; and play wrist-deep in magnetic liquids. Future exhibits include a robotic cyclist, hot-air balloons, and earth science displays.

The Omnimax Theatre has a huge projecting screen on which you can take a death-defying flight through the Grand Canyon and feel as though you're experiencing other spine-tingling acts in larger-than-life scale and surround sound. Call for presentation times and current productions.

When it's time for a break, the cafeteria and a science-oriented gift shop offer refreshments and shopping.

✪ Vancouver Maritime Museum

1905 Ogden Ave. in Vanier Park. ☎ **604/257-8300.** Admission $5 adults, $2.50 seniors and students, $10 family, children under 5 free. Tues–Sun 10am–5pm. Bus: 22. Walk 4 blocks north on Cypress. Boat: Granville Island Ferry or Aquabus.

The Maritime Museum overlooks English Bay, a fitting place to display Vancouver's nautical history. There are regularly scheduled guided tours of the RCMP Arctic patrol vessel *St. Roch*—the second vessel ever to navigate the Northwest Passage and the first to do it from west to east. An extensive collection of intricate ship models (some carved from bone by prisoners of war), antique wood and brass fittings, and prints and other documents line the other galleries.

The aft cabin of a schooner and the bridge of a modern tugboat lead the way to the Children's Maritime Discovery Centre, where there are computers loaded with navigational facts and fun; a wall of drawers bearing ship models and artifacts that are just the right height for browsing; and observation telescopes ready to spot real ships in English Bay. You can also maneuver an underwater robot in a large water tank or dress up in naval costumes.

✪ Vancouver Centennial Police Museum

240 E. Cordova St. ☎ **604/665-3346.** Admission $2 adults, $1 seniors and children. Mon–Fri 11:30am–4:30pm; May–Aug, Mon–Sat 11:30am–4:30pm. Bus: 4 or 7.

Lovers of the criminal underworld will revel in the morgue and simulated autopsy rooms as well as the re-creations of Vancouver's infamous murder and crime scenes. Not surprisingly, the museum was originally the Coroner's Court and City Morgue. Mug shots of notorious criminals and their captors are displayed along with seized artifacts—opium pipes, daggers, hatchets, pistols, zip guns, and counterfeit currency. There are also police equipment and a coroner's forensic exhibit. The Cop Shoppe carries mementos such as caps, pins, T-shirts, and books.

North Vancouver Museum & Archives

209 West 4th St., North Vancouver ☎ **604/987-5618.** Fax 604/987-5609. Admission by donation. Museum, Wed–Sun noon–5pm; archives Wed–Fri 9:30am–4:30pm. Take the SeaBus to Lonsdale Quay, then transfer to bus 239 or 246.

More than 70% of Canada's naval fleet was built in North Vancouver's two shipyards during World War II. This and other eras of the city's rich history are examined with photographs, documents, and artifacts, including items from local First Nations bands. You can also watch a video presentation of early lumbering techniques. The museum's archives contain approximately 15,000 historical photographs and film footage.

NEIGHBORHOODS

Vancouver's most touristed neighborhoods are **Gastown,** which is located on Water and Alexander streets from Richards Street to Columbia Street, and **Chinatown,** which lies on Pender and Keeler streets from Carrall Street to Gore Avenue (see Chapter 7). There are other, more residential neighborhoods worth strolling, including **Kitsilano**, **False Creek,** the **West End,** and **Shaughnessy.** The city's ethnic diversity has bred centers rich in sights and tastes that also merit your attention.

Between Granville Island and the UBC campus is **Greektown,** one portion of Kitsilano overflowing with Greek restaurants and grocery stores jammed with fresh squid, seawater-packed feta cheese, and jars of grape leaves. Bakeries with honey-sweetened baklava, lukumades, and buttery, nut-filled kourambiedes dusted with snow-white confectioner's sugar offer their wares in abundant window displays. **Pita Plus Bakery and Deli,** 2967 W. Broadway (☎ 604/733-9900), has hot-from-the-oven pita pockets filled with your choice of dozens of salads.

The Greektown area at West Broadway from MacDonald to Alma streets also bears vestiges of life in the old country. Men drink thick, sweet Greek coffee and play backgammon or billiards at the neighborhood *kaffenion* (men-only social clubs), and jewelers offer patrons evil eye talismans and anxiety-reducing bracelets of worry beads. With an atmosphere reminiscent of a general store, **Minerva Greek Imports,** 2924 W. Fourth Ave., sells everything from woolen sailor's hats, wooden wine gourds, baptismal candles, and coffeemaking *briki* to cassettes of down-and-dirty *rembetika* (Greek soul music), folk-style bouzouki instrumentals, and pop songs sung by famous chanteuses such as Melina Mercouri and Nana Mouskouri.

Women should not wear pants or shorts if they plan to view the Byzantine iconography and architecture at **St. George's Orthodox Church** (see "Churches/Temples," above). The most important annual service here takes place at midnight on Easter Sunday, when the priest and his attendants reopen the church with great pomp and circumstance, including a procession of candle-bearing worshippers through the solemn *Christos Anisti*. The **Greek Community Centre** (☎ 604/ 266-7148) sponsors a **Greek Food Feast** in late October where you can try all sorts of Mediterranean delicacies. You can get to Greektown by taking bus 4 or 10 to MacDonald Street.

At the opposite end of Broadway, running the length of Commercial Drive between Venables Street and East Broadway, is Vancouver's Grandview-Woodland **Italian community.** Many residents have Neapolitan and Sicilian ancestry. In the relaxed atmosphere here, people gossip on the street corners and friends argue about the day's events over tiny cups of strong espresso. Stroll along under the shade of the numerous large overhanging awnings of the restaurants, clothing, and grocery store-fronts. Take the bus 20 north from Granville Street.

The mouthwatering scent of cured meats, hearty cheeses, and eloquent sauces emanates from the restaurants. Rich, homemade gelati (Italian ice creams) refresh both mind and palette. Grocery stores are a visual delight: There are drawers of dried pasta waiting to be opened, fresh pasta being cut to order with chopping machines, gigantic cheese wheels being grated down to fluffy strands of Parmesan, and Parma prosciutto being sliced paper thin. Neighborhood cafes such as **Joe's Café,** 1150 Commercial Dr. (phone unlisted), serve the best espresso in town with more atmosphere than Starbucks could ever muster. Italian tailors and leather importers are ready to present patrons with the finest quality workmanship.

The **Italian Cultural Centre,** 3075 Slocan St. (☎ 604/430-3337), sponsors its own celebration, entitled **Italian Days,** in late June or early July. During Vancouver's winter rainy season, they also produce **Carnevale,** a two-day Mardi Gras celebration.

Vancouver's **Japanese community** was sizable before World War II, when Japanese-Canadians were sent to internment camps, as they were in the United States. On this one-block strip of Powell Street between Gore and Dunlevy Avenues, there are still a few shops, including the **Sunrise Market,** 300 Powell St., and the inexpensive, all-you-can-eat sushi bar **Japanese Deli House,** 381 Powell St. Vancouver's large Japanese population now primarily resides in Steveston and Rich-mond, but they return to Oppenheimer Park when the **Vancouver Buddhist Church,** 220 Jackson St. (☎ 604/253-7033), sponsors the **Obon Festival,** an an-nual event that takes place during the July full-moon cycle complete with kimonoed classical dancers and heart-quaking koto drummers. It's followed later in the month by the annual **Powell Street Japanese Festival.** To get here, take bus 4 or 7.

Established around the turn of the century as a Japanese fishing village, **Steveston** is the oldest portion of the widening Japanese community on the delta.

Weekend mornings are the best time visit the Fraser River harbor front, with its dockyards and venerable canneries. Walk along the boardwalk to **Government Wharf,** where fisherman are busy hawking their fresh catch straight off their boat decks. The **Steveston Salmon Festival** is worth the trip if you're in town on July 1. It includes a parade, salmon barbecue, and entertainment.

Stop at **Dave's Fish and Chips,** 3460 Moncton St. (☎ 604/271-7555), for a sea-food snack. Then head over to the **Gulf of Georgia Cannery National Historic Site,** near the wharf at Bayview Street and 4th Avenue (☎ 604/272-5045), where you can see how the fleet's catch was processed once it arrived at this vital port.

The **Steveston Historical Society,** 3811 Moncton St. (☎ 604/271-6868), is located above the town post office and offers a fascinating photographic portrayal of early Steveston history along with artifacts brought over by 19th-century Japanese immigrants. Admission is free. The museum is open Monday through Saturday from 9:30am to 5pm. There are also several Japanese grocery stores, restaurants, bookstores, and fishing supply stores on or near Moncton Street. To get here, take bus 401, 406, or 407.

The shopping district for Vancouver's **East Indian community** is a stretch of Main Street between East 49th and East 51st streets. Here, richly colored silk saris; sparkling 22-carat gold bangles; intricately detailed religious icons; videos and cassette tapes; sitars (traditional stringed instruments); and tablas (Indian drums) are crowded onto shelves, creating the illusion of a New Delhi bazaar. Grocery stores are scented by pungent spices such as cardamom, cumin, garam masala, coconut, and tamarind, while restaurants display a medley of pakoras, samosas, papadums, and curries. North America's first Sikh school, **Khalsa Elementary School,** 5987 Prince Albert St., is located nearby.

On the weekends, colorful late-morning wedding ceremonies take place at the Arthur Erickson–designed **Khalsa Diwan Gurudwara Temple** (see "Churches/Temples," above). Sikh festivals and parades, including the May **Sikh Sports Festival,** November **Festival of Lights,** and April **Baisakhi Day Parade** (Indian New Year), often begin in the streets and end up with vegetarian feasts at the temple.

OUTDOOR PLAZAS

In the heart of downtown, a waterfall serves as the centerpiece of the **Burrard Street Plaza,** between Alberni and Dunsmuir streets. You can rest here for a moment and ponder the Hotel Vancouver and Christ Church Cathedral or the harbor.

Robson Square, between Hornby and Howe streets from the Vancouver Art Gallery to the provincial courthouse, is a perfect downtown hideaway where you can sit and reflect in relative quiet among the shrubbery, cherry trees, sculptures, and a triple-tiered waterfall. The wheelchair-access ramp is beautifully disguised in the staircase leading to the courthouse. There are also two lower concourse cafes and a covered skating rink that don't obstruct the gardenlike surroundings above.

PARKS/GARDENS

In the city's parks and gardens, you can encounter raccoon families at Stanley Park's Lost Lagoon; go night skiing down Grouse Mountain; spot delta wetland inhabitants such as bald eagles and peregrine falcons; or watch T'ai Chi masters in a 500-year-old Chinese private garden. Scattered throughout Vancouver are publicly and privately maintained areas appealing to anyone wanting to escape for an hour or two from urban life.

Stanley Park (☎ 604/257-8400) is a 1,000-acre cedar forest near the busy West End (see Chapter 7 for a walking tour of Stanley Park). The park is brimming with abundant wildlife, pristine natural settings, and amazing marine views. This is where the locals go to run, skate, cycle, walk, or just sit. In addition to being 20% larger than New York's Central Park, it's 1,000 times safer. Take bus 19 or 52 (summer only) from the Stanley Park loop at the base of West Georgia Street.

There is a small, refreshing oasis in Chinatown, where gnarled limestone scholar rocks jut skyward amid pine, bamboo, winter-blooming plum, and dark reflective pools filled with koi (Japanese carp). The park is hidden from outside view by tall white walls topped with hand-fired clay roof tiles. **Dr. Sun Yat-Sen Classical Garden,** 578 Carrall St., is modeled after the private Taoist gardens found in China more than 500 years ago (see the walking tour of Gastown and Chinatown in Chapter 7) and was actually transported from China for Expo '86. To get here, take bus 19 or 22.

The *Other* Suspension Bridge

Lynn Canyon Park, situated in North Vancouver between Grouse Mountain and Mount Seymour Provincial Park on Lynn Valley Road, is a cheaper and possibly more impressive alternative to the Capilano Suspension Bridge for those who want to take a walk on the wild side. The 225-foot **Lynn Canyon Suspension Bridge,** originally built in 1912, is only half as long as the Capilano (see "The Top Attractions," above), but it's 10 feet higher above the canyon floor. And it's been a free attraction for more than 75 years.

The park in which the bridge is located is a heavily wooded, 617-acre, century-old Douglas fir forest that also includes an **Ecology Centre,** 3663 Park Rd. (☎ 604/987-5922), which presents natural history films, tours, and displays. Staff members lead frequent walking tours while the center is open daily from 10am to 5pm.

Four miles up Lynn Valley Road is the **Lynn Headwaters Regional Park** (☎ 604/985-1690 for trail conditions). Until the mid-1980s, this was an inaccessible wilderness and bear habitat. The park and the bears are now managed by the Greater Vancouver Regional Parks Department. The park has 12 marked trails of various levels of difficulty through beautiful forest scenery, including the former site of Cedar Mill and a waterfall. To get here, take the SeaBus to Lonsdale Quay, then transfer to bus 229; or take Trans-Canada Highway to the Lynn Valley Road exit.

Central Vancouver's **Queen Elizabeth Park,** Cambie Street at West 33rd Avenue, is the city's highest southern vantage point. Its well-manicured gardens sharply contrast with Stanley Park's wilder landscape. Lawn bowling, tennis, pitch-and-putt golf greens, as well as picnicking areas, are all well laid-out. A romantic dining spot, **Seasons in the Park**, Queen Elizabeth Park (☎ 604/874-8008), also shares this formal garden setting.

At the heart of Queen Elizabeth Park stands the **Bloedel Conservatory** (☎ 604/872-5513), a 140-foot-high domed structure with a commanding 360° city view. Named after a timber baron, it houses a tropical rain forest featuring more than 100 plant species and free-flying tropical birds. Conservatory admission is $3 for adults, $1.50 for seniors and children. To get here, take bus 15.

VanDusen Botanical Garden, 5251 Oak St.(☎ 604/266-7194), is another nearby formal garden. Within its 55 acres, there are rolling lawns, lakes, Elizabethan hedge mazes, and marble sculptures. The **Sino-Himalayan Garden** is just one of the distinctive international displays. Admission is $4.50 for adults, $2.25 for seniors, students, and children. Take bus 17 to visit this lovely garden in Shaughnessy.

The campus of the University of British Columbia incorporates gardens and parks. The **UBC Botanical Garden,** 6250 Stadium Rd., Gate 8. (☎ 604/822-4208), with 70 acres of formal alpine, herb, and exotic plantings, was established nearly a century ago. Admission is $4 for adults; $1.75 for seniors and children. Less than 2 miles away is the classically Zen construction of the Japanese **Nitobe Memorial Garden,** 6565 NW Marine Dr., Gate 4, (☎ 604/822-6038). Admission is $2.25 for adults; $1.50 for seniors and children.

Primeval **Pacific Spirit Park** contains 763 hectares of coastal rain forest, marshes, and beaches. Its nearly 22 miles of maintained trails are perfect for hiking, riding, mountain biking, and beachcombing. This university endowment land is free of admission and open to the public. To explore any of these gardens, take bus 4 or 10 to the UBC campus.

Racing cyclists and in-line skaters will enjoy the 50-acre **B.C. Parkway** that follows the SkyTrain's route from Main Street to New Westminster Station. The 7-Eleven Bicycle Path and John Molson Way running path interlink the parkway through 32 city parks. Floral gardens, heritage plazas, playgrounds, and an International Mile of Flags brighten riders' and runners' views.

Across Lions Gate Bridge toward North and West Vancouver are six regional parks that delight outdoor enthusiasts year-round. The publicly maintained **Capilano River Regional Park,** 4500 Capilano Rd. (☎ 604/666-1790), surrounds the Capilano Suspension Bridge and Park (see "The Top Attractions," above). Hikers can independently trek down the well-maintained **Capilano trails** for $4^{1}/_{2}$ miles to the Burrard Inlet and the Lions Gate Bridge or about a mile upstream to **Cleveland Dam,** the launching point for kayakers and canoers.

The **Capilano Salmon Hatchery** is located on the river's east bank a quarter mile below the dam (☎ 604/666-1790). About two million coho and Chinook salmon are hatched here annually in glass-fronted tanks in which you can observe the fishes' early life cycle and read the outdoor displays; it's open daily from 8am to 8pm (until 6pm in April and October; until 7pm in May and September). Take the SeaBus to Lonsdale Quay and transfer to bus 236; the trip takes less than 45 minutes.

Mount Seymour, Mount Seymour Road (☎ 604/986-2261), rises 4,767 feet above Indian Arm behind North Vancouver. The road to this provincial park roams through stands of Douglas fir, red cedar, and hemlock to the park's cafeteria and gift shop. At a higher altitude than Grouse Mountain, Mount Seymour has a spectacular view of Mount Baker in Washington state on clear days and challenging hiking trails that go straight to the summit. Mount Seymour is open daily from 7am to 10pm.

Five miles west of Lions Gate Bridge is **Lighthouse Park,** Marine Drive West, West Vancouver (☎ 604/922-1211), a 185-acre rugged-terrain forest that can be traversed via its eight miles of trails. One of the paths leads to the 60-foot **Point Atkinson Lighthouse,** on a rocky bluff overlooking the Strait of Georgia with a panoramic view of Vancouver. It's an easy trip on bus 250.

South of central Vancouver is the Fraser River delta, where thousands of migratory birds following the Pacific flyway rest and feed in the 850-acre **George C. Reifel Bird Sanctuary,** 5191 Robertson Rd., Westham Island (☎ 604/946-6980). Many other species have made this a permanent habitat for waterfowl. The sanctuary was created by a former bootlegger and wetland-bird lover. More than 250 species have been spotted, including a Temminck's stint, a spotted redshank, bald eagles, Siberian/trumpeter swans, peregrine falcons, blue herons, owls, and coots. The **Snow Goose Festival,** celebrating the annual migratory arrival of huge, snowy white flocks, is held here during the first weekend of November. The geese stay until mid-December, and high tide is the best time to visit. An observation tower, two miles of paths, free bird seed, and picnic tables make this wetland reserve an ideal outing spot from October through April. The sanctuary is wheelchair accessible and open daily from 9am to 4pm. Admission is $3.25 for adults and $1 for seniors and children.

The **Richmond Nature Park,** 1185 W. Minster Hwy. (☎ 604/273-7015), set on a natural wetland bog, features a Nature House with educational displays and a boardwalk-encircled duck pond. Take bus 401, 403, 406, or 407 and transfer on to the no. 3 Road bus at Cook Road.

VIEWS

The busy harbor at the **Port of Vancouver** can be seen from a variety of vantage points, each revealing a different aspect. You can look down at the harbor from the **Vanterm** public viewing area, at the foot of Clark Drive, or from **The Cannery Restaurant**'s picture windows facing the harbor (see Chapter 5 for restaurant review).

Lonsdale Quay has a great view of the northern end with a backdrop of Vancouver's skyline. Get in the middle of the action by taking the 15-minute **SeaBus** commute across the Burrard Inlet or by taking the **MPV** *Constitution,* a historic sternwheeler (see "Organized Tours," below).

Canada Place, at the north end of Burrard Street, has a pier-side view of landing and departing floatplanes as well as of commercial ferries leaving the nearby docks.

Vancouver's skyline can be seen from many vantage points and angles. The most popular (and most touristed) is high atop the space needle–roofed observation deck at **The Lookout!,** Harbour Centre Tower, 555 W. Hastings St. (☎ 604/689-0421). It's a great place for first-time visitors who want an overall city panorama. The glass Skylift whisks you 553 feet up to the observation deck in less than a minute. The 360° view is remarkable. (Yes, that is Mount Baker looming on the southeastern horizon.) Angled viewing windows, powerful telescopes, and descriptive point markers enhance the experience. A panoramic multiprojector historical presentation is shown regularly. Visitors can also take advantage of the lower concourse **Harbour Mall,** where there are 50 specialty shops and an international food fair. Admission to the Skylift is $7 for adults, $6 for seniors, and $4 for students. It is open in summer daily 8:30am to 10:30pm; in winter daily 10am to 9pm.

The **sunsets** at **English Bay Beach** are stupendous (see "Beaches," under "Outdoor Activities," below). Freighters are silhouetted against a broad, blazing sky while blue herons fly overhead. If you're lucky enough, you can turn toward the city to watch a sun-shower rainbow. **Milestone's** on Denman and Davie streets or the **lounge at the Sylvia Hotel** (see Chapter 4 for hotel review) are perfect retreats for dinner or cocktails.

The best **evening view** is from **Cloud Nine,** the revolving restaurant/lounge at The Landmark, 1400 Robson St. (☎ 604/687-0511). You can see the twinkling lights of Lions Gate Bridge and North Vancouver's night-ski runs. If you don't want a full meal, just have a cocktail, coffee, or desert at one of the smaller window-side tables. There is no admission, but you may have to be quick to get a table with a good view.

From the North Vancouver, the city's skyline is best seen from **Grouse Mountain** (see "The Top Attractions," above) or **Mount Seymour** (see "Parks/Gardens," under "More Attractions," above).

3 Especially for Kids

Kids of every age, inclination, and attention span will love Vancouver's wide variety of attractions. Pick up a copy of the free monthly newspaper *West Coast Families* at the Kids Only Market on Granville Island. The centerfold "Fun in the City," *West Coast Families'* event calendar, lists everything happening while you're here, including CN, IMAX, and OMNIMAX shows and free children's programs.

Young animal lovers will have a ball at **Stanley Park's petting zoo,** where peacocks, rabbits, calves, donkeys, and Shetland ponies eagerly await kids' attention (see "Parks/Gardens," under "More Attractions," above). The **Vancouver Aquarium,** with its playful sea otters, harbor seals, and whales is always a popular spot for children (see "The Top Attractions," above). Kids can also see domestic and wild

---

? **Did You Know?**

- Stanley Park was a military reserve in the mid-1880s; it was established to protect the entrance to Vancouver harbor from possible invasion by aggressive U.S. troops.

- The waters of Lost Lagoon, named by native poet Pauline Johnson, used to disappear daily at low tide. Now, it's a landlocked body of water and thus much easier to find.

- A boisterous old British sea cannon was placed in Stanley Park at the turn of the century and fired every evening to alert fisherman of the enforced end-of-the-day fishing limit. Now, the nine o'clock gun is a famous city tradition.

- The first meeting of Vancouver's city council was delayed because no one had a pen and paper to record minutes. A boy had to be sent to a local stationery store.

- The Vancouver Aquarium has the city's most innovative conference room: The Killer Whale Board Room's picture window has a scenic view of a tank of cavorting orcas.

- Movie theater crying rooms were commonplace when the Ridge Theatre opened in 1950. The eight-seat cubbyhole-supplied, soundproof, glass-enclosed seating was for baby- and toddler-toting families. The Ridge Theatre has British Columbia's last remaining crying room, used by the likes of Katherine Hepburn.

- The Lions, two handsome mountain peaks overlooking the Vancouver harbor, were named after London's pair of Trafalgar Square lion statues. Before that, the Coast Salish people called them the Two Sisters and believed that they watched over the area, ensuring peace and harmony.

- Lulu Island, south of central Vancouver, was named after Miss Lulu Sweet, a singer and dancer in a traveling troupe. In the late 1880s, the commanding officer of the Royal Engineers was so taken by the fair Miss Sweet during her performance that he dedicated the island to her as a token of his appreciation.

- During the test drive of Vancouver's first ambulance early in this century, an American tourist was run over and killed.

- False Creek got its named because a young naval officer entering the waters thought it was a creek, not an arm of the Burrard Inlet. It's only half its original size now, thanks to developers who filled in two sandbars to create Granville Island.

- Actress Yvonne de Carlo (of TV's *The Munsters*) was once an usher in the Orpheum Theatre. Back then, her name was Peggy Middleton.

---

animals at **Maplewood Farm,** 405 Seymour River Place, North Vancouver (☎ 604/929-5610). More than 200 domestic barnyard animals—cows, horses, ponies, pigs, sheep, donkeys, ducks, chickens, and more—live in this five-acre farm, which is open year-round. A few working farms operated here before the parks department converted this one into an attraction. The ticket booth, which is a former breeding kennel, also sells bird seed for the ducks and other fowl as well as guidebooks. Special events include the summertime **Sheep Fair,** the mid-September **Farm Fair,** the late-October **101 Pumpkins Day,** and the **Country Christmas** weekend. It is open daily from 10am to 4pm (closed nonholiday Mondays). Admission is $5.50 for families, $1.75 for adults, and $1.25 for seniors and children. Take bus 210 and transfer to 211 or 212.

Lion King fans can go on a safari through the **Vancouver Game Farm,** 5048 264th St., Aldergrove (☎ 604/856-6825), a lush 120-acre farm filled with lions, tigers, jaguars, ostriches, elephants, buffalo, and camels. In all, 100 species roam free or in spacious paddocks. Located 30 miles from Vancouver, this wildlife reserve also has food service and a playground. It is open daily from 8am until dusk. Admission is $9 for adults, $7.50 for children.

Budding scientists can get their hands into everything at **Science World British Columbia** (see "Museums/Galleries," under "More Attractions," above). They can go to the moon or just look at Mars in the **Pacific Space Center**'s flight simulator and observatory telescope (see "The Top Attractions," above). They can also maneuver the **Vancouver Maritime Museum**'s underwater robot or board the RCMP icebreaker *St. Roch* (see "Museums/Galleries," under "More Attractions," above).

Kids can travel back in time at the **Burnaby Heritage Village and Carousel,** 6501 Deer Lake Ave., Burnaby (☎ 604/293-6500 or 604/293-6501). At this nine-acre Victorian-era re-creation, you can walk along boardwalk streets among costumed townspeople; watch a Victorian blacksmith pounding horseshoes; shop in a general store; ride a vintage carousel; and wax nostalgic in a vintage ice cream parlor. The village is a little far from central Vancouver, but it's well worth the effort to get here. Admission is $6.10 for adults; $4.25 for seniors, physically disabled, or students; and $3.65 for children 6 to 12 (children under 6 free). It is open daily from 11am to 4:30pm; 10am to 4:30pm in the summer. Take bus 120 to Sperling Avenue.

Fort Langley Historic Site, 23433 Mavis Ave., Fort Langley (☎ 604/888-4424), dating from 1827, is the birthplace of British Columbia. This is where Hudson's Bay supplied its 1839 provincial posts; loggers, settlers, and fur traders bartered within the fortress wall. Today costumed craftspersons demonstrate blacksmithing, coopering, and woodworking skills. Admission is charged only in the summer. It is open daily from 10am to 4:30pm. Take the SkyTrain to Surrey Central Station, then transfer to bus 501.

Athletic kids can work up a good sweat at the **Participation Gallery** at the **B.C. Sports Hall of Fame and Museum** (see "Museums/Galleries," under "More Attractions," above). Here, they can run, jump, climb, race, and attempt to beat world records. At Granville Island's **Water Park and Adventure Playground,** 1496 Cartwright St. (☎ 604/665-3425), kids can really let loose with movable water guns and sprinklers. They can also just get wet on the water slides or wading pool in the summer from 10am to 6pm. Admission is free, and there are changing facilities right next door at Isadora's Restaurant.

Rainy days are no problem at **Bonkers: The Great Canadian Indoor Playground,** 1620-1185 W. Georgia St. (☎ 604/669-9230), where families can have a few dry hours of fun in this innovative play center. They are open Monday, Tuesday, and Saturday from 9:30am to 5:30pm; Wednesday through Friday from 9:30am to 9pm; and Sunday from 10am to 6pm. Admission for children is $5.95 on weekdays and $6.95 on weekends. Adults are always admitted for free.

For a more traditional family experience, go to **Playland Family Fun Park,** Exhibition Park, East Hastings Street at Carrier Street (☎ 604/255-5161). The price of admission includes all-day ride passes ($24 adults, $21 children). Anyone can relive their childhood at this amusement park by riding on an ornate carousel or a wooden roller coaster and playing miniature golf. Your kids will love the Nintendo Pavilion, Electric City Arcade, and the petting zoo. The park is open weekends April to May from 11am to 7pm; May through June on Saturday from 11am to 11pm, Sunday from 11am to 10pm; July through August on Friday and Saturday from

11am to 11pm, Sunday from 11am to 10pm; and September through October, Monday through Friday from 11am to 11pm, Saturday and Sunday from 10:30am to 11pm. Take bus 14 or 16.

The exciting prospect of walking high above the rushing waters is the attraction at the **Capilano Suspension Bridge** (see "The Top Attractions," above) or at the **Lynn Canyon Suspension Bridge** (see "Parks/Gardens," under "More Attractions," above). In both places, there are thrills and chills amid lush forests and roaring rivers. **Mount Seymour** (see "Skiing," under "Outdoor Activities," below) offers **Children's Ski Programs** (☎ 604/986-2261) for kids aged 4 to 16.

Kids who love to shop will find heaven in Granville Island's **Kids Only Market,** 1496 Cartwright St., open daily from 10am to 6pm (closed Mondays except in the summer). Playrooms and 21 shops filled with toys, books, records, clothes, and food are all child-oriented. Kids will also love taking the Aquabus or Granville Island ferry to get there.

Kids who like theater will enjoy the original works produced by the **Green Thumb Theatre for Young People,** 1895 Venables St. (☎ 604/254-4055), which presents more than 600 performances every year.

4 Special-Interest Sightseeing

For those of you who are always digging for places catering to your special interest— whether it's photography or simply stargazing at your favorite film or TV actors— we have found some one-of-a-kind attractions.

FOR THE LITERARY ENTHUSIAST   The down-and-out north shore home of *Under the Volcano* author Malcolm Lowry is concealed in a Cates Park thicket, which was the site of a 1940s shanty town. The **Malcolm Lowry Walk** is a well-marked, easy strolling trail located in North Vancouver's Cates Park, a small wooded point at the mouth of the Indian Arm fjord. To get there from Vancouver, take Trans-Canada Highway 1 across the Second Narrows Bridge. Exit onto the Dollarton Highway. Drive east for about 4 miles. The highway runs along the park's northern border. Follow the signs to the parking area, and then, get ready to walk back in time to the Beat Generation's era.

The ashes and memorial of First Nations princess-poet **Pauline Johnson** overlook Stanley Park's Third Beach near the Hollow Tree—even though she specifically asked that no monument be erected after her death. Her local claim to fame was that she named Lost Lagoon, while she is internationally known for *Legends of Vancouver*, her 1911 compilation of First Nations tales.

Vancouver's central library is anything but square. The new $100 million **Library Square** resembles a swirled version of the Roman Coliseum. It was designed by Moshe Safdie and Associates in association with Downs Archambault and Partners. Cozy window-side reading tables next to floor-to-ceiling windows in this seven-story complex make it a popular spot to do research or just sit and daydream.

The library has the Online Public Access Catalogue (OPAC), Internet, Freenet access, computer lab, and more than one million books, but that's just the beginning. The building also houses 15 stores and coffee bars, **Book-Mark** (the Library Shop), and a day-care center. The central branch is located at 350 West Georgia St. (☎ 604/ 331-3601). It's open Monday through Wednesday from 10am to 9pm (until 6pm Thursday through Saturday); and on Sundays from 1pm to 5pm from October through April.

Stargazing in "Hollywood North"

A stargazing expedition in Vancouver might turn up more constellations than a tour of the stars' homes in Beverly Hills. The **B.C. Film Commission** runs a hotline (☎ 604/660-3569) and posts a film list/fact sheet of who's doing what in town. Look for the list at the SeaBus terminal, 601 W. Cordova St. (open Monday through Friday from 8:30am to 4:30pm).

On one afternoon stroll, we found five different production sets between Stanley Park and Thurlow Street from Sunset Beach to Robson Street. The stars about town included Billy Dee Williams, Rick Moranis, Kelly LeBrock, and James Brolin. In just the past three years, such films as *Legends of the Fall, Little Women, Man of the House, Intersection* (with the best Vancouver scenery ever filmed), and *Jumanji* with Robin Williams have been shot here. Most of Sylvester Stallone's *Rambo: First Blood* was filmed in Lynn Canyon Park.

In addition, four hit TV programs continue to be shot in Vancouver: *The X-Files, The Commish, The Outer Limits,* and *Highlander.* You also might just see Katherine Hepburn, since Vancouver is her favorite escape from Hollywood.

Throughout the year, you can attend readings at the **Railway Club,** 579 Dunsmuir St. (☎ 604/681-1625); **Women in Print,** 3566 W. 4th St. (☎ 604/732-4128); **Octopus Books,** 1146 Commercial Dr. (☎ 604/253-0913); **Cafe Deux Soleils,** 2096 Commercial Dr. (☎ 604/254-1195); and the **WaaZuBee Cafe,** 1622 Commercial Dr. (☎ 604/253-5299).

FOR GOLFERS   Canada's only provincial golf museum, the **British Columbia Golf House Society,** 2545 Blanca St. (☎ 604/222-4653), is housed in a historic 1930s clubhouse filled with memorabilia about the evolution of this Scottish game as well as great golf moments and golfers. It's open from noon to 4pm Tuesday through Sunday.

FOR TRAVELERS INTERESTED IN BUSINESS AND INDUSTRY   Housed in a working sugar refinery built in 1890, the **B.C. Sugar Museum,** B.C. Sugar Refinery, 123 Rogers St. (☎ 604/253-1131), displays early 18th-century sugar beet and sugarcane processing machines, a plantation locomotive, historical photographs, and a 20-minute documentary film on the development of sugar manufacturing and Vancouver history. Admission is free. The museum is open Monday through Friday from 9am to 4pm. Take bus 4 or 7, then walk two blocks north from East Hastings Street.

The **Vancouver Stock Exchange Tower,** 609 Granville St. (☎ 604/643-6590), has a free-admission Visitor Centre open during trading hours. It is designed to give visitors a chance to observe the flurried action of the stock market. Self-guided tours are augmented by the help of on-site representatives. Also, there are noon-hour seminars, literature, and educational displays.

Those interested in forestry should visit the **Forest Alliance of B.C.,** 1055 Dunsmuir St. (☎ 604/685-7507), to view their video displays, on-line computer database, and exciting forestry exhibits.

FOR TRAVELERS INTERESTED IN PHOTOGRAPHY   When you want to take a break from shooting pictures, visit the **Presentation House Gallery** (☎ 604/986-1351). It shares exhibition space with the North Vancouver Museum and

Archives (see "Museums/Galleries," under "More Attractions," above). The gallery emphasizes historic and contemporary works by international, national, and regional photographers. It also has a professional drama and comedy theater. Admission to the gallery is $2 adults, $1 seniors and students; theater tickets range from $9 to $12. Open Wednesday through Sunday noon to 5pm. They also open Thursday evenings from 5pm to 9pm, free of charge.

HAUNTED PLACES/SCANDAL SITES   The **Vancouver Art Gallery** (see "The Top Attractions," above) has a ghost among its collections. The gallery was formerly a court house, and "Charlie," as the ghost is known, lives in the catacombs where the holding cells were located. He's said to be the spirit of William Charles Hopkinson, an immigration officer who was murdered there in 1914.

An architect haunts his own building at 207 Hastings Street. The terra–cotta **Dominion Bank Building** was designed by J. S. Helyer, who stumbled on the treads of his prized trapezoidal wrought-iron staircase and tumbled to his death.

The **B.C. Pavilion** at the Pacific National Exhibition has a ghost that presides—ashes and all—over one man's seven-year labor of love: an 1,800-square-foot British Columbia relief map made from a million handcut pieces of plywood. Created for the 1954 British Empire Games, the map has a plaque over the Pacific Ocean that conceals a paneled space containing the artist's ashes in an urn.

5 Organized Tours

If you don't have the time to arrange your own sightseeing tour, then let the experts take you around Vancouver. They will escort you by bus, seaplane, helicopter, boat, ferry, taxi, or vintage car.

BUS TOURS   **Gray Line of Vancouver,** 255 E. First Ave. (☎ 604/879-3363), escorts you on a four-hour Vancouver bus tour through Stanley Park, Gastown, Chinatown, Canada Place, Queen Elizabeth Park, Robson Street, Shaughnessy, and English Bay Beach year-round for $29.50 adults, $26.50 seniors, and $18.75 children. Departing at 9:15am and 1:45pm, they pick you up from downtown hotels a half hour before departure.

West Coast City and Nature Sightseeing, 4012 Myrtle St., Burnaby (☎ 604/451-5581), covers the same route (plus Granville Island) as Gray Line of Vancouver (see above) but in minicoaches. They run from March through October for $25.23 adult, $23.36 seniors, and $14.95 children. Departing at 9:30am and 2pm, they also pick up passengers from downtown hotels a half hour before departure. Other packages include a Grouse Mountain/Capilano Suspension Bridge half-day tour and a full-day Whistler/Shannon Falls excursion.

BOAT TOURS   **1st Tours,** Harbour Ferries, no. 1 North Foot of Denman St. (☎ 604/688-7246 or 800/663-1500), has a 90-minute, narrated Paddlewheel Harbour Tour aboard the MPV *Constitution,* an authentic, 19th-century, smoke-stacked, white stern-wheeler. Port of Vancouver harbor tours depart at 11:45am and 1:45pm Wednesday through Sunday and holiday Mondays from mid-May through mid-September. Tour fares are $16 adults, $13 seniors and students, $6 children 5 to 11, children under 5 free. They also offer sumptuous breakfast and lunch buffets as well as romantic sunset dinner cruises for $10.50 to $48 per person.

Gray Line Water Tours, 200-399 W. Sixth Ave. (☎ 604/681-8687), presents a two-hour Harbour Cruise Tour, departing daily at 9:30am and noon, July through mid-September. Fares are $25 adults, $22 seniors, and $13 children.

From mid-May through late September, the SS *Beaver* **Steamship Company,** 554 Cardero St. (☎ 604/682-7284) (not to be confused with the SS *Beaver* in Victoria), operates a three-hour Indian Arm Adventure Tour, which departs at 10:30am. They also offer a three-hour Sunset Dinner Cruise through English Bay, departing daily at 6:30pm. The fare of $49.95 per person includes a buffet salmon meal onboard this popular 19th-century paddle wheeler.

AIR TOURS   **Baxter Aviation,** Barbary Coast Marina (Mailing address: P.O. Box 1110, Nanaimo, Canada V9R 6E7) (☎ 604/683-6525 or 800/661-5599), operates 11 daily downtown Vancouver floatplane flights. The 30-minute "Vancouver Scenic" flies over Stanley Park and the North Shore mountains, and the five-hour Whistler Mountain Resort includes a three-hour stopover. Fares range from $59 to $229 per person. Other packages fly to Victoria, Johnstone Strait, glacial lakes, and fly-in fishing spots.

Harbour Air, 4760 Inglis Dr., Richmond (☎ 604/688-1277), will take you up in a seaplane for 30 minutes over downtown Vancouver, Stanley Park, and the North Shore for $65 per person.

Vancouver Helicopter, 5455 D Airport Rd. South, Richmond (☎ 604/ 270-1484), offers the following daily tours: a 30-minute Greater Vancouver Scenic Tour for $159 per person; a circle around the Lions in the "North Shore Discoverer" for $195 per person; and the "Pacific Rain Forest Coastal Mountain Odyssey," which includes a 10-minute stop on top of a glacier, for $295 per person. Custom mountaintop "heli-picnics" and trips to special destinations can also be arranged.

Grouse Mountain heli-tours from the resort's summit (see "The Top Attractions," above) circle Crown Mountain for $30 per person and Lions Peak for $60 per person.

SPECIALTY TOURS   **Early Motion Tours,** 1-1380 Thurlow St. (☎ 604/ 687-5088), offers private sightseeing tours around Vancouver in a restored 1930 Model A Ford Phaeton convertible, which holds four passengers plus the driver. Reservations are required, and there is a one-hour minimum for the $60 hourly rate. The office is open daily from 7:30am to 8pm.

6 Outdoor Activities

The city's hottest outdoor sports are year-round mountain biking and in-line skating, but just about every imaginable sport has a world-class outlet within the city limits. Alpine and Nordic skiing, parasailing, sea kayaking, canoeing, tidal water fishing, fly fishing, diving, and hiking are just a few of the options. Some activities can't really be done within the confines of metropolitan Vancouver but can be done close by, including river rafting and heli-skiing. If you don't find your favorite sport listed here, take a look at Chapter 17.

Pick up a copy of *Coast: The Outdoor Recreation Magazine,* which is published every other month. Available at many outfitter and recreational-equipment outlets, *Coast* let's you in on the latest snow conditions, bike trails, climbing spots, competitions, races, and the like and where to get vital bike tune-ups.

In the sections listed below, we have included specialized rental outfitters with each type of activity. If you want a one-stop shopping outlet, **Recreational Rentals,** 2560 Arbutus St. (☎ 604/733-7368), has one- and two-day package ski rentals as well as ice-skating, snowshoe, canoe, kayak, mountain-bike, camping, scuba, windsurfing, and in-line skating rental packages.

BEACHES Sunbathing is a serious Vancouver pastime. After the long rainy season, residents love to dry out on the local, sandy beaches. In addition to being a great place for viewing sunsets, **English Bay Beach,** at the end of Davie Street off Denman Street and Beach Avenue, has an interesting history behind it. It was the front yard of Joe Fortes, Vancouver's legendary lifeguard/bartender, for more than 35 years.

On Stanley Park's western end, **Second Beach** is a quick stroll north from English Bay Beach. A playground and a freshwater lap pool make this a convenient spot for sunning families. Secluded **Third Beach** is due north of Stanley Park Drive. The **hollow tree**, **Geographic Tree,** and **Siwash Rock** are sights of interest in the area. South of English Bay Beach near the Burrard Street Bridge and the Vancouver Aquatic Centre is **Sunset Beach.**

Kitsilano Beach, along Arbutus Drive near Ogden Street, is affectionately called Kits Beach by the locals. It's an easy walk from the Maritime Museum and the False Creek Ferry dock. A heated, saltwater swimming pool is open throughout the summer for people who just can't resist taking a quick dip but don't enjoy the rather bracing ocean temperatures. Admission is $2.85 for adults, $1.40 for seniors and students, $1.80 for children 6 to 12, and $5.70 for families. **Kitsilano Showboat,** the summertime amateur entertainment theater, attracts a local crowd for evening fun.

Further west, on the other side of Pioneer Park, is **Jericho Beach** (Alma Street off Point Grey Road), another local after-work social spot. **Locarno Beach,** off Discovery Street and NW Marine Drive, and **Spanish Banks,** NW Marine Drive, wrap around the northern point of the UBC campus and University Hill. (Be forewarned that the last beach-side rest rooms and concessions on the promontory end abruptly at Locarno Beach.) Below UBC's Museum of Anthropology is **Point Grey Beach,** a restored harbor defense site; it's the perfect deterrent for most people searching for **Wreck Beach,** Vancouver's nude beach, where au naturel sunbathers hide out. You get here by taking Trail 6 on the UBC campus near Gate 6 down to the water's edge. Though extremely popular with locals, the beach is also the most pristine and least developed city beach. The Wreck Beach Preservation Society sees to that.

Ambleside Park, at the northern foot of Lions Gate Bridge, is a popular North Shore spot. This ³/₄-mile-long beach faces the Burrard Inlet.

BOATING Bareboat rentals of power boats ranging from 15 to 56 feet are available for a few hours or several weeks. Don't forget to check the **marine forecast** (☎ 604/270-7411) before taking off. **Stanley Park Boat Rentals,** Coal Harbor Marina at the foot of Cardero Street (☎ 604/682-6257), maintains 15- to 17-foot speedboats for bareboat rental, plus rowboats and canoes. **Delta Charters,** 3500 Cessna Dr., Richmond (☎ 604/273-4211 or 800/661-7762), at the Delta Vancouver Airport Hotel and Marina, has weekly rates for 32- to 56-foot powered bareboat craft. **Granville Island Boat Rentals** (☎ 604/682-6287) also rents bareboat power boats by the hour or day.

CANOEING/KAYAKING Both placid, urban False Creek and the wilder 18.8-mile North Vancouver fjord known as Indian Arm have starting points that can be reached by bus. Granville Island's **Ecomarine Ocean Kayak Centre,** 1668 Duranleau St.(☎ 604/689-7575), offers daily and weekly kayak rentals for a minimum of two hours. They also offer paddling courses, equipment, and plenty of good free advice. They have another office at the Jericho Sailing Centre, 1300 Discovery St. Both branches offer guided tours, including coastal kayaking.

Curling: Tossing Rocks

Pop quiz: What sport involves a 40-pound stone, a couple of brooms, and a frozen lake? If you've never seen **curling** on the Winter Olympics or *The Wide World of Sports*, you may not believe this sport: It looks a bit like something from the Mad Hatter's tea party. In curling, you sling a highly polished granite disk with a handle on top down the ice while a couple of your teammates frantically sweep the ice ahead of it; you might recall the Beatles doing it in *Help!*

This is, nevertheless, a really serious sport. Think of curling as bowling on ice; it's about as popular in Canada as bowling is in the United States. If you're visiting in the winter, this is your chance to try it. There are more than 1,225 curling clubs in Canada, and a bunch of them are in Vancouver. You can contact **Curl B.C.,** 1367 W. Broadway (604/737-3040), to find out where to "toss some rocks." Rental equipment and instruction are available (wear sweats and running shoes and bring gloves). You can easily find a pick-up match, since curling is played with two teams of four. It's a great way to meet people, and Canadian curlers are friendly, welcoming, and, as we discovered, very kind to beginners.

Deep Cove Canoe and Kayak Rentals, at the foot of Gallant Street, Deep Cove (☎ 604/929-2268), is an easier starting point for anyone planning an Indian Arm run. They offer hourly and daily rowboat, canoe, and kayak rentals, plus customized tours.

CYCLING/MOUNTAIN BIKING   In Vancouver, it's time to put your car away and get a good mountain bike. Helmets are required both on and off-road. Marked cycle lanes traverse the entire central and downtown Vancouver area. Runners and cyclists have separate lanes on developed park and beach paths, so you don't have to worry about joggers and skaters getting in your way. Some West End hotels offer guests bike storage and rentals. The city's hot cycle runs include the following: **Stanley Park and the Seawall Promenade; English Bay to Sunset Beaches; Granville Island to Vanier Park; Kitsilano and Jericho Beaches; Pacific Spirit Park;** and the **7-Eleven Bicycle Path** along the B.C. Parkway.

Local mountain bikers love hitting **Hollyburn Mountain**'s cross-country ski trails in Cypress Provincial Park. The Secret Trail Society started building trails four years ago along **Grouse Mountain**'s backside, and they are now considered some of the best in the Lower Mainland. Mount Seymour's very steep **Good Samaritan Trail** connects to the Baden-Powell Trail and the Bridle Path near Mount Seymour Rd. This is recommended only for the roughest, toughest, world-class mountain bikers—the types who pour Gatorade on their Wheaties.

City rentals generally run around $3.50 to $5.60 per hour or $15.99 to $26 per day. Identification and a deposit are required at all shops. Mountain bikes, 6-speeds, 1-speed cruisers, tandems, helmets, locks, and child trailers are all available on an hourly or daily basis at **Spokes Bicycle Rentals and Espresso Bar,** 1798 W. Georgia St. (☎ 604/688-5141). **Alleycat Rentals,** 1779 Robson St. in the alley (☎ 604/682-5117), a very popular shop among locals, rents city or mountain bikes, child trailers, child seats, locks, helmets, and even in-line skates. **Bayshore Bicycle and Rollerblade Rentals,** at 745 Denman St. (☎ 604/688-2453) and 1601 W. Georgia St. (☎ 604/689-5071), rents 21-speed mountain bikes, bike carriers, tandems, city bikes, and kids' bikes.

The **Bicycling Association of British Columbia** has a group ride and special events hotline (☎ 604/731-7433).

DIVING   Winter sports enthusiasts in Vancouver aren't limited just to the slopes: They actually go scuba diving in the frigid winter waters between Vancouver Island and the mainland to view eel, giant octopus, and a rare type of brilliant red coral. Wreck diving on the thousands of ships that have sunk to the bottom is among the best sites in the world. More than 2,000 ships have sunk off-shore in the last two centuries. **Cates Park** in Deep Cove; **Whytecliff Park** near Horseshoe Bay; **Lighthouse Park** (see "Parks/Gardens" in "More Attractions," above); and **Telegraph Cove,** an underwater park in Howe Sound, are hot nearby dive spots.

Orca Dive & Charter Company, Box 38711, North Vancouver (☎ 604/551-1322), based in Coal Harbour, launches day or overnight dive trips and provides diving instruction. **The Diving Locker,** 2745 W. Fourth Ave. (☎ 604/736-2681), sells and rents equipment and offers diving courses and free information.

Join the **Underwater Archaeological Society of British Columbia,** Vancouver Maritime Museum, 1905 Ogden St., before you arrive in Vancouver. Then you can volunteer for the society's sponsored shipwreck excavations in the good name of marine heritage preservation and conservation.

FISHING   Salmon, rainbow trout, steelhead, and sturgeon abound in the waters around Vancouver. You need nonresident licenses—separately issued for tidal areas and freshwater—whether you've hired a charter guide or are striking out on your own. Tackle shops are your best source for purchasing licenses and getting copies of the current publications *B.C. Tidal Waters Sport Fishing Guide* and *B.C. Sport Fishing Regulations Synopsis for Non-tidal Waters.* Independent anglers should also pick up a copy of the *B.C. Fishing Directory and Atlas.* **Hanson's Fishing Outfitters,** 102-580 Hornby St. (☎ 604/684-8988), and **Granville Island Boat Rentals,** 1696 Duranleau St. (☎ 604/682-6287), are two convenient downtown Vancouver sources for tackle, licenses, and information.

Fly fishing in the surrounding national and provincial parks requires special permits, which you can get at any park site for a nominal fee. Once purchased, they're valid for all Canadian parks.

The **B.C. Department of Fisheries** has a 24-hour toll-free **information hotline** to keep you abreast of seasonal catches. They also offer tips on flies or lures and the best spots to hit (☎ 800/663-9333 or 800/666-2268 in Vancouver).

All good anglers look for charter guides, who offer more than a boat and a spot on the deck. A few local companies throw in rods, tackle, bait, foul-weather gear, and catch cleaning in their rates. Some of the more environmentally conscious companies encourage catch-and-release fishing and whale-watching charters. **Corcovado Yacht Charters,** 104-1676 Duranleau St., on Granville Island (☎ 604/669-7907); **Vancouver Sportfish Center,** 566 Cardero St. (☎ 604/689-7108); and **Hi-Liner Fishing Adventures,** 985 Crosscreek Rd., West Vancouver (☎ 604/926-8184), offer competitive rates and convenient tidal water launching locations. **Reel Adventures,** 1334 Larkspur Dr., North Vancouver (☎ 604/945-6755), specializes in wilderness sport fishing.

GOLF   In Vancouver, this is a year-round sport, except when it's raining hard. With five public 18-hole courses and pitch-and-putt courses, no golfer is far from his or her love. The **University Golf Club,** 5185 University Blvd. (☎ 604/224-1818), is a 6,560-yard par-71 course with a clubhouse, pro shop, locker rooms, a bar and grill, a sports lounge, and 280-car parking lot.

Leading private clubs are situated in the North Shore and central Vancouver. Check with your club at home to see if you have reciprocal visiting memberships with one of the following: **Capilano Golf and Country Club,** 420 Southborough Dr., West Vancouver (☎ 604/922-9331); **Marine Drive Golf Club,** W. 57th Ave. and SW Marine Drive (☎ 604/261-8111); **Seymour Golf and Country Club,** 3723 Mt. Seymour Pkwy., North Vancouver (☎ 604/929-2611); **Point Grey Golf and Country Club,** 3350 SW Marine Dr. (☎ 604/266-7171); and **Shaughnessy Golf and Country Club,** 4300 SW Marine Dr.(☎ 604/266-4141).

HIKING Relatively experienced and seriously seasoned hikers have access to some great trails through Vancouver's dramatic environs. Good trail maps are available from the **Ministry of Parks** (☎ 604/929-1291) and from the **Greater Vancouver Regional Parks District** (☎ 604/432-6350).

Stanley Park actually has some serious backtrails that are popular with flatlanders and runners. **Beaver Lake**, surrounded by thick cedar forests, is a great spot to get away from civilization (see Chapter 7).

Just a few yards from the entrance to Grouse Mountain Resort is one entry to the world-famous **Baden-Powell Trail,** a 26-mile span of thick forest, rocky bluffs, and snow-fed streams racing through ravines; it stretches from its eastern starting point at Cates Park on the Dollartin Highway to its western end at Horseshoe Bay. Even if you only want to cover the stretch from Grouse Mountain to Mount Seymour, start early and be ready for some steep ascents. The timer guide at the trail-head marker has been annotated by hikers who've found it takes longer to do the loop than is indicated: Give yourself a full day for this hike.

Lynn Canyon, Lynn Headwaters, Capilano Regional Park, Mount Seymour Provincial Park, and **Cypress Provincial Park** (see "Parks/Gardens," under "More Attractions," above) have good easy to challenging trails winding up through stands of Douglas fir and cedar and containing a few serious switchbacks. Pay attention to the trail warnings posted at the parks; some have bear habitats deep in the parks, and always remember to sign in with the park service at the start of your chosen trail. **Golden Ears** and **the Lions** are truly meant for seriously fit hikers.

ICE-SKATING Lace your skates (or rent a pair) at **Robson Square**'s free covered rink any time from November to early April (see "Outdoor Plazas," under "More Attractions," above). The **West End Community Centre,** 870 Denman St. (☎ 604/689-0571), rents them at its enclosed rink, which is open from October through March. UBC's **Thunderbird Winter Sports Centre,** 6066 Thunderbird Blvd. (☎ 604/822-6121), invites the public for ice-skating and casual hockey from September to April. (Hours are usually 8:30am to 4pm, but call ahead.)

IN-LINE SKATING In-line skates have definitely caught on in this outdoor city. You'll find locals rolling on beach paths, streets, park paths, and promenades. If you didn't bring a pair, go to **Alleycat Rentals,** 1779 Robson St. in the alley (☎ 604/682-5117). They are the local favorite, offering in-line skates for $4.50 an hour (two-hour minimum) or $15 per day or overnight. Protection packages, including helmet and pads, are $2 a day. Or try **Bayshore Bicycle and Rollerblade Rentals,** 745 Denman St. (☎ 604/688-2453) and 1601 W. Georgia St. (☎ 604/689-5071); both locations rent in-line skates.

JOGGING You'll find local fellow runners traversing Stanley Park's **Seawall Promenade, Lost Lagoon,** and **Beaver Lake.** If you're a dawn or dusk runner, take note that this is one of the world's safest city parks, but if you're alone, stick to open and lighted areas: Don't tempt fate. Molson Brewery B.C. constructed the 12-mile-long

John Molson Way along the B.C. Parkway (see "Parks/Gardens," under "More Attractions," above) as a part of its 200th-anniversary celebration in 1986. It's a good straight-away for marathoners.

PARASAILING   Summertime parasailing might be the ultimate Vancouver experience. Both **Aquila Para-Sail,** 167 E. Osborne Rd., North Vancouver (☎ 604/984-4333), and **Granville Island Watersports,** 1521 Foreshore Walk (☎ 604/662-7245), offer powerboat launchings that lift you high above the water. Bring your camera and take a few aerial shots before you land. Prices run about $55 to $95 per flight.

SAILING   Navigating sailboats in the unfamiliar surrounding straits is unsound unless you enroll in a local sailing course before attempting a bareboat sail rental. Knowing the tides, currents, and channels is essential. Multiday instruction packages sometimes combine guided Gulf Island cruises.

If all you want is to get out for a day, you can simply charter a three-hour yacht cruise with one of the following outfitters: **Cooper Boating Center,** 1620 Duranleau St. (☎ 604/687-4110), offers both cruises and sail instruction packages. The **Sea Wing Sailing School,** 1815 Mast Tower (☎ 604/669-0840), and **Blue Orca Sailing School,** 1818 Maritime Mews (☎ 604/683-6300), also offer lesson packages.

SKIING/SNOWBOARDING   Top-notch skiing lies outside the city at Whistler/ Blackcomb (rated by *Ski, Powder,* and *Snow Country* magazines as North America's number one ski resort), located 70 miles north of Vancouver (see Chapter 17). If you only have a day in Vancouver, you don't even have to leave the city to get in a few runs.

It seldom snows in the city's downtown and central areas, but Vancouverites can ski in the morning before work and take advantage of after-dinner night skiing. Just look up at the three ski resorts in the north shore mountains.

Grouse Mountain, 6400 Nancy Greene Way, North Vancouver (☎ 604/ 984-0661 or snow report 604/986-6262), is about 2 miles from Lion's Gate Bridge overlooking the Burrard Inlet and Vancouver's skyline (see "The Top Attractions," above). Four chairs, two beginner tows, and two T-bars take you up to the various alpine runs. Night skiing, special events, instruction, and a spectacular view enhance your enjoyment of the resort's 22 runs.

Beginners of all ages will enjoy the fresh mountain air at the Ski Wee Bowl, The Cut, or two other easy runs. Intermediate skiers and snowboarders can hone their skills on one of eleven runs. Five black diamond runs, including Coffin and Inferno, follow the east slopes from an elevation of 4,100 feet down to 2,500 feet. Devil's Advocate and Puragtory run the experts down chutes of towering Douglas fir.

Rental packages and a full range of facilities complete your experience. Lift tickets start at about $28 for adults with discounts for seniors and children.

Mount Seymour Provincial Park, 1700 Mt. Seymour Rd., North Vancouver (☎ 604/986-2261 or snow report 604/986-3444), has the area's highest base elevation; it's accessible via four chairs and a tow. In addition to day- and nighttime skiing, this facility offers snowboarding, snowshoeing, and tobogganing along their 22 runs. There are 16 miles of cross-country trails. They specialize in teaching first-timers. Camps for children and teenagers as well as adult clinics are available throughout the winter.

Mount Seymour has one of Western Canada's largest equipment rental shops; they will even keep your measurements on file for return visits. Lift tickets start at $26 for adults.

The McDonald's NW/98 Express Bus (☎ 604/986-2261) services skiers with round-trip transportation to Mount Seymour from various McDonald's restaurant locations citywide.

Cypress Bowl, 1610 Mt. Seymour Rd. (mailing address: P.O. Box 91252, West Vancouver, Canada V7V 3N9 ☎ 604/926-5612 or snow report 604/926-6007), has the area's highest vertical drop of 1,750 feet. Vancouver's best 10 miles of track-set cross-country skiing trails, in addition to 3 miles set aside for night skiing, are located here. Hollyburn Mountain is a local favorite in this 7,000-acre provincial mountain park. Serviced by four double chairs and a beginner's tow, they offer first-time skiers the Startracks program, which combines a lesson, trail ticket, and equipment rental starting at $39. Of the 24 downhill runs, some are set up for night-skiing, which makes this area an ideal multipurpose, all-day ski resort. To get here, take the Lion's Gate (Second Narrows) Bridge, and drive west on Highway 1/Highway 99 to Exit 22.

Cypress Bowl also operates **Cypress Mountain Sports,** 510 and 518 Park Royal South, West Vancouver (☎ 604/878-9229) at the Park Royal Mall. They stock a complete selection of downhill, cross country (including backwoods, skating, racing, and touring), and snowboarding equipment and accessories. The rental and repair department, staffed by avid skiers, offers a broad selection of equipment. And best of all, rental and repair prices are quite reasonable. A shuttle bus to Cypress Bowl ($7 round trip) departs from the store every hour during the ski season.

SWIMMING/WATER SPORTS   Vancouver's midsummer saltwater temperature rarely exceeds 65°F (18°C). Some swimmers opt for the fresh and saltwater pools located at city beaches (see "Beaches," above). Others take to the water at public aquatic centers. You can enjoy a full-size, heated, 50-meter Olympic pool, in addition to saunas, whirlpools, weight rooms, diving tanks, child care, and teaching pools at the **Vancouver Aquatic Centre,** 1050 Beach Ave. at the foot of Thurlow Street (☎ 604/665-3424). They charge $3.55 for adults, $1.75, for seniors, $2.30 for students, and $1.65 for children.

Located in the heart of downtown, the new **YWCA fitness center,** 535 Hornby St. (☎ 604/895-5777), has a six-lane, 25-meter ozone pool in addition to a steam room, whirlpool, conditioning gym, and aerobic studios.

UBC's **Aquatic Centre,** next door to the Student Union Building (☎ 604/ 822-4521), has open hours for the public.

TENNIS   Vancouver's 180 city-maintained, outdoor, public hard courts have one-hour limits to accommodate patrons on a first-come, first-serve basis from 8am until dusk. Local courtesy is that if someone is waiting, you surrender the court on the hour. Or use our trick: Invite them for doubles. (Heavy usage times are evenings and weekends, naturally.) With the exception of the Beach Avenue courts (which change a nominal fee), all city courts are free of admission.

Stanley Park has four courts near Lost Lagoon and 17 courts near the Beach Avenue entrance, next to the Fish House Restaurant. **Queen Elizabeth Park**'s 18 courts service the central Vancouver area, while **Kitsilano Beach Park**'s 10 courts service the beach area between Vanier Park and the UBC campus.

You can play nighttime tennis at the **Langara Campus** of Vancouver Community College, on West 49th Avenue between Main and Cambie streets.

The **UBC Tennis Training Centre,** on Thunderbird Boulevard (☎ 604/822-2505), has 10 outdoor and four indoor courts that you can reserve for $10 per hour.

Bayshore Bicycle & Rollerblade Rentals, at 745 Denman St. (☎ 604/688-2453) and at 1601 W. Georgia St. (☎ 604/689-5071), rents tennis rackets for $12 per day.

WILDLIFE WATCHING Where else will you find brant geese flying overhead on a major downtown thoroughfare and nesting on office buildings? Even in the city, nature hasn't lost the battle to civilization. Vancouver is an internationally famous stop for naturalists and ecotourists, so bring your cameras, binoculars, and spotting books! Orcas, salmon, bald eagles, herons, and numerous rare, indigenous, or migratory marine and waterfowl species all live within Vancouver's metropolitan area.

During the winter, thousands of bald eagles line the banks of **Indian Arm fjord** and the **Squamish, Cheakamus,** and **Mamquam** rivers to feed on spawning salmon (see Chapter 10). The area's official January 1994 eagle count recorded 3,700 eagles—the largest number ever seen in North America.

The annual summer salmon runs attract more than eagles. Tourists also flock to surrounding coastal streams and rivers to watch the waters turn red with leaping coho and sockeye. The salmon are plentiful at the **Capilano Salmon Hatchery** (see "Parks/Gardens," under "More Attractions," above), **Adams River** (see Chapter 17), **Goldstream National Park** (see Chapter 13), and numerous other fresh waters.

The Pacific Northwest's highest concentration of orcas (killer whales) also watch the salmon migration—it's their favorite food. A number of outfitters and charter companies that offer whale-watching cruises, floatplane flights, and guided kayaking trips include: **Corcovado Yacht Charters** (see "Fishing," below); **Firefly III Yacht Charters,** at Tradewinds Marina near Canada Place (☎ 604/377-7708); **Orca Dive & Charter Co.** (see "Diving," above); **Ecomarine Coastal Kayaking School** (☎ 604/689-7520) (see "Canoeing/Kayaking," above); and **Baxter Aviation** (see "Air Tours," under "Organized Tours," above). Many more launch from Vancouver Island and the Sunshine Coast.

Along the Fraser River delta, more than 250 bird species migrate to or perennially inhabit **George C. Reifel Sanctuary's** wetland reserve. The nearby **Richmond Nature Park** has a number of educational displays for young and first-time birders plus a boardwalk-encircled duck pond. (For more information about both attractions, see "Parks/Gardens," under "More Attractions," above.)

WINDSURFING Windsurfing is not allowed at the mouth of False Creek near Granville Island, between the Granville and Burrard Bridges. You can, however, rent or bring a board to Jericho and English Bay Beaches; there's good wind at both. Equipment sales and rental as well as instruction packages can be found at the following: **Windmaster,** at Denman and Pacific streets, at the English Bay Beach House (☎ 604/685-7245), and **Windsure Windsurfing School,** 1300 Discovery St. at Jericho Beach (☎ 604/224-0615). Instruction packages include board rentals and wet suits.

7 Spectator Sports

Spectators as well as participants find plenty of activity in Vancouver. From auto racing to soccer, Vancouver has world-class sports events.

You can get schedule information on all major sports events and purchase tickets at the Tourism Vancouver's **Travel InfoCentre,** 200 Burrard St. (☎ 604/683-2000).

You can also purchase tickets from Ticketmaster at the **Vancouver Ticket Centre,** 1304 Hornby St. (☎ 604/280-3311), which has 40 outlets in the greater Vancouver area, including at all Eaton's department stores and major shopping malls.

AUTO RACING   In early September, the CART Indy Series features its biggest annual event, the Labour Day **Molson Indy,** 765 Pacific Blvd.(☎ 604/684-4639 for information or 604/280-4639 for tickets). The race roars through Vancouver's streets around B.C. Place and the Concord Pacific site and attracts more than 350,000 spectators.

BASEBALL   The **Vancouver Canadians,** the AAA Pacific Coast league club for the California Angels, draws 6,500 spectators to their home at the **Nat Bailey Stadium,** 33rd Avenue at Ontario Street near Little Mountain Park (☎ 604/872-5232). It's a real grass field with a manual scoreboard: a ballpark that will warm any baseball fan's heart. Preseason Angels, Seattle Mariners, Montréal Expos, and Toronto Blue Jays exhibition games are also played here.

BASKETBALL   Vancouver has been awarded the National Basketball Association's 29th franchise. Basketball fever has caught on in this city as the **Vancouver Grizzlies** move in to the new **General Motors Place,** 800 Griffith Way (☎ 604/899-7469; event hotline 604/899-7444), where they tip off against the Charlotte Hornets, Chicago Bulls, Orlando Magic, New York Knicks, Boston Celtics, and the rest of the league.

CRICKET   Stanley Park's **Brockton Oval** in Stanley Park (see Chapter 7 for a walking tour of Stanley Park) is the spring-to-autumn venue of weekend test matches between the B.C. Cricket Association's amateur clubs.

CYCLE RACING   There are many small races both on and off-road throughout the year. Pick up a copy of *Coast* at local outfitters for a race calendar.

FOOTBALL   The Canadian Football League's **B.C. Lions** (☎ 604/585-3323) play their home and Grey Cup championship games in the 60,000-seat **B.C. Place Stadium,** Beatty and Robson streets (777 Pacific Blvd. South). Remember that Canadian football differs from its American cousin: It's a three-down offense passing game on a field that's 10 yards longer and wider. Some of the plays you see here will have NFL fans leaping out of their seats in surprise.

GOLF TOURNAMENTS   The 1996 Professional Golf Association Golf Tour's **Greater Vancouver Open,** featuring some of golf's greats going for the green, will be played on the Arnold Palmer–designed **Northview Golf and Country Club,** 6857 168th St., Surrey (☎ 604/574-0324).

HORSE RACING   Thoroughbred racehorses corner the track at **Hastings Park Racecourse,** Exhibition Park (☎ 604/254-1631), from mid-April to October. On Wednesday and Friday evenings, post time is 6:30pm. On weekends and holidays, post time is 1:30pm. There is a decent restaurant here, so you can make a full evening of dining and racing. Place a wager or two. Canadians true to their Commonwealth heritage are inveterate gentlemen and lady gamblers.

ICE HOCKEY   The National Hockey League's Stanley Cup–class **Vancouver Canucks** have played for 25 years at the Pacific Coliseum. With the opening of the **General Motors Place,** 800 Griffith Way (☎ 604/899-7469; event hotline 604/899-7444), they now share a new home with the Vancouver Grizzlies basketball franchise (see "Basketball," above).

LACROSSE   Canada's official national summertime sport, lacrosse was adopted from a traditional First Nations ball game that was once played across miles of rugged terrain. The sport is now played by the **Western Lacrosse League** at fields in **Renfrew Community Park, West Point Grey Park,** and **Hastings Community Centre Park**. Contact the **B.C. Lacrosse Association** (☎ 604/294-2122) for scheduled events and ticket information.

ROLLER HOCKEY   With the increasing popularity of in-line skating, roller hockey has become a fast-paced summer alternative for ice hockey fans. Watch the **Vancouver Voodoo** in action at the **Agridome,** Pacific National Exhibition (☎ 604/874-1900).

RUGBY   Another British sport, rugby, is played here through the fall and winter. The **Vancouver Rugby Union** (☎ 604/988-7660) and the **B.C. Rugby Union** (☎ 604/737-3065) schedule games at a variety of playing fields.

RUNNING   The **Sun Run** in April and the **Vancouver International Marathon** in May attract runners from around the world and even more spectators. Contact the Pacific Roadrunners (☎ 604/988-8899) for information.

SOCCER   The American Professional Soccer League's **Vancouver 86ers** (☎ 604/299-0086) play at **B.C. Place** (see "Football," above) until renovations are completed at their traditional home at Swangard Stadium, Kingsway and Patterson Avenue, Burnaby.

Vancouver Strolls

You can see Vancouver by floatplane, car, bike, helicopter, even kayak, but the most intimate way to enjoy the splendor of the city is by strolling along the miles of sidewalks and footpaths. It would take weeks of walking to see everything of interest, so we've selected four of the most popular areas for easy ambling.

WALKING TOUR 1
Downtown & the West End

Start: Canada Place.

Finish: Canada Place.

Time: 3 to 4 hours, not including shopping, sightseeing, and eating stops.

Best Times: Any weekday between 10am and 6pm.

Worst Times: Evenings, when the most of the stores and all the museums are closed.

Someone once said that to make a new start, you should see a cruise ship off. You don't need to know any of the passengers—just wish them bon voyage. With this advice in mind, start your downtown Vancouver tour by watching the Alaska- and Seattle-bound summer cruise ships departing from:

1. **Canada Place,** at the foot of Burrard Street. With its five trademark 80-foot-tall Teflon sails jutting from the pier, it more closely resembles the Sydney Opera House in Australia than it does a cruise ship terminal, outdoor promenade, and convention/exhibition center. The descriptive plaques along the **Promenade into History** provide an entertaining outdoor history lesson about the Burrard Inlet and Vancouver Harbour.

   The tri-level **Vancouver Trade and Convention Centre,** which hosts up to 11,000 people for events such as the International Wine Festival, and the **World Trade Centre** office complex share Canada Place's magnificent harbor and north shore views. Also in the complex are the luxurious **Pan-Pacific Hotel** and **Waterfront Centre Hotel** (see Chapter 4 for hotel reviews).

   If it's a rainy day, you can take in the five-story screen presentations at the **CN IMAX Theatre** (☎ 604/682-IMAX). There are three daily shows on the hour from noon to 3pm and two evening performances at 7 and 9:15pm. Matinee admission is $6.25 for adults, $5.25 for seniors and students, $4.25 for children; evening admission is $7.50 for adults and students, $4.50 for seniors and children.

Walk down Burrard Street past **Tourism Vancouver's Travel InfoCentre** at 200 Burrard St. to:

2. The art deco **Marine Building,** 355 Burrard St. at W. Cordova. It was the tallest office building in the British Commonwealth when it opened in 1930 (see "Architectural Highlights" in Chapter 6).

Continue walking down Burrard Street past a refreshing outdoor waterfall between Dunsmuir and West Georgia streets until you get to:

3. **Christ Church Cathedral** (Anglican Church of Canada), 690 Burrard St., a classically designed 19th-century stone church. It was nicknamed the "old root house." After the basement and foundation were finished, the congregation installed a temporary roof and began holding services that were literally underground. The existing structure wasn't completed until 1895. It was nearly demolished in the 1930s, when developers offered the clergy a great deal of money for the land. A local reporter, however, uncovered the clergy's plot to raze this landmark in exchange for a large profit while negotiations were in their final stages and publicized it. This caused a public outcry and perhaps the first shift in public sentiments toward the preservation of local heritage sites.

Next to the cathedral is the towering concrete, glass, and patina-green steel tower known as:

4. **Cathedral Place,** 925 W. Georgia St., which houses offices and the **Sri Lanken Gem Museum,** a unique, handcrafted treasure that will delight even the most jaded eyes (see "The Top Attractions" in Chapter 6).

Behind Cathedral Place is another gem:

5. **The Canadian Craft Museum,** 639 Hornby St., which displays and sells a magnificent selection of Canadian crafts (see "Museums/Galleries," under "More Attractions" in Chapter 6).

Across the street from Cathedral Place on West Georgia Street is:

6. The French Renaissance–style **Hotel Vancouver** (see Chapter 4 for hotel review; see "Architectural Highlights," under "More Attractions" in Chapter 6), built in 1929 by the Canadian-Pacific Railway.

Continue east on West Georgia one more block to Hornby Street to:

7. **Vancouver Art Gallery,** 750 Hornby St. (see "The Top Attractions" in Chapter 6), which was originally the provincial law courts building.

On the Gallery's Robson Street side, you can join an environmental protest, challenge a chess player or two, or listen to an impromptu grunge concert on the **courthouse steps** directly across from:

8. **Robson Square** (see "Outdoor Plazas," under "More Attractions" in Chapter 6), which is a quiet place to take a break next to a three-tier waterfall streaming from the new provincial courthouse or under a blossoming cherry tree. In the winter, you can also bring your ice-skates and do a few circles around the covered ice rink (see "Ice-Skating," under "Outdoor Activities" in Chapter 6). Keep an eye out for the pair of brant geese that have a nest on the courthouse roof.

Walk west down:

9. **Robson Street,** Vancouver's hottest shopping and dining district, which links downtown to the West End. You can buy a pair of outrageously cool cowboy boots at **David Gordon,** 790 Robson St.; an Inuit stone carving from **Rocks & Gems**

Walking Tour—Downtown

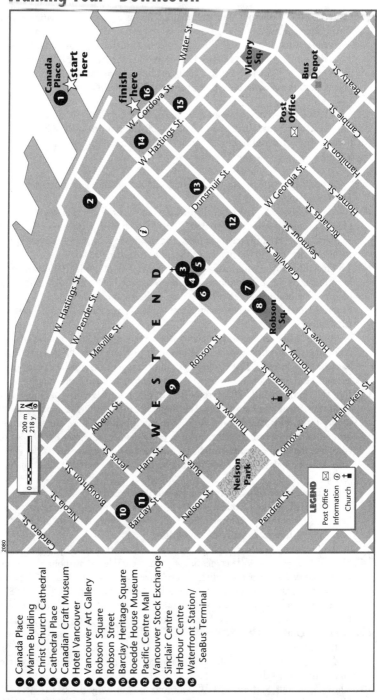

1. Canada Place
2. Marine Building
3. Christ Church Cathedral
4. Cathedral Place
5. Canadian Craft Museum
6. Hotel Vancouver
7. Vancouver Art Gallery
8. Robson Square
9. Robson Street
10. Barclay Heritage Square
11. Roedde House Museum
12. Pacific Centre Mall
13. Vancouver Stock Exchange
14. Sinclair Centre
15. Harbour Centre
16. Waterfront Station/ SeaBus Terminal

LEGEND
⊠ Post Office
ⓘ Information
✝ Church

Canada, 1066 Robson St.; or well-made fashions at any of the many clothing stores along the way.

People-watch at one of the sidewalk cafes or at such coffee bars as **Milestones,** 1145 Robson St., or **Blenz Coffee,** 1201 Robson St. Enjoy a plate of fish and chips at **Olympia's,** 1094 Robson St., while reading any of the world's daily newspapers from the **Manhattan Book Store and Newsstand** across the street.

☕ **TAKE A BREAK** For an elevated, rotating city view, go up to the **Cloud Nine** restaurant at the Landmark Hotel, 1400 Robson Street (see Chapter 4 for hotel review). You can have a full meal or just order dessert and a cappuccino or a drink and watch the world revolve around you.

Around the corner from the Landmark Hotel on Broughton Street between Haro and Barclay streets is:

10. **Barclay Heritage Square.** This is the only block in the city that has been completely protected from development. The original houses have been faithfully restored. Most are privately occupied, but the block is crisscrossed with garden paths that are open to the public. In this peaceful setting stands:

11. **The Roedde House Museum,** 1415 Barclay St. (☎ 604/684-7040), which is a beautiful example of what houses were like when the Edwardian West End was in bloom. The house was designed by Francis Rattenbury, architect of Victoria's Empress Hotel, Parliament Buildings, and Crystal Garden as well as the Vancouver Art Gallery.

As you return east on Robson Street, browse through souvenir or novelty shops, including the **Tacki Shop,** 1174 Robson St., or buy a watch at **Saatchi and Saatchi Fine Jewelry,** 1106 Robson St., until you get to Granville Street. Take a left and head up Granville, where you'll encounter the three-block-long:

12. **Pacific Centre Mall,** 701 Granville St. The complex contains more than 200 stores, including **Eaton's** and **The Bay** (the Hudson's Bay Company) department stores, plus eateries and ATM-equipped banks. There are also underground concourses for amusement on a rainy day (see Chapter 8). Also in the complex, the **Four Seasons Hotel's** glass-domed atrium looms over a three-story waterfall that splashes into a fountain-encircled pool (see Chapter 4 for hotel review).

You have a one-block shopping break until you reach:

13. The **Vancouver Stock Exchange,** 609 Granville St. You can watch money flow like so many numbers from the observation gallery overlooking the trading floor (see "Special-Interest Sightseeing" in Chapter 6).

If more sophisticated shopping is on your travel agenda, then by all means visit:

14. **Sinclair Centre,** 757 W. Hastings St., which is a complex created out of four early 20th-century buildings. Plaza Escada, exclusive European clothing retailers, and First Nations fashion designer Dorothy Grant have shops here (see Chapter 8).

If you didn't take in the view at Cloud Nine on Robson Street, then take a detour one block east on West Hastings Street, where you can visit:

15. **Lookout! Harbour Centre,** 555 W. Hastings St., which has a great 360° view of metropolitan Vancouver (see "Views," under "More Attractions" in Chapter 6).

Exit Harbour Centre on the Cordova Street side. Across the street on your left and a little farther down, is:

16. The **Waterfront Station,** 601 W. Cordova St. Formerly the Beaux Arts–style Canadian-Pacific Railway station. It's been restored and now contains the **SeaBus terminal** and offices of the **B.C. Film Commission.**

One block west on Cordova Street is the **Waterfront Centre,** where you can return to your starting point at Canada Place or relax over coffee or cocktails at the Pan Pacific Hotel's **Cascade Lounge** in front of the indoor/outdoor Pacific Rim fountain.

WALKING TOUR 2
Gastown

Start: The Landing, one block from the Waterfront Station SeaBus terminal.
Finish: R. J. Clarke's Tobacconist.
Time: Allow 1 hour, not including shopping and sightseeing stops.
Best Times: Late morning to early afternoon.
Worst Times: Late afternoon and evening.

Once the city center and industrial hub, Gastown is now a favorite film backdrop. It has appeared in dozens of movies and TV shows disguised as everywhere from Chicago to Boston to New Orleans.

Start your Gastown heritage tour at:

1. The Landing, 375 Water St. (☎ 604/687-1144), a restored Klondike gold-rush warehouse from 1905 which now houses an exclusive shopping/office complex (see Chapter 8). Head down Water Street past:

Walking Tour—Gastown

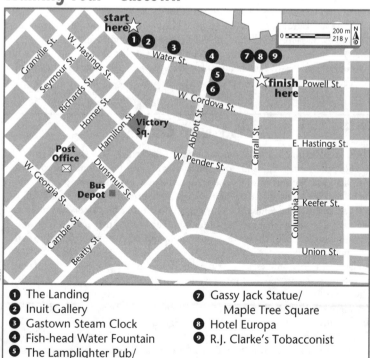

1 The Landing
2 Inuit Gallery
3 Gastown Steam Clock
4 Fish-head Water Fountain
5 The Lamplighter Pub/
    Dominion Hotel
6 Blood Alley

7 Gassy Jack Statue/
    Maple Tree Square
8 Hotel Europa
9 R.J. Clarke's Tobacconist

2. The **Inuit Gallery,** 345 Water St., and **Hill's Trading Post,** 165 Water St., two First Nations stores featuring excellent art, jewelry, and clothing selections by Pacific Northwest craftspeople (see Chapter 8). The famous Vancouver landmark standing at the next corner is:

3. The **Gastown Steam Clock,** at corner of Water and Cambie streets. It was built in the 1970s by local horologist (that is, a maker of time pieces) Ray Saunders, whose office is just upstairs from the clock. The same underground steam system that used to heat neighborhood buildings now powers the glass-enclosed clock-works. Every 15 minutes, the clock toots the Westminster Chimes theme and erupts in a cloud of steam. Walk one block further past more souvenir and gift shops until you get to the next corner where:

4. The **Fish-head Water Fountain,** at the intersection of Water and Abbott streets, stands across from:

5. The **Lamplighter Pub** in the **Dominion Hotel,** 210 Abbott St. This restored 1899 Heritage property was the first Vancouver establishment to serve women alcohol. Halfway down the block on Abbott Street and on the other side of the Dominion Hotel is:

6. **Blood Alley Square.** The lane between Abbott and Carrall streets, this is the place where nefarious dealings took place during Gastown's wild days of yore.

   Returning to Water Street and proceeding down one more block, you'll find:

7. **Maple Tree Square,** where a 1970 **bronze statue of Gassy Jack** proudly stands on a whiskey barrel. The likeness is from a vintage photo of an unknown person, since Gassy never had a portrait taken of himself. The square is at the intersection of Water, Carrall, Powell, and Alexander streets across from:

8. The **Hotel Europe,** 43 Powell St. (see "Historic Buildings/Monuments," under "More Attractions" in Chapter 6). Also at this intersection stands:

9. **R. J. Clarke's Tobacconist,** 3 Alexander St. (see chapter 8), Vancouver's first smoke shop. It still sells hand-rolled Cuban cigars and house blends of pipe tobaccos.

"Luckylucky" Gastown

The Coastal Salish called what is now Gastown "Luckylucky" or "beautiful grove." In 1867, the former Yorkshire river pilot "Gassy" Jack Deighton came to town with his First Nations mistress, a dog, and the only barrel of whiskey in town. He offered the locals all the free liquor they could drink in exchange for helping him to construct the Globe Saloon. (Legend has it that the saloon was built in one day.) The village that grew up around his pub was lovingly named Gastown, even though in 1870, the town's more sophisticated citizens preferred to call it Granville.

Gastown went commercial after the city burned to the ground 16 years later. Its genteel residents moved further west to establish Vancouver. By the 1940s, Gastown was a deserted part of skid row and Granville Island had become the city's industrial center. Fortunately, plans to demolish it were never realized, and by the time anyone took a serious look at the neighborhood, the buildings had gotten old enough to be quaint. It finally got a facelift in the early 1970s and was designated as a heritage area, filled with a touristy collection of boutiques, shops, restaurants, and nightclubs.

WALKING TOUR 3
Chinatown

Start: Chinese Freemasons' Building.
Finish: Kuomintang Building.
Time: Allow 1¹/₂ hours, not including shopping or sightseeing stops.
Best Times: Late morning through the afternoon.
Worst Times: Early morning and all evening.

If you are taking this tour after the Gastown tour, turn right onto Carrall Street and walk three blocks to West Pender Street. The area between Gastown and Chinatown is still part of a skid row and has not been restored by either community. Portions are slowly being reclaimed by the Gastown Business Improvement Society and a Hong Kong investor, but be forewarned that the renovation is still in the planning stages. In the early morning and late afternoons, this is a semideserted, three-block stretch where the homeless and skid-row outcasts roam through the lots. Be very careful during these off hours.

Vancouver's Chinatown is North America's third largest (after San Francisco and New York). Originally the area, measuring only six square blocks, was home to thousands of 19th-century Chinese immigrants who built the Canadian-Pacific railway. The community thrived until World War I, when anti-Chinese sentiment spread north from San Francisco and shut down immigration for three decades. After World War II, when both Canadian-born Chinese and newly-arrived refugees were finally granted citizenship, Chinatown was abandoned by many of its original residents, although it did remain a thriving shopping center for imported Chinese goods and services, and is still the first stop for many new immigrants.

By the 1960s, Chinatown had become an historic landmark. Today, it bustles with throngs of both Asian and non-Asian shoppers hunting bargains in ginseng, seafood, herbs, and spices as well as diners who regularly patronize the area's numerous restaurants for hard-to-find delicacies like authentic dim sum and fresh noodle soups.

Recently, many Hong Kong and Taiwanese emigrants have chosen to live in Richmond, where the vast majority of metropolitan Vancouver's quarter of a million Chinese-Canadians make their home.

Chinatown's past can still be seen in its upper-story recessed balconies, designed to cool building interiors, and its facades, which are still traditionally painted red (signifying happiness and prosperity), blue (for peace), or green (a symbol of fertility).

Your Chinatown tour begins at the corner of Pender and Carrall streets, where you'll find:

1. The 1901 **Chinese Freemasons' Building,** 3 W. Pender St. The building once housed a society that helped finance Dr. Sun Yat-sen's 1911 Chinese Revolution, which deposed the adolescent Manchu emperor Pu-Yi. Directly across the street is:

2. **The Sam Kee Building,** 8 W. Pender St., the world's narrowest building, according to the *Guinness Book of World Records* and Ripley's *Believe It or Not.* The dark-green structure is 5 feet 10 inches deep. The Jack Chow Insurance Co. now owns this two-story, steel-framed 1913 building, which has overhanging second-floor bay windows that increase its width by 50%. To the right of the Sam Kee Building is:

3. **Shanghai Alley,** which 40 years ago was a thriving lane packed with stores, restaurants, a pawnshop, a theater, rooming houses, and a public bath. Now, only three buildings remain. Catercorner from here is another, more infamous lane:

4. **Canton Alley,** near the corner of Pender and Carrall streets. It was once a concealed red-light district crammed with opium dens and rooming houses.

   Returning to Pender Street, take a left. Your first stop is:

5. The 1902 **Chinese Times Building,** 1 E. Pender St., which was the home of the first Chinatown newspaper. Between Carrall and Columbia streets is:

6. The **Chinese Cultural Centre,** 50 E. Pender St. (☎ 604/687-0729), nestled in a modern glass and concrete structure behind a traditional red archway gate. Rotating exhibits about local history and traditional culture are displayed in the lobby. The organization also sponsors the annual Chinese New Year parade. Directly behind the cultural center, you'll come to:

7. **Dr. Sun Yat-sen Classical Chinese Park and Garden,** 578 Carrall St. (see "Parks/ Gardens," under "More Attractions" in Chapter 6). The park is modeled after private Taoist gardens in Suzhou, China, from the Ming Dynasty (1368–1644). Every piece of the garden—from the hand-fired roof tiles and carved woodwork to the courtyard pebbles—was shipped from China in 950 crates and assembled by a 52-man Suzhou crew with four Chinese and Vancouverite master architects.

   Returning to busy Pender Street, take a right and stroll among the herb and grocery stores. Dried ginseng roots, live eels, century eggs, and geoducks overflow wooden crates and spill onto the sidewalk. Fascinating traces of the past linger amid the dim sum parlors, noodle shops, bakeries, and craft stores.

   Walk back through the Chinese Cultural Centre's arch. You will be back on East Pender Street. Directly across the street you will find the:

8. **Wing Sang Building,** 51-67 E. Pender St. This is Chinatown's oldest standing building. It was constructed in 1889, as the home of the first bank that catered to predominantly Chinese-speaking laborers and merchants.

   Continue walking a few doors down E. Pender to:

9. **The Chung Wing Geong Tong Building,** 79 E. Pender St., which was built in 1926 to house one of the merchants' association. At the turn of the century, the North American tong associations were organized in every major Chinatown. To the outside world, these societies united local tradesmen and merchants to facilitate the exchange of goods and services with mainland Chinese counterparts. Some tong groups, however, had underworld connections that most notably erupted during the 1920s and 1930s into the famous "Tong Wars"—a dispute over the control of the lucrative legal and illegal Asian import trade. Chinatowns worldwide became a battle zone where gunmen, street-fighters, and hatchet assassins ruled the nighttime streets.

   One block further down, across the street, and at the other end of the spectrum you will find:

10. The green-balconied **Chinese Benevolent Association,** 108 E. Pender St., which was established in 1909 to provide welfare services to Chinatown's new arrivals.

11. The 1921 **Won Benevolent Association,** 123 Pender St., on the other hand, was dedicated entirely to helping families named Won or Wong. Upstairs, the **Mon Keang School** offers Chinese classes at the high school level, as it has since the building's construction.

12. On the darker side of Chinatown's history, the 1907 **Lee Building,** 127–133 E. Pender St., once contained a concealed opium factory.

   When you get to the heart of Chinatown at the corner of Pender and Main streets, take a quick left turn and walk for one block to Hastings Street. At the corner you'll find:

13. The 1903 **Carnegie Library,** 1 E. Hastings St., which was built by Scottish industrial magnate Andrew Carnegie. Market Hall, the venue of many livestock

Walking Tour—Chinatown

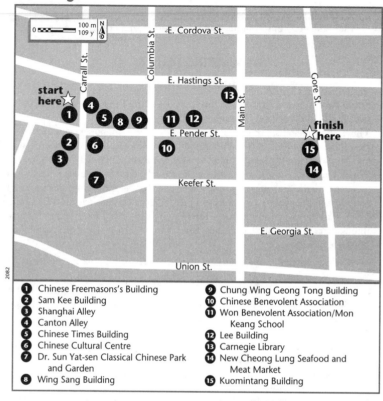

1. Chinese Freemasons's Building
2. Sam Kee Building
3. Shanghai Alley
4. Canton Alley
5. Chinese Times Building
6. Chinese Cultural Centre
7. Dr. Sun Yat-sen Classical Chinese Park and Garden
8. Wing Sang Building
9. Chung Wing Geong Tong Building
10. Chinese Benevolent Association
11. Won Benevolent Association/Mon Keang School
12. Lee Building
13. Carnegie Library
14. New Cheong Lung Seafood and Meat Market
15. Kuomintang Building

auctions and public events, stood here until 1896, when it became Vancouver's first city hall. In the 1930s, the building served as Vancouver's civic museum and public library. Now, it is a health and social services outreach office. Return to the corner of Pender and Main streets. Walk one block further on Main St. to the corner of Keefer St. if you want to:

🍵 **TAKE A BREAK** **Park Lock Seafood Restaurant,** 544 Main St. (☎ 604/688-1581), is a second-floor, spacious seafood restaurant. The fare includes an impressive, MSG-free selection of dim sum treats such as steamed pork or chicken buns, fresh garden pea and prawn *shu mai* (dumplings), pastry-wrapped sausage, and fried tofu served in a rich black bean sauce. (See Chapter 5 for dining review.)

Take Keefer Street or return to Pender St. and continue strolling past grill shops displaying roasted ducks and bakeries like Garden Bakery and Tea House, 249 E. Pender St., whose display counters are filled with freshly made *bao* (buns filled with sweetened pork or black beans) until you get to Gore Street, where you'll find:

14. The **New Chong Lung Seafood and Meat Market,** at Gore and Keefer Streets. The market packs geoduck, salmon, and smoked salmon for shipping anywhere in the world. The tour ends at:

15. The 1920 **Kuomintang Building,** 529 Gore St., which has remained unchanged since it was the Western Canadian political headquarters of the Chinese Nationalist Party, which overthrew the imperial Manchu government.

From here, you can either head back to downtown Vancouver via Pender Street or take the no. 3 bus from the corner of Main St. and Pender St.

WALKING TOUR 4
Granville Island

Start: Take either the Aquabus or the Granville Island Ferry to Granville Island.
Finish: The Aquabus and Granville Island Ferry terminal.
Time: About 3 hours, not including shopping or gallery-hopping stops.
Best Times: Anytime between 10am and 6pm, when most businesses are open, and Thursdays throughout the summer, when the Farmers' Market livens up the area.
Worst Times: Anytime if you're driving, because the one-way counterclockwise roadway can be backed up with slow-moving traffic three blocks up the street to the island even in the winter. Cars must yield to pedestrians (and there are a lot of them here). Parking is scarce and has a three-hour limit. Also, nonholiday Mondays throughout the winter are bad visiting times. That's when the Granville Island Public Market is closed.

After you land at the Granville Island ferry terminal, walk up the ramp. You will see:

1. Mulvaney's, 1455 Johnston St., a New Orleans–style seafood restaurant that has flourished at this same spot since Granville Island was a bustling, major industrial center (see Chapter 5 for a dining review).

To your right is the:

2. Arts Club Theatre (see Chapter 9), which presents a lively array of dramatic, music, and dance works by local and national performers.

Take the walkway in front of the Arts Club Theatre to the open courtyard facing False Creek. You are now at the entrance to:

3. The huge **Granville Island Public Market.** This 50,000-square-foot covered space is a major weekend draw. Locals and tourists come to sample a tantalizing variety of cuisine, do their food shopping, listen to street musicians performing in the market courtyard, or just sit by the water's edge and watch the parade of boats go by. From June through September, you can also join the locals shopping for fresh produce on Thursdays from 9am to 4pm at the **Farmer's Truck Market,** located right outside the Public Market.

Behind the Public Market on Johnston Street, musicians and magicians entertain passersby at **Triangle Square.** Head across the square past Bridges Restaurant (see Chapter 5 for dining review). Turn left and head down Duranleau Street through:

4. The **Maritime Market,** Duranleau Street from Triangle Square to Anderson Street. Here, **Mount Seymour Yacht Sales** or **Pacifica Yacht Sales** can sell you a yacht, and **Alder Bay Boat Company** can custom build your dream craft. You can stock up on fittings and nautical souvenirs at **Granville Island Marine Supplies;** get new lures at **Granville Island Tackle and Charters** (see "Fishing," under "Outdoor Activities" in Chapter 6); sign up for sailing lessons at **Sea Wing Sailing School and Yacht Charters** (see "Sailing," under "Outdoor Activities" in Chapter 6); or rent a kayak at **Ecomarine Ocean Kayak Centre** (see "Canoeing/ Kayaking," under "Outdoor Activities" in Chapter 6). The side streets along here are named Boatlift Lane, Mast Tower Road, and Maritime Mews.

Walking Tour—Granville Island

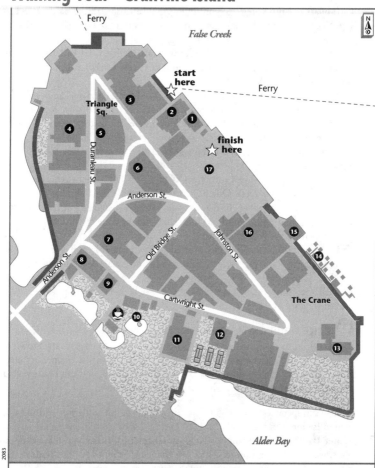

False Creek

Ferry

start here

Ferry

Triangle Sq.

finish here

Duranleau St.

Anderson St.

Old Bridge St.

Johnston St.

Anderson St.

Cartwright St.

The Crane

Alder Bay

2083

1. Mulvaney's
2. Arts Club Theatre
3. Granville Island Public Market
4. Maritime Market
5. Net Loft
6. Granville Island Information Centre
7. Granville Island Brewing Co.
8. Kids Only Market
9. Waterfront Theatre
10. Water Park
11. False Creek Community Center
12. Other galleries
13. Granville Island Hotel
14. Sea Village
15. Pier 32 Seafood Restaurant
16. Emily Carr College of Art and Design
17. Ocean Cement

If boats or kayaks aren't to your liking, you can also walk across the street to:

5. The **Net Loft,** between Duranleau and Johnston streets at Triangle Square, where you can buy handcrafted jewelry, fabrics, gifts, and objects or the elements for making your own creations at the **Circle Craft Gallery;** the **Bill Reid Studio; Molnar Glass Studio; Paperworks Gallery; Circle Craft Co-op; Beadworks;** and **Blackberry Books** (see Chapter 8).

Across the street, you can get a better idea of how Granville Island evolved at:

6. The **Granville Island Information Centre,** 1669 Johnston St. (☎ 604/ 666-5784), where you can stroll through an excellent historical exhibit, see an audiovisual presentation, and pick up a special events calendar.

Head south on Anderson Street toward Cartwright Street, where the first building on your left is the:

7. **Granville Island Brewing Company** (☎ 604/688-9927), at the corner of Anderson and Cartwright streets. One of British Columbia's most popular microbreweries, it offers free tours of the facilities and tastings of cold Island Lager, dark Island Bock, Island Light, and Lord Granville Pale Ale daily at 1pm and 3pm.

Across from the brewery is the:

8. **Kids Only Market** (see "Especially for Kids" in Chapter 6), which has 24 toy and clothing shops, rides, games, ice-cream stands, and even a day-care center.

Next door is the:

9. **Waterfront Theatre** (see Chapter 9), at Cartwright and Old Bridge Street. Across the street, you can:

☕ **TAKE A BREAK**   At **Isadora's** (☎ 604/681-3748), which is owned and operated by a co-op. The fare includes light entrées; fresh, organically grown salads; sandwiches; and a selection of wines. Pizzas and honey-sweetened ice cream at this two-story eatery will appeal to kids. And for $100, you can become a part owner of the restaurant. (See Chapter 5 for dining review.)

You can spend a few moments relaxing indoors or out while your kids have fun behind Isadora's in the:

10. **Water Park** (see "Especially for Kids" in Chapter 6). It has movable water cannons, water slides, and more. There are changing facilities at both Isadora's and the Community Center (see below) throughout the summer.

Along Cartwright Street, there are numerous performing and fine arts studios as well as galleries. Peek into the studio windows: You may see artisans throwing potter's clay, weaving cloth, blowing glass, hammering gold jewelry, or choreographing a new dance.

11. The **False Creek Community Center** (☎ 604/665-3425) has a variety of special events and facilities, including outdoor public tennis courts.

12. The **Gallery of B.C. Ceramics; Forge and Form; Harris-Jones Gallery; Performance Works;** and **Tanya Bolenz** are just a few of the galleries and studios you'll find along this stretch. (See Chapter 8.)

Cartwright ends and Johnston Street begins at the:

13. **Granville Island Hotel,** Cartwright and Johnston streets (see Chapter 4 for hotel review), on the island's eastern point.

Directly across the parking lot on the docks is:

14. **Sea Village,** where elaborate floating homes are moored along False Creek, and:

15. **Pier 32 Seafood Restaurant** (see Chapter 5 for dining review), which rests on the pier behind the:

16. Emily Carr College of Art and Design, 1399 Johnston St. (☎ 604/687 2345), where you can look at students' work in the school gallery or at the bronze Bill Reid sculpture in the open-air mall.

One of the last remnants of Granville's industrial days is:

17. Ocean Cement, between the college and the public market, which is still in operation.

You have now returned to the ferry terminal, where you can catch a boat ride to Vanier Park or back to downtown Vancouver.

WALKING TOUR 5
Stanley Park

Start: Lost Lagoon.
Finish: Lost Lagoon.
Time: 2¹/₂ hours around the seawall (less on skates) or 3¹/₂ hours through the interior, not including sightseeing and eating stops.
Best Times: Any day from dawn until dusk.
Worst Times: Any time you don't feel like communing with nature. Then just take the circle around Lost Lagoon before heading off to Robson or Denman Street.

Surrounded by the Burrard Inlet, First Narrows, and English Bay, Stanley Park is a thickly forested promontory with towering Douglas fir, red cedar, and hemlock. Sand beaches and beautiful views of the north shore mountains await you on the Seawall Walk—a 5¹/₂-mile (8.8 kilometers) stroll or run. If you take the interior route, you'll think you're in the untouched wilderness of the Pacific Northwest. Some of the trails were first cut by early Coastal Salish residents, but all are now well-maintained gravel paths. Either way you go, it's hard to believe you are in a city park.

You start your tour at the end of Robson Street at Lagoon Drive. Head north on Lagoon Drive. Walk past the public tennis courts and down to:

1. Lost Lagoon, named by First Nations princess-poet Pauline Johnson. The lagoon is inhabited by Canada geese, a few varieties of ducks, and rare trumpeter swans that forage amid the surrounding greens. Bring plenty of bird seed for these not-so-timid residents. (The park is trying to discourage people from feeding the animals bread—it's bad for their waistlines.) The squirrels you'll encounter love peanuts, which you can get in bulk at the Safeway store on Robson and Denman streets.

Right on the water's edge, you'll find:

2. The new **Nature Center,** where educational displays explain the park's ecosystem and wildlife. This urban park is larger than New York's Central Park. The wildlife includes raccoons, skunks, black-hued gray squirrels, beavers, owls, and waterfowl. The Center also conducts nature walks, if you want to learn about the park's unique flora. The next-door concession stand is open throughout the summer in case you forgot to bring a snack.

Follow the eastern edge of the lagoon and go through the Georgia Street underpass. Starting at the 0-km marker of the Seawall Promenade, go past:

3. The **Vancouver Rowing Club** on your right, where every morning you can watch crews launching their shells from the docks. On your left, you'll pass the **Queen Victoria Monument.**

As you look out onto Coal Harbour, you'll notice:

4. **Dead Man's Island,** the final resting place of the Coast Salish tribe. They buried the dead in ornately carved bentwood boxes and cedar lean-tos. During the smallpox epidemic of 1888, the city council unfortunately used the island to quarantine the stricken (primarily prostitutes and Chinese immigrants), despite the protests of the park commissioner. It is now used as a naval training base, and not surprisingly, they say the island's haunted.

    A few yards farther on your left is the entrance to the:

5. **Hummingbird Trail,** which takes you past **Malkin Bowl,** site of the summer Theater Under the Stars performances (see Chapter 9).

    You will reach a path that leads to the former site of the Vancouver Zoo and to one of the city's major attractions:

6. The **Vancouver Aquarium** (see "The Top Attractions" in Chapter 6), where you can watch trainers feeding and bonding with orcas (killer whales).

    If you continue up Hummingbird Trail instead of taking a detour to the aquarium, you'll reach:

7. The **Japanese Monument,** which was erected in 1920 to honor 190 Japanese-Canadians who served in World War I. The light at the top of the tower burns perennially to commemorate their actions. Two smaller plaques are dedicated to those who served in World War II and the Korean War.

    With your back to the monument, you will see a path that follows a tall wooden fence. This will lead you to:

8. The **Vancouver Children's Zoo** and **Variety Kids Farmyard** are on the two left-hand paths. Peacocks and rabbits placidly stroll the surrounding grounds in the evening, while Shetland ponies and other animals rest behind the farmyard's protective walls.

    Take a right at the Japanese Monument and follow the path that skirts the aquarium's northern side until you come to a paved road and parking area. Turn right and walk down the paved road a few yards until you see the Mallard Trail marker, then turn left onto:

9. **Mallard Trail,** which joins Brockton Oval Trail just before reaching **Brockton Oval** and the **cricket pitch,** where local teams from the B.C. Cricket Association hold their summer weekend test matches (see Chapter 6).

    Across the cricket pitch, still heading east, you'll come across:

10. A cluster of late 19th-century **totem poles** carved by the Kwakiutl and Haida.

    Follow the path north back to Park Drive and the Seawall Walk. Continue walking until you get a little past the 2.5-km marker. Close to the seawall's 3.0-km marker, you'll see:

11. *Girl in a Wet Suit,* a statue in the water that resembles *The Little Mermaid* in Copenhagen.

    About an eighth of a mile farther, you'll find:

12. The **Variety Kids Water Park** on your right. It's a water playground complete with a miniature railway and pony rides, which are located on the opposite side of the promenade walkway.

    From this point on, there are few human-made attractions. Cut into the interior of the park by taking:

13. **Ravine Trail** to **Beaver Lake** (yes, there are beavers here), where you'll pick up **Lake Trail.** This turns into **Squirrel Trail** (surprisingly, this is the one place we didn't see squirrels) after you cross the Bridle Path and into **Lovers Walk** after you cross Tatlow Walk. Take a left onto **Rawlings Trail.** Follow this until you get to

Walking Tour—Stanley Park

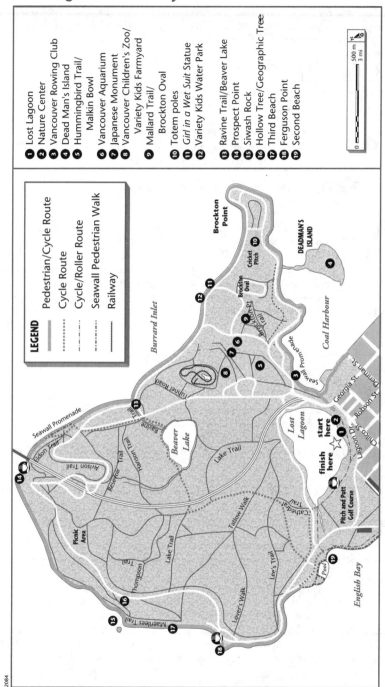

1. Lost Lagoon
2. Nature Center
3. Vancouver Rowing Club
4. Dead Man's Island
5. Hummingbird Trail/ Malkin Bowl
6. Vancouver Aquarium
7. Japanese Monument
8. Vancouver Children's Zoo/ Variety Kids Farmyard
9. Mallard Trail/ Brockton Oval
10. Totem poles
11. *Girl in a Wet Suit Statue*
12. Variety Kids Water Park
13. Ravine Trail/Beaver Lake
14. Prospect Point
15. Siwash Rock
16. Hollow Tree/Geographic Tree
17. Third Beach
18. Ferguson Point
19. Second Beach

LEGEND

— Pedestrian/Cycle Route
······ Cycle Route
—·—·— Cycle/Roller Route
——— Seawall Pedestrian Walk
········· Railway

0 ___ 500 m
0 ___ 3 mi

Burrard Inlet

Brockton Point

DEADMAN'S ISLAND

Cricket Pitch

Brockton Oval

Brockton Pt. Trail

Seawall Promenade

Coal Harbour

Seawall Promenade

Georgia St.

Denman St.

Robson St.

Chilco St.

Lagoon Dr.

Lost Lagoon

start here

finish here

Pitch and Putt Golf Course

Tunnel Road

Beaver Lake

Ravine Trail

Hanson Trail

Reservoir Trail

Eldon Trail

Avison Trail

Lake Trail

Lake Trail

Thompson Trail

Cathedral Trail

Tatlow Walk

Lee's Trail

Lover's Walk

Merilees Trail

Merilees Trail

Picnic Area

Pooh

English Bay

2084

Lees Trail, where you turn left. Follow Lees Trail to **Cathedral Trail** and turn right. This leads you across Park Drive and the **pitch-and-putt golf area** at Lost Lagoon's western edge. Here you can:

☕ **TAKE A BREAK**   The **Fish House in Stanley Park,** 2099 Beach Ave. (☎ 604/681-7275), has a great oyster and clam bar. During the summer, there is an outdoor fish-and-chips stand where you can try fresh shellfish and other Pacific Northwest seafood snacks.

If you choose to continue along the Seawall, follow the walk to:

14. Prospect Point, the park's northernmost lookout, near Lions Gate Bridge. It has a spectacular view from atop a sheer 200-foot basalt cliff.

☕ **TAKE A BREAK**   The casual **Prospect Point Café** on the lookout is a popular place to get a snack and take in the view.

Continue on the Seawall Walk around to the park's English Bay side. At the 6.0-km marker, you will see:

15. Siwash Rock, which was a World War I battery site and a key searchlight position during World War II. According to Salish legend, the Transformer rewarded the warrior Skalish for his unselfishness by turning him into this natural monolith. You often see Chinese fisherman here casting their morning lines.

16. The Hollow Tree is accessible by a series of winding trails. Close by is a red cedar measuring 30 meters in circumference. Declared by the National Geographic Society to be the largest tree in the world, it is unsurprisingly called the **Geographic Tree.**

Halfway between the Seawall's 6.5-km and 7.0-km markers is the city's most northern beach:

17. Third Beach, which has a picnic area, rest rooms, and concession stands open for sunbathers who prefer a quieter spot than those at the other English Bay beaches. Many locals come here during the summer to have barbecues.

At the 7.0-km marker, you'll find:

18. Ferguson Point, another World War II artillery battery site. This is a good point to:

☕ **TAKE A BREAK**   The **Teahouse Restaurant,** converted from a 1920s army barracks, has been repeatedly touted as Vancouver's most romantic restaurant (see Chapter 5 for dining review).

At the 8.0-km marker, you'll find:

19. Second Beach. A popular family beach, it sports a saltwater swimming pool and Opperley Playground.

Just past the playground, a path heading south and inland leads back into the park. Take this path and you'll finally end up on Park Drive, which turns into Lagoon Drive. Walk along the roadside path. Stop at the tennis courts next to the Fish House Restaurant.

From here, you can either stroll to Lost Lagoon or return to the Seawall Walk and continue strolling along the bay side all the way to **English Bay Beach.**

Vancouver Shopping

8

Whether you're looking for a simple memento of your Vancouver visit or planning to "shop 'til you drop," be sure to allow some time in your schedule to explore Vancouver's hundreds of stores, specialty shops, and shopping centers. The selection of designer clothing boutiques, arts and crafts galleries, and sports and camping equipment outfitters won't disappoint you. The downtown area attracts a daily crowd of international shoppers from the U.S. and Europe and as far away as Japan and China.

1 The Shopping Scene

With such great shopping areas as **Robson Street** for the latest trendy fashions; **Granville Island** for crafts and kids' items; **Kerrisdale** for reasonably priced clothing to suit every taste; **Gastown** for First Nations art; and up-and-coming **Yaletown** for hip designer wear and furniture, it's hard to spend any time in Vancouver without gleefully going on a shopping spree.

Downtown Vancouver has attracted an international collection of name-brand designers, including **Salvatore Ferragamo, Chanel, Gianni Versace, Polo/Ralph Lauren,** and many more. Vancouver's real finds, however, are the bold, exciting, collectible, and often wearable art made by local fashion designers and craftspeople. Local artists are applying elements of First Nations, European, and Asian traditions to silk, leather, wood, gold, and silver.

Stroll along such neighborhoods as **West Point Grey** and **Kerrisdale** in Central Vancouver, where you'll find the locals shopping for everything from haute couture to funky and casual wear. Discover the hidden treasures in the city's ethnic areas such as **Chinatown, Richmond, Steveston, Little Italy, Greektown,** and the **Punjabi Market** (see "Neighborhoods," under "More Attractions" in Chapter 6).

Don't miss the bold Haida-influenced appliquéd leather vests and coats at **Dorothy Grant**'s boutique; **Zonda Nellis**'s sumptuously soft handwoven and hand-painted creations; or **Martha Sturdy**'s colorful yet functional handblown glass decorated with gold leaf.

You will find First Nations art in abundance. You don't have to purchase an impossible-to-find antique to acquire a original, quality Coast Salish or Haida work of art. As the experts at the Museum of Anthropology will tell you, if an item is crafted by any of the native Northwest Coast artisans, it's a real First Nations piece of art.

Pick up a copy of *Publication No. 10: A Guide to Buying Contemporary Northwest Coast Art* by Karen Duffel (available at the Museum of Anthropology), which explains how to identify and care for these beautifully carved and woven works. Then feast your eyes on the totem poles, ceremonial masks, bowls, sculptures, carvings, Cowichan sweaters, and beaded or metal jewelry at such shops as **The Inuit Gallery, Hill's Indian Crafts, Khot-La-Cha,** or the **Museum of Anthropology's Gift Shop.**

British Columbian wines—especially rich, honey-thick icewines (made by harvesting the grapes after the first frost has ruptured their skins and started the fermentation process, resulting in a particularly sweet flavor) such as Eric von Krosigk's gold-medal **Summerhill Estate 1992 Reisling Icewine** and bold Merlots such as Anne Sperling's gold medal **Cedar Creek 1992 Merlot**—are worth buying by the case. Five years of restructuring, reblending, and careful tending by French and German master vintners have brought these local vineyards world recognition. John Simes of Mission Hill won the Avery's Trophy in 1994 for his **1992 Grand Barrel Reserve Chardonnay** at the London International Wine and Spirits Competition. Knowledgeable staffs will help you discover the region's best at such shops as **Marquis Wine Cellars; The Okanagan Estate Wine Cellars;** and the government-operated **LDB stores.**

Salmon is all around you in Vancouver, and you can even send or bring a taste of this fish home. Shops throughout the city carry delectable smoked salmon in safe, vacuum-packed containers. Some shops offer decorative cedar gift boxes for an additional charge. If you decide to ship your catch home, you'll find most shop-keepers offer overnight delivery.

Don't stop at traditional salmon. Try such treats as **salmon jerky,** a chewy, unsalty West Coast alternative to the meat variety, or **Indian candy,** whose texture more closely resembles smoked salmon than jerky and whose meat is marinated and smoked with spices and a dash of honey or whiskey. The fishmongers at public markets, including Lonsdale Quay Market and Granville Island Public Market, are good places to taste these treats. The **Salmon Village** and **Olympia Fish and Chips** (see Chapter 5 for dining review) are also great places to pick up decoratively boxed gifts from the sea.

2 Shopping A to Z

ANTIQUES

With a little more than a century under its belt, Vancouver is a relatively young city, but you can find some great Chinese, Japanese, and European antiques here at the following places:

Potter's Gallery

Westin Bayshore Hotel, 1601 W. Georgia St. ☎ **604/685-3919** or 604/685-7412. SkyTrain: Burrard.

Established in 1924, this store sells Chinese and Japanese art as well as Kurf Sutton's fine porcelain flowers. Open daily from 8:30am to 6pm.

Three Centuries Shop

321 Water St. ☎ **604/685-8808.** Bus: 1 or 50.

French and English decorative arts, especially from the art deco and art nouveau periods, are featured at this store three doors down from the Gastown Steam Clock. Open Tuesday to Sunday from 10:30am to 5:30pm.

Uno Langmann Ltd.

2117 Granville St. ☎ **604/736-8825.** Bus: 10 or 20.

This world-famous gallery specializes in European and North American paintings from the 18th through early 20th centuries and a carefully selected collection of furniture, silver, and art objects. Open Tuesday through Saturday from 10am to 5pm, Monday by appointment only.

ART

Modern and First Nations artists are well represented in Vancouver. Even if you're not in the market, go gallery-hopping to see works by Haida artists **Bill Reid** (perhaps the best-known native artist) and **Richard Davidson** and by Kwakwaka'wakw artist/photographer **David Neel.** Contemporary Vancouver painters such as **Terence Johnson, Tiko Kerr,** photographer **Ed Olsen,** and sculptor **Alexander Schick** are just a small cross section of the creative talent you'll find here.

✪ Images for a Canadian Heritage

164 Water St. ☎ **604/685-7046.** Bus: 1 or 50.

Both this store and the Inuit Gallery of Vancouver (see below) are government-licensed First Nations galleries featuring traditional and contemporary art and artifacts. This spacious setting is not just an experience in buying art: It's also the perfect place to get an overall view of the range of materials and styles used in this marvelous art heritage. Open daily from 10am to 6pm.

Inuit Gallery of Vancouver

345 Water St. ☎ **604/688-7323.** Bus: 1 or 50.

This gallery contains one of Canada's foremost collections of Inuit and Northwest Coast First Nations art, displayed in a rich environment where you can really step back and see each piece. Open Monday to Saturday from 10am to 6pm, Sunday from noon to 5pm.

✪ Leona Lattimer Gallery

1590 W. 2nd Ave. ☎ **604/732-4556.** Ferry: Aquabus to Granville Island.

This beautiful gallery presents museum-quality displays of Pacific Northwest First Nations art—ceremonial masks, totem poles, limited-edition silkscreen prints, argillite sculptures, gold and silver jewelry—of the highest quality. The contemporary artists that are represented work in a variety of media and all of them are of a caliber not often seen. The gallery is open Monday through Saturday from 10am to 6pm; Sunday from noon to 5pm.

Marion Scott Ltd.

481 Howe St. ☎ **604/685-1934.** Bus: 401.

For more than 20 years, this gallery has been well regarded for its Inuit and Northwest Coast First Nations collections. Open Monday to Saturday from 9:30am to 5:30pm, Sunday from 10am to 5pm; closed Sundays during the winter.

BOOKS

Vancouver publishing houses produce a book a day. There's certainly a book-hungry local market—there are actually lines of people waiting to get into the bookstores and public libraries every morning. Check out titles by local Vancouverites and other British Columbians such as William Gibson, Nick Bantock, Anne Cameron, and Malcolm Lowry.

Blackberry Books

1663 Duranleau St. ☎ **604/685-4113** or 604/685-6188. Bus: 51. Boat: Granville Island Ferry or Aquabus.

Books about art, architecture, and fine cuisine are the specialties of this Granville Island store. The Kitsilano branch at 2855 W. Broadway (☎ 604/739-8116) has a great selection of fiction. New titles are displayed with staff reviews posted beside them. Both stores are open daily from 9am to 9pm.

Duthie Books
919 Robson St. ☎ **604/684-4496.** Bus: 3 or 8.

Since 1957, this six-branch, full-service, well-stocked, chain with a knowledgeable staff has carried a huge inventory of Canadian and American titles. They offer services such as special, mail, and out-of-print ordering. Open Monday to Friday from 9am to 9pm, Saturday from 9am to 6pm, Sunday from noon to 5pm. There are other branches at the following locations: Library branch, 345 Robson St., in Library Square (☎ 604/602-0610); University branch, 4444 W. Tenth Ave. (☎ 604/224-7012); Kitsilano branch, 2239 W. 4th Ave. (☎ 604/732-5344); Arbutus Shopping Centre, 4255 Arbutus St. (☎ 604/738-1833).

✪ Manhattan Books and Magazines
1089 Robson St. ☎ **604/681-9074.** Bus: 3 or 8.

In this very comfortable, packed-to-the rafters bookstore, you can find new releases; remainders; foreign-language titles in French, Spanish, and German; and international newspapers and periodicals. Open Monday to Wednesday 9am to 9pm, Thursday to Saturday from 9am to 10pm, Sunday from 10am to 6pm.

The Travel Bug
2667 W. Broadway. ☎ **604/737-1122.** Bus: 10.

This is an ideal place to discover your next travel destination. The store carries travel guides, travelogues, maps, globes, and any other printed matter travelers need. Open Monday to Wednesday plus Saturday from 10am to 6pm, Thursday and Friday from 10am to 8pm, Sunday from noon to 5pm.

White Dwarf
4368 W. 10th Ave. ☎ **604/228-8223.** Bus: 10.

Sci-fi fans will love browsing the stacks at this specialty bookstore. Open Monday to Friday from 10am to 8pm, Saturday from 10am to 6pm, Sunday from noon to 5pm.

Worldwide Books and Maps
736A Granville St. ☎ **604/687-3320.** Bus: 4 or 10.

Across from Eaton's department store on Granville St., there's a narrow staircase that leads down to the best selection of travel books and maps in town. Among the books, maps, and globes there is an impressive selection of special-interest B.C. guides with topics ranging from backcountry skiing and minimum impact hiking to off-road four wheeling. This is the hikers best source of detailed topographic maps of the entire province. Open Monday to Saturday 9am to 6pm.

CHINA, SILVER & CRYSTAL

You can observe the potters, silversmiths, and glassblowers on Granville Island while they create both whimsical and elegant tableware. Another local, **Martha Sturdy,** has a downtown shop. There is a great array of sophisticated international china and crystal in downtown stores.

Atkinson's
3057 Granville St. ☎ **604/736-3378.** Bus: 20.

Baccarat and Lalique crystal, Cristofle silver, Haviland Limoges, Hermès china, and Liberty's of London linens are just a few of the items you can buy here to grace your table settings or bed. Open Tuesday to Saturday from 10am to 5:30pm.

Gallery of B.C. Ceramics

1359 Cartwright St. ☎ **604/669-5645.** Bus: 51. Boat: Granville Island Ferry or Aquabus.

This Granville Island gallery loft, owned and operated by the Potters Guild of British Columbia, presents a lively, juried collection of more than 70 sculptural and utilitarian ceramic works. Open Tuesday to Sunday from 10:30am to 5:30pm; open daily May through October.

✪ Martha Sturdy Designs

775 Burrard St. ☎ **604/685-7751.** Bus: 17.

Jewelry designer Martha Sturdy creates collectible, useable, handblown glassware trimmed in gold leaf. Open Monday to Friday from 10am to 6pm, Saturday from 10am to 8pm, Sunday from noon to 5pm.

DEPARTMENT STORES

An important player in Canadian history, the **Hudson's Bay Company** was instrumental in developing Canada's western territories and setting up trading posts along the pioneer trails and in the forts. It still maintains a major presence in Vancouver. A window-shopping tour of "The Bay's" sporting equipment department alone will give you a feel for its high standards of quality.

The Bay (Hudson's Bay Company)

674 Granville St. ☎ **604/681-6211.** SkyTrain: Granville. Bus: 8.

From its early trading posts and forts in the 1670s to its modern coast-to-coast chain, "The Bay" has sold quality Canadian goods. Instead of lingerie on the second floor, however, you'll find camping and sports equipment. You can still buy a Hudson's Bay woolen point blanket (the colorful stripes originally represented how many beaver pelts were traded), but you'll also find Tommy Hilfiger, Polo, DKNY, Ellen Tracy, Anne Klein II, and Liz Claiborne. Open Monday to Wednesday from 9:30am to 6pm, Thursday and Friday from 9:30am to 9pm, Saturday from 9:30am to 5:30pm, Sunday from 11am to 5:30pm.

Eaton's

Pacific Centre Mall, 701 Granville St. ☎ **604/685-7112.** SkyTrain: Granville. Bus: 8.

Eaton's is a lot like Saks Fifth Avenue: It carries fashions that range from classic to outrageous, china and crystal, kitchenware, gourmet foods, and books. The seventh-floor bargain annex sells discount children's and men's clothing. Open Monday to Wednesday from 9:30am to 6pm, Thursday and Friday from 9:30am to 9pm, Saturday from 9:30am to 5:30pm, Sunday from noon to 5pm.

DISCOUNT SHOPPING

If a great deal is what you're after, you can find substantial discounts on high-quality merchandise from designer clothing to sporting goods.

Second Suit for Men & Women

2036 W. Fourth Ave. ☎ **604/732-0338.** Bus: 4.

This resale/sample clothing store has the best in men's and women's designs from Hugo Boss, Armani, Donna Karan, and Alfred Sung. Open Monday to Friday from 10am to 6pm, Saturday from 10am to 5:30pm, Sunday from noon to 5pm.

SportMart Discount Superstore
2300 Cambie St. ☎ **604/873-6737.** Bus: 9, 15, or 17.

Great deals on skiing, in-line skating, running, and snowboarding equipment as well as clothing and accessories. Open daily from 10am to 9pm.

Turn Me Loose for Men
1813 W. First Ave. ☎ **604/739-1080.** Bus: 22.

This store sells men's designer casual and evening clothes plus accessories at discounted prices year-round. There's also a consignment section for used clothes. Open Monday to Thursday from 10am to 6pm, Friday from 10am to 8pm, Saturday from 10am to 5:30pm, Sunday from noon to 5pm.

FASHIONS
CHILDREN'S

Why dress your kids in Gap and Esprit when you can delight them with the one-of-a-kind, colorful clothes created by Vancouver's local designers?

✪ Iago-go
1496 Cartwright St. ☎ **604/689-2400.** Bus: 51.

This Granville Island shop, located in the Kids Only market, has a beautiful selection of colorfully printed, handcrafted children's fashions. Open Monday to Thursday and Saturday and Sunday from 10am to 6pm, Friday from 10am to 9pm.

Isola Bella
5692 Yew St. ☎ **604/266-8808.** Bus: 41st St.

This store carries an exclusive collection of imported newborn, boys', and girls' clothing from designers such as Babar, Babymini, and Paul Smith. Open Monday to Saturday from 10am to 5:30pm or by appointment.

Please Mum
2951 W. Broadway St. ☎ **604/732-4574.** Bus: 10.

This Kitsilano store sells attractively designed, Vancouver-made toddler's and children's cotton clothing. Open Monday to Thursday and Saturday from 9:30am to 6pm, Friday from 9:30am to 8pm, Sunday from noon to 5pm.

MEN'S & WOMEN'S

Vancouver has the best collection of clothes from Paris, London, Milan, and Rome in the Pacific Northwest in addition to the greatest assortment of locally made cutting-edge fashion. Check out **Patricia Fieldwalder**'s silky lingerie at fine stores; or if you're in the market for bridal wear, don't miss **Christine and Company**'s romantic gowns and trousseau items.

International designers represented here include the following: **Chanel Boutique,** 103-755 Burrard St. (☎ 604/682-0522); **Salvatore Ferragamo,** 918 Robson St. (☎ 604/669-4495); **Romeo Gigli,** 769 Hornby St. (☎ 604/669-8080); **Gianni Versace's Istante,** 773 Hornby St. (☎ 604/669-8398); **Versace's Versus,** 1008 W. Georgia St. (☎ 604/688-8938); **Polo Ralph Lauren,** The Landing, 375 Water St. (☎ 604/682-7656); and **Plaza Escada,** Sinclair Centre, 757 W. Hastings St. (☎ 604/688-8558).

It seems like almost every week, a new, local designer boutique is opening in Yaletown, the once industrial loft and studio area filled with home-furnishings showrooms and restaurants. Key local designers and international specialty stores carrying men's and women's fashions include the following:

✪ Christine and Company
250 18th St., West Vancouver. ☎ **604/922-0350**. Bus: 250.

More than 20 years ago, Vancouverite Christine Morton started out selling delicate antique lacy things along with a few of her own lingerie creations. She expanded to romantic silky blouses and heirloom-quality trousseau lingerie. She's regarded as the hottest bridal-wear designer in town. Open Monday to Friday from 9am to 5pm, Saturday from 10am to 4pm.

✪ Dorothy Grant
Sinclair Centre, 250-757 W. Hastings St. ☎ **604/681-0201**. SkyTrain: Waterfront. Bus: 22.

In a shop modeled after a Haida longhouse, First Nations designer Dorothy Grant exhibits her husband Robert Davidson's collection of exquisitely detailed Haida motifs appliquéd on coats, leather vests, jackets, caps, and accessories. Their clothes are gorgeous. She also carries contemporary Haida art and jewelry. Open weekdays from 10am to 6pm, Saturdays from 10am to 5:30pm, Sundays from noon to 5pm.

E. A. Lee Ltd.
466 Howe St. ☎ **604/683-2457**. Bus: 10, 14, or 20.

A historic 1920s building complete with a centerpiece fountain is the home of this classic European men's and women's clothing store. It features Versace, Cerutti, Karl Lagerfeld, Luciano Soprani, and Zilli in luscious cashmere, leather, cotton, and silk. Open Monday to Saturday from 9am to 5:30pm.

Leone
Sinclair Centre, 757 W. Hastings St. ☎ **604/683-1133**. SkyTrain: Waterfront. Bus: 22.

Gianni Versace, Donna Karan, Byblos, Armani, and fabulous Italian and French accessories are sold in this beautiful architectural masterpiece frequented by film stars and celebrities. Open Monday to Friday from 9:30am to 6pm, Saturday from 9:30am to 5:30pm, Sunday from noon to 5pm.

Look Sharp
150-12240 2nd Ave., Richmond. ☎ **604/275-5860**. Bus: 401 or 406.

This store features Canadian-made wearable art, including high fashion, casual styles, jewelry, and shoes, by local designers. Open Monday to Saturday from 10am to 6pm, Sunday from noon to 6pm.

LuLu Island Designs
Steveston Landing, 119-3800 Bayview St., Richmond. ☎ **604/275-5858**. Bus: 401 or 406.

Inside this historic cannery amid artifacts from Steveston's days as a 19th-century Japanese fishing village are high-quality embroidered and screened shirts. Open daily from 10am to 5pm.

Straiths
Hotel Vancouver, 900 W. Georgia St. ☎ **604/685-3301**. SkyTrain: Granville.

If Valentino, Ungaro, Bally, and Testoni are your preferences, then visit this well-known establishment, which features the best clothing and accessories from the world's leading designers. Open Monday to Wednesday from 8:30am to 6pm, Thursday and Friday from 8:30am to 8pm, Saturday from 8:30am to 5:30pm, Sunday from 8:30am to 12:30pm.

✪ Zonda Nellis Design Ltd.
2203 S. Granville St. ☎ **604/736-5668**. Bus: 10 or 20.

Rich colors and patterns highlight this Vancouver designer's imaginative handwoven separates, pleated silks, sweaters, vests, and soft knits. Nellis has also introduced a new line of hand-painted silks and velvets that coordinate with her signature weaves. Open Monday to Saturday from 11am to 5pm.

FIRST NATIONS ARTS & CRAFTS

Bold, traditional, and innovative designs; intricate carvings; strong primary colors; and rich wood stains are just a few of the elements you'll find in First Nations works. Pacific Northwest Coastal tribes, including the Haida, Coast Salish, and Kwakwaka'wakw, create crafts, jewelry, and art.

Authentic Cowichan Indian Knits
424 W. 3rd St., North Vancouver. ☎ **604/988-4735.** Bus: 242.

Freda Nahanee's cottage-industry shop, on the North Vancouver Squamish Band Reserve, carries Vancouver Island–made sweaters; carved-silver Kwakiutl jewelry; Squamish woodcarvings; beaded leather moccasins; and woven baskets. Open Monday to Saturday from 10am to 6pm.

Hill's Indian Crafts
165 Water St. ☎ **604/685-4249.** Bus: 1 or 50.

In the re-created interior of a trading post, this First Nations shop features moccasins; ceremonial masks; Cowichan sweaters; wood sculptures; totem poles; serigraphic prints; soapstone sculptures; and gold, silver, and argillite jewelry. Open daily from 9am to 9pm.

Khot-La-Cha Salish Handicrafts
270 Whonoak St., West Vancouver. ☎ **604/987-3339.** Bus: 210.

Hand-tanned moosehide crafts; carvings; Cowichan sweaters; porcupine quill jewelry; and bone, silver, gold, and turquoise accessories are just a few of the selections at this Coast Salish crafts shop. Open Monday to Friday from noon to 5pm, Saturday from 10am to 5pm.

✪ Museum of Anthropology
University of British Columbia, 6393 NW Marine Dr. ☎ **604/822-5087.** Bus: 4 and 10.

Works by contemporary First Nations artisans as well as cultural books and publications on identifying and caring for Pacific Northwest crafts are the highlights of this museum store. Open Wednesday to Monday from 11am to 5pm, Tues from 11am to 9pm. Closed Monday September through mid-May.

FOOD

Even though salmon is the most popular item to buy in Vancouver, coffee flows like water—as does Belgian chocolate.

✪ Au Chocolat
1702 Davie St. ☎ **604/682-3536.** Bus: 3 or 8.

If you are a true chocolaholic, you must stop at this coffee bar/chocolatier. They craft the most delectable Belgian chocolate truffles and shaped chocolates. The owner/pastry chef developed his own recipes, and the result is decadent perfection. You can have chocolates shipped to anywhere in lovely little boxes. You can even taste a few truffles with a good espresso or a scoop of handmade ice cream inside or out on the tree-shaded sidewalk patio. Open Monday to Friday from 7:30am to 10pm, Saturday and Sunday from 7:30am to 11pm.

Cheena B.C. Limited
667 Howe St. ☎ **604/684-5374.** Bus: 401; or walk.

If fresh seafood is on your list of items to bring home, then place your order in advance from this downtown shop. They will pack your catch (or selection) in a sturdy carton surrounded by ice packs and have it ready for pickup on the day of your departure. Open daily 9am to 7pm; open Thursday and Friday until 9pm.

The Lobsterman
1807 Mast Tower Rd. ☎ **604/687-4531.** Bus: 51. Boat: Granville Island Ferry or Aquabus.

Live lobsters, Dungeness crab, oysters, mussels, clams, geoduck, and scallops are just a few of the varieties of seafood swimming in the saltwater tanks at this Granville Island fish store. They steam the food fresh on the spot for free. Salmon and other seafood can be packed for air travel if you don't get your fill. Open daily from 9am to 6pm.

Murchie's Tea & Coffee
970 Robson St. ☎ **604/662-3776.** Bus: 8.

This Vancouver institution has been the city's main purveyor of tea and coffee for more than a century. You'll find everything from Jamaican Blue Mountain and Kona coffees to Lapsing Souchong and Kemun teas. Their knowledgeable staff will help you decide which flavors and blends fit your tastes. They even carry bone china and crystal serving ware as well as coffeemakers and teapots. Open Monday to Wednesday and Saturday from 9:30am to 6pm, Thursday to Friday from 9:30am to 9pm, Sunday from noon to 5pm. There is also a shop at 1200 Homer St. (☎ 604/662-3776), which is open daily from 9:30am to 5pm.

Salmon Village
779 Thurlow St. ☎ **604/685-3378.** Bus: 8.

Smoked salmon (from their own plant), salmon jerky, Indian candy, and caviar are a few of the gourmet specialties you can have wrapped and shipped to deserving loved ones back home. They also have a great selection of prepackaged gift boxes for last-minute purchases. Open daily from 9am to 10pm.

Ten Ren Tea & Ginseng Co.
550 Main St. ☎ **604/684-1566.** Bus: 19 or 22.

Whether you prefer the pungent taste of Chinese black teas or the exotic fragrances of chrysanthemum, jasmine, or ginger flower–laced teas, you must try the numerous varieties of drinking and medicinal teas in this Chinatown shop. They also carry Korean, American, and Siberian ginseng in the forms of extract, tea, and dried root for a lot less than what you might pay elsewhere. Open daily from 9:30am to 6pm.

GIFTS/SOUVENIRS
Here are some unconventional places to buy items that won't look like they were made somewhere else.

Canadian Impressions at the Station
601 Cordova St. ☎ **604/681-3507.** SkyTrain: Waterfront.

This souvenir shop stocks good, plain lumberjack shirts and Cowichan sweaters next to printed T-shirts and baseball caps. You'll also find salmon jerky, maple syrup, and shortbread cookies. There are the requisite mugs, plates, and other memorabilia amid more unique items. Open Monday to Friday and Sunday from 9am to 9pm, Saturday from 9am to 10pm.

Cows Vancouver
1301 Robson St. ☎ **604/682-2622.** Bus: 3 or 8.

Everybody knows at least one cow memorabilia collector, and this is the perfect place to buy a gift for that special person in your life. T-shirts, tableware, accessories, children's clothes, and towels are just a few of the bovine items sold. They also serve delicious handmade ice cream in fresh waffle cones. Open Monday through Thursday 10am to 10pm; Friday and Saturday 10am to 11pm; and Sunday noon to 10pm.

Nikaido Gifts

150-3580 Moncton St., Richmond. ☎ **604/275-0262.** Bus: 401 or 406.

Wedding kimonos, antique Hina dolls, yukata, plates, dishes, and many other lovely Oriental items fill this gift store in Steveston Village. Open Monday to Thursday from 10am to 5pm, Friday and Saturday from 10am to 8pm, Sunday from 10am to 5pm.

The Ocean Floor

1525 Duranleau. ☎ **604/681-5014.** Bus: 51. Boat: Granville Island Ferry or Aquabus.

If you want to bring home a few gifts from the sea, then select from among this Granville Island shop's collection of shells, shell jewelry, ship models, lamps, chimes, corals, and marine brass. Open daily from 9:30am to 5:30pm, Saturday from 10:30am to 5:30pm.

Return to Sender

1076 Davie St. ☎ **604/683-6363.** Bus: 3 or 8.

This card and novelty shop has all sorts of fun postables, from Canadian wildflower seed postcards to some rather risqué and ribald cards you wouldn't send to Mom. Open Monday to Wednesday from 11am to 8pm, Thursday and Friday from 11am to 9pm, Saturday from 10:30am to 7pm, Sunday from noon to 6pm.

JEWELRY

With influences ranging from European and Asian to First Nations, Vancouver jewelers offer baubles for every taste and budget.

Forge and Form

1334 Cartwright St. ☎ **604/684-6298.** Bus: 51. Boat: Granville Island Ferry or Aquabus.

Master Granville Island metal designers Dietje Hagedoorn and Jürgen Schönheit specialize in customized gold and silver jewelry. Curvaceous settings accentuate brilliant gemstones. Strong lines are a hallmark of their designs. Open daily from 9:30am to 6pm.

Henry Birks & Sons Ltd.

Vancouver Centre, 710 Granville St. ☎ **604/669-3333.** SkyTrain: Granville. Bus: 4, 10, or 20.

Established in 1879, Birks has a long tradition of designing and creating beautiful jewelry and watches, as well as selling jewelry to an array of international designers. Open Monday to Wednesday from 9:30am to 6pm, Thursday and Friday from 9:30am to 9pm, Saturday from 9:30am to 5:30pm.

Jade World

1696 W. First Ave. ☎ **604/733-7212.** Bus: 22; then walk one block west to Burrard and one block north at Cornwall.

The shop's three master carvers conduct free tours of their factory and studio. Jade World mines its own northern British Columbian jade, fashioning it into numerous specially designed items. Open Monday to Friday from 8am to 4:30pm; open Saturdays from May through September.

✪ Karl Stittgen + Goldsmiths
2203 Granville St. ☎ **604/737-0029.** Bus: 4 or 10.

Stittgen's cleanly designed gold pins, pendants, rings, and other accessories show his commitment to fine craftsmanship. Each work is a miniature architectural wonder. Open Tuesday to Saturday from 10am to 5pm.

MALLS/SHOPPING CENTERS

To ensure that the rain doesn't make shopping problematical, city developers have established great shopping centers, some of which stretch for more than three blocks through underground concourses and plazas. They're filled with everything you could ever want—from boutiques to casual wear stores; from formal restaurants to food courts; from accessories to outdoor equipment. There are even a few downtown shopping centers created from renovated landmark buildings that are worth walking through for their architecture alone.

The Landing
375 Water St. ☎ **604/687-1144.** SkyTrain: Waterfront.

This 1905 Gastown heritage building was renovated from a warehouse into a complex of shops and offices. Designer boutiques such as Polo Ralph Lauren and Fleet Street as well as diverse restaurants offer unique ways to indulge yourself. Open Monday to Wednesday and Saturday to Sunday from 9:30am to 5:30pm, Thursday to Friday from 9:30am to 9pm.

Pacific Centre Mall
700 W. Georgia St. ☎ **604/688-7236.** SkyTrain: Granville.

This three-block complex contains 200 shops and services, including Godiva, Benetton, Crabtree and Evelyn, and Eddie Bauer. Underground concourses make this a pleasant experience on rainy days. Open Monday to Wednesday from 9:30am to 6pm, Thursday and Friday from 9:30am to 9pm, Saturday from 9:30am to 5:30pm, Sunday from 11am to 5pm.

Park Royal Shopping Centre
2002 Park Royal South, West Vancouver. ☎ **604/925-9576.** Bus: 250 or 253.

Park Royal really consists of two malls facing each other on Marine Drive. The Gap, Disney, Eaton's, The Bay, Eddie Bauer, and its own Public Market are just a few of the 200 stores in this full-service center. There are also cinemas, bowling lanes, a golf driving range, community and special events, and a food court. Open Monday to Wednesday from 10am to 6pm, Thursday and Friday from 10am to 9pm, Saturday from 9:30am to 5:30pm, Sunday from noon to 6pm.

Sinclair Centre
757 W. Hastings St. ☎ **604/666-4438.** SkyTrain: Waterfront. Bus: 22.

Four restored landmark buildings—the Post Office (1910), Winch Building (1911), Customs Examining Warehouse (1913), and Federal Building (1937)—house such elite shops as Leone and Dorothy Grant, as well as other boutiques, art galleries, a food court, and year-round afternoon entertainment. Most stores open Monday to Friday from 10am to 5:30pm, Saturday from 10am to 5pm.

Vancouver Centre
650 W. Georgia St. ☎ **604/684-7537.** SkyTrain: Granville.

The Bay, Birks jewelers, a restaurant, food fair, and more than 115 specialty stores connect underground to the adjoining Pacific Centre (see above). Open Monday to

Wednesday and Saturday from 9:30am to 6pm, Thursday and Friday from 9:30am to 9pm, Sunday from noon to 5pm.

MARKETS

Vancouverites love shopping at the **green markets** scattered throughout the city. You don't have to go grocery shopping to have fun at these enclosed atriums and multi-level spaces; you just need to enjoy sampling food, looking at crafts, tasting B.C. wines, or people-watching. In the commercial harbor area, you'll also find a huge **flea market** in one of the old wharf-side terminal complexes with as great a mix of stuff as you could possibly imagine.

GREENMARKETS

✪ Granville Island Public Market

1669 Johnston St., Granville Island. ☎ **604/666-5784.** Bus: 51. Boat: Granville Island Ferry or Aquabus.

The 50,000-square-foot public market features produce, meats, fish, wines, cheeses, and lots of fast-food counters where you can get a plate of Chinese, vegetarian, Mexican, or just about any other kind of food. Open daily from 9am to 6pm; closed Monday in winter except public holidays. From mid-June through September, the farmers' truck market operates on Thursday from 9am to 6pm.

Lonsdale Quay Market

123 Carrie Cates Court, North Vancouver. ☎ **604/985-6261.** SeaBus: Lonsdale Quay.

Located right at the entrance to the SeaBus terminal, this public market is filled with produce; meats; fish; specialty fashion; gift shops; food counters; coffee bars; its own hotel; and Kids' Alley, a section dedicated to children's shops with a play area. The upper floor houses a variety of fashion stores, bookstores, gift shops. Open Saturday to Thursday from 9:30am to 6:30pm, Friday from 9:30am to 9pm.

Robson Public Market

1610 Robson St. ☎ **604/682-2733.** Bus: 8.

On your way to Stanley Park, stop into this market in a modern glass atrium that houses produce sellers, great bakeries, fishmongers, and butchers. The food courts offer French, Italian, Greek, Chinese, and Japanese delights as well as bagels, pita sandwiches, and other picnic foods. Open daily from 9am to 9pm.

FLEA MARKETS

Vancouver Flea Market

703 Terminal Ave. ☎ **604/685-0666.** Bus: 3, 8, or 19.

Located near the bus terminal, Vancouver's largest flea market houses more than 350 stalls in an old warehouse. Admission is 60¢ for adults; children under 12 free. Open Saturday, Sunday, and holidays from 9am to 5pm.

MEMORABILIA

The Canadian-Pacific Railway made Vancouver a great metropolis. **Railway World** in Gastown carries a fine collection of CP's engines, passenger and freight cars, and volumes of nostalgic reminiscences about the building and running of this railroad giant.

Railway World

150 Water St. ☎ **604/681-4811.** Bus: 1 or 50.

Lovers of model trains, cars, and planes will be in seventh heaven in this small but packed-to-the-rafters shop. There are some great Canadian model trains in both N and O gauges, as well as collectors' books. Open Monday to Thursday from 11am to 6pm, Friday from 11am to 8pm, and Saturday from 11am to 7pm.

MUSIC

You'll find a good assortment and great prices on recorded music throughout the city. No matter what your musical tastes are, Vancouver's got a store that caters to you.

Crosstown Music

518 W. Pender St. ☎ **604/683-8774.** Bus: 19.

For used CDs, tapes, and albums with rock, jazz, and blues, you can't beat the quality and selection at this small but packed shop. Open daily from 10am to 6pm.

MC Productions

505–1701 Powell St. at Commercial Drive. ☎ **604/255-7869.** Bus: 20.

Vintage-record collector Mickey Clark has a huge library of 37,000 vaudeville, personality, jazz, blues, operatic, and classical recordings dating from the 1900s. He produces preprogrammed and special-request cassette tapes of these collected 78s and 33s in both 60- and 90-minute formats for under $20. Hours are by appointment only.

Sam the Record Man

568 Seymour St. Phone number unlisted. Bus: 3, 8, or 19.

Don't ask us why Sam doesn't have a phone at any of his four locations—we don't know. With four floors of tapes, CDs, and videos that cover a full range of sounds, he sure should have his own number. Open daily from 10am to 6pm.

SHOES

A walking city has to have some great outlets for buying good shoes. In Vancouver you'll find ornate cowboy boots, sturdy Dr. Martin's, funky clogs, weatherproof hiking shoes, and boots along with fine Swiss and Italian footwear.

John Fluevog Boots & Shoes Ltd.

837 Granville St. ☎ **604/688-2828.** Bus: 4 or 10.

This native Vancouverite has a growing following of designers and models who are clamoring for his under- $200 creations. You'll find outrageous platforms and clogs, Angelic Sole workboots, and a few bizarre experiments for the truly daring foot fetishist. Open Monday to Friday from 10:30am to 6:30pm, Saturday from 10:30am to 7:30pm, Sunday from noon to 5pm.

David Gordon

790 Robson St. ☎ **604/685-3784.** Bus: 8.

This is Vancouver's oldest Western boot, hat, and accessories store. Its boot selection includes Tony Lama, Boulet, and Dan Post. Open Monday to Wednesday and Saturday from 10am to 6pm; Friday from 10am to 9pm, Sunday from 11am to 5pm.

Roots Canada

Pacific Centre, 701 W. Georgia St. ☎ **604/683-5465.** SkyTrain: Granville.

For more than 20 years, this chain has featured sturdy, rugged, causal clothing made in Canada for the whole family. Their wares include leather jackets, leather bags, footwear, outerwear, and athletic wear. Open Monday to Wednesday from 9:30am to 6pm, Thursday and Friday from 9:30am to 9pm, Saturday from 9:30am to 5:30pm, Sunday from 11am to 5pm.

TOBACCO

Vancouver has a special treat for pipe and cigar aficionados alike: tobacconists who feature real Havana cigars and custom pipe blends made from Latakia and Perique imported leaves.

R. J. Clarke Tobacconist
3 Alexander St. ☎ **604/687-4136.** Bus: 1 or 50.

Vancouver's oldest custom tobacconist, R. J. Clarke has maintained its original 19th-century Gastown shop. If you've never had a real imported Cuban cigar (it puts a Tampa to shame), then choose a smoke from two floor-to-ceiling glass humidor cabinets of the best. Many American visitors come here to buy a few types (to consume in Canada, of course). You can also select a custom-blend pipe tobacco. Open Monday to Saturday from 10am to 5:30pm, Sunday from noon to 5pm.

TOYS

Kids Only Market
1496 Cartwright St. ☎ **604/684-0066.** Bus: 51.

This 24-shop Granville Island complex has everything to fulfill any kid's desire for fun, including toys, craft kits, games, computer software, and books. Open Monday to Thursday and Saturday to Sunday from 10am to 6pm, Friday from 10am to 9pm.

Kites on Clouds
The Courtyard, 131 Water St. ☎ **604/669-5677.** Bus: 1 or 50.

This little Gastown shop has every type of kite you could ever want for a pleasant afternoon at the beach or the park. Prices range from $10 to $20 for nylon or Mylar dragon kites to under $200 for more elaborate ghost clippers and nylon hang glider kites. Open Monday to Saturday from noon to 5:30pm.

VINTAGE CLOTHING

Vintage clothing is not trendy here, but there is one place where you can go if you're looking for a few hip items to round out your wardrobe.

True Value Vintage Clothing
710 Robson St. ☎ **604/685-5403.** Bus: 3, 4, 8, or 10.

This place has a funky collection of fashions from the '30s through '90s, including tons of fake furs, leather jackets, denims, sweaters, and accessories. Open daily 11am to 7pm; Sunday noon to 6pm.

WINE

British Columbian wines are being widely recognized by international connoisseurs. They've recently garnered praise from wine competitions in London and Paris. Look for the VQA (Vintner Quality Alliance) seal on the label—a guarantee that all grapes used are B.C.-grown and meet European standards for growing and processing. (VQA wines are accredited through lengthy blind tastings by a jury of winemakers and industry experts.)

   Summerhill, Cedar Creek, Mission Hill, and **Okanagan Vineyards** are just of few of the more than 50 local estates producing hearty Cabernet Sauvignons, honey rich icewines, and oaky Merlots. These wines can be found at incredibly good prices at any government-owned **LDB** liquor store such as the one on 1716 Robson St. (☎ 604/660-4576 or call 604/660-9463 for the nearest location) and some privately owned wine stores (see below).

Marquis Wine Cellars
1034 Davie St. ☎ **604/684-0445** or 604/685-2246. Bus: 3 or 8.

The owner and staff of this West End wine shop are dedicated to educating their patrons about wines with monthly newsletters and stacks of pamphlets in the entrance of their large Davie Street establishment. They also conduct evening wine tastings, which feature selections from their special blends. In addition to carrying a full range of B.C. wines, they also have a beautiful array of international wines. Open Monday to Wednesday from noon to 8pm, Thursday to Saturday from noon to 9pm.

The Okanagan Estate Wine Cellar
The Bay, 674 Granville St. ☎ **604/681-6211.** SkyTrain: Granville. Bus: 8, 10, or 20.

This annex in The Bay offers a great selection of British Columbian wines on the Vancouver Centre mall level. Open Monday to Wednesday from 9:30am to 6pm, Thursday and Friday from 9:30am to 9pm, Saturday from 9:30am to 5:30pm, Sunday from noon to 5pm.

9

Vancouver After Dark

There are a lot of exciting things going on after dark in Vancouver, from Pavarotti at the Queen Elizabeth Theatre to Andrew Lloyd Weber's next premiere. There's also plenty of original material presented by local talent throughout the year. If you want to get an overview of Vancouver's nightlife, pick up a copy of *The Georgia Straight*, a weekly tabloid, or a copy of *Xtra! West*, the gay and lesbian biweekly tabloid. You can find both at bookstores, venues, and curbside boxes. The monthly *Vancouver Magazine* is a lot like *New York* magazine: It's filled with listings and strong views about what's really hot in the city. On the Internet, you can check out Vancouver club listings, band profiles, and movie reviews on http://www.axionet.com/euphony/clubs.html.

The Vancouver Cultural Alliance Arts Hotline, 938 Howe St., in the Orpheum Theatre (☎ 604/684-2787), is a great source of information about all major cultural events, including where and how to get tickets (which are not always easy to get here). The office is open Monday to Friday from 9am to 5pm.

You can purchase tickets for many major performances at the Travel InfoCentre. If you are willing to pay a service charge, you can also buy tickets at **TicketMaster (Vancouver Ticket Centre),** 1304 Hornby St. (☎ 604/280-3311), which has 40 outlets in the greater Vancouver area, including all Eaton's department stores and major shopping malls.

Tickets and reservations for the smaller theater and community events, lectures, and special attractions in Vancouver are handled through **Community Box Offices,** 1234 W. Hastings St. (☎ 604/280-2801). They sell tickets for events at the Commodore Ballroom, Massey Theatre, Firehall Arts Centre, Station Street Arts Center, and Richard's on Richards. The office is open Monday to Saturday from 9am to 5:30pm.

There are three major Vancouver theaters where touring performers play. **The Orpheum Theatre,** 801 Granville St., an elegant 1927 theater that once hosted the Chicago-based Orpheum vaudeville circuit, is the refurbished home of the Vancouver Symphony Orchestra. Its ornate interior is filled with crystal chandeliers, gilded arches, domes, and an original Wurlitzer organ. The theater also hosts pop, rock, and variety shows.

The Queen Elizabeth Complex, 600 Hamilton St. (☎ 604/280-4444), consisting of the Queen Elizabeth Theatre and the Vancouver Playhouse, hosts major national touring musical and theater productions. It is also home to the Vancouver Opera and Ballet British Columbia. The small, 670-seat **Vancouver Playhouse** presents chamber music performances and recitals.

The Ford Center for the Performing Arts, on Homer Street off Robson Street, opened its doors in November 1995 with its production of *Showboat.*

Located in a converted turn-of-the-century church, the **Vancouver East Cultural Centre,** 1895 Venables St. (☎ 604/254-9578), has an impressive program, including avant-garde theater productions; performances by international musical groups; festivals and cultural events; children's programs; and art exhibitions. The box office is open Monday to Friday from 10am to 5pm.

1 The Performing Arts

THEATER

The dramatic stage is very much alive and well in Vancouver. There are a number of well-recognized groups performing classic works as well as new, controversial dramatic pieces. Theater isn't only an indoor pastime here; it goes outdoors in the summertime, with events such as the Shakespearean series Bard on the Beach (in Vanier Park) and Theatre Under the Stars (in Stanley Park). Major Broadway productions also stop in Vancouver, so you can see *Kiss of the Spider Woman, Showboat,* or even an Andrew Lloyd Weber premiere without ever touching foot in London or Manhattan.

Arts Club Theatre

1585 Johnston St. ☎ **604/687-1644.** Tickets $8.50–$24.50. Student and senior discounts. Box office open Monday–Saturday 10am–7pm. Bus: 51 .

Originally founded in 1958 as a private club for artists, musicians, and actors, this complex has two theaters. The 425-seat Granville Island Mainstage, established in 1979, presents major dramas, comedies, and musicals with post-performance entertainment in the Backstage Lounge. The Arts Club Revue Stage is an intimate, cabaret-style showcase for small productions, improvisation nights, and musical revues such as *Ain't Misbehavin'.*

Firehall Arts Centre

280 E. Cordova St. ☎ **604/689-0926.** Ticket prices usually $12–$15. Senior and student discounts. Box office open Tues–Fri 5pm–show time; Sat 6:30pm–show time; Sun 5:30pm–show time. Bus: 8.

Originally Vancouver's Firehouse No. 1, this center is the 20-year home of three cutting-edge companies—the Firehall Theatre Co., the Touchstone Theatre, and Axis Mime. The companies present dance events, arts festivals, and concerts in addition to their regular programs.

Frederic Wood Theatre

Gate 4, University of British Columbia. ☎ **604/822-2678.** Tickets $10 adults, $7 students; summer season, all seats $10. Box office open Mon–Fri 8:30am–4:30pm. Bus: 10.

Talented UBC students stage year-round productions from classic dramatic works to Broadway musicals. They present lighter material during their summer season.

Theatre Under the Stars

Malkin Bowl in Stanley Park. ☎ **604/687-0174.** Tickets $16 adults, $10 seniors and children. Box office open Mon–Sat 7–8:30pm (curtain time). Bus: 8.

From mid-July to mid-August, professional and amateur popular musical productions are performed outdoors in the bandshell. Bring a blanket and a picnic dinner for a relaxing evening of summer entertainment.

Vancouver Little Theatre

Heritage Hall, 3102 Main St. (enter from the back alley). ☎ **604/876-4165.** Ticket prices usually $7–$12. Senior and student discounts. Box office open 30 minutes before show time. Bus: 3.

Works by new Canadian playwrights as well as controversial international dramatists are presented by a variety of professional, local, and traveling companies.

Vancouver Playhouse

543 W. 7th Ave. ☎ **604/876-4165.** Ticket prices usually $7–$12. Senior and student discounts. Box office open 30 minutes before show time. Bus: 4 or 10.

Now in its third decade of entertaining more than 18,000 patrons per production, the company presents six plays each season.

Waterfront Theatre

1412 Cartwright St. ☎ **604/685-6217.** Ticket prices usually $11–$22. Box office open Mon–Fri 9am–5pm. Bus: 51.

This theater is home to the Carousel Theatre and School. It also hosts both touring and local dance, music, mime, and theater companies.

OPERA

English supertitles projected above the stage of the Queen Elizabeth Theatre help you follow the dialogue of the lavish Vancouver Opera productions presented here from October through June.

Vancouver Opera

500-845 Cambie St. ☎ **604/682-2871.** Ticket prices usually $29.50–$79.75. No discounts. SkyTrain: Stadium.

For 35 years, this company has produced works often featuring international stars at the Queen Elizabeth Theatre. Their repertoire ranges from classics by Puccini, Verdi, Gounod, and Bizet to 20th-century works by Benjamin Britten and Kurt Janacek as well as esoteric modern productions by lesser-known artists.

CLASSICAL MUSIC

Whether you like baroque fugues, Russian romantic symphonies, or popular show tunes, you'll find world-class performances to soothe or stimulate your soul.

Festival Concert Society

3737 Oak St. ☎ **604/736-3737.** Tickets $5. Box office open Sunday at 10am until show time. SkyTrain: Stadium.

The society's Coffee Concert series takes place every Sunday at 11am September through June at the Queen Elizabeth Theatre. The one-hour concerts feature classical, jazz, folk, dance, theater, or operatic music. Babysitting is provided for free.

University of British Columbia School of Music

Recital Hall, Gate 4, 6361 Memorial Rd. ☎ **604/822-5574.** Tickets $17 adults, $9 seniors and students. Box office open Mon–Fri 8:30am–4:30pm. Bus: 4 or 10.

Between September and November as well as during January and March, UBC presents eight faculty and guest-artist concerts featuring piano, piano and violin, opera, or quartets.

Vancouver Bach Choir

5730 Seaview Rd., West Vancouver. ☎ **604/921-8012.** Ticket prices vary depending on performance and venue. Bus: 4 or 10.

Vancouver's international, award-winning amateur choir, this 150-voice ensemble presents five major concerts a year at the Orpheum Theatre. One popular concert is a sing-along performance of Handel's *Messiah* during the Christmas season.

Vancouver Cantata Singers

5115 Keith Rd., West Vancouver. ☎ **604/921-8588.** Tickets $20 adults, $15 seniors and students.

This semiprofessional, 40-person, mixed choir specializes in early music. They perform works by Brahms, Stravinsky, and Handel as well as Eastern European choral music. The season usually includes three programs in November, December, and March at different locations.

Vancouver Chamber Choir

1254 W. Seventh Ave. ☎ **604/738-6822.** Tickets, Orpheum series: $15–$35 adults, $13–$25 students and seniors; Ryerson and Hotel Vancouver series: $15 adults, $12 students and seniors.

Western Canada's only professional choral ensemble, the Chamber Choir presents an annual concert series in the Orpheum Theatre, Hotel Vancouver, and Ryerson United Church. Under conductor John Washburn, the choir has gained an international reputation from its 19 recordings as well as its concerts.

Vancouver New Music Society

207 W. Hastings St. ☎ **604/874-6200.** Tickets $14 adults, $10 students. Bus: 20.

This company presents seven annual concerts, which feature the works of contemporary and avant-garde composers as well as mixed media performances combining dance and film, at the Vancouver East Cultural Centre between September and April.

Vancouver Society for Early Music

1254 W. Seventh Ave. ☎ **604/732-1610.** Tickets, UBC: $18 adults, $8.50 seniors and students; informal concerts: $5 adults, $4 seniors and students.

This society performs Medieval, Renaissance, and baroque music played on period instruments at various locations, including UBC Recital Hall and St. Andrew's Wesley Church (1012 Nelson St.). The society also presents the Festival of Early Music in July and August, featuring musicians from all over North America.

Vancouver Symphony Orchestra

601 Smithe St. ☎ **604/684-9100** or 604/876-3434 for ticket information. Tickets $12.75–$38 adults; discounts for students and seniors. SkyTrain: Stadium.

At their home in Orpheum Theatre, Vancouver's extremely active orchestra presents the following series: the Masterworks series of great classical works; Air Canada Favourites (light classics); Tea & Trumpets (modern classics and ethnic); VSO Pops (popular and show tunes); and a children's series. Their traveling summer concert series takes them from White Rock and Cloverdale on the U.S. border to the Whistler area.

DANCE

If you love dance, make sure you're in town for the September Dancing on the Edge Festival, which presents 60 to 80 pieces over 10 days. That's when you can get a healthy sampling of works by local companies, including the Anna Wyman Dance Theatre (see below); Judith Marcuse Dance Company (☎ 604/985-6459); and the Karen Jamieson Dance Company (☎ 604/872-5658). Call the Dance Centre (☎ 604/872-0432) for more information about performances around the city.

Anna Wyman Dance Theatre

1705 Marine Dr., West Vancouver. ☎ **604/926-6535.** Tickets for indoor performances $15–$17.

This internationally famous contemporary dance troupe performs bold and dramatically colorful original creations from fall through early spring before taking its act on the road. Catch one of its free late-summer outdoor appearances on Granville Island or Robson Square.

Ballet British Columbia

502-68 Water St. ☎ **604/669-5954.** Tickets $17–$42 adults; senior and student discounts. SkyTrain: Stadium.

This 10-year-old ballet company regularly performs at the Queen Elizabeth Theatre. The innovative company presents works by choreographers such as John Cranko and William Forsythe. Ballet B.C. also hosts visiting soloists such as Mikhail Baryshnikov and companies such as the American Ballet Theatre and the National Ballet of Canada.

2 The Club & Music Scene

COMEDY CLUBS

Punchlines Comedy Theatre

15 Water St. ☎ **604/684-3015.** Cover Tues $3.50, Wed–Thurs $6.50, Fri–Sat $9.65. Drinks $3. Box office open Mon–Fri noon–4pm. Doors open at 8pm; show time at 9:30pm. Bus: 1 or 50.

Jay Leno, Howie Mandel, and other famous comedians have performed at this Gastown club before they made it big. Tuesday is Amateur Night. Wednesday nights are dedicated to improv groups, while stand-up comics take the weekend stage. They don't take reservations, so get here at least a half-hour before show time.

Yuk Yuk's Komedy Kabaret

Plaza of Nations, 750 Pacific Blvd. ☎ **604/687-5233.** Cover Wed $3, Thurs $6, Fri–Sat $10. Drinks $4.75. Show times Wed–Thurs 9pm, Fri–Sat 9pm and 11:30pm. SkyTrain: Stadium.

Paul Wildman and J. O. Mass host a leading lineup of Canadian and American stand-up comics. Amateurs take the stage on Wednesday nights. It's a small theater (capacity 200), so it's hard to get a bad seat.

JAZZ, BLUES & FOLK CLUBS

In June, the du Maurier International Jazz Festival spreads over a number of venues in Vancouver and outdoors at the Plaza of Nations. The Vancouver Folk Festival takes place outdoors in July at Jericho Beach Park. Both festivals have free as well as admission events. The Coastal Jazz and Blues Society (☎ 604/682-0706) has information on all current and upcoming music events throughout the year.

Alma Street Cafe

2505 Alma St. ☎ **604/222-2244.** Cover for special performances only. Drinks $3.75; entrées $8.95–$14.95. Reservations recommended. Entertainment Wed–Sat 8pm–11:30pm. Bus: 10 or 22.

Ethnomusicologist Stephen Huddart's Kitsilano cafe (see Chapter 5 for dining review) is a great place to catch modern jazz performers from Canada and the United States.

Bacchus Piano Lounge

Wedgewood Hotel, 845 Hornby St. ☎ **604/689-7777.** No cover. Drinks $4.50. Entertainment begins around 7pm. SkyTrain: Granville.

At this elegant hotel lounge, you can catch Wes Mackey playing blues guitar nightly except Sunday and sit before the fireplace, which is especially cozy on rainy evenings. People show up wearing everything from suits to jeans. The richly appointed room is filled with high-backed chairs and a presiding painting of the god Bacchus behind the grand piano. There's an excellent light snack menu featuring a few items from the adjoining Bacchus Ristorante plus a great wine and drink list (see Chapter 5 for dining review).

Glass Slipper

185 E. 11th Ave. ☎ **604/877-0066.** Cover $5; more for special acts. Located downstairs from the Cinderella Ballroom. Open Wed–Thurs 9pm–2am; Fri–Sat 8:30pm–2am; Sun 9pm–midnight. Bus: 3.

A performance venue for the Coastal Jazz and Blues Society and the New Orchestra Workshop, this place features modern and improv jazz in an intimate, inexpensive setting.

Hogan's Alley

730 Main St. ☎ **604/689-8645.** Cover Fri–Sat $2. Drinks $3.50. Bus: 3 or 8.

Live local and U.S. bands perform nightly before a very savvy and seriously devoted blues audience.

Hot Jazz Society

2120 Main St. ☎ **604/873-4131.** Cover $6–$8 for special acts. Drinks $3.50. Open Wed 8pm–midnight; Fri–Sat 8:30pm–1am. Bus: 3 or 8.

Playing everything from Dixieland to swing and progressive, this club caters to dedicated jazz fans. The dance floor is permanently packed no matter who is playing.

✪ Yale Hotel

1300 Granville St. ☎ **604/681-9253.** Cover Thurs–Sat usually $5–$7. Drinks about $4.50. Entertainment Mon–Sat 9:30pm–1:30am; jam sessions Sat–Sun from 3pm. Bus: 8, 10, or 20.

Long John Baldry, Junior Wells, Koko Taylor, John Hammond, Kathi McDonald, Clarence "Gatemouth" Brown, and many other blues masters have played at this club located in a late 19th-century hotel. If you are a serious blues fan, this is *the* place. The room is set up for sitting back or boogying down. There's also a billiard corner set away from the stage.

ROCK MUSIC

Rock clubs bloom and fade here as rapidly as they do in many metropolitan areas. Vancouver also has top talent giving major concerts at the Orpheum, Queen Elizabeth Theatre, and other halls.

Commodore Ballroom

870 Granville Mall. ☎ **604/681-7838.** Drinks about $5. Open most nights from 8pm. Cover from $5. Bus: 10.

This 1929 ballroom hosts major rock, rap, jazz, blues, reggae, and other performers such as Buddy Guy and Sonny Landreth, Ice-T and Body Count, Queen Ida and the Bon Temps Zydeco Band, The Wailers, Little Feet, Vancouver Men's Chorus, and Burning Spear. It's a disco on Tuesdays and gives a Friday night dance party. The Commodore has four bars, six video screens, and a huge dance floor.

Gastown Music Hall

6 Powell St. ☎ **604/685-1333.** Open Thurs–Sat. Cover from $5. Drinks $4. Bus: 1 or 50.

This 125-seat hall has a dance floor and two bars. As the name suggests, they get all kinds of acts from rock, country, and jazz to R&B, spoken word, and rap. Wednesday is blues night.

The Mighty Niagara (Falls Pub)

435 W Pender St. ☎ **604/688-7574.** Cover $4–$5 Drinks $3. Entertainment Thurs–Sat 8pm–midnight. Bus: 22.

This is a venue for local bands playing for a young, hip audience. Groups include Daisy Chain, Funkyard, and Fine Tooth Combine.

Roxy

932 Granville St. ☎ **604/684-7699.** Cover Mon–Wed $3, Thurs $5, Fri–Sat $6, Sun free. Drinks $3.95. Open Mon–Sat 7pm–2am, Sun 7pm–midnight. Bus: 8, 10, or 20.

Live bands play '50s, '60s, and '70s classic rock in this casual club with showmen bartenders. Theme parties (often with vacation giveaways), old movies, and Wednesday "Student Nights" add to the entertainment.

The Starfish Room

1055 Homer St., near Helmcken Street. ☎ **604/682-4171.** Cover Tues–Wed $2; Thurs $4 for men only (after 10pm); Fri–Sat $6. Prices vary for larger acts. Drinks $4.35. Open Tues–Sat 8pm–2am. Bus: 4, 7, 8, 10, 14, or 20; then walk three blocks west on Granville Street.

This large club has a huge dance floor and hosts international recording stars as well as local artists. Jon Spencer Blues Explosion, Offspring, Jonathan Richman, Jimmie Dale Gilmore, and Jeff Buckley are just a few of the acts that have played here. Monday and Tuesdays are DJ nights.

Town Pump

66 Water St. ☎ **604/683-6695.** Cover $5–$20. Drinks about $4. Entertainment Mon–Fri 8pm–2am, Sat 7:30pm–2am (earlier in summer), Sun 7:30pm–midnight. Bus: 8.

One of Vancouver's favorite social spots, this Gastown club attracts top local and national acts to its casual, antique-filled premises. You can have dinner in the restaurant (open from 5 to 9pm) before the show starts.

Twilight Zone

7 Alexander St. ☎ **604/632-8550.** Cover $2–$5. Drinks $3. Bus: 1 or 50.

This is a cyberpunk venue with DJ Atomic as your host. Wear your best cyberpunk outfit and win a door prize. This is Vancouver's industrial Gothic punk alternative. Call before you go since venues change from month to month. Punk nights here are not for spectators. Be sure to bring your Docs.

DANCE CLUBS

Big Bamboo

1236 W. Broadway. ☎ **604/733-2220.** Cover $3. Drinks run $3.50. Open Wed–Sat 8pm–2am. Bus: 10.

This large club is Vancouver's hottest Top 40 dance spot. The crowd is mostly Kitsilano and UBC locals. Wednesday is ladies' night, and on Saturday, DJ Hype and the Flygirls take over the turntables.

Blue Note

455 W. Broadway. ☎ **604/872-8866.** Cover Fri–Sat $2. Drinks $6 minimum all week. Open 8pm for dinner, 10pm for music. Bus: 10.

A New York–style supper club, this place has no connection to the Manhattan Blue Note. While the music is on par, it's about a quarter of the price and the drinks and food are better. The generally relaxed audience contains a lot of couples.

Hungry Eye

23 W. Cordova St. ☎ **604/688-5351.** Cover varies per event. Drinks $3.50. Open daily 8:30pm–2am. Bus: 50.

A mixture of new bands, thrash, and DJs attract alternative music lovers—mostly young ones.

MaRs

1320 Richards St. ☎ **604/662-7077.** Cover usually $3–$7. Drinks $3.95. Open Tues–Sat 9pm–2am. Bus: 8, 10, or 20.

This is a Generation X industrial dance music warehouse space with really cool lighting effects and a Wednesday reggae night. Wear your best grunge cyberwear to dance here.

Luv-A-Fair

1275 Seymour St. ☎ **604/685-3288.** Cover Mon–Tues $3, Wed–Thurs $2, Fri–Sat $6, Sun free. Drinks around $3.75. Open Mon–Sat 9pm–2am, Sun 9pm–midnight. Bus: 8, 10, or 20.

This place is a costume party of skins, post-punks, drag queens, and college students. It features a great dance floor and serious imported music and videos.

Rio Rio

102 Water St. ☎ **604/685-1144.** No cover. Drinks $3.50–$6. Open daily 5pm–1am. Bus: 50.

Learn to Lambada and have a few Spanish and Mexican tapas to rejuvenate yourself at this live-music supper club, which also features a full list of tequila drinks.

3 The Bar Scene

The bar scene is closely linked with the restaurant scene. Due to local liquor laws, most bars also have full menus. Places for dinner and drinks include **Yaletown Brewery,** a microbrewery offering more than a half dozen delicious brews, and **Delilah's,** an elegant yet informal restaurant featuring an extensive martini menu. Delilah's attracts an upscale, mostly gay clientele, but everyone is welcome (see Chapter 5 for dining reviews).

Bimini

2010 W. 4th Ave. ☎ **604/738-2714.** Drinks $4. Open Mon–Fri 11am–midnight, Sat 11am–1am, Sun noon–midnight. Bus: 4.

This two-story bar appeals to the local Kitsilano crowd. It features sport events on TV and occasional live entertainment.

Checkers

1755 Davie St. ☎ **604/682-1831.** Drinks $4.35. Open Mon–Sat 11am–2am, Sunday from 11am to midnight. Bus: 8.

This is a friendly West End bar where you can listen to classic rock amid the checkerboard decor. The view of English Bay provides a withdrawn spot for people-watching.

Joe Fortes Seafood House

777 Thurlow St. ☎ **604/669-1940.** Drinks $3.50–$7. Open daily 11:30am–11pm, Fri–Sat until midnight. Bus: 8.

Named after the burly Caribbean seaman who became English Bay's first lifeguard and a popular local hero, this spacious, dark-wood, immensely popular bar is filled throughout the day with Vancouver's young and successful. The single-malt list scotch is the best in town. You can even get a few oysters—try the pan-fried variety—to go with your drink.

The Rusty Gull

175 E. 1st St., North Vancouver. ☎ **604/988-5585.** Drinks $4.20–$5.50. Open daily 10am–midnight. SeaBus: Lonsdale Quay.

Gourmet-beer drinkers will love the 13 local brews on tap at this watering hole. And, if your musical tastes run more towards R&B and blues, you'll appreciate the local talent that comes to play at this spot.

Stamp's Landing

610 Stamp's Landing. ☎ **604/879-0821.** Drinks $4. Open daily 11am–midnight. Bus: 50; then walk $1/4$ mile south on West 6th Avenue.

With a cheerful neighborhood pub flavor, this two-story restaurant/bar is a casual, friendly place to spend the evening. Twelve brews on tap and a classic British pub menu—shepherd's pie, steak and mushroom pie, plus bangers and mash—is topped off with freshly baked cheesecake or apple pie. The False Creek Marina yachting crowd packs into this pub adjacent to Monk McQueen's restaurant.

✪ **Steamworks Pub & Brewery**

375 Water St. ☎ **604/689-2739.** Drinks $3.50–$6. Open daily 11:30am–10pm. Bus: 50.

This new spot at The Landing in Gastown appeals to a broad clientele ranging from office types to casual locals. The interior has comfortable upholstered chairs and wood paneling. There are pool tables downstairs for those who are jaded by the harbor view. They serve a dozen great in-house brews from dark Australian-style ales to light, refreshing wheat lagers and have a full menu as well.

4 The Gay & Lesbian Scene

Vancouver's gay and lesbian scene is comfortable and open without the cloistered feeling you'll find in other cities. A lot of the clubs feature theme nights and dance parties.

Celebrities

1022 Davie St. ☎ **604/689-3180.** Drinks $3.50–$5.50. Open daily 9pm–2am. Bus: 3 or 8.

The West End's largest gay dance club, Celebrities has DJs who spin everything from techno pop to disco. On Wednesday, Queen Myria LeNoir's drag show takes the stage. On "Phallic Phriday's" house music plays, while on Saturday "Club Kid Nights" cover every musical taste.

Heritage House Hotel

455 Abbott St. ☎ **604/685-7777.** Drinks $3.60. Open Mon–Sat 11am–1am, Sun 11am–midnight. Bus: 19.

This Gastown gay bar has a main-floor lounge and pub that attracts both men and women. The downstairs lesbian bar is open Tuesday through Saturday; only women are admitted on Wednesday and Friday.

The Odyssey

1251 Howe St. ☎ **604/689-5256.** Cover Tues $2, Fri–Sat $4. Drinks $3.75. Open Mon–Sat 9pm–2am, Sun 9pm–midnight. Bus: 8.

This big dance club offers live entertainment: Male strippers on Mondays, shower contests on Tuesdays, male go-go dancers on Fridays and Saturdays, and live drag on Sundays. A DJ spins nightly for the mixed audience. There's a heated patio open year-round, and the back entrance is for men only.

Red Lounge

818 Richards St. ☎ **604/688-2923.** Cover ranges from none to $4, depending on the night. Drinks $4. Open 9pm–2am. Bus: 8, 10, or 20.

DJs spin disks Tuesday through Saturday with special events, including Thursday night acid jazz, Friday male stripper nights, and a Leather Levi's Cruise Bar on Saturday.

The Underground

1082 Granville St. ☎ **604/681-3020.** Cover $2–$4. Drinks $4. Open Thurs–Sun. Doors open 7pm. Bus: 4 or 10.

This premier dance club and mainly male cruise bar features wet boxer contests, dance contests, and fetish parties—wear what you dare. The Underground is definitely not for the white-sneaker-and-cardigan set or the faint of heart.

5 More Entertainment

MOVIES

Vancouver is a great place to see films. From the Vancouver Film Festival (see "Vancouver Calendar of Events" in Chapter 2) to first-run, second-run, and revival theaters, you can get your fill of good flicks.

First-run ticket prices are about $8 for adults, with student and senior discounts. Sometimes there are $4.50 matinees. Just a few of the downtown theaters include the following: **Capital 6,** 820 Granville St. (☎ 604/669-6000); **Vancouver Centre,** 620 W. Georgia St. (☎ 604/669-4442); **Granville Theatre,** 855 Granville St. (☎ 604/684-4000); and **Royal Centre,** 1055 W. Georgia St.(☎ 604/669-9791).

Second-run double- and triple-feature Vancouver cinemas include the **Paradise Theatre,** 919 Granville St. (☎ 604/681-1732), which shows three films for $2.50; the **Hollywood Theatre,** 3123 W. Broadway (☎ 604/738-3211), which shows two films for $3.25; and our favorite, the **Denman Place Discount Cinema,** on Comox at Denman (☎ 604/684-2202), which presents three films for $4.50. The first and second shows (if you only want to sit for one) are $4, while the last show is $2.50. Five stamps on your discount card (issued the first time you go) gets you one free pass to a $4 show.

The Starlight Cinema, 935 Denman St. (☎ 604/689-0096); the **Park Theatre,** 3440 Cambie St. (☎ 604/876-2747); and the **Varsity Theatre,** 4375 W. 10th Ave. (☎ 604/222-2235), all offer first-run, foreign-language, independent, art, and political films. Admission for these Festival Cinemas theaters is $5 for members ($3 for seniors and children); $8 for nonmembers ($4 on Tuesdays and $4 for seniors and children). Students pay only $4 on Sundays.

The Pacific Cinematheque, 1131 Howe St.(☎ 604/688-3456), features classic and contemporary foreign films and series such as the Jean Luc Godard film festival, Michael Powell film festival, and International Women's Week films. It also presents experimental, independent North American features. This is also the head-quarters cinema of the Vancouver Film Festival, held every September and October. Films are presented here as well as at the Hollywood, Park, Starlight, Varsity, Ridge, and University of British Columbia theaters. Admission is $5.50 adults, $4 seniors and students for a single billing; double features cost $1 extra. Annual membership is $5. Vancouver Film Festival tickets are $7.50 per show.

The Ridge Theatre, 3131 Arbutus St. (☎ 604/738-6311), is where you're likely to catch a Cannes Film Festival award-winner, an uncut print of an old classic, an unpublicized rock movie, or a sensational underground sleeper. The Ridge Theatre's glass-enclosed crying room (originally designed for parents with infants whose crying might upset other patrons) is Katherine Hepburn's favorite place to catch a movie undisturbed by fans. This theater also has an induction-loop system for hearing-impaired patrons. Admission to first-run films is $6 adults, $3 for seniors and children; double features are $4 adults, $2 for seniors and children. Seniors get in free on Mondays. Bus: 18.

GAMBLING CASINOS

Casinos here are not on par with those in Las Vegas, London, or Monte Carlo, but you can still try your luck at blackjack, roulette, sic-bo, red dog (diamond dog), and Caribbean stud poker. They are not open 24 hours like their counterparts in other places nor do they offer floor shows. There are betting limits here so you won't lose your shirt in the process. Half of the gambling proceeds are allocated to city social services, so your losses actually go to a good cause.

The **Royal Diamond Casino,** 1195 Richards St. (☎ 604/685-2340), is informal and very friendly. It's open seven nights a week from 6pm to 2am.

6 Caffeine Nation

"I've never seen so much coffee in all my life. The whole town is on a caffeine jag, and still nothing gets done any faster," said Bette Midler when she performed in Vancouver. The reason coffee is king here is the weather: It rains at least half of the year, and coffee helps soothe the soul amid all that grayness and pouring rain. This city has hundreds of coffeehouses, from cafes for leather-clad-bikers to espresso joints for businesspeople in suits.

Above and beyond the generic Starbucks/Benz/Roastmastirs' scene, the city's best java joint is **Joe's Cafe,** 1150 Commercial Dr. (unlisted phone), located in the heart of the Italian community. Here, you can get a cappuccino with two inches of foam and sit amid local intellectuals, bohemians, poets, feminists, and political agitators. There's also the classic coffee spot **Ciao Espresso Bar,** 1074 Denman St. (☎ 604/ 682-0112), where smoking is not only permitted, but practically mandatory.

And since playing pool while sipping cafe latte is a hot pastime, you may want to polish up your cue stick. **Benny's Bagels,** 2505 W. Broadway in Kitsilano (☎ 604/ 736-4686) and 1095 Hamilton St. in Yaletown (☎ 604/688-8018), is a coffee bar/ pool hall with the best bagel toppings in town. Down the street at **Bar None,** 1222 Hamilton St. (☎ 604/689-7000), pool is played in a slightly more conventional bar with live and canned music. Yaletown hipsters swig beer and wine between racks. **Automotive,** 1095 Homer St. (☎ 604/682-0040), has a drive-in/garage atmosphere and serves a good cappuccino along with a light selection of snacks, sandwiches, and alcoholic drinks. On Sunday afternoons, you can play cut-throat to cool live jazz. **Barracuda Billiards and Bistro,** 562 Beatty St. (☎ 604/683-8448), in a cavernous former warehouse loft, has foosball tables as well.

7 Late-Night Bites

The Bread Garden
812 Bute St. (south of Robson St.) ☎ **604/688-3213.** Daily 24 hours.

The Bread Garden is one spot (actually, there are nine locations in Vancouver) where you can get a light breakfast, lunch, or dinner at any hour. Light wood paneling, glass, and terra-cotta tiles give it a casual feel; the scent of fresh coffee and herb tea permeate the air. The food—baked goods, salads, quiches, lasagnes, frittatas, and desserts—is decent, and the prices are reasonable.

The Edge
1142 Davie St. ☎ **604/688-3395.** Mon–Thurs 7am–4am; Fri–Sat 24 hours; Sunday 7am–2am.

This laid-back cafe serves light food and great coffee to a mostly gay crowd. On warm afternoons, the windows come off and the pace slows even more, but that's exactly what draws people here.

Hamburger Mary's Diner
1202 Davie St. ☎ **604/687-1293.** Daily 6am–4am.

Since 1979, this popular casual eatery has served a selection of classic diner dishes in-cluding salads, pastas, steaks, huge milkshakes, and about 20 different kinds of hamburgers. On a recent night, the customers included a table of Japanese tourists, a Molson Indy pit crew, dozens of locals, and a pair of ravenous travel writers. None of them left hungry.

Getting to Know Victoria 10

New York tycoon Pierpont Morgan and actor John Wayne spent their summers here. The Nixons honeymooned here. And they all got to Victoria, British Columbia's provincial capital, by ferry. If you're in a hurry you can arrive by plane or helicopter, but getting here by ferry is romantic and scenic. What follows are a few tips for getting around once you're on Vancouver Island.

1 Orientation

VISITOR INFORMATION

Located right on the Inner Harbour wharf, across from the Empress Hotel, the **Tourism Victoria Travel InfoCentre,** 812 Wharf St. (☎ 604/382-2127), is a great source of tourist information. If you didn't reserve a room before you arrived, you can go to this office or call its **reservations hotline** (☎ 800/663-3883) for last-minute bookings at hotels, inns, and bed-and-breakfasts. They'll even help you locate discounts and stay within whatever price range you specify. The InfoCentre is open daily: September through March, from 9am to 5pm; May and June, from 9am to 8pm; and July and August, from 9am to 9pm. **Tourism Victoria**'s executive offices are at 710-1175 Douglas St. (☎ 604/382-2127).

If you want to explore the rest of the 285-mile-long island, then contact the **Tourism Association of Vancouver Island,** Bastion Square (☎ 604/382-3551).

CITY LAYOUT

Victoria sits on the southeastern tip of Vancouver Island, sheltered by suburban residential districts from the Strait of Juan de Fuca across from Washington state's snow-capped Olympic peninsula. The **downtown/Olde Town** area embraces the **Inner Harbour,** an offshoot of Victoria Harbour that leads to the **Upper Harbour,** while the **Ross Bay** and **Oak Bay** residential areas around Dallas Road and Beach Drive reach the open waters of the strait.

Victoria's most central landmark is the **Empress Hotel** on Government Street located right on the Inner Harbour wharf. If you turn your back to the hotel, you'll be facing the northern edge of the residential community of **James Bay,** where the Seattle-Port Angeles ferries dock. To your immediate left are the provincial **Legislative Buildings** on Belleville Street.

MAIN ARTERIES & STREETS   Three **main north-south arteries** intersect with just about every destination you would want to reach in Victoria:

Government Street goes through Victoria's main downtown shopping and dining district. (Wharf Street, a frontage road that edges the harbor, merges with Government Street at the Empress Hotel) **Douglas Street,** running parallel to Government Street, is the main business thoroughfare as well as the road to Nanaimo and the rest of the island. (This is also Trans-Canada Highway 1. The Mile-0 marker sits at the corner of Douglas and Dallas roads.) Also running parallel to Government and Douglas streets is **Blanshard Street** (Highway 17). This street merges with Douglas Street at Southgate Street, which is the opening of Beacon Hill Park. It's also the route to Saanich Peninsula, including the Sidney-Vancouver ferry terminal, and Butchart Gardens.

East-west streets to know include the following:

Johnson Street lies at the northern end of downtown/Olde Town where the E&N Rail station sits opposite from Swan's Hotel at the corner of Wharf Street. The Johnson Street Bridge is the demarcation line between the Upper Harbour and the northern edge of the Inner Harbour. **Belleville Street** is the boundary line of the Inner Harbour's southern edge. The Legislative Buildings and the ferry terminal are both located here. Belleville Street loops around westward toward Victoria Harbour before heading south, becoming Dallas Road. **Dallas Road** follows the water's edge past residential areas and beaches before it winds northward up to Oak Bay.

FINDING AN ADDRESS   Victoria addresses are written like those of Vancouver: The suite or room number precedes the building number. For instance, 100–1250 Government St. refers to suite 100 at 1250 Government St.

Victoria's streets are numbered from the city's southwest corner and increase as you go north and east. The numbers on Douglas Street, for example, begin with 1 Douglas St. at Dallas Road and increase on their way north. Fort Street starts its 500 block at Wharf Street, increasing as its heads due east.

STREET MAPS   Free, detailed street maps are available at the **Tourism Victoria Travel InfoCentre** (see "Visitor Information," above). The best map of the surrounding area is the B.C. Provincial Parks map of Vancouver Island, which is also available at the InfoCentre.

NEIGHBORHOODS IN BRIEF

Many people refer to Victoria as being more "British than the British." This is a misquotation of native Victorian Emily Carr—the wildly independent artist was actually referring to her father's personality and gardening habits, not to the city. The best description comes from Rudyard Kipling:

> To realize Victoria you must take all that the eye admires in Bournemouth, Torquay, the Isle of Wight, the happy valley at Hong Kong, the Doon, Sorrento and Camp's Bay—add reminiscences of the Thousand Islands and arrange the whole around the Bay of Naples with some Himalayas for the background.

Downtown and Olde Town   These two areas have been the city's social focal points since the turn of the century, when settlers first arrived by ship. This is also the city's most heavily touristed area, filled with shops and restaurants. The area recalls its fascinating history, which includes rum smuggling, opium manufacturing, gold mining, whaling, and shipping.

There is a large Scottish population here (not to be confused with the British). The Scottish-owned Hudson's Bay Company was the earliest and largest European establishment here in the 1800s. St. Andrews, Victoria's oldest charitable foundation, was founded to aid the many Highlander-born trappers and traders who had made the perilous continental crossing to this Eden.

Chinatown   Victoria's Chinatown is the oldest in North America. The oldest Chinese school in the western hemisphere is still in operation on Fisgard Street. There are still strong, visible historic sites in this community such as **Fan Tan Alley**—one of the world's narrowest streets—where legal opium manufacturing took place in the hidden courtyard buildings flanking this four-foot-wide way.

James Bay, Ross Bay, and Oak Bay   These beautiful residential communities have a more modern West Coast feel. Houses perched on hills overlooking the straits are nestled amid lushly landscaped floral gardens. Intermittent golf courses, marinas, and a few cozy inns edge the waters, where you can take advantage of the city's temperate climate.

2 Getting Around

BY PUBLIC TRANSPORTATION

BY BUS   The **Victoria Regional Transit System (B.C. Transit),** 520 Gorge Rd. (☎ 604/382-6161), runs 40 bus routes through greater Victoria, Sooke, and Sidney. You can even take the bus to Butchart Gardens and the Vancouver ferry terminal at Sidney. Regular service on the main routes runs from 6am to just past midnight.

Schedules and routes are available at the Tourism Victoria Travel InfoCentre (see "Visitor Information," above), where you can pick up a copy of *Victoria Rider's Guide* or *Discover Vancouver on Transit: Including Victoria*. These publications provide transit routes for many city neighborhoods, landmarks, and attractions.

Popular bus routes include the following: no. 2 (Oak Bay); no. 5 (downtown, James Bay, Beacon Hill Park); no. 14 (Victoria Art Gallery, Craigdarroch Castle, University of Victoria); no. 24 (Anne Hathaway's Cottage); no. 30 (James Bay night route from downtown); no. 61 (Sooke); no. 70 (Sidney, Swartz Bay); and no. 75 (Butchart Gardens).

Fares are charged on a per-zone basis. One-way, single-zone fares are $1.35 for adults and 90¢ for seniors and children 5 to 13; two zones are $2 for adults, $1.35 seniors and children 5 to 13. Transfers are good for travel in one direction only with no stopovers.

A **DayPass** ($4 adults, $3 seniors and children 5 to 13) gives you unlimited travel throughout the day. You can buy passes at the Tourism Vancouver Travel InfoCentre (see "Visitor Information," above), convenience stores, and ticket outlets throughout Victoria.

BY FERRY   Crossing the Inner, Upper, and Victoria Harbours by one of blue miniferries of **Victoria Harbour** (☎ 604/408-0971) is cheap and fun. It's the scenic way to start a tour in either direction. Ferries to the Empress Hotel, Coast Harborside Hotel, and Ocean Pointe Resort Hotel leave about every 15 minutes from 10am to 10pm. The cost is $2.50 for adults, $1.25 seniors and children.

BY CAR

If you're planning any out-of-town activities, rent a car or bring your own. If you have a city-bound agenda, make sure that your hotel has parking. Street parking is at a premium in Victoria, just as it is in Vancouver, and the downtown area is small enough to be easily explored on foot. Be forewarned that gas prices are high. Gas is sold by the liter, and speeds and distances are posted in kilometers.

RENTALS   Car rental agencies in Victoria include the following: **ABC,** 2507 Government St. (☎ 604/388-3153); **Avis,** 843 Douglas St. (☎ 604/386-8468); **Budget,** 757 Douglas St. (☎ 604/388-5525); **Hertz Canada,** 655 Douglas St. (☎ 604/388-4411); and **Tilden International,** 767 Douglas St. (☎ 604/386-1213). Car rentals cost about $25 to $35 per day.

PARKING   Metered **street parking** is hard to come by in the downtown area, and rules are strictly enforced. Unmetered parking on side streets is risky.

All major downtown hotels have guest parking with rates varying from free to $20. There are parking lots at **View Street** between Douglas and Blanshard streets; **Johnson Street** off Blanshard Street; **Yates Street** north of Bastion Square; and at **The Bay** on Fisgard at Blanshard Street.

DRIVING RULES   Canadian driving rules are similar to regulations in California; stopping for crossing pedestrians is the most notable law. Seat belts and daytime headlights are mandatory. Children under five must be in child restraints. Motorcyclists must wear helmets. It's legal to turn right on a red light after you've come to a full stop.

AUTO CLUB   Members of the American Automobile Association (AAA) can get assistance from the **Canadian Automobile Association (CAA)** (☎ 800/222-4357).

BY BICYCLE/SCOOTER

Cycling is the easiest way to get around the downtown and beach areas. There are bike lanes throughout the city and paved paths along parks and beaches. Helmets are mandatory, and riding on sidewalks is illegal, except where bike paths are indicated.

You can rent cycles and scooters for $5 to $8 per hour or $15 per day from **Budget,** 757 Douglas St. (☎ 604/388-5525). **Cycle Victoria Rentals,** 327 Belleville St. (☎ 604/385-2453), rents scooters, cycles, in-line skates, tandems, and strollers for about the same price.

ON FOOT

Strolling along the Inner Harbour's pedestrian walkways and streets is as relaxing as it should be in a seaport city. The terrain is flat for the most part, and with few exceptions, everything is accessible within less than a half hour on foot.

BY TAXI

Within the downtown area, you can expect to travel for less than $6. It's best to call for a cab; they don't always stop on city streets (especially when it's raining). Call for a pickup from **Empress Cabs** (☎ 604/383-8888) or **Blue Bird Cabs** (☎ 604/382-8294).

FAST FACTS: Victoria

Airport   See "Getting to Victoria" in Chapter 2.

American Express   The American Express office is at 1203 Douglas St. (☎ 604/385-8731). It's open Monday through Friday from 8:30am to 5:30pm, Saturday from 10am to 4pm.

Area Code   The telephone area code for all of British Columbia is 604.

Babysitters   Most major hotels can arrange babysitting service; look through your room's guest services directory for the phone number or hotel extension.

Business Hours   Victoria banks are open Monday through Thursday from 10am to 3pm and Friday until 6pm. Business hours are Monday through Friday from 9am to 5pm (lunch time is from noon to 1pm). Stores are generally open Monday through Saturday from 10am to 6pm. Some are open on Sundays during the summer. Last call at the city's restaurant bars and cocktail lounges is 2am.

Camera Repair   City Photo Centre, 1227 Government St. (☎ 604/385-5633), is a good repair shop for new and old cameras.

Car Rentals   See "Getting Around," earlier in this chapter.

Climate   See "When to Go" in Chapter 2.

Currency   See "Money" in Chapter 2.

Currency Exchange   The best exchange rates in town can be found at banks. They don't charge service or transaction fees.

Dentist   Most major hotels have a dentist on call. Cresta Dental Centre, 3170 Tillicum Rd. at Burnside Street (☎ 604/384-7711), is an accessible service.

Doctor   Hotels usually have a doctor on call. James Bay Treatment Center, 100-230 Menzies St. (☎ 604/388-9934), is a local medical facility.

Documents Required   See "Visitor Information and Entry Requirements" in Chapter 2.

Driving Rules   See "Getting Around," earlier in this chapter.

Drugstores   See "Pharmacies," below.

Electricity   The same 110 volts, alternating current as in the United States.

Embassies/Consulates   See "Fast Facts: Vancouver" in Chapter 3.

Emergencies   Dial **911** for fire, police, ambulance, and poison control.

Etiquette   See "Fast Facts: Vancouver" in Chapter 3.

Eyeglass Repair   Eyeglass repair and replacement can be done at Lenscrafters (☎ 604/361-1977) in Eaton Center.

Holidays   See "When to Go" in Chapter 2.

Hospitals   Local hospitals include Royal Jubilee Hospital, 1800 Fort St. (☎ 604/370-8000; emergency 604/370-8212); and Victoria General Hospital, 35 Helmcken Rd. (☎ 604/727-4212; emergency 604/727-4181).

Hotlines   Hotlines include the following: Royal Canadian Mounted Police (☎ 604/380-6261); Emotional Crisis Centre (☎ 604/386-6323); Sexual Assault Centre (☎ 604/383-3232); Poison Control Centre (☎ 604/595-9211); Help Line for Children (dial 0 and ask for Zenith 1234); SPCA animal emergency (☎ 604/385-6521); Better Business Bureau (☎ 604/386-6348); Lawyer Referral Service (☎ 604/382-1415); B.C. Road Conditions (☎ 604/380-4997).

Information   See "Visitor Information," earlier in this chapter.

Language   See "Fast Facts: Vancouver" in Chapter 3.

Libraries   The Greater Victoria Public Library (☎ 604/382-7241) is located at the corner of Broughton and Blanchard streets.

Liquor Laws   See "Fast Facts: Vancouver" in Chapter 3.

Lost Property   Call the Victoria City Police (see "Police," below).

Luggage Storage/Lockers   Most hotels will store bags for guests who are about to check in or who have just checked out. Otherwise, coin lockers ($1) are available outside the bus station (behind the Empress Hotel) and across the street from the Royal British Columbian Museum.

Mail   see "Fast Facts: Vancouver" in Chapter 3.

Maps   See "City Layout," earlier in this chapter.

Newspapers   The *Times Colonist* comes out every morning, seven days a week. The weekly entertainment paper *Monday Magazine* comes out, believe it or not, on Thursday.

Pharmacies   Shopper's Drug Mart, 1222 Douglas St. (☎ 604/384-0544), is open Monday through Wednesday from 7am to 7pm; Thursday and Friday from 7am to 8pm; Saturday from 9am to 7pm; and Sunday from 10am to 7pm. McGill and Orne, 649 Fort St. (☎ 604/384-1195), is open Monday through Friday from 8:30am to 8pm; Saturday from 9am to 6pm; and Sunday from 11am to 6pm.

Police   Dial **911**. The Vancouver City Police can be reached by calling 604/665-3321. The Royal Canadian Mounted Police (☎ 604/380-6261) handle most cases for tourists.

Post Office   The main post office is at 714 Yates St. (☎ 604/595-2552).

Radio   FM stations include 98.5 CFMS (easy listening), 100.3 CKKU (album rock), and 102 CFUV (jazz, classical, and alternative music). AM radio stations include 900 CJVI (classic rock), 1070 CFAX (easy listening), and 1200 CKDA (soft rock).

Restrooms   Hotel lobbies are your best bet for downtown facilities. The shopping centers have them as well.

Safety   Crime rates are relatively low in Victoria, but there are transients panhandling throughout the downtown and Olde Town areas. As in any city, be aware that crimes of opportunity are partly the fault of careless victims.

Taxes   See "Fast Facts: Vancouver" in Chapter 3.

Taxis   See "Getting Around," earlier in this chapter.

Telephone/Fax   See "Fast Facts: Vancouver" in Chapter 3.

Television   CHEK (Channel 6), a Canadian network affiliate, is Vancouver Island's only local TV station. Victoria receives all the same channels as Vancouver (see "Fast Facts: Vancouver" in Chapter 3).

Time   See "Fast Facts: Vancouver" in Chapter 3.

Tipping   See "Fast Facts: Vancouver" in Chapter 3.

Transit Information   The B.C. Transit phone number is 604/832-6161.

Water   Victoria's tap water is safe to drink.

Weather   Call 604/656-3978 for weather updates; you can get marine forecasts by dialing 604/656-7515.

Victoria Accommodations

Victoria has a wide choice of fine accommodations in all price ranges. Lodgings can be found in the greatest numbers in the picturesque **Inner Harbour, Downtown/Olde Town,** and **James Bay** areas, all of which are all close to the city action. **Beach Drive** is another alternative if you want to be close to boats, sand, and sea. The areas immediately outside of Victoria, such as **Sooke, Malahat,** and **Brentwood Bay,** have wonderful hideaways if you want peaceful accommodations away from the madding crowd.

Room rates have been sorted into the following categories: **Very Expensive** ($200 and up a night); **Expensive** ($150 to $200); **Moderate** ($100 to $150); and **Inexpensive** (under $100). All rates are listed in Canadian dollars. They are not inclusive of the 10% provincial accommodations tax nor the 7% goods and services tax (GST). Non-Canadian residents can receive a rebate for the GST on short-stay accommodations by filling out the Tax Refund Application available at most hotels and at tourist information offices.

RESERVATIONS   Reservations are absolutely essential in Victoria from June to September and during other holiday periods. If you arrive without a reservation and have trouble finding a room, call **Tourism Victoria** (☎ 604/382-1131 or 800/663-3883). They can make reservations for you at hotels, inns, or bed-and-breakfasts.

BED-AND-BREAKFAST REGISTRIES   If you prefer to stay in a bed-and-breakfast other than those listed in this chapter, the following agencies specialize in matching guests to establishments which best suit their needs:

- **Beachside Bed and Breakfast Registry,** 4208 Evergreen Ave., West Vancouver VTV 1H1(☎ 604/922-7773 or 800/563-3311). (See Chapter 4 for more information.)
- **Born Free Bed and Breakfast of B.C.,** 4390 Frances St., Burnaby V5C 2R3(☎ 604/298-8815 or 800/488-1941). (See Chapter 4 for more information.)
- **Canada-West Accommodations Bed and Breakfast Registry,** P.O. Box 86607, North Vancouver V7L 4L2(☎ 604/929-1424 or 800/561-3223). (See Chapter 4 for more information.)
- **Town and Country Bed and Breakfast,** P.O. Box 74542, 2803 W. Fourth Ave V6K 1K2(☎ 604/731-5942). (See Chapter 4 for more information.)

1 Best Bets

- **Best Historic Hotel:** Built by Francis Rattenbury for the Canadian-Pacific Railway and opened in 1908, **The Empress Hotel,** 721 Government St. (☎ 604/ 384-8111), is Victoria's grandest, most historic hotel. The rooms are filled with an eclectic mix of Victorian and Edwardian antique furnishings, and the afternoon tea here is a Victoria tradition.
- **Best for Business Travelers:** The **Ocean Pointe Resort,** 45 Songhees Rd. (☎ 604/360-2999 or 800/667-4677), has all the amenities businesspeople look for in a hotel: service, excellent facilities, and a great staff.
- **Best for a Romantic Getaway:** The **Aerie Resort,** 600 Ebedora Ln., P.O. Box 108, Malahat (☎ 604/743-7115), high atop Malahat is the perfect place to run away from it all and get spoiled in the process. It's completely secluded, but it's also the height of luxury. From the hand-carved king-size beds, fireplaces, and chandeliered Jacuzzis, to the stellar service in the dining room, the Aerie was designed to be the best hideaway in the world, and it just might be.
- **Best Hotel Lobby for Pretending that You're Rich:** The lobby of **The Empress Hotel,** 721 Government St. (☎ 604/384-8111 or 800/441-1414), will make you feel like one of its royal guests, who have included the king of Siam and Her Royal Majesty Queen Elizabeth II. The three-story atrium lobby boasts huge flower arrangements, throne-sized arm chairs, and the ideal staircase for making a grand entrance.
- **Best for Families:** The **Royal Scot,** 425 Quebec St. (☎ 604/388-5463 or 800/ 663-7515), is a converted apartment building with spacious suites that will make your family feel like they're in their home away from home. Suites come with fully equipped kitchens, VCRs, and many even have balconies.
- **Best Moderately Priced Hotel: Dashwood Manor,** 1 Cook St. (☎ 604/ 385-5517 or 800/667-5517), is an Edwardian showcase. Inside, the halls are richly carpeted and the walls are covered in dark wook paneling with polished brass accents. The suites aren't palatial, but neither is the price.
- **Best Inexpensive Hotel:** The **Victoria International Youth Hostel,** 516 Yates St. (☎ 604/385-4511), is a clean, efficient IYHA accommodation with lockers, bike storage, and dining facilities in a supportive atmosphere, and it's located right near the wharf.
- **Best B&B:** You can pretend to be the Great Gatsby at **Andersen Bed and Breakfast,** 301 Kingston St. (☎ 604/388-4565). You have a choice of sleeping either in their 1891 Queen Anne Victorian sea captain's home or on their 1927 yacht in Inner Harbour.
- **Best Alternative Accommodation:** The **Boathouse,** 746 Sea Dr. (☎ 604/ 652-9370), is a real boathouse, complete with a private dock and a rowing dinghy. There's only one room, built at the water's edge in a secluded cove, so it's a perfect spot for people who want privacy. It's small, but it has a full kitchen, a nice sitting area, and it's wonderful going to sleep to the sound of the waves.
- **Best Service:** The superb service at the **Aerie Resort,** 600 Ebedora Ln., P.O. Box 108, Malahat (☎ 604/743-7115), has all the magnificent European touches you rarely see on this continent. Leo and Maria Schuster, the owners, personally greet every guest. The maître d' and waitstaff of the hotel's restaurant were recruited from some of the world's best restaurants. And though there are only 24 rooms, full spa service is available on the premises.
- **Best Location:** Overlooking the Inner Harbour, the **Empress Hotel,** 721 Government St. (☎ 604/384-8111 or 800/441-1414), is the centerpiece of the Inner

Harbour. The Parliament Buildings (which are completely outlined in lights at night), the historic boat harbor (filled with antique sailing vessels), and the Royal British Columbia Museum are all within a block of the hotel.

- **Best Health Club:** The **Ocean Pointe Resort,** 45 Songhees Rd. (☎ 604/360-2999 or 800/667-4677), takes great pains to provide guests with the best spa in the Pacific Northwest. Complete skin and body treatments, exercise and pool facilities, aesthetic and aromatherapy treatments pamper the body and spirit.
- **Best Hotel Pool:** The **Ocean Pointe Resort,** 45 Songhees Rd. (☎ 604/360-2999 or 800/667-4677), has a lovely pool enclosed in a greenhouse facing the inner harbor. Glass doors open out onto the surrounding sundeck.
- **Best Views:** Harbor-view rooms at the **Ocean Pointe Resort,** 45 Songhees Rd. (☎ 604/360-2999 or 800/667-4677), have a wonderful view of both the Empress Hotel and the Parliament Buildings across the Inner Harbour with the Olympic Mountains in the distance.

2 The Inner Harbour

VERY EXPENSIVE

Coast Victoria Harbourside Hotel

146 Kingston St., Victoria B.C., Canada V8V 1V4. ☎ **604/360-1211** or 800/663-1144. Fax 604/360-1418. 132 rms, 6 suites. Nonsmoking rooms. Wheelchair-accessible rooms. A/C MINIBAR TV TEL. May–Sept, $164–$184 double; Oct–Apr, $114 double; year-round $300 suite. Children under 18 stay free in parents' room. AE, DC, ER, MC, V. Free underground parking. Bus: 30 from Superior and Montreal.

Located on the eastern shore of Inner Harbour, this new Coast hotel offers fine views from most rooms and suites. The best views are on the harbor side. The small standard rooms have only a single telephone and tiny balconies, but the modern furnishings are attractive and new. If you want luxury, try rooms and suites on the limited-edition service floor. These accommodations have balconies large enough to use as well as significantly better furnishings and amenities. The staff is outgoing and helpful, but be sure to use your "do not disturb" sign or they may start knocking very early to service the room. Follow the lovely garden path along the water's edge from the front of the hotel into downtown or catch the miniature Harbour Ferry that stops at the marina.

Dining/Entertainment: The intimate Blue Crab Bar and Grill offers West Coast cuisine and a view of the pleasure boats docked at the hotel's marina. The menu features fresh local seafood. There's live entertainment on Thursday, Friday, and Saturday nights.

Services: 24-hour room service, complimentary downtown shuttle, laundry and valet.

Facilities: Indoor/outdoor pool; small fitness center; whirlpool; private marina; conference facilities for up to 150.

The Empress Hotel

721 Government St., Victoria B.C., Canada V8W 1W5. ☎ **604/381-8111** or 800/441-1414. Fax 604/381-4334. 452 rms, 29 suites. MINIBAR TV TEL. Early May–mid-Oct, $180–$235 double; mid-Oct–early May, $129–$170 double. Year-round, $325–$1,400 suite. AE, CB, DC, DISC, ER, MC, V. Underground parking $9 (24 hours), valet $15. Bus: 5.

Conrad Hilton once said that the three most important things in a successful hotel are location, location, and location. The Empress, a Canadian-Pacific hotel, has them all. Opened in 1908 and extensively renovated in 1988, this ivy-covered grand château at the heart of the Inner Harbor is the crowning achievement of architect

Francis Rattenbury (of Vancouver Art Gallery fame). The hotel has had its share of celebrities, including Rudyard Kipling, the king of Siam, John Wayne, Bob Hope, and Queen Elizabeth II. But you don't have to be famous to stay here—all their guests feel a bit like royalty.

All guest rooms have Victorian decor and richly restored antique furnishings. Deluxe rooms have harbor views, while moderately priced rooms face the new Victoria Conference Centre. Eight honeymoon suites, accessible only by a private stairway, have four-poster canopy beds. Rooms for the hearing-impaired are equipped with strobe-light fire alarms.

Dining/Entertainment: The Empress has quite a few restaurants, but it is perhaps best known for afternoon tea in the Tiffany glass–domed Palm Court. Tea, which comes with an assortment of scones, crumpets, and the like, runs $16.95 per person. People who are serious about afternoon tea may prefer the James Bay Restaurant and Tea Room (see Chapter 12 for dining review) a few blocks away, but nothing beats the Empress for atmosphere.

Services: Concierge, room service, dry cleaning, laundry, secretarial service, massage.

Facilities: Indoor swimming pool; health club; sauna; whirlpool; shopping arcade; meeting/banquet space for up to 1,500 in the conference center; car-rental desk.

Harbour Towers Hotel

345 Quebec St., Victoria B.C., Canada V8V 1W4. ☎ **604/385-2405** or 800/663-5896. Fax 604/385-4453. 99 rms, 86 suites. Nonsmoking rooms. A/C TV TEL MINIBAR. Apr 20–June 15, $180 double; $220–$500 suite. June 16–Oct 15, $206 double; $286–$566 suite. Oct–Apr, $162 double; $202–$500 suite. AE, CB, DC, ER, MC, V. Underground parking $2. Bus: 30 to Superior and Oswego.

The modern 12-story Harbour Towers is the headquarters of the annual Victoria Jazz Festival, which is held in June. Light jazz music wafts year-round beneath the glass chandeliers of the marble-floored lobby.

All rooms have floor-to-ceiling sliding windows, especially important in harbor-view rooms. (You can guarantee a harbor view for an additional $10 to $15.) Costing $40 extra, "royal treatment" rooms on the 10th and 11th floors include continental breakfast, upgraded amenities, hairdryer, newspaper, free local calls, bathrobes, and unobstructed views. Suites have kitchens with two-burner stoves, microwave ovens, and small refrigerators. The deluxe penthouse suites on the twelfth floor even have fireplaces and stereo systems.

Dining/Entertainment: The "California-style" Art Deco restaurant serves three meals daily. Steak and seafood dinners are in the $14 to $18 range.

Services: Room service (6:30am to 1am), courtesy van, babysitting service.

Facilities: Fitness center; indoor swimming pool; sauna; whirlpool; beauty salon; gift shop; meeting space for up to 300.

✪ Ocean Pointe Resort

45 Songhees Rd., Victoria B.C., Canada V9A 6T3. ☎ **604/360-2999** or 800/667-4677. Fax 604/360-1041. 222 rms, 28 suites. Nonsmoking rooms. Wheelchair-accessible rooms. A/C MINIBAR TV TEL. May–Sept, $160–$220 double; $200–$650 suite. Oct–Apr, $150–$180 double; $175–$600 suite. AE, DC, ER, MC, V. Underground valet parking $9. Bus: 24 to Colville, or take the Harbour Ferry to the hotel's private dock.

A two-minute walk across the Johnson Street bridge from downtown and Market Square, this luxurious independent hotel built in 1992 stands on the Inner Harbour's north shore. It has Victoria's most commanding city and harbor views against a

Victoria Accommodations

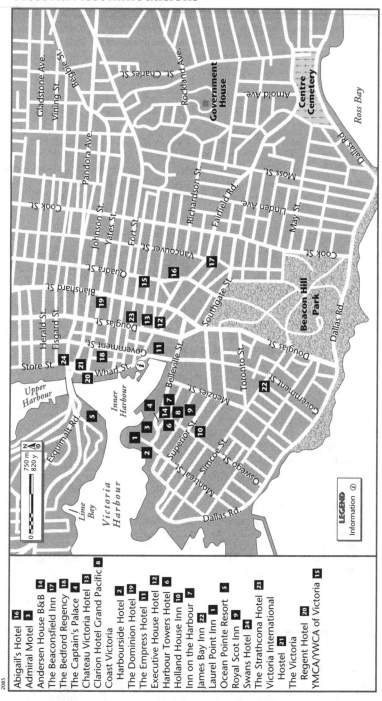

Abigail's Hotel **16**
Admiral Motel **3**
Andersen House B&B **14**
The Beaconsfield Inn **17**
The Bedford Regency **18**
The Captain's Palace **4**
Chateau Victoria Hotel **13**
Clarion Hotel Grand Pacific **8**
Coast Victoria
  Harbourside Hotel **2**
The Dominion Hotel **19**
The Empress Hotel **11**
Executive House Hotel **12**
Harbour Towers Hotel **6**
Holland House Inn **10**
Inn on the Harbour **7**
James Bay Inn **22**
Laurel Point Inn **1**
Ocean Pointe Resort **5**
Royal Scot Inn **9**
Swans Hotel **24**
The Strathcona Hotel **23**
Victoria International
  Hostel **21**
The Victoria
  Regent Hotel **20**
YMCA/YWCA of Victoria **15**

LEGEND
Information (i)

2085

backdrop of the Olympic Mountains. It offers some of the most complete spa services in the Pacific Northwest and an ever-increasing range of activities, including whale-watching expeditions that depart from their private dock. The Inner Harbour rooms have the best view, but rooms facing the outer harbor have floor-to-ceiling bay windows. On the executive floor, there are suites, a boardroom, lounge, and a fully equipped business center.

Dining/Entertainment: The Victorian, with views of Olde Town and the Parliament Buildings, offers elegant West Coast and spa cuisine. Casual dining is also available.

Services: 24-hour room service; concierge; complimentary shuttle service; valet; laundry; activities coordinator; babysitting.

Facilities: Heated glass-enclosed pool; health club; racquetball/squash and tennis courts; wine shop; European spa with massage, hydrotherapy, aromatherapy, facial and body treatments, and aesthetics salon; conference facilities for up to 400.

EXPENSIVE

The Captain's Palace

309 Belleville St., Victoria B.C., Canada V8V 1X2. ☎ **604/388-9191** or 800/563-9656. Fax 604/388-7606. 16 suites in two buildings. Apr 15–Oct 15, $125–$250 double suite. Oct 16–Apr 14, $75–$135 double suite. Rates include full breakfast. AE, DC, MC, V. Free parking. Bus: 5 to Belleville and Government.

Originally built in 1897, this small, quaint, white clapboard Victorian hotel (located just around the corner from the Empress Hotel) has been faithfully restored and preserved. It resembles a period museum—from the foyer, with its hand-painted, ceramic-tiled fireplace and rich wood paneling to the crystal chandeliers hanging from frescoed ceilings to the stained-glass windows and velvet tapestries. The staff completes the picture by dressing as liveried butlers and pinafored maids. Every suite is fully furnished with estate antiques, down to the carpeted private baths. There are no elevators, but the stairs add to the charm. Some rooms have harbor views; others feature private parlors.

The Captain's Palace is located right across from the ferry landings and a block from the legislative buildings. The hotel draws its share of the passing crowds of tourists, so don't look for solitude here.

Three meals and tea are served daily in several lovely ground-floor rooms, including the verandah, and are very popular. Dinner prices are in the $15–$20 range.

Clarion Hotel Grand Pacific

450 Quebec St., Victoria B.C., Canada V8V 1W5. ☎ **604/386-0450** or 800/228-5151. Fax 604/386-8779. 145 rms, 19 suites. A/C MINIBAR TV TEL. Jan–May 15, $195 double; $132–$352 suite. May 16–June, $140 double; $180–$400 suite. July–Sept 15, $92 double; $215–$425 suite. Sept 16–Dec 31, $110 double; $175–$400 suite. AE, DC, DISC, MC, V. Free parking. Bus: 30 to Superior and Oswego.

The Grand Pacific has two wings—an eight-story nonsmoking west wing and a six-story east wing. Opened in 1989, the hotel has already undergone major renovations.

Each of the richly decorated rooms has a balcony. Junior suites have French doors separating the bedroom and sitting room. Each executive suite features a double Jacuzzi, fireplace, three balconies, and a wet bar.

Dining/Entertainment: The dining room serves three meals daily, including a buffet breakfast in the summer. The bar offers light dining.

Services: Room service (6am to 11pm), concierge, valet cleaning, courtesy limousine.

Facilities: Athletic club with 25-meter ozonated indoor pool, separate kids' pool, weight room, aerobics classes, racquetball courts, sauna, whirlpool, massage therapist, equipment sales; fully equipped business center.

✪ Holland House Inn

595 Michigan St., Victoria B.C., Canada V8V 1S7. ☎ **604/384-6644.** Fax 604/384-6117. 10 rms. Wheelchair-accessible room. TV TEL. Apr–Oct, $120–$225 double. Nov–Mar, $80–$155 double. AE, DC, MC, V. Bus: 5 to Superior and Government.

Owned by noted avant-garde artist Lance Olsen, this impeccably clean and tidy home is a veritable fine-art museum displaying the work of Olsen, sculptor David Toresdahl, and other B.C. artists. The romantic three-story 1934 house with a white picket fence is tucked away on a tree-lined street less than two blocks behind the Parliament Buildings.

All rooms are furnished with antiques, private baths, wood floors, and four-poster beds with goose-down comforters. Two rooms have wood-burning fireplaces, but smokers are requested to use the outside balconies.

There is room service available. Complimentary gourmet breakfasts, featuring such treats as German apple pancakes or baked eggs with Brie and ham, are served between 7 and 9am.

Laurel Point Inn

680 Montreal St., Victoria B.C., Canada V8V 1Z8. ☎ **604/386-8721** or 800/663-7667. Fax 604/386-9547. 130 rms, 72 suites. Nonsmoking rooms. Wheelchair-accessible rooms. A/C TV TEL. May–Sept, $165 double; $235 junior suite; $325 bedroom suite; $595 full suite. Oct–Apr (including breakfast), $99 double; $169 junior suite; $235 bedroom suite; $450 full suite. Children under 12 stay free in parents' room. AE, CB, ER, MC, V. Free parking. Bus: 30 to Montreal and Superior.

The Laurel Point occupies a promontory that juts into the Inner Harbour, where visiting vessels make their final turn through the narrow channel toward downtown. All guest rooms have harbor views and small balconies. Many overlook a sculptured harborside garden. Room interiors are stark and uncluttered. There is a Japanese design throughout this attractive new property (almost half of the hotel is a 1989 addition). People in search of activity, however, may prefer the Ocean Pointe Resort (see above).

Dining/Entertainment: *Monday Magazine*, a free local paper, has declared the Sunday luncheon buffet in the cafe the "best in Victoria." There's live piano music nightly in the lounge.

Services: 24-hour room service, concierge, valet laundry.

Facilities: Heated indoor swimming pool, Jacuzzi, sauna, exercise bikes, gift shop, meeting/banquet space for up to 250.

MODERATE

Admiral Motel

257 Belleville St., Victoria B.C., Canada V8V 1X3. ☎ and fax **604/388-6267.** 18 rms, 11 suites. TV TEL. May–Sept, $89 double; $129 double with kitchen; $139 suite. Oct–Apr, $65 double; $79 double with kitchen; $85 suite. Additional person $6 extra. Children under 12 stay free in parents' room. Senior and off-season discounts. AE, DISC, ER, MC, V. Free parking. Bus: 5 to Belleville and Government.

The small, family operated Admiral Motel is an attractive '60s modern-style building. It's located right on the Inner Harbour near the Seattle-bound ferry landing and close to restaurants and shopping. The combination of comfortable rooms and reasonable rates attracts young couples, families, and other travelers in search of a harbor view without the attendant price.

The rooms are attractive and comfortably furnished. All have refrigerators. Some can sleep up to six people (though they might get a little cramped) and have kitchens. The owners are very friendly and provide assistance with sightseeing. They offer guest laundry, courtesy vehicle, and a car-rental desk.

⑨ Andersen House B&B

301 Kingston St., Victoria B.C., Canada V8V 1V5. ☎ **604/388-4565.** 5 rms. TEL. $75–$165 double. Rates include breakfast. MC, V. Free limited parking. Bus: 30 from Superior and Montreal.

A short walk from downtown, Andersen House was built in 1891 for a sea captain. It's an ornate Queen Anne-style Victorian wooden structure with high ceilings and stained-glass windows. Each room has a private bath/Jacuzzi, a stereo, and a king- or queen-size bed; three rooms overlook a lovely English garden. Our favorite room is the cabin of Janet and Max Andersen's gorgeous 50-foot teak 1927 motor yacht. It's docked in the harbor two blocks from the house. Breakfast for all guests is served in the house. Smoking is not allowed in the house or on the boat. Children over 8 are welcome.

Inn on the Harbour

427 Belleville St., Victoria B.C., Canada V8V 1X3. ☎ and Fax **604/386-3451.** 69 rms. TV TEL. May–Sept, $110–$120 double; $115–$125 twin. Oct–Apr, $66–$72 double; $69–$75 twin. Children under 12 stay free in parents' room. Winter discounts available. AE, DC, DISC, MC, V. Parking $2 per night. Bus: 5 to Belleville and Government.

This very welcoming hotel opposite the MV *Coho* ferry terminal has a subtle nautical decor. In the lobby, there's a scale model of the HMS *Royal Sovereign*, a 17th-century English vessel. The restaurant and lounge are named for the HMS *Swiftsure*—the last of the tall ships serving duty in the Pacific from 1882 to 1890.

Half the rooms face the Inner Harbour. Standard units are decorated in forest-green and floral prints with standard furnishings and a step-up bathtub; 18 have kitchenettes, including a stove and refrigerator.

Dining/Entertainment: The Swiftsure Restaurant offers three meals daily; dinners are in the $12 to $17 range. The handsome Swiftsure Lounge also serves light meals and features late-night fondues. In summer, there's an outdoor barbecue.

Services: Room service, valet laundry, courtesy van, secretarial service, safe-deposit boxes, automated teller machine, and postal services.

Facilities: Indoor/outdoor swimming pool, sauna, whirlpool, and meeting space for up to 60.

Royal Scot Inn

425 Quebec St., Victoria B.C., Canada V8V 1W7. ☎ **604/388-5463** or 800/663-7515. Fax 604/388-5452. 28 rms, 150 suites. TV TEL. May 16–June 30, $99–$112 double; $123–$249 suite. July 1–Sept 30, $107–$129 double; $144–$281 suite. Oct 1–May 15, $83–$93 double; $115–$225 suite. Weekly, monthly, and off-season discount rates. AE, ER, MC, V. Free parking. Bus: 5 to Belleville and Government.

A converted former modern apartment house, the Royal Scot is just half a block from the Parliament Buildings. The spacious suites that comprise most of the hotel have fully equipped kitchens and VCRs (there's in-house video rental); many also have balconies. Studio suites have a room divider separating the bedroom from the living room, dining area, and kitchen. One-bedroom suites have separate bedrooms with king-size, queen-size, or twin beds. All suites have sofa beds in the living room. In summer, the Royal Scot fills up with families; in winter, it's favored by retirees from the prairie provinces escaping subzero weather.

The fully licensed restaurant, which offers summertime outdoor seating, serves three meals and high tea daily. Room service is available, along with valet and guest laundry. Local phone calls are free. There's also an indoor swimming pool, sauna, Jacuzzi, exercise room, gift/sundries shop, games room, fax transmission service, courtesy van, and meeting space for up to 55.

INEXPENSIVE

✪ The James Bay Inn

270 Government St., Victoria B.C., Canada V8V 2V2. ☎ **604/384-7151.** Fax 604/381-2115. 50 rms (41 with bath). TEL TV. Apr 30–May 31, $52–$89 double. Oct 1–Apr 30, $38–$49 double. Jun 1–Sept 30, $72–$109 double. MC, V. Free, limited parking. Bus: 5 or 30 to Government and Superior.

A 1907 Edwardian manor facing Beacon Hill Park, this popular inn was the last home of famed painter Emily Carr, a Victoria native. The newly renovated lobby and rooms reflect a subtle Spanish design. The restaurant serves three meals daily, and there is also a well-patronized neighborhood pub. Guests of the inn receive 15% off in both establishments. The tranquillity of the James Bay Inn makes this place popular with vacationing retirees.

3 Downtown/Olde Town

EXPENSIVE

✪ The Beaconsfield Inn

998 Humboldt St., Victoria B.C., Canada V8V 2Z8. ☎ **604/384-4044.** Fax 604/721-2442. 6 rms, 3 suites. Oct 18–April 30, $120–$200 double. May 1–Oct 17, $175–$300 double (2 nights minimum on weekends). Rates include full breakfast. MC, V. Free parking. Bus: 1 or 2.

This charming inn is an impressively restored 1905 Edwardian mansion. Originally commissioned as a wedding gift, the Beaconsfield is now a romantic retreat (no children or pets) just four blocks from downtown. The inn boasts rich mahogany paneling, antique English furnishings throughout, hardwood floors, and delicate stained-glass window trim. The cozy library has wall-to-wall books and a games table.

Guests receive complimentary champagne in their rooms upon arrival. Each lavishly decorated room and suite is unique; some have fireplaces or skylights and French doors opening out onto the garden. None has televisions or phones. Smoking is not permitted. Each suite has a Jacuzzi for two and a fireplace in the sitting room. Beware of the cancellation and refund policy, which is rather unforgiving.

Dining/Entertainment: A full gourmet breakfast is served daily in the sunroom or the dining room, and there's afternoon tea (featuring self-service tea, port, sherry, fruit, and cheese) in the library.

Services: Concierge, complimentary umbrellas.

The Bedford Regency

1140 Government St., Victoria B.C., Canada V8W 1Y2. ☎ **604/384-6835** or 800/665-6500. Fax 604/386-8930. 40 rms. TV TEL. Oct 1–Apr 30, $110–$150 double. May 1–Sept 30, $150–$200 double. Rates include full breakfast and afternoon tea. AE, MC, V. Parking $15.65. Bus: 5.

This small hotel, hidden in the heart of Olde Town and surrounded by Victoria's finest shopping and dining, is a real find. Built in 1930, it was thoroughly gutted and renovated in 1987 and 1988. Today, the colorful flowerpots on its window ledges above Government Street and its spacious art deco lobby only hint at its charm.

Typical of many older hotels, the rooms vary considerably in size, shape, and decor. Most have brass accents, stocked bookshelves, goose-down comforters, and luxurious amenities. Some even have wood-burning fireplaces and Jacuzzis. Children are welcome, but the rooms only have one queen-size bed; the hotel recommends booking a separate room for children.

Dining/Entertainment: The restaurant serves three meals daily in summer, breakfast and lunch in winter, and classic British afternoon tea year-round. Garrick's Head Pub offers pub meals from 11am to 11pm daily in summer, Monday through Saturday in winter.

Services: Concierge, free local phone calls, valet laundry, morning coffee delivered to room, overnight shoeshine.

Chateau Victoria Hotel

740 Burdett Ave., Victoria B.C., Canada V8W 1B3. ☎ **604/382-4221** or 800/663-5891. Fax 604/380-1950. 61 rms, 117 suites. 8 nonsmoking floors. A/C TV TEL. $99–$136 double; $159–$270 suite. Seasonal discounts offered. AE, CB, DC, ER, MC, V. Free parking. Bus: 2.

This 18-story hotel was constructed in 1975 on the former site of the "Bird Lady's" house. Victoria Jane Wilson lived in a big white manor on the hill behind the Empress (see above). When she died in 1949, she left her fortune to her parrot, Louis. The loquacious bird continued to live in the house until his caretaker's death in 1966, at which time he was moved to a retirement home. His spirit—and that of his mistress—are alive at the château.

Though the exterior and immediate surroundings are rather plain (parking lots extend down the hill to the Empress), the interior is lovely. The rooms were completely renovated in 1989; two-thirds of them are elegant one- and two-bedroom suites. Every suite has a balcony, a king-size bed or two queen-size beds, a coffeemaker, and a small refrigerator. Some have kitchenettes.

Dining/Entertainment: The Parrot House Restaurant, offering magnificent views, is Victoria's only rooftop restaurant. It's open daily for breakfast and dinner.

Services: Room service (6:30am-10:30pm), concierge, valet laundry, courtesy van, secretarial services, babysitting referral.

Facilities: Skylit indoor swimming pool, whirlpool bath, business center, meeting space for up to 50.

Swans Hotel

506 Pandora Ave., Victoria B.C., Canada V8W 1N6. ☎ **604/361-3310** or 800/668-7926. Fax 604/361-3491. 29 suites. Oct 1–Apr 30, $79–$99 suite. May 1–June 30, $99–$119 suite. July 1–Sept 30, $145–$165 suite. AE, MC, V. Parking: $8. Bus: 23 or 24.

This 1913 building on the Inner Harbour was a feed warehouse when historic preservationist Michael Williams saw its potential in 1988 as a hotel/restaurant/brewery complex. Today, it's one of Olde Town's best-known buildings and is within a few blocks of most downtown attractions.

Swans is a boutique hotel—small, friendly, and charming. Unlike the diminutive lobby, the suites are spacious. Many are split level and have open lofts and exposed beams. All have full kitchens, separate dining areas, and living rooms. The two-bedroom suites are great for families as they can accommodate up to six people comfortably. Furnishings are basic, but original artwork and fresh flowers add to the pleasant atmosphere.

Dining/Entertainment: The new Fowl Fish Café is open for lunch and dinner daily. The often-crowded pub (see Chapter 12 for dining review), with a new glassed-in patio, serves a wide variety of pub snacks and traditional British-style ales brewed on the premises. Buckerfield's Brewery produces a dozen highly regarded draft ales.

Services: Room service, guest laundry.

The Victoria Regent Hotel

1234 Wharf St., Victoria B.C., Canada V8W 3H9. ☎ **604/386-2211** or 800/663-7472. Fax 604/386-2622. 15 rms, 33 suites. MINIBAR TV TEL. Apr 15–June 30, $125 double; $180–$365 suite. Jul 1–Sept 30 $150 double; $200–$320 suite. Oct 1–Apr 14, $95 double; $155–$295 suite. Rates include full breakfast. Children under 16 stay free in parents' room. AE, DC, DISC, ER, MC, V. Free, underground parking. Bus: 23 or 24 at the Johnson Street Bridge.

Originally slated to be a convention center in the 1970s, this condominium hotel consists in part of individually owned apartments. The hotel, with its wedding-cake architecture jutting into the Inner Harbour, is unmistakable from the water. The units are fairly large. There are full kitchens in each suite equipped with a stove, refrigerator, toaster, and even a dishwasher. All suites have king-size beds.

Dining/Entertainment: The ground-floor restaurant is a converted suite that actually extends out over the water. It serves three meals daily in summer but only breakfast and lunch in winter.

Services: Guest laundry, morning newspaper, babysitting referrals, secretarial service.

Facilities: Boat charters, meeting space for 30.

MODERATE

○ Abigail's Hotel

906 McClure St., Victoria B.C., Canada V8V 3E7. ☎ **604/388-5363.** Fax 604/388-7787. 16 rms. $120–$225 double. Rates include full breakfast. Midweek rates discounted about 30%. MC, V. Free parking. Bus: 1.

A four-story, gabled Tudor building surrounded by a beautiful garden, Abigail's is the quintessential small European-style luxury inn. This friendly, nonsmoking hotel is only a four-block walk east of the Empress, but it seems like another world.

The rooms seem tailor made for honeymooners or young lovers. Decorated in pastel colors, rooms have crystal chandeliers with dimmer switches, stained-glass windows, fresh flowers, and goose-down comforters. Most have either a private Jacuzzi or a deep soaking tub. Some also have fireplaces and four-poster canopy beds. Maybe best of all, there's no TV or telephone (there's a pay phone in the lobby). Once you're here, you've escaped from the real world. Be sure to check in before 10pm, when the doors are locked; unless you already have your room key, you won't get in.

A filling breakfast is served in the sunroom between 8 and 9am. There's an afternoon social hour with mulled wine and snacks from 4 to 7pm in the library. The library's piano and games table are popular with guests.

The Dominion Hotel

759 Yates St., Victoria B.C., Canada V8W 1L6. ☎ **604/384-4136** or 800/663-6101. Fax 604/382-6416. 101 rms. TV TEL. May–Sept, $114 double. Oct–Apr, $44.50–$49.50 double. Children under 16 stay free in parents' room. AE, DC, ER, MC, V. Free parking. Bus: 10, 11, or 14.

Victoria's oldest surviving hotel, the Dominion opened in 1876. Today, following a $7 million restoration, it's a lovely family oriented heritage property decorated with rich woods, marble floors, brass trim, and red velvet upholstery on antique chairs. Rooms have more modern appointments but maintain the flavor of times past with ceiling fans, brass lamps, and steam rooms. There are dozens of types of rooms, all of which have been fully renovated in the past few years.

The excellent gourmet restaurant, Central Park, features continental and nouvelle dinners in a turn-of-the-century decor for $16 to $25. The Lettuce Patch coffee shop serves three meals a day. The intimate Gaslight Lounge has carved solid-oak paneling, while the Barbary Coast Lounge is a bustling, garish, Victorian brass, wood, and stained glass sports bar reminiscent of San Francisco's turn-of-the-century dockside saloons. Room service and valet laundry are offered, and there is a health club available for guest use.

INEXPENSIVE

⑤ Executive House Hotel

777 Douglas St., Victoria B.C., Canada V8W 2B5. ☎ **604/388-5111** or 800/663-7001. Fax 604/385-1323. 108 rms, 71 suites. A/C TV TEL. $99–$159 double; $179–$495 suite. 10$–50% seasonal discount, depending on availability. AE, CB, DC, ER, MC, V. Parking $2. Bus: 2.

This 17-story luxury high-rise, across the street from the Victoria Conference Centre, offers spectacular city and harbor views. A clean and quiet hotel, it's a haven for business travelers and mature tourists.

The lobby is as small as the rooms are spacious. From standard rooms to one- and two-bedroom suites, all have balconies and floor-to-ceiling windows. Superior rooms and suites have kitchenettes with a stove and refrigerator (utensils can be rented for an additional $15). Each penthouse-level room and suite has a Jacuzzi, fireplace, garden patio, dining table, and fully equipped kitchen. Standard rooms have small fridges. All rooms include complimentary tea and coffee.

Barkley's Grill Room serves outstanding steaks and reasonable seafood. For more casual dining, the hotel has an informal restaurant, a pub, and an oyster bar. Guest services include room service (7am to 10pm), a concierge, valet laundry, and courtesy van. There's also a health spa with a steam room, tanning bed, and salon that offers facials, waxing and herbal wraps, as well as meeting space for up to 70.

The Strathcona Hotel

919 Douglas St., Victoria B.C., Canada V8W 2C2. ☎ **604/383-7137** or 800/663-7476. Fax 604/383-6893. 83 rooms, 2 suites. TV TEL. Oct 1–Mar 30, $48–$70 double; $110 suite. Apr–June, $55–$78 double; $125 suite. July–Sept, $60–$88 double; $135 suite. AE DC DISC MC V. Free, limited parking. All city buses stop within one block.

One block from the Inner Harbour in the heart of downtown, the five-story Strathcona Hotel, which dates from 1912, has been owned and operated by the Olson family for 49 years. A row of popular pubs and restaurants—the Sticky Wicket Pub on the corner, Big Bad John's Hill Billy Bar, and the Cuckoo's Nest Pub—nearly

---

🅐 Family-Friendly Hotels

Most Victoria hotels welcome children, but a few go further to make sure kids—and their parents—enjoy their stay.

Admiral Motel *(see p. 165)*   Friendly prices, a central location, refrigerators, and harbor views attract families year-round.

The Captain's Palace *(see p. 164)*   With a costumed staff and a wonderfully Victorian vintage decor, it's almost like staying in a museum—and an interesting one at that.

Royal Scot Hotel *(see p. 166)*   Apartment-style suites come with fully equipped kitchens, dining rooms, and living rooms.

Ocean Pointe Resort *(see p. 162)*   A gracious staff, loads of facilities, and activities will keep your kids occupied for days.

Swans Hotel *(see p. 168)*   Duplex suites filled with homey furnishings (and full kitchens) make this small hotel a home away from home.

hide the hotel from view. All part of the hotel, these establishments are connected to each other. Pool tables, a big rooftop patio with two sand-filled beach volleyball courts, horse racing via satellite with on-site wagering, and a host of other diversions attract a lively crowd. Upstairs, the rooms are surprisingly clean and well kept. Furnishings are basic. Rooms on the back side, away from the action, are reasonably quiet.

Victoria International Hostel

516 Yates St., Victoria B.C., Canada V8W 1K8. ☎ **604/385-4511.** Fax 604/385-3232. 104 beds. $14.50 International Youth Hostel members, $18.50 nonmembers. MC, V. Bus: 23 or 24 at the Johnson Street Bridge.

In the heart of Olde Town, this hostel has everything the serious backpacker needs. Facilities include two kitchens (stocked with utensils), dining room, TV lounge with VCR, games room, common room, library, laundry facilities, indoor bicycle lockup, and hot showers. An extensive ride board helps those in need of transportation arrangements, and the collection of outfitter and tour information rivals that of the tourism office. Most beds are in dormitories separated by gender, but there are a couple of family rooms. There's a 2am curfew, but the town gets a little sleepy by then, so you won't be missing much by turning in early.

YMCA/YWCA of Victoria

880 Courtney St., Victoria B.C., Canada V8W 1C4. ☎ **604/386-7511.** Fax 604/380-1933. 25 beds. A/C. $46 double. Payment required in advance. MC, V. Bus: 1.

Although exercise facilities for both genders are located in this big, brown-brick building, the residence is *for women only*. The entrance, which has a new lobby overlooking the work-out area, is on the Broughton Street side. The "Y" has a cafeteria (closed on Sunday), a swimming pool, and a cozy TV lounge. Rooms are small and simply furnished but very clean. There are shared bathrooms and pay telephones on each floor.

4 Outside the Central Area

EXPENSIVE

✪ The Aerie

P.O. Box 108, Malahat B.C., Canada V0R 2L0. ☎ **604/743-7115.** Fax 604/743-4766. 24 suites. A/C TV TEL. Apr 15–Oct 10, $165–$230 double; $270–$360 suite. Oct 11–Apr 14, $145–$190 double; $240–$300 suite. Rates include breakfast. AE, MC, V. Free parking.

This little bit of heaven, nestled high above the Malahat summit, is reached via a scenic 30-minute drive from Victoria. A steep, winding driveway leads up to the elegant Mediterranean villa, surrounded by a profusion of flowers, rock gardens, and lily ponds.

They recently installed phones in each suite, but the sense of tranquillity remains: Each suite is a perfect hideaway with a large, handcrafted bed; a sumptuous bathroom; a relaxing indoor Jacuzzi with mountain view; a few carefully selected books and magazines; and a fireplace in front of a white leather sofa. Most of the suites have decks positioned to ensure complete privacy. There are acres of private (guests-only) walking trails up to the summit.

The inn is the creation of gracious owner/managers Leo and Maria Schuster, who built the Aerie in 1991 after an extensive search for the perfect piece of land. Though the Aerie has been featured on *Lifestyles of the Rich and Famous*, there's no pretension here; whether you arrive by helicopter or Hyundai, you can expect the same warm welcome and pampering throughout your stay.

To get here, take Highway 1 (The Trans-Canada Highway) north from Victoria (or south from Nanaimo) to the Spectacle Lake turnoff near the Malahat Summit viewpoint. Take the first right and follow the winding driveway up to the inn.

Dining/Entertainment: The restaurant (see Chapter 13 for dining review) serves three meals daily but is only open to the public for dinner.

Services: In-room wet bar and fridge, in-room coffeemaker.

Facilities: Helipad, heated indoor pool, outdoor hot tub, tennis courts (racquets and balls available), full spa treatments, outdoor wedding chapel, conference facilities for 20.

Oak Bay Beach Hotel

1175 Beach Dr., Victoria B.C., Canada V8S 2N2. ☎ **604/598-4556** or 800/668-7758. Fax 604/598-4556. 46 rms, 5 suites. TV TEL. Apr 15-Oct 15, $103–$128 standard double; $154–$188 deluxe double; $158–$220 junior suite; $265–$395 executive suite. Oct 16–Apr 14, $88 standard double; $128 deluxe double; $142–$198 junior suite; $238–$355 executive suite. AE, DC, ER, MC, V. Free parking. Bus: 2.

This very British, Tudor-style inn perched above shore of the Haro Strait, $3\frac{1}{2}$ miles east of downtown Victoria, attracts an older crowd. Extensive flower gardens extend to the water, and there are views of the San Juan Islands and snow-capped Mount Baker. The hotel is casual and comfortable. The lobby is a huge living room with a century-old baby grand piano, antiques, and a big fireplace. Rooms, each of which is unique, are priced according to size and view. The third-story junior suites, with bay windows and balconies facing the sea, are the best rooms.

Dining/Entertainment: A popular restaurant with outdoor seating serves West Coast cuisine. An authentic English pub serves light meals and desserts.

Services: Room service, valet laundry, morning coffee and newspaper, complimentary seasonal shuttle service.

Facilities: The hotel's two private yachts offer dinner cruises, sightseeing, and fishing charters.

Sooke Harbour House

1528 Whiffen Spit Rd., Sooke B.C., Canada V0S 1N0. ☎ **604/642-3421.** 13 rooms. TEL. $123–$225. Rates include breakfast and lunch; dinner $56 additional.

This inn boasts the scenery of the island's secluded southern coast as well as refined British service and excellent cuisine. Owners Sinclair and Frederica Philip blend an innovative cooking style with fresh natural ingredients.

Each uniquely decorated room has views of the Strait of Juan de Fuca. The Victor Newman Longhouse Room has a Pacific Northwest First Nations' decor. The Herb Garden Room, decorated in shades of mint and parsley throughout, opens onto a private patio. The hosts leave a bouquet of flowers or a decanter of port in each room. TVs are available on request.

MODERATE

The Boathouse

746 Sea Dr. (Rt. 1), Brentwood Bay, Victoria B.C., Canada V0S 1A0. ☎ **604/652-9370.** 1 unit. TEL. $120 double. Rate includes continental breakfast. MC, V. Free parking.

True to its name, this single-unit bed-and-breakfast cottage is a converted boathouse built on pilings in the Saanich Inlet. It's a short stroll, or row, to Butchart Gardens, but it's very secluded. The only passers-by are likely to be seals, bald eagles, otters, herons, and raccoons. This is a great spot for a romantic getaway.

This charming red cabin is reached by descending a very long flight of stairs behind the owner's home. Inside, there are a sofa bed, dining table, kitchen area with small refrigerator and toaster oven, electric heat, and a reading alcove overlooking the floating dock. Full toilet and shower facilities are in a separate bathhouse a short way back uphill. All the makings for a delicious continental breakfast are provided the evening before. Guests have use of a rowing dinghy.

ⓢ Dashwood Manor

1 Cook St., Victoria B.C., Canada V8V 3W6. ☎ **604/385-5517** or 800/667-5517. Fax 604/383-1760. 15 suites. TV. Nov 1–Mar 31, $45–$155 suite. Jun 1–Sept 30, $135–$285 suite. Oct and Apr 1–May 31, $95–$215 suite. AE DC ER MC V. Free parking. Bus: 5.

This cozy Tudor manor, built in 1912 and renovated in 1994, looks south over the Straits of Juan de Fuca toward the Olympic Mountains. The beach is just across Dallas Street, one of the most scenic drives in Victoria, and Beacon Hill Park borders the manor on the west. Downtown is 20 minutes away, but the walk through the park is worth the trip.

The lobby is an Edwardian showcase: Deep-stained oak paneling and burgundy carpeting lead up to the 15 guest suites. Each unique suite has a queen-size bed and a well-stocked kitchen (breakfast is self-catered). Select suites have a fireplace, Jacuzzi, balcony, or perhaps a chandelier. The basement suites are the least expensive, but staying upstairs is worth the extra money. Complimentary sherry, port, and wine are laid out in the lobby in the evenings. Don't expect a crowd though—the clientele here is mostly couples, and the romance of the manor is hard to avoid.

INEXPENSIVE

ⓢ The Medana Grove

162 Medana St., Victoria B.C., Canada V8V 2H5. ☎ **604/389-0437** or 800/269-1188. Fax 604/389-0425. 2 rms. TV. May 16–Sept 14, $70–$85 double. Sept 15–May 15, $49 double. MC, V. Street parking. Bus: 5 to Simcoe.

This charming 1908 home in the James Bay district is a short walk from downtown and the Inner Harbour. Tucked away on a one-block-long, tree-lined street, the Medana Grove can be a little difficult to find, but it's worth the effort. Friendly hosts Garry and Noreen Hunt took it over in 1993 and have renovated both the cozy guest rooms and the public areas. The antique-filled living room, which has a welcoming fireplace, and dining room are comfortable and cheery. Both guest rooms are decorated in subtle floral patterns and have private baths. A full gourmet breakfast is served in the dining room. Smoking and pets are not permitted.

University of Victoria

Housing and Conference Services, P.O. Box 1700, Sinclair at Finerty Rd., Victoria B.C, Canada V8W 2Y2. ☎ **604/721-8395.** Fax 604/721-8930. May–Aug, $51.65 twin; $75.05 suite. Rates include full breakfast and taxes. Parking $4. Closed Sept–Apr. Bus: 4 or 14.

Victoria's major university opens its dormitories to summertime visitors for the four months when classes are not in session. All rooms have single or twin beds and basic furnishings. There are bathrooms, pay phones, and TV lounges on every floor. Linens, towels, and soap are provided. Each suite has four bedrooms (add $17.55 for each additional bedroom used), a kitchen, living room, and 1 1/2 baths. Each building has a coin-op laundry. Guests may use campus cafeterias; dining rooms; and athletic facilities, including the weight room, swimming pool, and tennis and squash courts for additional charges. Discounts are available for longer stays.

12 Victoria Dining

You've had a wonderful time wandering along the wharf and through the shops in Olde Town, and now you're famished. You've passed dozens of eateries of all shapes and sizes, but which one do you pick? Flip this way: in this chapter we've culled the real gems. *Bon appétit*!

They're all located in three geographical areas: **the Inner Harbour, Downtown/Olde Town,** and **Outside the Central Area.** Inner Harbour and Downtown/Olde Towne restaurants are all accessible on foot, while establishments outside the central area require a car.

Price ranges are based on the cost of entrées: **Very Expensive** (more than $20); **Expensive** ($15 to $20); **Moderate** ($10 to $15); and **Inexpensive** (less than $10). There's no provincial tax on restaurant meals in British Columbia—just the 7% federal goods and services tax (GST).

Restaurant hours vary. Lunch is typically served from noon to 1pm. British Columbians rarely dine before 7pm and eat even later in the summer. **Reservations** are recommended at most restaurants, especially the popular places.

1 Best Bets

- **Best Spot for a Romantic Dinner:** High atop Malahat Summit, overlooking Spectacle Lake, the **Aerie Resort,** 600 Ebedora Ln., P.O. Box 108, Malahat (☎ 604/743-7115), is the most romantic dining spot on the whole island.
- **Best Spot for Business Lunch:** The **Harvest Moon Café,** 1218 Wharf St. (☎ 604/381-3338), is a great place for afternoon negotiations. Located near the Inner Harbour, Olde Towne, and downtown areas, you can rendezvous with clients without anyone needing to commute too far out of the way. Tables are set far enough apart to allow privacy no matter how crowded it gets.
- **Best Spot for a Celebration: Rebecca's,** 1127 Wharf St. (☎ 604/380-6999), light, open, airy dining room has storefront-style windows that look out on to Wharf Street. A refreshingly light Pacific Northwest menu includes dishes like fresh halibut with almonds and a strawberry-balsamic vinaigrette. They even

bake their own cakes and pastries on the premises! During the summer, you can also move the party to their outdoor cafe garden.

- **Best Decor:** You'll feel "to the manor born" in **Olde English Inn's,** 429 Lampson St. (☎ 604/ 388-4353), with its baronial interior, complete with arms and armaments on the walls.
- **Best View: Milestone's,** 812 Wharf St. (☎ 604/381-2244), has Victoria's best wharf-side Inner Harbour view. You can watch the twinkling lights that outline the Parliament Buildings as they dance on the water in a comfortable rich, dark-wood setting.
- **Best Wine List:** The **Herald Street Café**'s, 546 Herald St. (☎ 604/381-1441), award-winning wine list is closely seconded by the **Harvest Moon Café**'s collection of B.C. wines and by the **Aerie's** international-vintage cellar.
- **Best Value:** The **James Bay Tea Room,** 322 Menzies St. (☎ 604/382-8282), offers healthy portions of classic British fare like roast beef with Yorkshire pudding as well as great service at a surprisingly moderate price.
- **Best for Kids: Millos,** 716, Burdett Ave. (☎ 604/382-4422 or 382-5544), treats your kids to a night on the town with a kids' menu, children-loving waiters, and exciting Greek dishes like stuffed grape leaves or egg and lemon soup.
- **Best Chinese Cuisine: Don Mee,** 538 Fisgard St. (☎ 604/383-1032), offers the finest Hong Kong–style dining experience in Chinatown. This large dining establishment offers a wide variety of meat, poultry, noodle, rice, and seafood dishes cooked with exotic spices and fresh vegetables.
- **Best Continental Cuisine:** The **Marina Restaurant,** 1327 Beach Dr. (☎ 604/ 598-8555), in Oak Bay creates a wide-ranging continental cuisine that appeals to a broad dining audience. Whether you prefer seafood such as fresh clams and oysters or perfectly roasted beef, ham, or chicken, you'll find hearty portions served here against a magnificent waterfront view.
- **Best French Cuisine:** The **Aerie Resort**'s, P.O. Box 108, Malahat (☎ 604/ 743-7115), chef/owner Leo Schuster creates the most remarkable classic French dishes. You can savor a cassoulet of smoked duck and venison sausage with a vintage Chateau Margaux Pavilion Rouge under a 24-carat gold ceiling, next to an open-hearth fireplace.
- **Best Italian Cuisine: Pagliacci's,** 1011 Broad St. (☎ 604/386-1662), brings southern Italian fare directly from Manhattan's Little Italy to your Victoria table. If you miss the taste of rich tomato-based sauces, veal parmesano resting on a mountain of spaghetti, or ricotta-stuffed cannelloni served in a lively, crowded atmosphere, then this is heaven. The expatriate New York owner guarantees it.
- **Best Seafood: Sooke Harbour House,** 1528 Whiffen Spit Rd. (☎ 604/ 642-3421), not only serves the best gifts from the sea and its own garden—like red sturgeon in a raspberry, sweet cicely, and sake-butter sauce with glazed beets, maple-roasted celeric and a wild rice parmesan—it's a favorite spot among some of Vancouver's most successful restaurateurs.
- **Best Pacific Northwest:** The **Harvest Moon Café**'s, 1218 Wharf St. (☎ 604/ 381-3338), new owner, Terry Jackson has completely revamped its already outstanding regional cuisine. Pacific-Northwest cuisine is famous for its preparation of fresh, locally grown produce, meats, wines, and seafood without disguising them in too many fats or cream sauces. Grilled, wood-smoke, and baked dishes are accented by a wide repertoire of herbs and spices.

- **Best West Coast:** The **Herald Street Café,** 546 Herald St. (☎ 604/381-1441), has the best of what West Coast cuisine has to offer: fresh ingredients combined with imaginative blends of both eastern and western influences. Try the delectable combination of fettucine imaginatively served with prawns sautéed in ginger and wine topped with roasted cashews and stir-fried vegetables.
- **Best Burgers and Beer: Fogg 'N' Suds,** 711 Broughton St. (☎ 604/383-BEER), may be a regional chain, but who else offers you a "passport" to more than 250 varieties of ales and lagers accompanied by big, juicy grilled burgers? (The passport gets stamped everytime you try a new brew.)
- **Best Desserts:** The Belgian Chocolate Bag filled with fresh fruit, mousse, and ice cream at **Met Bistro,** 1715 Government St. (☎ 604/386-1512), is absolutely heaven-sent.
- **Best Late-Night Dining: Pagliacci's,** 1011 Broad St. (☎ 604/386-1662), *is* Victoria's late-night dining spot. Noisy, crowded, and "very New York," this is where to be seen while you munch on a plate of spaghetti bolognese or a piping hot sausage and mushroom pizza.
- **Best Outdoor Dining: Milestone's,** 812 Wharf St. (☎ 604/381-2244), has an outdoor patio that overlooks the fishing boats on the Inner Harbour, the illuminated Parliament Buildings, and the Grand Empress Hotel. Claim your seat before sunset and enjoy the view.
- **Best People Watching:** Even though **Vin Santo,** 620 Trounce Alley (☎ 604/480-5560), is tucked away in Trounce Alley, it is the best people-watching spot. The floor-to-ceiling windows give you a perfect view of shoppers as they make their way through the numerous fashionable gift and clothing shops. And Vin Santo's clientele are as beautiful as the original art prominently displayed on the rich, dark walls.
- **Best Afternoon Tea:** The **James Bay Tea Room,** 332 Menzies St. (☎ 604/382-8282), makes you feel as if you've been transported to a cozy Cotswalds cottage tea room. Freshly baked scones, thick Devonshire cream, and strawberry jam are served with a piping hot pot of tea in true British fashion.
- **Best Brunch:** Overlooking Oak Bay, the **Marina Restaurant's,** 1327 Beach Dr. (☎ 604/598-8555), huge, all-you-can-eat buffet of everything from breakfast foods to fresh seafoods and sumptuous desserts is not just a great value, it's delicious!
- **Best Fast Food: Wah Lai Yuen,** 560 Fisgard St. (☎ 604/381-5355), makes a variety of Chinese-style baked and steamed buns filled with beef, pork, curried chicken, or vegetables. Made fresh daily and prominently displayed on racks, they cost about 85¢ each. But you better get there before 2pm. They're a popular alternative to grabbing a hamburger around here.

2 Restaurants by Cuisine

CANTONESE
Don Mee Restaurant
   (Downtown/Olde Town, *I*)
Wah Lai Yuen (Downtown/Olde
   Town, *I*)

CONTINENTAL
The Marina Restaurant
   (Outside the Central Area, *E*)
Pablo's Dining Lounge
   (Inner Harbour, *E*)

Key to abbreviations: *I*=Inexpensive; *M*=Moderate; *E*=Expensive; *VE*=Very Expensive

ENGLISH

James Bay Tea Room (Inner
   Harbour, *E*)
Olde England Inn (Downtown/
   Olde Town, *E*)

FRENCH

The Aerie (Outside the Central
   Area, *VE*)

GREEK

Millos (Downtown/Olde Town, *M*)

INDIAN

Taj Mahal (Downtown/
   Olde Town, *M*)

INTERNATIONAL

Fogg 'N' Suds (Downtown/
   Olde Town, *I*)

ITALIAN

Pagliacci's (Downtown/
   Olde Town, *M*)

JEWISH

Pagliacci's (Downtown/
   Olde Town, *M*)

MEXICAN

Café Mexico
   (Downtown/Olde Town, *I*)

NORTHERN INDIAN

Da Tandoor
   (Downtown/Olde Town, *M*)

PACIFIC NORTHWEST

Harvest Moon Café
   (Downtown/Olde Town, *E*)

Met Bistro (Downtown/
   Olde Town, *M*)
Rebecca's (Downtown/
   Olde Town, *E*)

PASTA

Herald Street Café
   (Downtown/Olde
   Town, *M*)
Vin Santo (Downtown/
   Olde Town, *E*)

PUB GRUB

Six Mile Pub (Outside the
   Central Area, *I*)

RIBS

Cherry Bank Spare Rib House
   (Downtown/Olde Town, *M*)

SZECHUAN

Don Mee Restaurant (Downtown/
   Olde Town, *I*)

WEST COAST

Banana Belt Café
   (Inner Harbour, *I*)
Camille's (Downtown/
   Olde Town, *M*)
Herald Street Café
   (Downtown/Olde Town, *M*)
Milestone's (Downtown/
   Olde Town, *I*)
Reebar (Downtown/Olde
   Town, *M*)
Sooke Harbour House
   (Outside the Central Area, *VE*)
Vin Santo (Downtown/
   Olde Town, *E*)

3 The Inner Harbour

EXPENSIVE

Pablo's Dining Lounge

225 Quebec St. ☎ **604/388-4255.** Reservations recommended. Main courses $13.95–$25.
AE, MC, V. Daily 5pm–around 11pm. CONTINENTAL.

Pablo Hernandez's paella valenciana has been a Victoria favorite for 17 years. This
intimate restaurant is housed in an Edwardian house near Laurel Point. Special

dinners for two include a Salt Spring rack of lamb and chateaubriand forestière. Try one of Pablo's seafood dishes prepared in classic French style. Live music serenades you (Wednesday through Saturday) while you sip Spanish coffee and nibble on flambéed crepes and ice cream.

MODERATE

⑤ James Bay Tea Room

332 Menzies St. ☎ **604/382-8282.** Reservations recommended. Lunch $4.25–$8.25; dinner $9.25–$11.25. MC, V. Breakfast Mon–Sat 7–11:30am, Sun 8am–12:30pm; lunch Mon–Sat 11:30am–4:30pm; tea daily 1–4:30pm; dinner daily 4:30–9pm. ENGLISH.

This has been Victoria's best spot for afternoon tea for decades. A pot of tea, accompanied by scones with clotted cream and jam, is served in this simple British country home a block from the Parliament Buildings. Traditional dishes such as eggs and kippers for breakfast or steak-and-kidney pie and Cornish pasties for lunch are served daily. A favorite dinner dish at this very British restaurant is, unsurprisingly, roast prime rib of beef with Yorkshire pudding. They also serve stew and dumplings, filet of salmon, and more. There's often a line for tea—but it's a civil one.

INEXPENSIVE

Banana Belt Café

281 Menzies St. ☎ **604/385-9616.** Breakfast and lunch $4.25–$9.25. No credit cards. Tues–Sun 8am–3pm. WEST COAST.

If you're looking for a fresh quesadilla stuffed with cheese and avocados, a fresh juice shake, or a good old-fashioned burger, then go to this favorite hangout of James Bay locals. Breakfast, serious business here, features huge omelets served with fruit salad. Don't let names such as the Sensitive New Age Guy Omelet (filled with Monterey jack, Brie, and avocados) fool you—a hearty appetite is necessary to eat here. The interior is rather plain and the outside even plainer. But if it looked quaint, it wouldn't be this cheap.

4 Downtown/Olde Town

EXPENSIVE

✪ Harvest Moon Café

1218 Wharf St. ☎ **604/381-3338.** Reservations recommended. Lunch $6.95–$9.50; main courses $14.50–$18.50. AE, MC, V. Daily 11am–11pm. PACIFIC NORTHWEST.

This place serves up roast pork lion with apple-garlic relish, fresh asparagus, and grilled yams in one of western Canada's oldest buildings: the 1858 Steam Victoria warehouse. The exposed-brick walls (made of ballast collected from British ships) are warmed by original art and floral arrangements, creating an intimate setting.

The restaurant's motto is "fresh, local, seasonal." Smoked salmon and Indian candy are made on the premises and served with black bean and ginger, caper and dill, or hot oil sauces. The award-winning wine list includes an extensive collection of great B.C. wines. Bread pudding and Belgian chocolate cookies are house specialties, but if you're lucky enough to eat here on a night when they feature white Belgian chocolate cheesecake, you'll be truly blessed.

Olde England Inn

429 Lampson St. ☎ **604/388-4353.** Reservations recommended. Main courses $14–$30. AE, DC, MC, V. Lunch daily 11:30am–3:30pm; dinner daily 5–9pm. ENGLISH.

Victoria Dining

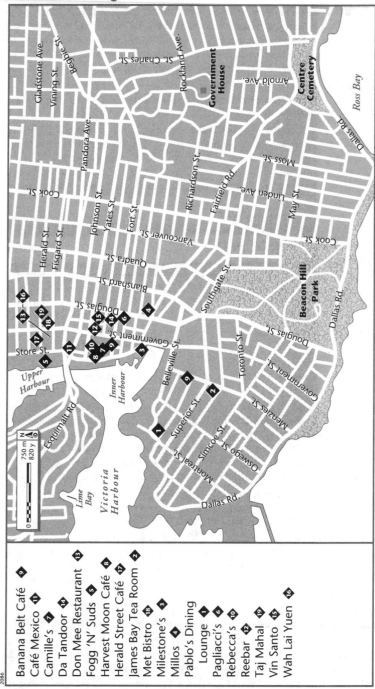

Banana Belt Café ◆ 9
Café Mexico ◆ 11
Camille's ◆ 7
Da Tandoor ◆ 14
Don Mee Restaurant ◆ 13
Fogg 'N' Suds ◆ 5
Harvest Moon Café ◆ 8
Herald Street Café ◆ 17
James Bay Tea Room ◆ 2
Met Bistro ◆ 18
Milestone's ◆ 3
Millos ◆ 4
Pablo's Dining
  Lounge ◆ 1
Pagliacci's ◆ 6
Rebecca's ◆ 10
Reebar ◆ 12
Taj Mahal ◆ 19
Vin Santo ◆ 15
Wah Lai Yuen ◆ 16

2086

You'll feel pampered in this aristocratic British setting complete with swords on the walls. The costumed staff serves a banquet of classic fare including Cumberland broth (mushrooms in a beef stock laced with port); mixed grill of lamb chop, kidney, and steak; rabbit with juniper berries and currants; and, in true British tradition, a roast loin of beef. Their "puddings" include sherry trifle and rich cakes served with custard sauce.

Rebecca's

1127 Wharf St. ☎ **604/380-6999.** Main courses $12.95–$18.95. AE, MC, V. Daily 11:30am–10pm. PACIFIC NORTHWEST.

A team of eight chefs creates the pastas and baked goods served at this spacious, wharf-front restaurant with a light, open atmosphere. The seasonal menus include such specials as whole Dungeness crab with Chardonnay and fresh halibut with almonds and a strawberry balsamic vinaigrette. There is a cappuccino bar and a cocktail bar that's perfect for people watching. The outdoor cafe is open in the summer.

Vin Santo

620 Trounce Alley. ☎ **604/480-5560.** Main courses $13–$18. AE, MC, V. Mon–Sat 11am–midnight, Sun 11am–10pm; brunch Sat–Sun 11am–3pm. PASTA/WEST COAST.

Vin Santo, which is located down a short side street, is an art gallery-cum-bistro filled with impressive works by local artists. Fresh northern Italian pasta dishes (by the half or full order), Santa Fe wraps, caribou sausage with apple compote, lamb burgers, grilled salmon, and brunch omelets are artistically executed with tasty herb and wine sauces. When Vin Santo hosts its occasional jazz evenings, the place is transformed into a Chicago-style jazz and supper club (call for current information).

MODERATE

Camille's

45 Bastion Sq. ☎ **604/381-3433.** Reservations recommended. Main courses $12.25–$16.95. MC, V. Tues–Sat 5:30–10pm. WEST COAST.

Concealed in the basement of the Old Law Chambers, Camille's is a romantic restaurant with exposed brick softly illuminated by Tiffany glass lamps. On Sunday evenings, wine tastings introduce you to the best selections from their cellar. Smoked salmon pinwheels with avocado and horseradish cream and Portuguese pork tenderloin with clams baked with sherry, paprika, and caramelized apples are just two of the sumptuous seasonal menu choices at this intimate hideaway.

Cherry Bank Spare Rib House

825 Burdett Ave. ☎ **604/385-5380.** Reservations accepted. Three-course rib special $11.95. AE, DC, MC, V. Lunch daily 11:30am–2pm; dinner daily 5–9pm. RIBS.

For more than 40 years, this has been Victoria's top rib house. Located in an 1897 landmark hotel, this place has a friendly atmosphere and staff. They serve up large, tangy racks of ribs accompanied by salad, potatoes, vegetables, and garlic bread to a family oriented clientele. You'll also find scampi, fresh fish, seafood, and steaks on the menu.

Da Tandoor

1010 Fort St. ☎ **604/384-6333.** Reservations recommended. Main courses $6.95–$14.95; combination dinners $12.95–$17.95. MC, V. Daily 5pm–10:30pm. NORTHERN INDIAN.

Tandoori-baked chicken, seafood, and lamb are the house specialties at this elegant northern Indian restaurant, whose service and atmosphere rival those of the best establishments in New York or London. The extensive, well-prepared menu also includes masalas, vindaloos, goshts, and vegetarian dishes as well as classic appetizers such as vegetable or meat samosas, pakoras, and papadums.

Herald Street Café

546 Herald St. ☎ **604/381-1441.** Reservations required. Lunch $5.50–$9, dinner $10.95–
$19.95. AE, ER, MC, V. Lunch Wed–Sat 11:30am–3pm; dinner Sun–Wed 5:30–10:30pm, Thurs–
Sat 5:30pm–midnight; brunch Sun 10am–3pm. PASTA/WEST COAST.

Young Olde Town locals frequent this light, casual restaurant for its excellent
Sunday brunch. Housed in a Victoria heritage building, the café is filled with
potted palms and flowers. The walls are decorated with local artists' works, which
you can buy if the desire strikes. Freshly made pastas; delicate venison medaillons;
and steamed mussels served with prawns, ginger, and roasted cashews are just
a few of the dinner creations. Desserts are fabulous, and their award-winning wine
list has won them almost as much recognition as their food. The dessert menu
changes at every meal, and each item is freshly-made as well as remarkably inventive:
Imagine rolling a ripe banana in rain forest crunch and topping it with red-bean
ice cream.

✪ Met Bistro

1715 Government St. ☎ **604/381-1512.** Reservations recommended. Main courses $9.50–
$18.50. MC, V. Daily 4:30pm–11pm. PACIFIC NORTHWEST.

This Chinese-style, balconied building once served as the Chinatown Community
Settlement House. (There's still a Buddhist temple upstairs.) Now the ground floor
serves hungry patrons from a delightful menu that changes considerably every month.
The fare includes oyster stew, brimming with large Fanny Bay oysters, leeks, back
bacon, cream, and potatoes; smoked duck sausage served with caramelized pear, blue
cheese, and flat bread; and herb-and-spice-crusted loin of lamb topped with a rosemary and red wine demi-glacé. Tables are set up in a cozy, bistro-style arrangement
so the restaurant remains intimate even when crowded.

The wine list comes from the Okanagan valley, France, South Africa, and Australia.
For dessert, it's worth the 20-minute wait to receive your shell-shaped Belgian chocolate bag filled with fresh fruit, white chocolate mousse, and ice cream.

⑤ Millos

716 Burdett Ave. ☎ **604/382-4422** or 604/382-5544. Reservations recommended.
Main courses $8.95–$24.95. AE, DC, ER, MC, V. Lunch Mon–Sat 11:30am–4:30pm; dinner daily
4:30–11pm. GREEK.

Millos is not hard to find: Just look for its life-size namesake—a blue-and-white wind-
mill behind the Empress Hotel. Flaming *saghanaki* (sharp cheese sautéed in olive oil
and flambéed with Greek brandy); grilled halibut *souvlaki*; baby back ribs; and succulent, fresh salmon grilled with lemon, oregano, and herbs are just a small portion
of the menu at this five-level, lively, Mediterranean restaurant. You become part of
the family for the evening, and your kids get their own special menu. If the staff and
food aren't entertaining enough, folk and belly dancers perform on Friday and
Saturday nights.

Pagliacci's

1011 Broad St. ☎ **604/386-1662.** Reservations not accepted. Main courses $8–$14. MC, V.
Daily 11:30am–12:30am (light menu 3–6pm). ITALIAN/JEWISH.

Transplanted New Yorker Howie Segal re-created a little bit of home in this incredibly popular hangout. You can get a good, hearty plate of southern Italian pasta;
veal Parmesan; chicken soup like Mother used to make; and cappuccino and *dolce*
(Italian pastries) in a lively, noisy, casual atmosphere. Tables are so close together
that you'll know your neighbor's life story. It's one of the few late-night eateries in
town, so even if you have to stand in line for while, you can be sure you'll eventually
get to eat.

Reebar

50 Bastion Square. ☎ **604/361-9223.** Main courses $5.25–$8.95. AE, MC, V. Lunch daily from 11:30am (noon on Sat); dinner daily 5:30–10pm. WEST COAST.

This "modern-food" restaurant attracts a young, casual clientele. The simple offerings include a vegetable and almond patty served with red onions, sprouts, and fresh tomato salsa on a multigrain kaiser roll; crisp salads loaded with toasted pine nuts, feta cheese, market-fresh vegetables, and sun-dried tomato vinaigrette; and blue corn crepes filled with vegetable salsa and three cheeses and served with chipotle chile cream sauce.

Taj Mahal

679 Herald St., near Douglas Street. ☎ **604/383-4662.** Reservations recommended. Main courses $11.95–$17.95. AE, DC, MC, V. Lunch Mon–Fri 11:30am–2pm, Sat noon–2:30pm; dinner daily 5:30pm–about 10:30pm. Bus: 4, 10, or 14 to Douglas Street. INDIAN.

Domes and minarets trimmed in blue and gold tiles grace the exotic exterior of this establishment. You'll feel as though you had stepped into a fairy tale as waiters and waitresses in saris serve you in this elaborate re-creation of a Punjab prince's palace. Dishes include fish in coconut sauce, Pacific prawn biriyani, vindaloos, tikkas, and tandooris. There is also an extensive selection of delectable vegetarian dishes. Fresh mango and homemade yogurt drinks as well as *chai* (spicy tea) and *kawa* (coffee made with cinnamon, cardamom, and cloves) are refreshing beverages.

INEXPENSIVE

Café Mexico

1425 Store St. ☎ **604/386-1425.** Main courses $6.95–$13.95. AE, DC, MC, V. Sun–Thurs 11:30am–11pm, Fri–Sat 11:30am–midnight. MEXICAN.

Cacti and bullfight posters decorate this exposed-brick Market Square cantina, where you can get enchiladas, tacos, burritos, chiles rellenos, chimichangas, and fajitas. The Vista del Mar (a grilled flour tortilla topped with prawns and scallops in a wine-cream sauce and covered with melted cheese, avocado, and sour cream) is our favorite special. If you're just looking for a light bite, nibble on some nachos as Latin music plays in the background.

Don Mee Restaurant

538 Fisgard St. ☎ **604/383-1032.** Four-course dinner for two $16.95; main courses $4.95–$10.35. AE, DC, MC, V. Lunch Mon–Fri 11am–2:30pm, Sat–Sun and holidays 10:30am–2:30pm; dinner daily 5pm–closing. CANTONESE/SZECHUAN.

Serving since the 1920s at the same location, Don Mee's is still preparing genuine Hong Kong–style dim sum, San Francisco–style chop suey and chow mein, piquant Szechwan seafood dishes, and Cantonese sizzling platters. You can't miss this second-story restaurant with its huge, brightly illuminated neon Chinese lantern above the small doorway. A four-foot-tall, gold-leafed, laughing Buddha greets you at the foot of the stairs leading up to the large Hong Kong–style room. The dinner specials for two, three, or four people are a great deal.

Fogg 'N' Suds

711 Broughton St. ☎ **604/383-BEER.** Main courses $5.95–$12.95. AE, MC, V. Mon–Sat 11am–1am, Sun 11am–11pm. INTERNATIONAL.

This theme-oriented Canadian chain restaurant is named after Phineas T. Fogg, the character in Jules Verne's *Around the World in 80 Days*. It's an absolutely delightful place to bring the kids. The dark-wood, pub-style decor belies its family friendly ambience and eclectic menu. If you think that the beer list of 250 international brews

> ### 👪 Family-Friendly Restaurants
>
> **Banana Belt Café** *(see p. 178)*   Here, kids can savor yogurt smoothies, fruit shakes, quesadillas, and other fun food in a casual atmosphere.
>
> **Cherry Bank Spare Rib House** *(see p. 180)*   In this rib house with finger-licking fare, you and your kids can enjoy a warm, friendly atmosphere while you're digging in.
>
> **Fogg 'N' Suds** *(see p. 182)*   Even the pickiest eater in your family will find something appealing here.
>
> **Millos** *(see p. 181)*   Victoria's best Greek restaurant, offers a children's menu; lively, friendly waiters who love kids; and new tastes.

is impressive, then take a look at the food selections from around the world: Hamburgers, nachos, pastas, stir-fries, calamari, and schnitzel are just the beginning.

Milestone's

812 Wharf St. ☎ **604/381-2244.** Reservations not required. Main courses $5.95–$9.95 at brunch, $5.95–$12.95 at dinner. AE, DC, MC, V. Brunch Mon–Fri 11am–4pm, Sat–Sun 10am–4pm; dinner Sun–Thurs 4–10pm, Fri–Sat 4–11pm. WEST COAST.

You'll find the best waterside view of the Inner Harbour from this highly successful Vancouver chain restaurant located just below the Travel InfoCentre. Bountiful grilled chicken Caesar salad, seafood, ribs, and steak as well as overstuffed sandwiches are served up in an upscale, casual atmosphere. The drink specials are refreshing, especially if you manage to get a table on the outdoor patio.

🆂 Wah Lai Yuen

560 Fisgard St. ☎ **604/381-5355.** Main courses $5.95–$13.95. No credit cards. Tues–Sat 10am–9pm, Sun 10am–7pm. CANTONESE.

Whor wonton is not your basic noodle dumpling soup—it's a brimming bowl of wontons, sliced barbecue pork, black mushrooms, prawns, and bok choi in a clear, rich chicken stock. It's also one of the many delights you'll find in this brightly lit, Formica-filled Chinatown diner. You may find yourself sharing one of the large round tables with a Chinese family or a couple who've discovered this unlikely source of excellent Chinese food. Favorite selections include hot pot dishes such as chicken steamed with black mushrooms and ginger and served with a bowl of steamed rice; and their generously large baked buns (around 85¢) filled with barbecue pork or black bean paste.

5 Outside the Central Area

VERY EXPENSIVE

⊘ The Aerie

600 Ebedora Ln., P.O. Box 108, Malahat. ☎ **604/743-7115.** Reservations required. Main courses $26.75–$29; seven-course menu $55 per person. AE, MC, V. Daily 5–10pm. (*Note:* Breakfast and lunch are for overnight guests only.) FRENCH.

Leo and Maria Schuster built their "Castle in the Mountains" with beautiful dining rooms overlooking Spectacle Lake from high atop Malahat Summit. From every room, panoramic windows look out at bald eagles soaring from treetop nests and deer grazing down below.

An appetizer plate of grilled, marinated tiger prawns in a ginger-lime cream sauce or shrimp and lobster bisque with fresh basil are just the overtures to this dining symphony. Impeccable service accompanies the meal. A 24-carat gold-leaf ceiling and a large, open-hearth fireplace warm the room. Cassoulet of smoked duck, venison sausage with red onion marmalade, or masterfully prepared halibut filet are accompanied by the region's best wine list, which even includes a vintage Château Margaux Pavilion Rouge. A luscious orange cappuccino mousse topped with white Belgian chocolate sauce and an excellent selection of brandies and Kona coffee complete the experience.

Sooke Harbour House

1528 Whiffen Spit Rd., Sooke. ☎ **604/642-3421.** Reservations required. Main courses $16–$28. AE, ER, MC, V. Daily from 5:30pm–10pm. (*Note:* Breakfast and lunch for overnight guests only.) WEST COAST.

This highly acclaimed establishment is in a rambling white house on a bluff overlooking the Whiffen Spit in Sooke. A huge living room with a fireplace and two adjoining rooms have been converted into this restaurant with a spectacular view of Sooke Harbour. You immediately feel at home in the quiet, relaxed atmosphere as you dine on local seafood and organically farmed herbs and vegetables (fresh from Frederica and Sinclair Philip's own garden) prepared West Coast style. Sooke continues to live up to its fine reputation.

EXPENSIVE

The Marina Restaurant

1327 Beach Dr., Oak Bay, Victoria. ☎ **604/598-8555.** Lunch $9.25–$11.25; main courses $14.95–$24.95; brunch $19.95. Lunch daily 11:30am–2:30pm; dinner Mon–Thurs 5–10pm, Fri–Sat 5–11pm; brunch Sun 10am–2:30pm. CONTINENTAL.

The fashionable Oak Bay marina and surrounding palatial California-style homes provide a romantic backdrop for dinner or Sunday brunch at this dock-side restaurant. There are two levels of seating and panoramic table-to-ceiling windows throughout the semicircular dark-wood dining room. No matter where you sit, your view of the marina is unobstructed.

The customers here are on the conservative side. The service is friendly and efficient: While we helped ourselves to the buffet at the popular Sunday brunch, our coffee cups and water glasses were never empty. The splendid, all-you-can-eat buffet is overflowing with oysters, clams, prawns, prime rib, poached salmon, garden-fresh salads, marinated vegetables, sparkling fruit salads, breakfast foods, as well as an exhaustive array of handmade Belgian chocolate truffles, tall cakes, and puddings. Though we never made it for dinner, we've heard rave reviews.

INEXPENSIVE

Six Mile Pub

494 Island Hwy., View Royal. ☎ **604/478-3121.** Main courses $4.50–$7.50. ER, MC, V. Lunch daily 11:30am–2pm; dinner daily 6–9pm. Pub, Mon–Sat 11am–1am, Sun 11am–midnight. ENGLISH PUB.

This pub, in a building dating from 1898, has a loyal local clientele who come for both the atmosphere and the dinner specials. The food is seasoned with fresh herbs from the pub's own garden. You can enjoy the warm ambience of the fireside room, which has an oak bar with stained glass and other classic British touches, or the beautiful scenery from the outdoor patio. Start with one of their 10 brews on tap and then enjoy a hearty cornish pasty, steak-and-mushroom pie, or juicy prime rib. If meat isn't part of your diet, try one of their tasty veggie burgers.

What to See & Do in Victoria

13

Steeped in history, this quiet, friendly, seaside community is filled with attractions to suit every interest. The outdoors is as much a part of life here as it is in the rest of the province. If your plans include long strolls and relaxation, then Victoria is also the ideal place for you: There are magnificent rolling estates, gardens, beaches, and harbors to discover here.

SUGGESTED ITINERARIES

If You Have 1 Day

Stroll along the Inner Harbour. Start out by looking at Francis Rattenbury's great architectural gems: the Empress Hotel and the Parliament Buildings, which are both located right on the southern harbor. Then check out the Royal British Columbia Museum, which has a fascinating collection of First Nations artifacts and natural wonders from the region. After lunch, head north to Butchart Gardens, easily accessible by public transit, car, cycle, moped, or tour bus. When you return to Victoria, have a seafood dinner and take an evening walk on the waterfront promenade in front of the illuminated Parliament Buildings.

If You Have 2 Days

Explore the Inner Harbour itself on your second morning. Check out Madame Tussaud's work at the Royal London Wax Museum and play hide-and-seek with a baby harbor seal at the Pacific Undersea Gardens before descending the glass-enclosed stairs to the harbor's bottom. Stroll along the pedestrian promenade in Centennial Park and watch the fishing fleet come in at Fisherman's Wharf. Have lunch in James Bay before heading north to the shops and restaurants in downtown and Olde Town, where you can still catch glimpses of Victoria's past as well as visit North America's oldest Chinatown.

If You Have 3 Days

Venture beyond the safe harbor waters of Victoria proper and go to Craigdarroch Castle, Robert Dunsmuir's Scottish castle, and to his son James's Dunsmuir Castle, which now houses the Royal Roads Military College. Take a drive up to the opulent natural wonders of Goldstream Regional Park. (If you're here during the autumn, you can watch the salmon run through the clear, shallow, rushing waters.) Then spend the afternoon discovering First Nations culture at the Native Heritage Center in Duncan (about 30 minutes further north). You can also take a whale-watching cruise (they supply the waterproof gear) from the docks at the Ocean Pointe Resort. If a romantic dinner is on your agenda, then make reservations at the Aerie Resort, which overlooks Spectacle Lake high above Malahat.

If You Have 5 Days or More

Discover the rest of southern Vancouver Island. Explore the Horn Lake Caves or go island-hopping to Quadra, Salt Spring, or Pender Islands in the central island area. There are challenging hiking trails; thick, old-growth rain forest paths leading to quiet, secluded beaches; and excellent diving spots along the islands' southwestern shores. If you're traveling during the winter, then take in a little skiing just outside of Port Alberni or further north. You could spent weeks finding new adventures on this 320-mile-long island.

1 The Top Attractions

Butchart Gardens

800 Benvenuto Ave., Brentwood Bay. ☎ **604/652-4422** or 604/652-5256 for a recording (24 hours). Admission $13 adults, $6.50 students 13–17, $1.50 children 5–12. Discounts available during winter off-season. Open daily at 9am. Call for seasonal gate closing times. Bus: 75.

These internationally acclaimed, heavily touristed gardens lie 13 miles north of Victoria. They are the creation of Jenny Butchart, the ingenious wife of Canadian cement manufacturer Robert Butchart. When her husband had exhausted the limestone quarry near their Tod Inlet home at the turn of the century, Jenny decided to re-landscape the deserted eyesore. Importing topsoil, she converted the pit into the stunning Sunken Garden. Butchart himself populated the garden with ducks, peacocks, and trained pigeons. Four years later, they added a Japanese Garden, then an Italian Garden, and finally an English Rose Garden.

As the fame of the 50-acre gardens grew, the Butcharts turned the rest of their house into an attraction with a bowling alley, indoor saltwater swimming pool, paneled billiard room, and self-playing Aeolian pipe organ. They named their spectacular 130-acre estate Benvenuto (Italian for "welcome"). Butchart's grandson now owns and operates the gardens, which have more than a million plants blooming year-round. (You won't find sea views here, except through one or two peepholes in the protective hedge rows.)

The gardens are illuminated on summer nights for evening strolls. Fireworks explode on Saturday nights in July and August. You can have lunch, dinner, or afternoon tea in one of the two restaurants or the summer-only snack bar. You can bring home seeds to plant your own garden from the Seed and Gift Store.

✪ Royal British Columbia Museum

675 Belleville St. ☎ **604/387-3701** or 800/661-5411. Two-day passes, $5 adults, $2 children. Daily July–Sept 9:30am–7pm; Oct–June 10am–5:30pm. Closed Christmas and New Year's Day. Bus: 5, 28, or 30.

Human interaction with the environment is the focal point of this three-story modern concrete-and-glass museum. Outside of the museum, you will encounter a beautiful glass-encased display of First Nations house posts, funerary pots, and other large works. Be sure to check out the ceremonial longhouse and contemporary poles in Thunderbird Park, located behind the museum, especially when guest carvers demonstrate their skills.

What's Special About Victoria

Beaches
- Willows Beach, a great place to build a sand castle.
- Ross Bay Beach, where you can stroll along the breezy shore just minutes from downtown.

Buildings
- Market Square, completely restored from its 1850s origins and filled with shops and restaurants.
- The Empress Hotel—unquestionably the centerpiece of the Inner Harbour.

Museums
- The Royal British Columbian Museum, where humans and their environment are on display.
- Craigdarroch Castle, built in the 1880s and now open to visitors.

Parks/Gardens
- Goldstream Provincial Park, once a gold miner's camp and now the home of bald eagles and other island wildlife.
- Beacon Hill Park, which stretches from downtown to Ross Bay; it's a great spot for a picnic or a walk.

Events/Festivals
- The Victoria International Folk Fest staged each summer attracts talent and spectators from around the world.
- The Dragon Boat Festival, which draws hundreds of competitors every August to the Inner Harbor.

For Kids
- The Royal London Wax Museum, filled with the same wonderfully macabre historic figures as Madame Tussaud's in London.
- The Pacific Undersea Gardens, where you can walk to the bottom of the harbor without getting wet and stare back at wolf eels, baby seals, and a giant octopus.

Natural Spectacles
- The Olympia Mountains, whose snowy peaks frame the southern skyline from their location across the straits.

Zoos
- The Beacon Hill Children's Petting Zoo, home of a bevy of farm animals.

Great Neighborhoods
- Downtown/Olde Town, worthy of at least a full-day stroll, whether your interest is in shopping, history, architecture, or food.
- Victoria's Chinatown, which is the oldest in North America—don't miss Fan Tan Alley.

On the ground floor, Newcombe Auditorium has hosted such speakers as explorer Sir Edmund Hillary. A tea room and gift shop are also located here. Upstairs, you enter *Living Land, Living Sea*—a world of prehistoric fossils; local vegetation; dioramas of a coastal temperate rain forest; and a live tidal pool filled with West Coast marine life. The *Open Ocean* exhibit takes you from the water's surface down through the depths to the ocean floor. In the *First Peoples Gallery*, you can learn how archeologists study ancient New World cultures. Art and artifacts from a wide range of regional coastal bands include ceremonial masks, sculptures, clothing, and house posts. The influence of European settlement on indigenous culture is also explored.

Pacific Undersea Gardens

490 Belleville St. ☎ **604/382-5717.** Admission $6 adults, $5.50 seniors, $4.50 students 12–17, $2.75 children 5–11, free for children under 5; $17.50 families. May–Sept, daily 9am–5pm; Sept–Apr, daily 10am–5pm. Bus: 5, 27, 28, or 30.

To get to the glass-enclosed viewing area of this marine observatory, you descend a gently sloping stairway. Some 5,000 marine creatures feed, play, hunt, and mate in the protected waters at the bottom of Inner Harbour. Among them are sharks, wolf eels, poisonous stonefish, flowerlike sea anemones, starfish, and salmon. One of the harbor's star attractions is a huge, remarkably photogenic octopus. Rescued seals and pups are also cared for in holding pens alongside the observatory.

2 More Attractions

ARCHITECTURAL HIGHLIGHTS

Much of Victoria's historic architecture has been refurbished or renovated in the past few decades to nearly its original mid- to late 19th-century beauty. The Scottish and British settlers who made their way to Vancouver Island built stately homes along the harbor and even more magnificent structures further north of the city.

Francis Rattenbury, the architect who designed the Vancouver Art Gallery and Roedde House, constructed his two crowning achievements along the Inner Harbour. He designed the provincial **Parliament Buildings,** 501 Belleville St., in 1897 to commemorate Queen Victoria's diamond jubilee. Illuminated by more than 3,000 white lights, this government seat is an exquisitely beautiful landmark, especially at night. In 1908, Rattenbury designed the opulent **Empress Hotel,** 721 Government St., for the Canadian-Pacific Railway. Guests have included Rudyard Kipling, the king of Siam, John Wayne, Bob Hope, and Queen Elizabeth II.

Similarly grandiose, **Craigdarroch Castle,** 1050 Joan Crescent (☎ 604/592-5323), is an 1880s Rockland-district mansion. More nearly resembling a Highland lord's keep than a coal baron's estate, it was formerly the four-story, 39-room home of Scottish mining magnate Robert Dunsmuir. Complete with stone turrets, 18 fireplaces, fine wood paneling, Persian carpets, Art Nouveau stained glass, fine art, and parquet flooring throughout, the castle is filled with opulent late-Victorian splendor that Dunsmuir and his wife collected. It was prominently featured in the 1994 film *Little Women.* The castle is open daily from 10am to 4:30pm (during the winter, until 5pm); the admission charge is $6 for adults, $5 students, $2 children, free for children under 6.

The Dunsmuir legacy continued in 1908 when Robert's son James Dunsmuir commissioned architect Samuel Maclure to design **Dunsmuir Castle.** James positioned his home, three times the size of his father's mansion, in the 650-acre Hatley Park, which was maintained by a 100-man landscaping crew. Today, the castle houses **Royal Roads Military College,** 2050 Sooke Rd., Colwood (☎ 604/363-2000), but the gardens and grounds are open to the public from 10am to 4pm daily. Admission is free.

To get a taste of how upper-middle-class Victorians lived, take a tour of the **Carr House,** 207 Government St. (☎ 604/387-4697), where artist Emily Carr was born

Victoria Attractions

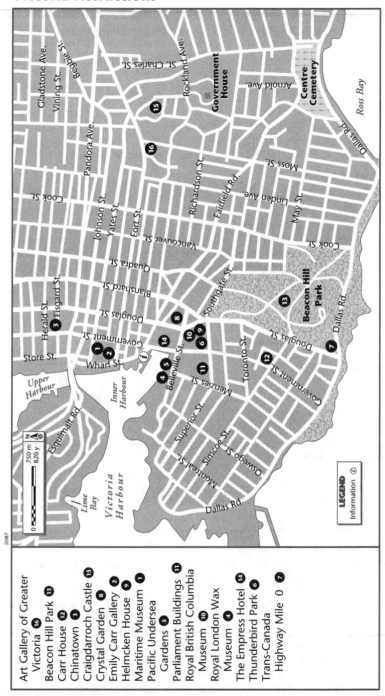

Art Gallery of Greater Victoria 16
Beacon Hill Park 13
Carr House 12
Chinatown 3
Craigdarroch Castle 15
Crystal Garden 8
Emily Carr Gallery 2
Helmcken House 9
Maritime Museum 1
Pacific Undersea Gardens 5
Parliament Buildings 11
Royal British Columbia Museum 10
Royal London Wax Museum 4
The Empress Hotel 14
Thunderbird Park 6
Trans-Canada Highway Mile 0 7

and her father meticulously maintained his very British garden. **Helmcken House,** 675 Belleville St. (☎ 604/387-4697), adjacent to Thunderbird Park, is the 1850s residence of a pioneer doctor. It still contains the original imported British furnishings and the doctor's medicine chest. **Craigflower Farmhouse,** 110 Island Hwy., View Royal (☎ 604/387-3067), was built in 1856 by a Scottish settler. One of Vancouver Island's first permanent agricultural settlements, the farmhouse has been painstakingly restored with many of its original Scottish furnishings.

Carr House, Helmcken House, and the Craigflower Farmhouse are all open during the summer Thursday through Monday from 11am to 5pm. Admission is $3.25 for adults, $2.25 seniors and students, $1.25 children, free for children under six. If you want to see all three, there is a package discount pass available.

CEMETERIES

There are two great cemeteries in Victoria. **Pioneer Square,** on the corner of Meares and Quadra streets beside Christ Church, is one of British Columbia's oldest cemeteries. Hudson's Bay Company fur traders, ship captains, sailors, fishermen, and crew members from British Royal Navy vessels lie beneath the worn sandstone markers. The peaceful, woodland setting of **Ross Bay Cemetery,** between Dallas and Fairfield roads, overlooks the beaches. The man who found gold in B.C.'s interior, Billy Barker, is buried here. Contact the **Old Cemetery Society** (☎ 604/384-0045) for more information.

HISTORIC BUILDINGS/MONUMENTS

Fisgard Lighthouse National Historic Site
501 Belmont Rd., Colwood. ☎ **604/380-4662.** Admission free. Daily 10am–5:30pm. Bus: 50, then transfer to no. 52.

Built in 1860, this was Canada's first permanent lighthouse on the Pacific coast. Still in operation today, it guides ships through the entrance to Esquimalt Harbour's Constance Cove naval base.

Fort Rodd Hill National Historic Park
603 Fort Rodd Hill Rd., Colwood. ☎ **604/363-4662.** Admission free. Daily 10am–5:30pm. Bus: 50, then transfer to no. 52.

Fort Rodd Hill was constructed between 1895 and 1900 to protect ships anchored in Esquimalt Harbour against attack. After the British garrison withdrew in 1906, the fort became a Canadian naval base until the mid-1950s.

MUSEUMS & GALLERIES

Art Gallery of Greater Victoria
1040 Moss St. ☎ **604/384-4101.** Admission $4 adults, $2 seniors and students, free for children under 12; free for everyone Thurs 5–9pm. Mon–Wed and Fri–Sat 10am–5pm, Thurs 10am–9pm, Sun 1–5pm. Bus: 10, 11, or 14.

The Victorian Spencer mansion in the Rockland district houses this art gallery, which features permanent and rotating collections of works by leading Canadian contemporary artists as well as classical to modern European, American, and Asian masters. The extensive Japanese and Chinese collection includes a magnificent Shinto shrine. The building, with its classic turn-of-the-century exterior and Minton-tiled fireplace illustrated with scenes from the Arthurian legend, is an exhibit in itself. There is a Gallery Shop containing books and reproductions, as well as an art rental and sales office where you can purchase original work by regional artists.

Emily Carr Gallery

1107 Wharf St. ☎ **604/384-3130.** Admission $2 adults, $1 students, free for children under 12. May–Sept, Tues–Sun 10am–5:30pm; Oct–Apr, phone for hours. Bus: 5 to Fort and Government.

The works of Victoria native Emily Carr depict coastal First Nations life. If you enjoyed viewing her work in the Vancouver Art Gallery (see Chapter 6), then you must see the concentrated display of her work at this gallery.

Maritime Museum

28 Bastion Sq. ☎ **604/385-4222.** Admission $5 adults, $4 seniors and students, free for children under 6. Family discounts available. July–Aug, daily 9am–8:30pm; June and Sept, daily 9am–6pm; Oct–May, daily 9:30am–4pm. Bus: 5.

This museum is housed in the former B.C. provincial courthouse built in 1889. There are more than 5,000 artifacts on display, including two European shipping vessels and an array of ship models, photographs, and journals.

Royal London Wax Museum

Belleville St. ☎ **604/388-4461.** Admission $7 adults, $3 children. May–Aug, daily 9am–9pm; Sept–Apr, daily 9:30am–4:30pm. Bus: 5, 27, 28, or 30.

The wax museum stands opposite the Pacific Undersea Gardens. Direct from London, 300 of Madame Josephine Tussaud's costumed wax figures—including some of her world-famous Chamber of Horrors characters with accompanying macabre sound effects—are on display. The lines to get in are considerably shorter than those at the London counterpart, so making this a rainy-day destination won't dampen your spirits.

NEIGHBORHOODS

From the time that the Scottish-based Hudson's Bay Company settled here in the 1800s, historic **Olde Town** was the center of the city's bustling business in shipping, fur trading, and legal opium manufacturing. Market Square and the surrounding warehouses once brimmed with exports bound for England and the United States.

Just one block north on Fisgard Street is **Chinatown**. Founded in 1863, it's the oldest Chinatown in North America. One of the more dramatic structures is a three-story school built by the Chinese Benevolent Society in the early part of this century when non-Canadian Chinese children were banned from public schools.

The **James Bay** area on the southern shores of Inner Harbour is still a quiet, middle-class residential community. As you walk through its tree-lined streets, you'll find a few older private residences which have maintained their original Victorian flavor.

Beautiful residential communities such as **Ross Bay** and **Oak Bay** have a more modern West Coast appearance. Houses perch on hills overlooking the beaches amid lusciously landscaped gardens. Private marinas in these areas are filled with perfectly maintained sailing craft.

PARKS/GARDENS

The great natural beauty of **Goldstream Provincial Park** (☎ 604/387-4363), just 20 minutes north of Victoria on Highway 1, will astound you. Towering red cedars and clear, rushing waters beckon you to walk the paths. More than 90 bald eagles were sighted here in January 1995, and the salmon swim upstream every year from October through December. The E&N Railroad runs through this magnificent wonderland on its way to Nanaimo, but you'll want to explore this area on foot. The visitor's center is open daily from 9am to 4:30pm.

Back in the town proper, the 154-acre **Beacon Hill Park** stretches from behind the Royal B.C. Museum (Southgate Street) to the beach (Dallas Road) between Douglas and Cook streets. Stands of Garry oaks, indigenous to the island, and manicured lawns are interspersed with floral gardens and at least a half dozen wildlife sanctuary ponds. You'll encounter blue herons, brant geese, and a variety of ducks placidly enjoying their quiet havens. You can hike up to the top of Beacon Hill, where there is a clear view all the way across the Strait of Juan de Fuca to Washington's Olympic Mountains. The children's farm (see "Especially for Kids," below), aviary, tennis courts, bowling green, putting green, cricket pitch, wading pool, playground, and picnic area all make this a wonderful place in which to stroll or relax.

The Trans-Canadian Highway's Mile-0 marker stands at the Dallas Road end of the park. Two small plaques dedicated to two brave athletes are also placed here. Runner Al Howie started his transcontinental Tomorrow Run in 1991 at this point. Seventy-two days and 10 hours later, he arrived in St. John, Newfoundland. Nineteen-year-old cancer patient Terry Fox also started his ill-fated run against cancer here.

Butchart Gardens (see "The Top Attractions," above) should also be on your local garden tour. If it's raining, don't worry—there's an indoor garden near the park. Originally a 1925 Olympic saltwater pool and later a big-band dance hall, the **Crystal Garden,** 731 Douglas St. (☎ 604/381-1277), is now filled with rare and exotic tropical flora and fauna. Don't let the ground-floor souvenir plaza fool you—47 species of birds, including roaming flamingoes and macaws, pygmy marmosets, wallabies, butterflies, and other wildlife, live in this jungle setting. Open daily from 8am to 5:30pm; admission is $6.50 for adults ($4 seniors and children).

VIEWS

You can see across the Strait of Juan de Fuca and the San Juan Islands to the mountains of the Olympic Peninsula from the **Oak Bay Inn** on Beach Drive or from the top of the hill in **Beacon Hill Park.**

Walk along the pedestrian path in front of the **Ocean Pointe Resort** off the Johnson Street Bridge. From here, you can see the Parliament Buildings and the boats docked along the southern shore of Inner Harbour. The promenade behind the **Travel InfoCentre** on Wharf Street offers another great view of the city.

When the fishing fleets come in, head over to **Fisherman's Wharf** at St. Lawrence and Erie streets, where you can watch the activity as the fisherman unload their catches.

Take in the sunset from **the wharf along the eastern edge of the Inner Harbour,** or from the **Parrot House Restaurant,** 740 Burdett Ave. (☎ 604/382-9258), or take a drive out to **Sooke Harbour House** on Whiffen Spit Road in Sooke.

At the top of Little Saanich Mountain (about 10 miles north of Victoria) stands the **Dominion Astrophysical Observatory**, 5071 W. Saanich Rd. (☎ 604/363-0001), where you can survey all that's around you during the day; on Saturday evenings from 7pm to 11pm, you can observe the starlit skies overhead.

3 Especially for Kids

Victoria opens up a world of discovery for kids of all ages, especially if they're fascinated by nature, animals, or history.

Animal lovers can ride a pony or pet the goats, rabbits, and other barnyard animals at the **Beacon Hill Children's Farm** (☎ 604/381-2532), in Beacon Hill Park (see "Parks/Gardens," under "More Attractions," above). They are open from mid-March to mid-October, daily from 10am to 6pm. Admission is by donation.

❓ Did You Know?

- One morning in 1862, Victoria's citizenry gasped at the sight of 23 Bactrian camels plodding along the main road between Esquimalt and Victoria. An enterprising young Californian named Colbreath brought the creatures to Victoria to pack gold miner's supplies in the Cariboo. Shortly after their arrival, a camel was born in Victoria, causing a great sensation. The camels didn't last long because they wouldn't work in the winter months and their feet were too soft for the rocky soil.

- Architect Francis Mawson Rattenbury won his first design competition at the age of 25 right after his arrival from England. The design would become one of his most famous commissions: Victoria's Parliament Buildings.

- The only notable person who didn't attend the 1898 opening of the Parliament Buildings was their architect Francis Rattenbury.

- Nineteenth-century Victorians did not take callers on Sunday afternoons because their Chinese servants—all male—took off religiously as soon as the lunch table was cleared and didn't return until Monday morning.

- When she wasn't working on her magnificent landscapes, artist Emily Carr ran a not-so-proper boarding house. She turned a garden hose on a roomer who refused to take in his washing and terrorized her other guests with her animal menagerie, which included a monkey named Woo, a white rat, stray cats, and bobtailed sheep dogs.

- Billy Barker, the man who struck it rich in the Cariboo's largest gold claim, is buried in Ross Bay Cemetery. Barker was a Cambridge, England canal man before he immigrated to Canada in search of his fortune. He found it on Williams Creek, where the town of Barkerville still stands, but he died a pauper.

Hitch 'N' Post Ranch, 4120 Sooke Rd. (☎ 604/474-3494), conducts pony rides and has a petting zoos with llamas, pot belly pigs, and other gentle animals. The tropical fauna and flora at the **Crystal Garden** (see "Parks/Gardens," under "More Attractions," above) will make even a rainy day outing a pure delight. At the **Pacific Undersea Gardens'** underwater observatory (see "The Top Attractions," above), kids can eye a wolf eel or giant octopus up close, and they can watch cavorting harbor seals.

If your kids are interested in First Nations culture, then take them to the **Royal British Columbia Museum** (see "The Top Attractions," above), which presents many aspects of tribal life as well as myriad artifacts such as ceremonial masks and feast bowls. (Don't miss the carving demonstrations in the Thunderbird Park longhouse.)

At the **Native Heritage Center** (see "Special-Interest Sightseeing," below), kids can observe or participate in regularly scheduled events, including ceremonial dances and dinners. They can see master and apprentice carvers at work throughout the year.

Another entertaining place for you and your kids is the **Royal London Wax Museum** (see "Museums/Galleries," under "More Attractions," above), where you can see Madame Tussaud's world-famous waxworks and Chamber of Horrors.

Beaver Lake, off Highway 17, is a great freshwater spot where your children can enjoy swimming with lifeguards in attendance. **Swan Lake Nature Sanctuary,** Ralph Road, Victoria (☎ 604/479-0211), becomes even more fun when it rains! You and your kids can enjoy a wet walk around the floating boardwalk that rings the 100-acre park. The resident swans love to be fed, and the Nature House will supply grain upon request.

4 Special-Interest Sightseeing

FOR TRAVELERS INTERESTED IN FIRST NATIONS' CULTURE   About an hour's drive out of Victoria is the **Native Heritage Center,** 200 Cowichan Way, Duncan (☎ 604/746-8119). The longhouses built along the Cowichan River contain an impressive collection of cultural artifacts and presentations of tribal life. More interestingly, there are regularly scheduled events, including ceremonial dances and dinners, to which the public is invited. Master and apprentice carvers create poles as well as masks here throughout the year. The two gift shops in the complex sell some of their works as well as jewelery, clothing, serigraphic prints, and other items. They are open daily from 9:30am to 5pm; admission is $6.96 for adults, $6.15 for seniors and children.

FOR COLLECTORS OF MINIATURES AND DOLLHOUSES   After they returned from their life on the road as circus performers, owners Don and Honey Ray created 40 lifelike miniature dioramas depicting historic battles, Dickens tales, the trans-Canadian railway, a circus under the big top, and a remarkably elaborate 24-room dollhouse. The small museum, known as **Miniature World,** 649 Humboldt St. (☎ 604/385-9731), is open daily from 8:30am to 10pm (during the winter from 9am to 5pm). Admission is $6.75 adults, $5.75 students, and $4.75 children.

FOR BIRD-WATCHERS   **Goldstream Regional Park** (see Parks/Gardens above) and **Malahat**—both off Highway 1 north of Victoria—are filled with dozens of varieties of migratory and local birds. Ninety-seven eagles were spotted at Goldstream on one January day alone in 1995. **Elk and Beaver Lake Regional Park,** off Highway 17, has some rare species such as the rose-breasted Grosbeak and Hutton's Vireo. Osprey also nest here. **Cowichan Bay,** off Highway 1, is the perfect place to observe osprey, bald eagles, a few great egrets, and purple martins.

FOR WINE LOVERS   You don't have to go all the way to Okanagan to take a winery tour—there are five B.C. vintners located between Mill Bay and Duncan off Highway 1 that offer winery tours and tastings. **Merridale Estate Cidery,** 1230 Merridale Rd., Mill Bay (☎ 604/743-4293), has tours Monday through Saturday from 10:30am to 4:30pm. **Cherry Point Vineyards,** 840 Cherry Point Rd., Cobble Hill (☎ 604/743-1272), offers tours by appointment only, as does **Venturi-Schulze Vineyards,** 4235 Trans Canada Highway, Cowichan Station (☎ 604/743-5630). **Blue Grouse Vineyards,** 4365 Blue Grouse Rd., Cowichan Station (☎ 604/743-3834), conducts tours on Wednesday plus Friday through Sunday from 11am to 5pm. **Vigneti Zanatta Vineyards,** 5039 Marshall Rd., Duncan (☎ 604/748-2338), conducts tours on Saturday and Sunday from 1pm to 4pm.

5 Organized Tours

If you are uncomfortable with public transportation or worried about admissions and opening hours, a guided tour is the best way to see Victoria. There are bus tours, but Victoria has a few fun alternatives if that's not your style.

BY BUS   **Gray Line of Victoria,** 700 Douglas St. (☎ 604/388-5248), tours Victoria and the Butchart Gardens. The 1¹/₂-hour Grand City Tour costs $13.75 for adults and $6.95 for children. The schedule varies by season; daily summer departures are every half hour from 9:30am to 7pm, and from December through mid-March, tours run once daily (at 11:30am or 1:30pm).

SPECIALTY TOURS   Heritage Tours and Daimler Limosine Service, 713 Bexhill Rd. (☎ 604/474-4332), offers you a chance to tour the city, Butchart Gardens, and Craigdarroch Castle in a six-passenger British Daimler limousine. Rates start at $62 per hour per vehicle, not per person.

You can usually find the bicycle rickshaws operated by **Kabuki Kabs,** Unit 15, 950 Government St. (☎ 604/385-4243), in front of the Empress hotel on Government Street. The cost runs about $30 to $40 per hour, but the drivers negotiate their own prices. For the right price, the drivers will take you anywhere.

Since 1903, **Tallyho Tours,** 180 Goward Rd. (☎ 604/479-1113), has conducted horse-drawn carriage city tours of Beacon Hill Park, the waterfront, and nearby heritage homes. The starting point is at the corner of Belleville and Menzies streets. The cost is $9.50 for adults, $6 for students, and $5 for children 17 and under. They also offer discount family rates. Tours operate every 20 minutes from 9:30am to 7pm from mid-March through September (10am to 5:30pm in April, May, and September).

Black Beauty Carriage Tours (☎ 604/479-1113) has private carriages that will take you on their regular route or on a special tour.

To get a bird's-eye view of Victoria, take a flight on **Go Island Hopper Helicopter,** 103-9800 Lysander Lane, Sidney (☎ 604/656-7627), or **Harbour Air Ltd.,** 1234 Wharf St. (☎ 604/361-6786).

6 Outdoor Activities

Year-round mountain biking, kayaking, ecotouring, and in-line skating are popular sports in Victoria, but that's just a smattering of what you can do here. Alpine and Nordic skiing, parasailing, sea kayaking, canoeing, tidal water fishing, fly fishing, diving, and hiking are a few more options. Pick up a copy of *Coast: The Outdoor Recreation Magazine,* which is published every other month and is available at many outfitter and recreational equipment outlets. *Coast* lets you in on the latest snow conditions, bike trails, climbing areas, competitions, races, and the like and where to get vital services such as bike tune-ups.

In the sections below, specialized rental outfitters are listed with each activity so you don't have to lug all your personal equipment with you. If you get inspired, you can try something new. **Sports Rent,** 3084 Blanshard St. (☎ 604/385-7368), is a general-equipment and water-sport rental outlet you should keep in mind if you forget to pack anything.

BEACHES   Since you are on the sunny side of western Canada, you should take advantage of the beaches in and around the area. The most popular is Oak Bay's **Willows Beach,** at Beach and Dalhousie roads along the Esplanade. The park, playground, and snack bar make it a great place to spend the day building a sand castle. **Gyro Beach Park,** Beach Road on Cadboro Bay, is another good spot for winding down. At the **Ross Bay Beaches** below Beacon Hill Park, you can stroll or cycle along the promenade at the water's edge.

Two inland lakes give you the option to swim in freshwater. **Elk and Beaver Lake Regional Park,** on Patricia Bay Road, is located 7 miles north of downtown Victoria; **Thetis Lake,** about 6 miles west, is where locals shed all their clothes but none of their civility.

BICYCLING Cycling is the fastest way to get around Victoria, especially during the summer. The 8-mile Scenic Marine Drive, following Dallas Road and Beach Drive along the city's south shore and returning to downtown via Oak Bay Avenue, is also the perfect alternate route if you want to cycle to Butchart Gardens without breathing in auto exhaust the entire way. There's also an off-road pedestrian/cycle promenade you can follow for much of the journey.

The **Bicycling Association of British Columbia** has a group ride and special events hotline (☎ 604/731-7433). Rentals run around $3.50 to $5.60 per hour, $16 to $26 per day. Bikes, helmets, locks, and child trailers are all available on an hourly or daily basis at **Budget Cycle Time,** 727 Courtney, Victoria (☎ 604/388-4442); **Oak Bay Bicycle,** 1968 Oak Bay Ave., Victoria (☎ 604/598-4111).

BOATING Bareboat or skippered rentals lasting for a few hours to a couple of weeks are available from Brentwood Inn Resort Boat Rentals, 7176 Brentwood Dr., Brentwood Bay (☎ 604/652-3151). They are located five minutes from Butchart Gardens. There are also a few smaller outfits on the docks at the Oak Bay Marina Group, 1327 Beach Dr. (☎ 604/598-3369).

Don't forget to check the **marine forecast** by calling 604/656-7515.

BUNGY JUMPING Did you ever want to jump off a bridge? Well, you can fulfill your dreams from a 140-foot trestle at **The Bungy Zone** (☎ 604/753-5867) near Nanaimo. North America's only legally sanctioned bridge jump, it has given a wedding party a flying start and sponsored more than one nude jumping weekend to benefit charity. Leaping high over the Nanaimo River from a specially constructed steel trestle bridge, you will pay $95 for your first leap (the second is $75). You can even choose how far into the icy mountain waters you want to go. The Bungy Zone is open daily from 10am to 4:30pm year-round. For a small admission fee (around $2 to $4), you can just be a wide-eyed observer. Reservations are recommended June through August. The Bungy Zone is located 41 miles north of Victoria or 8 miles south of Nanaimo, off Highway 1. There's also a free shuttle service from both Victoria and Nanaimo.

CANOEING/KAYAKING Southeastern Vancouver Island has numerous inlets to explore as well as tiny Gulf Islands accessible by ocean kayak or canoe. **Ocean River Sports,** 1437 Store St. (☎ 604/381-4233), can equip you with everything you need from kayak and canoe rentals to jackets, tents, and dry-storage camping equipment. They also offer group tours as well as lessons and clinics for adults and kids.

DIVING The coastline of **Pacific Rim National Park** is known as "the graveyard of the Pacific." The park offers views of dozens of 19th- and 20th-century sunken shipwrecks and the marine life that has taken up residence at the bottom. According to the Cousteau Society, this dive site is second only to the Red Sea. Underwater interpretive trails help you identify what you see in these artificially created reefs. If you want to take a look for yourself, contact the **Ocean Centre,** 800 Cloverdale (☎ 604/475-2202), or **Seaker Adventure Tours,** 1-1035 Pakington St. (☎ 604/479-0244).

FISHING Pacific salmon, halibut, cutthroat trout, and ling cod are just a few of the varieties of saltwater catch you can get in the island's gulf and ocean waters. **Elk and Beaver Lakes** off Patricia Bay Road just north of Victoria are well stocked with freshwater fish such as steelhead and rainbow trout as well as kokanee, Dolly Varden char, and smallmouth bass. You will need to get a fishing license—one for saltwater and another for freshwater (see "Fishing," under "Outdoor Activities" in Chapter 6). **Robinson's Sporting Goods Ltd.,** 1307 Broad St. (☎ 604/385-3429), is a good source of lures, licenses, and equipment.

East Sooke Fish Company, 6638 E. Sooke Rd., Sooke (☎ 604/642-7078), combines the excitement of salmon fishing with the pleasures of ecotouring in its charters. While you're trying your hand at catching Chinook or coho, you are entertained by orcas, seals, bald eagles, and porpoises that are also trying their luck at salmon fishing. Another outfit, **Reel Action Fishing Charters**, 961 Haslam Ave. (☎ 604/478-1977), also offers salmon fishing charters in the areas around the Strait of Georgia.

GOLF   Given Victoria's Scottish-English heritage and its rolling landscape, it's no wonder that golf is a popular sport here. The **Cedar Hill Municipal Golf Course,** 1400 Derby Rd. (☎ 604/595-3103), is a public course located just 2 miles from downtown. The **Cordova Bay Golf Course,** 5333 Cordova Bay Rd. (☎ 604/658-4075), northeast of downtown, was designed by Bill Robinson with 66 challenging sand traps and some tight fairways. If your U.S. club has reciprocal privilege arrangements, then check out the 17th hole at the **Olympic View Golf Course,** 643 Latoria Rd. (☎ 604/474-3671), where designer Bill Robinson placed a 417-yard hole with a slight turn and downhill toward the green, backdropped by a waterfall.

HIKING   **Goldstream Provincial Park** is a tranquil site for a day hike through towering cedars and clear, rushing waters. Minimum-impact hiking and camping are the rule in these parts. Bring your portable stove and pitch your tent only in established areas.

For a serious backpacking run, go to **Pacific Rim National Park,** 65 miles west on Highway 14 to Port Renfrew. The challenging **West Coast Trail,** extending 48 miles from Port Renfrew to Bamfield, was originally established as a life-saving trail for shipwrecked sailors. Plan a seven-day trek if you want to do the whole route. The trail is rugged and often wet, but the scenery changes from old-growth forest to magnificent secluded sand beaches, making it worth every step. You might even spot a few whales along the way. **Robinson's Sporting Goods Ltd.,** 1307 Broad St. (☎ 604/385-3429), is a good place to gear up before you go.

If you want to learn more about what's around you, you can book a naturalist-guided tour of the island's rain forests and seashore with **Coastal Connections-Interpretive Nature Hikes,** 1027 Roslyn Rd. (☎ 604/598-7043).

HORSERIDING   You can take a ride through a wooded trail up to Buck Mountain's summit or an overnight ride if you're up for serious backcountry packing. Make arrangements through **Hitch 'N' Post Ranch,** 4120 Sooke Rd. (☎ 604/474-3494).

SAILING   The **Horizon Yacht Centre,** 1327 Beach Dr. at Oak Bay Marina (☎ 604/595-2628), offers lessons and navigational tips to familiarize you with the waters around the sounds and straits. They also offer sailboat rentals.

SKIING   **Mount Washington Ski Resort,** P.O. Box 3069, Courtenay (☎ 604/338-1386 or 604/338-1515 for snow report), in the Comox Valley, is British Columbia's third-largest ski area. It's a five-hour drive from Victoria. A 1,600-foot vertical drop and 20 groomed runs are serviced by four chair lifts and a beginners' tow. Nineteen miles of track-set Nordic trails connect to Strathcona Provincial Park. Full-day rates are $29 for adults; equipment rentals are available at the resort. It's open daily all winter.

The family oriented **Forbidden Plateau,** 2050 Cliffe Ave., Courtenay (☎ 604/334-4744, or 604/338-1919 for snow report), is the island's oldest ski resort (opened in 1950). The 1,150-foot vertical and 12 groomed runs are geared more to novices. One chair lift, three T-bars, and a rope tow service the runs. Full-day adult rates are $23 with complete equipment rentals available. Open Friday, Saturday and Sunday, it's a casual place where you can avoid the crowds during the mid-December to mid-April season.

SWIMMING/WATER SPORTS   The **Crystal Pool and Fitness Centre,** 2275 Quadra St. (☎ 604/380-7946 or 604/380-4636 for schedule), is Victoria's aquatic facility. The 50-meter lap pool; separate children's pool; diving pool; sauna; whirlpool; and steam, weight, and aerobics rooms are open daily for 15 hours, from 6:30am to 1:30pm; and from 3:30pm to 11:30pm. **Beaver Lake** in Elk and Beaver Lake Regional Park, off Highway 17, has lifeguards on duty as well as picnicking facilities.

   All Fun Recreation Park, 650 Hordon Rd. (☎ 604/474-4546 or 604/474-3184), has a ³/₄-mile water slide complex.

   Ocean Wind Water Sports Rentals, 5411 Hamsterly Rd. (☎ 604/658-8171), has everything you need for water sports, including parasails.

WILDLIFE WATCHING   You can take a two- or three-hour tour from Victoria's Inner Harbour into the Gulf Islands to see orcas, harbor seals, sea lions, bald eagles, and porpoises from May through September. **Sea Coast Expeditions,** Ocean Pointe Resort, 25 Songhees Rd. (☎ 604/383-2254), has biologist guides aboard its high-speed, open Zodiac boats during its 20- to 50-mile trips. They supply the wet gear. Rates are $50 to $75 for adults, $30 to $45 for children 6 to 16. Boats depart seven times daily from 8am to the last launch at 4pm. If you don't want to get wet, sail along with **Island Breeze Sailing** (mailing address: P.O. Box 1233, Victoria V8W 2T6, ☎ 604/744-7327); or take one of the power yachts run by **Chinook Charters** (mailing address: P.O. Box 501, Tofino VOR 200, ☎ 604/725-3431).

WINDSURFING   In addition to cavorting in the Inner Harbour, windsurfers skim along **Elk Lake,** which is just 8 miles north of Victoria. Beginners can learn how to manage their craft through **Active Sports,** 1620 Blanshard St. (☎ 604/381-SAIL) in about three days.

Victoria Strolls

14

Unlike Vancouver, Victoria has a strong historic presence that has been preserved with great care. Throughout the downtown area, you can see glimpses into the city's nefarious past as well as its charming present.

WALKING TOUR 1
The Inner Harbour

Start: The Empress Hotel, 321 Government St.
Finish: The Empress Hotel.
Time: 2 hours, not including shopping, sightseeing, and eating stops.
Best Times: Any weekday, year-round.
Worst Times: Summer weekends, when the streets are packed with people, and any day after 6pm, when the shops are closed and the streets empty.

You can get a good sense of the city's present in this tour of the Inner Harbour, where two of the Victoria's most impressive landmarks are situated.

In front of you is:

1. The **Empress Hotel** (see Chapter 11 for hotel review and "Architectural Highlights," under "More Attractions" in Chapter 13), designed by Francis Rattenbury for Queen Victoria's diamond jubilee.

    Walk one block south of this grand Victorian château to reach another of Rattenbury's crowning works known as the:

2. **Parliament Buildings,** 501 Belleville St. (see "Architectural Highlights," under "More Attractions" in Chapter 13), where the provincial parliament conducts its meetings on affairs of state. The buildings are generally closed to the public, but you are welcome to wander through the gardens.

    Next door to the Parliament Buildings is the:

3. **Heritage Court,** the beautiful legislative lawns. You get to the gardens, filled with native plants, by stepping over a petrified dinosaur footprint. You'll also find the tall white tower known as the **Netherlands Carillon**. A gift from the Dutch people, it rises 88 feet and houses bells weighing more than five tons.

    Opposite the lawns, at Belleville and Menzies streets, is the:

4. **Confederation Garden,** which has a monument to the country's provincial confederation as its centerpiece. The huge bronze sculpture displays the Canadian coat of arms surrounded by the 10 provincial heraldries. Here, you can catch a horse and carriage for a quick spin around the area.

Across Belleville Street is the:

5. **Royal London Wax Museum,** 470 Belleville St. (see "Museums and Galleries," under "More Attractions" in Chapter 13), the Victoria branch of the world-famous Madame Tussaud's of London. Next door, you'll find more natural creations at the:

6. **Pacific Undersea Gardens,** 490 Belleville St. (see "The Top Attractions" in Chapter 13), where you can descend to the harbor floor without getting wet and view marine life in its natural habitat.

Keep walking past the ferry terminal, where the Port Angeles ferry loads and unloads passengers from Washington state, until you get to a curve in the road. Next to the Admiral Motel, you will see a sign indicating the entrance to a pedestrian promenade. Once you enter this paved path, you have arrived in:

7. **Centennial Park,** a beautifully maintained stretch of city-owned shoreline with trees, shrubbery, and floral gardens. If you take the lower pathway, you cross over small wooden footbridges; keep an eye on the clear water's edge for beavers swimming past. There is also a great view of the Empress Hotel from this side of the harbor. You will pass Laurel Point and the Inner Harbour ferry dock along the way.

The Promenade ends near the Coast Harbourside Hotel and its marina. Keep following Belleville Street as it winds its way around the point. Within a few blocks, you'll come to:

8. **Fisherman's Wharf,** at St. Lawrence and Erie streets, where the fishing fleets dock to unload their catches.

Walk one block north on St. Lawrence Street and turn left on Superior Street. Continue walking four blocks to Government Street and turn right. You'll find the:

9. **James Bay Inn,** 270 Government St. (see Chapter 11 for hotel review), a 1907 Edwardian manor that was artist Emily Carr's last Vancouver Island home before the structure was converted into a hotel. If you are in need of fuel, you can:

☕ **TAKE A BREAK** Drop into the **Unwinder** pub or **Rib Tickler's restaurant** in the James Bay Inn. You can get a quick bite or a pint in this old Victoria hotel/neighborhood gathering place.

Walk two blocks east on Toronto Street to Douglas Street, then turn left, heading back toward the Parliament Buildings. Across the street, you'll see the north end of:

10. **Beacon Hill Park** (see "Parks/Gardens," under "More Attractions" in Chapter 13), which stretches from Southgate Street down to the water's edge at Dallas Road. Take a few minutes to stroll along the well-manicured lawns and floral gardens before you come to the end of the park. Diagonally across from you is:

11. **Thunderbird Park,** where wooden totem poles preside over the landscape and the longhouse where master carvers demonstrate their skills. You'll find two 1850s heritage buildings nestled behind the longhouse:

12. **Helmcken House,** the home of a mid-1800s pioneer doctor (see "Architectural Highlights," under "More Attractions" in Chapter 13), and:

Walking Tour—The Inner Harbour

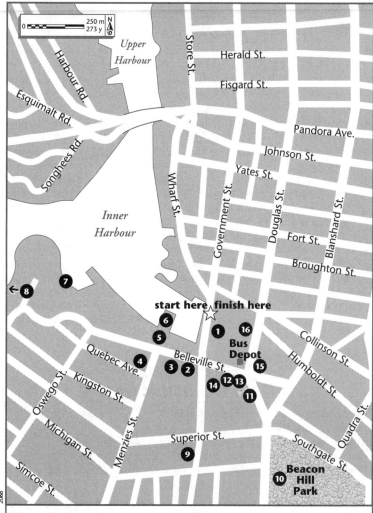

1 The Empress Hotel
2 Parliament Buildings
3 Heritage Court
4 Confederation Garden
5 Royal London Wax Museum
6 Pacific Undersea Gardens
7 Centennial Park
8 Fisherman's Wharf
9 James Bay Inn
10 Beacon Hill Park
11 Thunderbird Park
12 Helmcken House
13 St. Ann's Schoolhouse
14 Royal British Columbia Museum
15 Crystal Garden
16 Victoria Conference Centre

13. **St. Ann's Schoolhouse,** a small settlement school established around the same time.

Beyond these structures is the:

14. **Royal British Columbia Museum,** 675 Belleville St., which is filled with natural and human-made wonders (see "The Top Attractions" in Chapter 13).

Continue north on Douglas across Belleville Street. On your left is the city bus depot, where you can catch the ferry bus and other coaches heading further up the island. Directly across from that, hidden behind souvenir shops, is the:

15. **Crystal Garden,** 731 Douglas St. (see "Parks/Gardens," under "More Attractions" in Chapter 13), where Johnny Weismuller (who played Tarzan in the 1940s film series) once broke the world swimming record in the largest saltwater pool in the British Empire. The 1925 Olympic pool and building were designed by Francis Rattenbury, but little remains of the original interior design. During the 1940s, the space was turned into a big-band dance hall. The pool was removed more than 20 years ago and replaced with a tropical greenhouse garden filled with exotic vegetation and equally colorful birds and animals.

Across the street, north of the bus depot, is the:

16. **Victoria Conference Centre,** 720 Douglas St. (☎ 604/361-1000). Opened in 1989, this very modern brick-and-glass structure also contains public gardens and a foyer gallery filled with provincial artists' works, including a totem pole by master carver Tony Hunt.

Turn left on Douglas Street and walk to the corner of Humboldt Street, where you'll make another left. Within one block, you'll be back on Government Street at the Empress Hotel.

WALKING TOUR 2
Olde Town & Chinatown

Start: The Empress Hotel, 321 Government St.
Finish: The Empress Hotel.
Time: 2 hours, not including shopping, sightseeing, and eating stops.
Best Times: Any weekday, year-round.
Worst Times: Summer weekends, when the streets are packed with people, and any day after 6pm.

This tour also begins at one of Victoria's most impressive landmarks. In front of you is:

1. The **Empress Hotel** (see Chapter 11 for hotel review and "Architectural Highlights," under "More Attractions" in Chapter 13), designed by Francis Rattenbury for Queen Victoria's diamond jubilee.

Walking north up Government Street, you'll find a number of historic buildings. British Columbia's oldest brick structure is the:

2. **Windsor Hotel** building, 901 Government St. Dating from 1858, it now houses gifts shops and has been timbered over to give it a warmer facade.

On the next block, you'll find a brass sidewalk plaque indicating the former site of:

3. **Fort Victoria,** 1022 Government St., which was constructed in 1843 by the Hudson's Bay Company as the western headquarters of its fur-trading empire. Bounded by Broughton Street between Government and Wharf streets to Bastion

Walking Tour—Olde Town/Chinatown

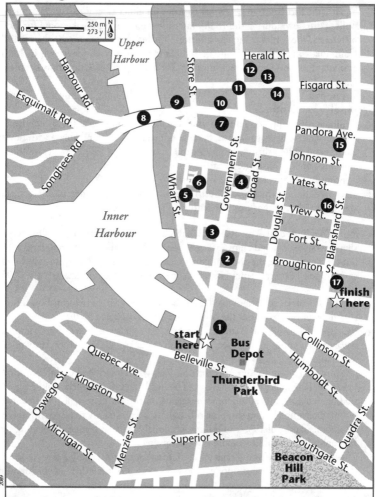

0 | 250 m / 273 y | N

Upper Harbour

Harbour Rd.

Esquimalt Rd.

Songhees Rd.

Store St.

Herald St.

Fisgard St.

Pandora Ave.

Johnson St.

Government St.

Broad St.

Wharf St.

Yates St.

Douglas St.

View St.

Fort St.

Blanshard St.

Broughton St.

Inner Harbour

finish here

start here

Bus Depot

Belleville St.

Thunderbird Park

Quebec Ave.

Kingston St.

Oswego St.

Collinson St.

Humboldt St.

Menzies St.

Michigan St.

Superior St.

Southgate St.

Quadra St.

Beacon Hill Park

2089

❶ The Empress Hotel
❷ Windsor Hotel building
❸ Fort Victoria
❹ Trounce Alley
❺ Bastion Square
❻ Maritime Museum
❼ Market Square
❽ Johnson Street Bridge
❾ Via Rail/E&N Railway Station
❿ Fan Tan Alley
⓫ Gate of Harmonious Interest
⓬ Chinese Settlement House
⓭ Chinese Imperial School
⓮ McPherson Playhouse
⓯ Congregation Emanu-El Synagogue
⓰ St. Andrew's Roman Catholic Church
⓱ Royal Theatre

Square, the fort had two octagonal bastions on either side of its tall cedar picket walls. Torn down during the 1858 Fraser River gold rush to make room for more businesses, the fort was the city's historic birthplace. The first school in British Columbia was built on this site in 1849, and the first bank (dedicated in 1886) also stood on this spot, which now houses **The Spirit of Christmas** shop (see Chapter 15).

Just past View Street, a little byway cuts off on the right, running one block to Broad Street Known as:

4. **Trounce Alley,** this is where miners and mariners spent their extra cash on ladies. The alley is still lit by gas lamps, hung with heraldic crests, and ablaze with flower baskets and potted shrubs. You can stroll through shops selling jewelry, fashions, and crafts or stop for a bite to eat.

From Broad Street, circle back west down View Street. You will reach:

5. **Bastion Square,** which was a bustling area with waterfront hotels, saloons, and warehouses during the late 19th century. This is a good place to:

☕ **TAKE A BREAK** **Garrick's Head Pub,** 64 Bastion Square, serves shepherd's pie, fish and chips, bangers, and mash (in other words, pub fare) without the chain-restaurant prices or glitz that some of the neighboring so-called pubs sport. Open 11am to 11pm, Garrick's serves meals and a pint for less than $7.95.

The provincial courthouse and hangman's square were once located on this restored pedestrian mall, but the courthouse is now occupied by the:

6. **Maritime Museum,** 28 Bastion Sq., where you can get a glimpse into Victoria's naval and shipping history (see "Museums/Galleries," under "More Attractions" in Chapter 13).

More than a century ago, Victoria's business was transacted in this area of winding Olde Town alleys and walkways. The hustle and bustle of the gold rush, far trading, whaling, and shipping were carried on behind these walls. Warehouses, old mariner's hotels, and shipping offices have been carefully restored into shops, restaurants, and galleries. You'll find occasional historical plaques explaining the function of each building before it was renovated.

Turn north up Commercial Alley. Cross Yates Street, and a few steps farther west, turn north again up Waddington Alley. On the other side of Johnson Street is:

7. **Market Square,** a restored historic site that was once a two-story complex of shipping offices and supply stores. It now contains more than 40 shops that sell everything from sports equipment and crafts to books and toys. There are also seven restaurants in the square; some have outdoor seating in the large open-air court where musicians often perform in the summertime.

On its western side, Market Square faces the:

8. **Johnson Street Bridge,** which divides the Inner and Upper Harbours and serves as the main link between downtown Victoria and the Esquimalt peninsula.

Across Store Street is the:

9. **VIA Rail/Esquimalt and Nanaimo Railroad Terminal,** where you can board a train that rambles through Goldstream Provincial Park on its way to Nanaimo.

Go north one block on Store Street and turn right onto Fisgard Street. You are now in North America's oldest **Chinatown.** Established in 1858 when the first Chinese arrived as gold-seekers and railroad workers, this was a six-block district that fell into decline after World War I (as did many West Coast Asian districts when the U.S. and Canadian governments restricted immigration from Asia until well after World War II). What remains is a fascinating peek into a well-hidden and exotic heritage. Halfway up the block, you'll find:

10. **Fan Tan Alley,** one of the world's narrowest streets. It is no more than four feet wide at either end and expands to a little over six feet in the center. Through the maze of doorways, which still have their old Chinese signage, there are entries to small courtyards leading to more doorways. In the late 19th century, this was the main entrance to "Little Canton," where the scent of legally manufactured opium wafted from the courtyards out into the streets. Opium dens, gambling parlors, and brothels sprung up between the factories and bachelor rooms, where immigrants would share cramped quarters to save money.

   Today, you'll find only a few little shops selling crafts and trinkets, but you can still feel the intrigue of yesteryear as you walk through the alley and back up Fisgard Street.

   At the corner of Government and Fisgard streets is the:

11. **Gate of Harmonious Interest.** This lavishly detailed dragon-headed red and gold archway was built in 1981 to commemorate the completion—after years of deterioration—of Chinatown's revitalization by the city and the Chinese Consolidated Benevolent Association. The gate is guarded by a pair of hand-carved stone lions from Suzhou, China.

   One-half block up Government Street is the former location of the:

12. **Chinese Settlement House,** 1715 Government St. Newly arrived mainland Chinese families once lived in the upstairs of this balconied building and received social services here until they were able to secure work and living quarters. The ground floor now houses **Met Bistro** restaurant (see Chapter 12 for dining review). The original Chinese Buddhist temple has been moved to the second floor, but it's still open for tours.

   A half block up from the Gate of Harmonious Interest on Fisgard Street is the:

13. **Chinese Imperial School (Zhongua Xuetang),** 36 Fisgard Street. This red and gold pagoda-style building with a baked-tile roof and recessed balconies was built by the Chinese Benevolent Society. In 1907, the Victoria School Board banned non-Canadian Chinese children from attending public school, and in response, the society opened its own community elementary school the following year. The school is open to everyone during the week and gives children and adults instruction in Chinese reading and writing on weekends.

   Just east of the school is the:

14. **McPherson Playhouse,** 3 Centennial Sq. (☎ 604/386-6121). Formerly a 1912 Edwardian baroque-style vaudeville theater known as the Pantages, it was restored into this dramatic theater, which is now Victoria's main performing arts center. City Hall and the police department are located in the 1960s office plaza surrounding the playhouse.

   When you get to the southeast corner of Centennial Square, walk up one more block on Pandora Ave. to Blanshard St. Here you will find:

15. **Congregation Emanu-El Synagogue,** the oldest surviving Jewish temple on North America's west coast. Built in 1863, it has been proclaimed a national heritage site.

   Turn south on Blanshard Street and go past a number of movie theaters until you reach the impressive:

16. **St. Andrew's Roman Catholic Cathedral,** at the corner of View St. Built by the St. Andrew's Scottish Benevolent Society in the late 19th-century, this house of worship stands as testimony to the good works performed by its members—who set up the Hudson Bay Company's operations in Victoria—to help Scottish

immigrants settling on Vancouver Island. After making the arduous journey from the Maritime Provinces across the continent, many of these late arrivals were in dire need of the shelter, food, clothing, employment, and medical attention that the society provided.

Two blocks further down is the:

17. Royal Theatre, 805 Broughton St. (☎ 604/361-0820), which is home of the Victoria Symphony and host of many touring and local groups.

Walk west on Broughton Street to Government Street. Then walk two blocks south past a number of gift, clothing, and souvenir shops. This will bring you back to your starting point at the Empress Hotel.

Victoria Shopping 15

Victoria has dozens of little specialty shops to appeal to your every taste and whim. You won't find high-fashion boutiques, but you will find high-quality classics and ethnic clothing. Adventurous types will enjoy the great selection (which even includes some bargains) of marine and camping gear. Many of the stores are renovated heritage structures, so a shopping spree can quickly become a stroll through Victoria's history. Stores are generally open Monday through Saturday from 10am to 6pm; some are open on Sundays during the summer, but not many.

1 The Shopping Scene

Downtown/Olde Town is Victoria's principal shopping district; **Government Street** is the main location of specialty shops. You can buy warm and cozy Irish knits from **Avoca Handweavers,** sturdy Scottish woolens at the **Edinburgh Tartan Shop**, or locally made Cowichan raw wool sweaters at **Cowichan Trading Ltd.**

Whether you're a lover of land or sea, you'll find dozens of outfitters in Olde Town to suit you up for your next trip. You can pick up a few field guides at **The Field Naturalist** or look at the latest in whitewater, paddling, or kevlar-bottom ocean kayaks at **Ocean River Sports.** There are a number of year-round Christmas shops selling beautiful ornaments and decorations, including **The Spirit of Christmas** on Government Street. Along Fort Street, you'll find European and American antiques at **Kilshaw Auctioneers.**

2 Shopping A to Z

ANTIQUES

Victoria's 19th- and early 20th-century homes might inspire you to bring home a piece of history. You'll find some deals on lovely authentic antiques and reproductions along Fort St. **Kilshaw's Auctioneers,** 1115 Fort St. (☎ 604/384-6441), specializes in estate sales of beautiful Edwardian and Victorian furnishings as well as accessories. **Jeffries and Co.,** 1026 Fort St. (☎ 604/383-8315), has great deals on antique silver. **Chintz and Company,** 1720 Store St. (☎ 604/384-2404), creates beautiful reproductions to suit most budgets.

ART

Pacific Northwest First Nations works are plentiful here. **Alcheringa Gallery,** 665 Fort St. (☎ 604/383-8224), handles the work of Kwakiutl master carver Richard Hunt and Haida printmaker Robert Davidson, among dozens of other regional artists. **Eagle's Moon Gallery,** 1010 Government St. (☎ 604/361-4184), deals in serigraphic prints, wood sculpture, and paintings by artists such as Tsimshian painter Roy Henry Vickers. **Small Pressings Gallery and Paper,** 103-3 Fan Tan Alley (☎ 604/380-2479), is tucked away on one of the world's narrowest streets. Specializing in Canadian paper arts, they carry colorful handmade paper and books as well as origami.

BOOKS

There are a number of excellent local authors such as Anne Cameron living on Vancouver Island and the Gulf Islands. Their works weave wonderful tales about early and modern life in this natural paradise. **Munro's Book Store,** 1108 Government St. (☎ 604/382-2464), is a Victoria landmark as well as a great source for regional books and fiction by local authors. You can find bargains on remainders at the **Book Warehouse,** 1301 Government St. (☎ 604/386-5711). If you want to find a good field guide before setting out to explore the natural wonders of the island, go to **The Field Naturalist,** 1126 Blanshard St. (☎ 604/388-4174). They also sell binoculars, telescopes, spotting charts, and other critical naturalist equipment.

CHINA & CRYSTAL

You can find Waterford crystal, Royal Worcester bone china, and other delightful British wares at **Victoria Limited Editions,** 919 Fort St. (☎ 604/386-5155), or **Sidney Reynolds,** 801 Government St. (☎ 604/383-3931).

CHINESE ARTS & CRAFTS

Although small, Victoria's Chinatown has plenty of import shops that carry a wide variety of Asian goods. **Magpie Studio,** 556 Fisgard St. (☎ 604/383-1880), stocks small, intricate Chinese decorative items such as jade-and-brass-inlay rosewood boxes. **Eastern Interiors**, 572 Fisgard St. (☎ 604/385-4643), has larger furniture pieces and accessories.

CHRISTMAS ORNAMENTS

Victoria has year-round Christmas shops where you can buy ornaments and decorations ranging from intricate Victorian and Edwardian replicas to very modern creations. The largest store in town, located in a heritage building, is **The Spirit of Christmas**, 1022 Government St. (☎ 604/385-2501).

DEPARTMENT STORES/SHOPPING MALLS

The same two department stores that service Vancouver also have branches in Victoria. At **The Bay (Hudson's Bay Company),** 1701 Douglas St. (☎ 604/382-7141), you'll find camping and sports equipment and Hudson's Bay woolen point blankets as well as fashions by Tommy Hilfiger, Polo, DKNY, Ellen Tracy, Anne Klein II, and Liz Claiborne. **Eaton's,** Victoria Eaton Centre between Government and Douglas streets off Fort and View streets (☎ 604/382-7141), has a lot of boutiques carrying classic to outrageous fashions, china and crystal, kitchenware, gourmet foods, and books.

DISCOUNT SHOPPING

There are no discount shops in Victoria; hop a ferry to Vancouver (see Chapter 8).

FIRST NATIONS CRAFTS

The Cowichan bands living in the valley near Duncan are famous for their warm, durable Cowichan sweaters, which are knit with bold motifs from hand-spun raw wool. In addition to these beautiful knits, the bands make moccasins; moosehide boots; ceremonial masks; sculptures carved from argillite or soapstone; intricate basketry; bearskin rugs; and jewelry.

The gift shop and gallery at the **Native Heritage Center,** 200 Cowichan Way, Duncan (☎ 604/746-8119), is owned and operated by the Cowichan band. In addition to selling beautiful crafts, they also have an excellent selection of books and publications on First Nations history and lore. You can also watch artisans at work at this fascinating center. In town, **Cowichan Trading Ltd.,** 1328 Government St. (☎ 604/383-0321), has been dealing in crafts and clothing at this location for almost 50 years. Also in town is **Chinook Trading,** 1315 Government St. (☎ 604/ 383-7021), which has a beautiful collection of basketry, beading, and jewelry.

FASHIONS

You can purchase men's, women's, and children's woolen fashions in Victoria at great prices. **Avoca Handweavers,** 1009 Government St. (☎ 604/ 383-0433), specializes in Irish clothing, blankets, and crafts. Colorful Nova Scotia woolens can be found in between the shelves of maple syrup and hand-carved duck decoys at **James Bay Trading Co.,** 1102 Government St. (☎ 604/388-5477). **The Edinburgh Tartan Shop,** 921 Government St. (☎ 604/388-9312), caters to those who prefer sturdy woolens. For something out of the ordinary, **Carnaby Street,** 538 Yates St. (☎ 604/382-3747), carries a marvelous selection of caftans, djellabas, and other ethnic clothing as well as rare, imported textiles, jewelry, and carpets.

Outdoor gear isn't just important to have here—it's *the* style of choice in the Pacific Northwest. You can suit up at the following places: **Bosun's Locker Ltd.,** 580 Johnson St. (☎ 604/383-7774); the century-old **Jeune Bros. Great Outdoors Store,** 570 Johnson St. (☎ 604/386-8778); **Coastline Surf and Sport,** 152-560 Johnson St. (☎ 604/382-2123); **Pacific Trekking,** 1305 Government (☎ 604/388-7088); or at our favorite outfitter, **Ocean River Sports,** 1437 Store St. (☎ 604/381-4233).

FOOD

Murchie's, 1110 Government St. (☎ 604/383-3112), has a branch in Victoria where you can buy coffee, tea, and chocolates (see Chapter 8). If your taste buds crave a box of chocolate-covered tea digestives or a jar of lemon curd, then head to **Marks and Spencer,** Victoria Eaton Centre (☎ 604/386-6727), which is a branch of the time-honored British food and clothing chain.

Wah Yuen Grocery, 534 Fisgard St. (☎ 604/383-2813) is worth a visit just to take in the scents and sights of this exotic Chinese food and herb shop.

JEWELRY

You'll find unique ethnic pieces; locally made jewelry; semiprecious stones; amber; horn; seed beads; and other items to make your own creations at **Jewellations,** 542 Johnson St. (☎ 604/383-3250). Also check out the jewelry at the stores we mentioned under "First Nations Crafts," above.

PUBLIC MARKET

Market Square, 560 Johnson St. (☎ 604/386-2441), near Chinatown, was constructed from the original warehouses and shipping offices built here in the

19th century. Small shops and restaurants surround a central courtyard where live performances take place throughout the summer.

SOUVENIRS

You can bring a bit of Canada home with you, including maple syrup, salmon jerky, decals, and lapel pins, from the **James Bay Trading Co.,** 1102 Government St. (☎ 604/388-5477); or from **Canadian Impressions,** 811 Government St. (☎ 604/ 383-2641).

TOBACCO

The century-old tradition of custom-blended pipe tobacco is still maintained at **Old Morris Tobacconist Ltd.,** 1116 Government St. (☎ 604/382-4811).

TOYS

There's a wonderful selection of toys, including kites and games, for children of all ages at **Fox Glove Toys,** 162-560 Johnson St. (☎ 604/383-8852). At **East Bay,** 1889 Oak Bay Ave. (☎ 604/595-8338), you and your kids will discover a cornucopia of toys and gifts for the gardener, naturalist, hiker, astronomer, traveler, or adventurer.

WINE

The Wine Shoppe at Ocean Pointe Resort, 45 Songhees Rd. (☎ 604/360-5804), carries a great selection of Vancouver Island, Okanagan, French, and Australian wines. It is open from noon to 8pm Wednesday through Sunday.

Victoria After Dark

16

Though it's sleepy and outdoors-oriented, Victoria *does* have a few diversions to fill your evening hours. There are jazz festivals (jazz is very popular here), dance and theater productions, and concerts.

The **Community Arts Council of Greater Victoria,** 511–620 View St. (☎ 604/381-ARTS or 604/381-2787), runs a hotline to keep you informed about what's happening where in Victoria. You can buy tickets and get schedules from the **Travel InfoCentre,** 812 Wharf St. (☎ 604/382-2127). *Monday Magazine,* a weekly tabloid actually published on Thursdays, and the bimonthly *Arts Victoria* are the best quick references for information about current goings-on.

1 The Performing Arts

There are two major Victoria performance halls where theater, dance, and musical productions take place. **The Royal Theatre,** 805 Broughton St. (☎ 604/361-0820; box office 604/386-6121), was built in the early 1900s and renovated in the 1970s. It hosts concerts, dance recitals, and touring stage plays. The box office is located at the McPherson Playhouse. **The McPherson Playhouse,** 3 Centennial Sq., at Pandora Avenue and Government Street (☎ 604/386-6121), is a baroque Edwardian theater that was built in 1914 as the Pantages Vaudeville Theatre. The box office is open Monday through Saturday from 9:30am to 5:30pm, and on performance days it's also open from 6 to 8:30pm.

THEATER

Victoria's largest theatrical event is hosted by the **Intrepid Theatre Company,** 602-620 View St. (☎ 604/383-2663), which produces the annual **Victoria Fringe Festival** from late April until mid-September. Fifty alternative-performance companies from around the world perform at seven downtown venues from noon to midnight daily. Tickets for these performances are $8 or less; all proceeds go to the performers. In the last week of January, the same production company also presents the **Focus on Women Arts Festival,** featuring a variety of plays, visual arts, film, and music showcasing women artists. Tickets for this event are $12 per performance.

The **Belfry Theatre,** 1291 Gladstone St. (☎ 604/385-6815), is a nationally acclaimed theatrical group that stages five productions from October to April in a small, intimate playhouse. Dramatic works by contemporary Canadian playwrights as well as master international dramatists such as Eugene O'Neill, Harold Pinter, and Stephen Sondheim are part of their repertoire. Tickets are $16 for adults (senior and student discounts are available). The box office is open weekdays from 9am to 5pm with extended hours on performance days.

The **Kaleidoscope Theatre,** 715 Yates St. (☎ 604/475-4444), has both a critically acclaimed resident company and a touring company. Both perform plays, dances, and concerts for younger audiences.

The **Theatre Inconnu,** based in Market Square (☎ 604/380-1284), performs avant-garde material in the square's courtyard and elsewhere around town on an irregular basis.

OPERA

The **Pacific Opera Victoria,** 1316B Government St. (☎ 604/385-0222; box office 604/386-6121), presents three productions annually in September, February, and April at the McPherson Playhouse. Their repertoire ranges from light Mozart operas to Gilbert and Sullivan operettas with an occasional Tchaikovsky work such as *Eugene Onegin* thrown in for good measure. Tickets range from $15 to $52 and are available at the McPherson Playhouse box office.

The **Victoria Operatic Society,** 798 Fairview Rd. (☎ 604/381-1021), established in 1945, has year-round performances of light Broadway musicals such as *Evita, The Mikado,* and *Into the Woods* at the McPherson Playhouse. Ticket prices range from $12.50 to $19.50.

ORCHESTRAL & CHORAL MUSIC

Another big Victoria cultural event is the **Victoria International Festival,** held each year from the second week of July through the third week of August. Concerts, recitals, ballet performances, and a host of other events featuring world-renowned musicians are presented at the McPherson Playhouse, Royal Theatre, University Centre Auditorium and Recital Hall, Christ Church Cathedral, and the St. Michael's University School. The entire series subscription is $160 to $220 ($142 to $198 for seniors and students), but you can also buy individual event tickets at the McPherson Playhouse box office.

The **Victoria Symphony Orchestra,** 846 Broughton St. (☎ 604/385-9771), performs under the direction of maestro Peter McCoppin every week from August through May. The orchestra kicks off each season with its internationally acclaimed Symphony Splash—a free concert performed on a downtown barge. Summer Pops is a favorite Friday evening event at the Royal Theatre. Masterworks, Concerts for Kids, and Primetime Classics, performed at different venues, fill out their schedule during the rest of the year. Tickets are $12 for most concerts; senior, student, and group discounts are available.

DANCE

Dance recitals and full-scale performances by local and international dance troupes are scheduled throughout the year. Call the **Community Arts Council of Greater Victoria** (☎ 604/381-ARTS or 604/381-2787) to find out who's performing when you're in town.

2 The Club & Music Scene

Even though the city seems to close down at sunset, there are some good places to listen to music, to dance, and to chuckle.

COMEDY CLUBS

If you want a few laughs, go to **Stu's Comedy Feast** at the Ingy Pub, Ingraham Hotel, 2915 Douglas St. (☎ 604/385-6731). Drinks and admission are each $3 to $5. Stu's laughs it up daily from 7pm to 1am.

JAZZ, BLUES & FOLK CLUBS

The **Victoria Jazz Society** (☎ 604/388-4423) is the local hotline listing jazz events taking place throughout the year. **Harpo's,** 15 Bastion Sq. (☎ 604/385-5333), is Victoria's intimate waterfront venue for high-profile performers. The Joanne Brackeen Trio, Koko Taylor, the Oyster Band, plus popular reggae and rock bands play here. Admission depends on who's playing but generally ranges from $3 to $15. Drinks run $3 and up. Harpo's is open Monday through Saturday from 8:30pm to 2am.

Jazz is hot in Victoria. The **TerrifVic Dixieland Jazz Festival** (☎ 604/381-5277) takes place at venues all over Victoria in late April. Bands from New Orleans, England, and Latin America perform swing, dixie, honky-tonk, fusion, and improv before devoted audiences. The **International Jazz Fest** (☎ 604/386-2441) is a big June event in the Market Square courtyard. Swing, bebop, fusion, and improv are presented at noon-hour and evening performances. **Sunfest** is the end-of-summer jazz festival held on the third weekend of August at Market Square.

Hermann's Dixieland Inn, 753 View St., near Blanshard St. (☎ 604/388-9166), is regarded locally as the best jazz venue in town. This low-lit supper club with framed photos and posters plastered all over its walls specializes in Dixieland but occasionally features fusion and blues bands. It's open Monday from 5pm to midnight, Tuesday through Friday from 11:30am to 12:30am, and Saturday from 4pm to 12:30am. Entrées cost $9.95 to $11.95. Drinks are $3, and there's usually no cover charge.

Local rock bands perform at **The Forge,** in the Strathcona Hotel, 919 Douglas St. (☎ 604/383-7137). It's a big, noisy venue that attracts blue-collar workers and hip University of Victoria students. The $3 to $5 cover charge and $3 drinks make it a reasonable place to boogie down nightly.

DANCE CLUBS

There are a few canned dance track and singles clubs here. Most are open Monday through Saturday until 2am, Sunday until midnight. **Merlin's,** 1208 Wharf St. (☎ 604/381-2331), is a waterfront club with theme nights (including male dancers and ladies-only nights). It attracts a cool 20-something crowd. There's a $3 cover after 9:30pm on weekends, and drinks are about the same price. Events change constantly, so call for information.

Pier 42, 1605 Store St., in the basement of Swans Pub (☎ 604/381-7437), is a Top 40 club with a very congenial local crowd that likes to dance. It's open Wednesday through Sunday from 8pm. There's no cover charge, and drinks are around $3.

The Drawing Room Dance Hall, on the top floor of 751 View St. (☎ 604/920-7798), is open Tuesday through Saturday nights. They feature funk jazz, indy jazz, rock jazz, and a local house band on Wednesday. As of this writing, the Drawing Room seems to be the upscale place of choice for the young and beautiful. Drinks and admission are each $4.

Sweetwaters Niteclub, 27-570 Store St. (☎ 604/383-7844), is a basement singles club featuring classic tracks and top 40s. It's open Tuesday through Saturday; an admission charge of $3 is charged on weekends only. Drinks are around $3.50.

3 The Bar Scene

As in Vancouver, Victoria's bar scene is closely linked with food because of the liquor laws. There are three exceptionally good watering holes in town. **Garrick's Head Pub,** 64 Bastion Sq. in the Bedford Regency Hotel (☎ 604/384-6835), serves pub fare such as shepherd's pie, fish and chips, bangers and mash but without the chain-restaurant prices or glitz of neighboring so-called pubs. You can enjoy a meal and a pint for less than $7.95. They're open from 11am to 11pm.

Spinnaker's Brew Pub, 308 Catherine St. (☎ 604/386-BREW or 604/ 386-2739), offers ales and lagers from its own microbrewery. Overlooking Victoria Harbour on the west side of the Songhees Point Development, its bar draws local old-timers as well as smart, young professionals. You can even take a brewery tour if you call ahead. They sometimes have live music. Meals start at $5.50; ales cost $4 and up. Spinnaker's is open daily from 11am to 11pm. Take bus 23 to Esquimalt Rd.

Swans Pub, 506 Pandora Ave. (☎ 604/361-3310), is part of Swans Hotel, which is in a beautifully converted 1913 feed warehouse across from the Johnson Street Bridge and the E&N Rail Station. This is the hottest night spot in town for Victoria's young professionals. The adjoining cafe with a wraparound sidewalk-level greenhouse serves entreés priced from $9 to $18. Drinks are around $3.50. They're open daily from 11am to 2am.

4 The Gay & Lesbian Scene

The scene here is small and intimate but friendly. After having cocktails and dinner at **Met Bistro** (see Chapter 12 for dining review), try **Rumors,** 1325 Government St. (☎ 604/385-0566). This is where Victoria's gays, bisexuals, lesbians, and transvestites go to hang out, dance, and socialize. They're open daily 9pm until 2am (but call ahead to check). There's no cover charge. Drinks start at $2.75, and there are nightly drink specials.

5 Gambling Casinos

Victoria has two casinos that, like those in Vancouver, cater mainly to patrons who want to play blackjack, roulette, sic-bo, red dog (diamond dog), and Caribbean stud poker. **Casino Victoria,** 716 Courtney St. (☎ 604/380-3998), and the **Great Canadian Casino,** 3366 Douglas St. (☎ 604/384-2614), are both open from 6pm to 2am. They don't offer floor shows or any other side entertainment—just genteel gambling.

Side Trips from Vancouver & Victoria

17

After traveling less than two hours from Vancouver by ferry, rail, or car, you will find yourself amid the best nature has to offer. Our favorite getaways from Vancouver include trips to Whistler/ Blackcomb, one of North America's premier ski resorts, and to laid-back Bowen Island.

From Victoria, we like to take day hikes in the majestic provincial park less than one-half hour away by car; or stop in for a glass of wine at one of the wineries just off Hwy. 1 as we make our way north along the island highway toward the cities of Duncan and Nanaimo. The first is famous for its raw wool sweaters, the second for its proximity to Vancouver Island's north and west coasts—both are great places for outdoor recreation.

1 Whistler & Squamish

Whistler is one North America's most popular winter destinations— especially with west coast and Canadian residents. This world-class ski resort, located 75 miles north of Vancouver on Highway 99, has the west's longest alpine, heli-skiing, and snowboard season: Blackcomb Mountain has year-round glacier skiing. The regular season (including excellent Nordic and backcountry skiing) starts on the last week of November and ends in late May. How good is the skiing? This year, *Ski, Snow Country* and *Powder* magazines named Whistler North America's best ski resort for the third consecutive year. It surpasses Vail, Colorado and Banff for quality, variety, and price.

The fun doesn't end there. During the summer, glacier skiers stand in line with hikers, backpackers, paragliders, horseback riders, and mountain bikers to take the lifts to choice alpine trails on the lower elevations. Kayakers, canoeists, and campers traverse the wilderness below the towering peaks. Restaurants, nightclubs, and shops attract not only outdoor enthusiasts, but city dwellers who drive up on weekends to get a breath of fresh mountain air.

ESSENTIALS

You can drive up the scenic **Sea-to-Sky Highway** (Highway 99) to Whistler, but there are more interesting ways to get here.

The **Royal Hudson Steam Train,** run by B.C. Rail (☎ 604/ 984-5246), is a 1930s steam locomotive that chugs its way up Howe Sound to the logging town of Squamish through forests, mountains, and glaciers in about two hours. You can take this spectacular, nostalgic ride from June through mid-September from Wednesday to Sunday. The train leaves North Vancouver daily at 10am and returns at 4pm. Bring your camera: There's an observation car for picture-taking. Round-trip fares, which include lunch on the way up and tea on return in the parlor car, are $35 for adults, $30.50 for seniors and students, and $10 for children.

B.C. Rail also operates the **Whistler Explorer,** which follows a series of rushing rivers, deep lakes, and canyons to Whistler. Lunch and afternoon tea are included in the round-trip price of $88. This train runs from mid-May through mid-October; it departs from North Vancouver at 8:30am and returns at 6:10pm.

The **Whistler Travel InfoCentre,** 2097 Lake Placid Road, Whistler (☎ 604/ 932-5528), is open year-round. Besides having a wealth of travel information and the best map of the area, the staff can help you find last-minute accommodations and tickets to special events, such as music festivals.

WHAT TO SEE & DO

The mountain resort offers hiking, golfing, fishing, river-rafting, horseback riding, canoeing, and kayaking areas during the summer months and the world's best skiing in the winter and spring. If that isn't enough, there are also plenty of shops and restaurants to explore. If you plan to stay for more than a couple of days, you might want to consider renting a condo or camping in Nairn Falls, between Whistler and Pemberton. Eating out can get expensive, so if you're camping or taking a condo, you'll find plenty of provisions at the Nester's Village grocery store and the IGA supermarket in Whistler Village.

There are numerous music and art festivals scheduled in the village, including the **Whistler Country and Blues Festival** in July; the **Whistler Classical Music Festival** and the concert series held by the **Vancouver Symphony Orchestra,** both in August; the **Whistler Fall for Jazz Festival** in September; and **Oktoberfest.**

CYCLING   The ski trails are open for mountain biking throughout the summer, and there are numerous competitions as well. Tour cyclists take to the trails following Highway 99 up to Pemberton and Mount Currie. You can rent a mountain bike from the following places: **Blackcomb Ski and Sports,** located at the base of the mountain in the Daylodge (☎ 604/938-7788); **Trax and Trails,** in the Chateau Whistler Hotel (☎ 604/938-2017); and **McCoo's Too,** in Whistler Village Centre (☎ 604/938-9954).

GOLF   **Chateau Whistler Golf Club,** at the base of Blackcomb Mountain (☎ 604/938-2095; pro shop 604/938-2092), was designed by Robert Trent Jones. The first few holes feature a gradual 300-foot ascent over cascading creeks and granite rock faces. Midcourse, there's a panoramic view of the Coast Mountains. **Nicklaus North at Whistler** (☎ 604/938-9898) is five minutes north of the Village on Green Lake. The mountain views on this par-71 course are spectacular. The driving range was scheduled to open by summer 1996.

MOUNTAINEERING   One of the ascents most highly recommended by local mountaineers is **The Chief,** a stark wall that looms above Squamish at the head of Howe Sound. Another favorite rock-climbing spot is **Smoke Bluffs.** Backpacking trips in and around this area are organized by the **Federation of Mountain Clubs of B.C.,** 1367 W. Broadway (☎ 604/737-3053).

RIVER RAFTING   White-water rafting down the Squamish or Elaho Rivers is incredibly exhilarating. Aiton's Alley and Steamroller rapids await you and your rubber raft! A riverside barbecue lunch is your reward for shooting the rapids. If you want to experience the thrill of this sport for the first time, try paddle rafting on the Green River instead. **Whistler River Adventures,** Box 202, Whistler V0N 1B0 (☎ 604/932-3532), has package trips that include equipment and ground transport for $38 to $104.

SKIING Skiers take note: **Whistler Mountain** has a 5,006-foot vertical and 100 marked runs. The mountain is serviced by one high-speed gondola, eight chairs, and five other lifts and tows. Helicopter skiing makes another 100-plus runs accessible on nearby glaciers. **Blackcomb Mountain** has a 5,280-foot vertical and 100 marked runs. It's serviced by nine chairs and three other lifts and tows. Heli-skiing is at its best up here. Year-round skiing is possible on **Blackcomb Glacier** (bring plenty of sunblock). If you find yourself up there on a clear summer Saturday night, then join Blackcomb's weekly guided stargazing and moonrise expeditions.

A full-day lift ticket to either Blackcomb or Whistler Mountains is $49 for adults ($35 for seniors, $38 for children over 12, $21 for children 12 and under) and a dual-mountain pass—good for both—is only $51 ($37 for seniors, $46 for children over 12, $28 for children 12 and under). Ski rental packages are available at numerous village sports shops, some major hotels, and the base lodges at both mountains. A complete alpine or snowboard rental package runs about $39, while Nordic, skate, and telemark packages cost between $13 and $20.

Whistler Resort itself has cross-country trails on both the Whistler Golf Course and Chateau Whistler Golf Course. Just off Nancy Greene Road, you'll find the ticket booth and trail head for **Lost Lakes** which has expert, intermediate, beginner, and lit night trails for nordic skiers and ski-skaters. A day pass costs $9, and lessons are available for $30 an hour. **Mad River Nordic Centre,** south of Whistler, has 38 miles of groomed trails equipped with warming huts.

If you want to ski some serious verticals, contact **Whistler Backcountry Adventures** (☎ 604/938-1410), which arranges both heli-skiing and heli-fishing trips.

For more information, contact the **Whistler Resort Association,** 4010 Whistler Way, Whistler (☎ 604/932-3928 or 800/944-7853). For **snow reports,** call 604/687-6761 for Whistler, 604/932-4211 for Blackcomb.

WILDLIFE WATCHING An annual January bald-eagle count takes place between Brackendale and Squamish. In 1994, 3,700 bald eagles were counted by observers watching the eagles as they gathered to feed on salmon. There is an abundance of wildlife here. Rafting expeditions to this exciting spot can be booked through **Canadian Outback Adventure Company,** 206-1110 Hamilton St., Vancouver (☎ 604/688-7206), or **Rivers and Ocean Unlimited Expeditions,** 206–1110 Hamilton St., Vancouver (☎ 604/685-3732).

WHERE TO STAY & DINE

There are more than 1,500 hotel and luxury condominium units as well as dozens restaurants and shops ranging from chic to funky in the village area. We recommend the following two places:

✪ **Canadian-Pacific Chateau Whistler,** 4599 Chateau Blvd., Whistler V0N 1B4 (☎ 604/938-8000), is a 342-room Upper Village hotel that has sterling service and excellent accommodations right next to the Blackcomb ski lift. The two-story executive suites are amazing. The rooms and smaller suites all feature comfortable sitting areas and wonderful views. The lobby resembles a hunting chalet with rustic wood and country antiques. Ski and bike storage as well as a full-service spa and health club are located downstairs. The village's best buffet-style brunch is served daily amid a fascinating collection of bird houses.

Rooms at the Chateau Whistler range from $125 to $225 per night double or triple. Off-season discounts are offered throughout the summer.

Durlacher Hof, Box 1125, 7055 Nesters Rd. V0N 1B0 (☎ 604/932-1924), is a lovely Swiss mountain chalet run by Peter and Erika Durlacher. As their guest, you will be totally spoiled with the grace and charm of excellent European service. Rooms feature goose-down duvets; a choice of private baths, Jacuzzis, or showers; and mountain-view balconies. The fireside cocktail lounge, sauna, and whirlpool are welcome comforts after a day on the slopes. Dinners here on selected evenings are often prepared by a celebrated guest chef.

Double occupancy room rates range from $85 to $150 and include a full breakfast.

If you prefer to have all of the comforts of home including a full kitchen and dining area, then consider renting a studio, one or two bedroom condo suite at the **Whistler Resort & Club** on Nita Lake or a trailside house on the slopes of Whistler Mountain. Rates vary from $75 to $150 during the spring and fall and from $120 to $240 during peak ski season weeks. To make a reservation at this peaceful complex, contact Rainbow Retreats Accommodations, 2129 Lake Placid Rd., Whistler B.C., Canada V0N 1B0 (☎ 604/932-2343).

Pick your favorite Vancouver restaurant, and it probably has a branch in Whistler. You'll find an abundance of fine-dining establishments, and not all of them are connected to hotels or inns.

Citta Bistro, in Whistler Village Square (☎ 604/932-4177), appeals to a young, casual crowd. This locals' hangout is the best deal in town. The pizzas, burgers, homemade soups, and crisp, fresh salads are served in tasty, healthy portions, for reasonable prices. It's also the best place in town for people-watching. **Monk's Grill,** near the Blackcomb ski lifts (☎ 604/932-9677), has spectacular mountain views. The menu includes everything from fresh seafood and pasta dishes to lobster and Alberta prime rib. You can sit in their formal dining area or in their casual lounge and outdoor patios.

Heading north toward Mount Currie, you'll come to the **Spirit Circle Art, Craft, and Tea Company,** on Route 99 (☎ 604/894-6336), where owner Deanna Pilling serves a huge all-day Canadian breakfast for $6.25 and lunch specials starting at $4.95. You can't miss this wood building with red-and-black carved doors. You eat surrounded by a collection of First Nations art and crafts.

2 Bowen Island

In the 1930s and 1940s, weekending Vancouver couples used to romance their way to Bowen Island (known as the "Happy Isle") aboard the *Lady Alexandra* and follow the popular big-band orchestras of the day up to British Columbia's largest dance pavilion. This lovely island off Horseshoe Bay is still a great place to get away from it all and enjoy historic walks, a brewery tour, hiking paths, and beaches. There are a number of artists, writers, as well as baby boomers who have taken up residence on this 36-square-mile, forested island.

ESSENTIALS

Whether you're on foot or bike or driving a car, the only way to get to Bowen Island is to take a pleasant 20-minute ride on the **B.C. Ferry** (☎ 604/669-1211) from Horseshoe Bay, near West Vancouver. Ferries leave hourly. Passengers pay $4.25 round-trip. Your car pays another $15.50 to join you.

Once you get off the ferry, turn right to reach the renovated red building that once housed the Union Steamship Company and now serves as the summertime drop-in **tourist center and gas station,** which is open 9am to 5pm daily. (They don't have a phone or address, but are easy to find.) You can pick up a copy of *Undercurrent*, the weekly paper covering island events, and a map.

WHAT TO SEE & DO

Take a stroll through town to the site of the **old dance pavilion** and the old **Union Steamship Company** rental cottages near the ferry landing. For an easy hike, you can take to the woods via the trails in **Crippen Regional Park.** When you get off the ferry, take the first right and turn and walk a short distance down the road to the entrance. If you're up for a magnificent view of the surrounding islands, then hike up to **Mount Gardiner.** You can also go for a refreshing swim at **Killarney Lake** or at **Bowen Bay's public beach.**

If you're in the mood for a true Canadian experience, then take a tour of the **Bowen Island Brewing Company** (☎ 604/947-0822), a microbrewery that produces the award-winning ales. After all, as author Stephen Beaumont commented in his *Great Canadian Beer Guide*: "Along with back bacon, winter, and hockey, beer practically defines Canada." Tour hours vary, but if you call ahead they're open seven days a week.

WHERE TO STAY

If you become enamored of the beauty of this happy isle, then stay overnight and see why so many couples over the years have loved escaping city life by coming to this spot. Contact **Bowen Island Bed and Breakfast,** 981 Grafton Rd., Bowen Island B.C., Canada V0N 1G0 (☎ 604/947-2013). There are three rooms in this bed-and-breakfast run by Cindy and Ron Burrows. All have private baths. Rates are $75 to $85. A garden, guest lounge, library, games, barbecue, pool, and hot tub are available to guests.

WHERE TO DINE

When you get hungry, stop in at **Caroline's Deli,** Trunk Rd. (☎ 604/947-2907) for a sandwich. Or if you want a full meal and a pint of local ale, stroll down to the ferry landing to **Doc Morgan's Inn,** Snug Cove (☎ 604/947-0808). Their plain, simple and hearty menu includes burgers, sandwiches, pasta dishes, and on weekends they cook up a juicy prime rib roast.

3 Goldstream Provincial Park

The great natural beauty of south-central Vancouver Island is perhaps best seen in Goldstream Provincial Park (☎ 604/387-4363), just 20 minutes north of Victoria on the Island Highway (also called Highway 1 or Route 19). This majestic and tranquil setting was once a bustling goldrush site. Park trails take you past abandoned mine shafts and tunnels, plus 600-year-old rainforest stands of Douglas fir, red cedar, indigenous yew, and arbutus. In the autumn, an annual chum salmon run draws bald eagles and other spectators. Every January, a bald eagle count is held here; in 1995, 97 of these magnificent birds were spotted. The **Freeman King Visitor Centre** (☎ 604/ 478-9414) offers guided walks, talks, displays, and programs throughout the year.

While the E&N Railroad runs through this magnificent wonderland on its way to Nanaimo, you'll want to spend some time here and do some walking to really explore the park in depth.

WHERE TO STAY & DINE NEARBY

✪ The Aerie

600 Ebedora Lane, P.O. Box 108, Malahat, B.C. V0R 2L0. ☎ **604/743-7115.** Fax 604/ 743-4766. 24 suites. A/C TV TEL. Apr 15–Oct 10 $165–$230 double, $270–$360 suite; Oct 11–Apr 14 $145–$190 double, $240–$300 suite. Rates include full breakfast. AE, MC, V. Free parking. Take Highway 1 to the Spectacle Lake turn-off; take the first right and follow the winding driveway up.

Nestled high above the Malahat summit is a little bit of heaven, complete with an incredible restaurant. In this elegant Mediterranean villa, each hideaway suite has a large hand-crafted bed, a sumptuous bathroom, an indoor Jacuzzi, a wet-bar and fridge, and a fireplace in front of a white leather sofa. Most of the suites have decks positioned to ensure complete privacy. Though it's the kind of exclusive opulent get-away you'd expect to see featured on *Lifestyles of the Rich and Famous* (in fact, it's appeared three times on the TV show), there's no pretension here.

Dining/Entertainment: The wonderful in-house restaurant, with a 24-carat gold-leaf ceiling, an open-hearth fireplace, and views of Spectacle Lake, serves three meals each day, but is only open to the public for dinner (served 5 to 10pm); reservations are required. Grilled tiger prawns in a ginger-lime cream is just one overture in master chef Leo Schuster's dining symphony, served with impeccable service. A masterfully prepared halibut filet can be accompanied by a selection from the region's best wine list. A luscious orange cappuccino mousse topped with a white Belgian chocolate sauce, plus an excellent brandy and Kona coffee completes your experience. Main courses run $26.75 to $29; a seven-course menu is $55.

Facilities: Five acres of private walking trails, a helipad, a heated indoor pool, outdoor hot tub, tennis courts, full spa treatments, and an outdoor wedding chapel.

4 Duncan

The Island Highway continues north from the park, and in about 30 miles you'll reach the verdant Cowhican Valley and the city of Duncan.

You can even do some wine tasting as you travel north from Victoria to Duncan. There are five wineries located between Mill Bay and Duncan that offer tours and tastings; all are just off Highway 1. **Merridale Estate Cidery,** 1230 Merridale Rd., Mill Bay (☎ 604/743-4293), conducts tours Monday through Saturday from 10:30am to 4:30pm.

Cherry Point Vineyards, 840 Cherry Point Rd., Cobble Hill (☎ 604/743-1272) provides tours by appointment only, as does **Venturi-Schulze Vineyards,** 4235 Trans-Canada Highway, Cowichan Stn. (☎ 604/743-5630). **Blue Grouse Vineyards,** 4365 Blue Grouse Rd., Cowichan Stn. (☎ 604/743-3834), has tours on Wednesday plus Friday through Sunday from 11am to 5pm; and **Vigneti Zanatta Vineyards,** 5039 Marshall Rd., Duncan (☎ 604/748-2338), conducts tours on Saturday and Sunday from 1 to 4pm.

ESSENTIALS

The **Duncan Travel InfoCentre** is located at 381 Trans-Canada Highway (☎ 604/ 746-4636).

EXPLORING THE TOWN

The Cowichan Valley tribes living near Duncan are famous for their warm, durable sweaters knit with bold motifs from hand-spun raw wool. Visiting the **Native Heritage Center,** 200 Cowichan Way (☎ 604/746-8119), is a rich cultural experience where you can observe master and apprentice carvers at work on totem poles and ceremonial masks, have a native meal, or join in their summer song and dance festival. Shoppers will find a wide assortment of authentic Cowichan sweaters and jewelry in the two gift shops, as well as books, serigraphic prints, handcrafted ceremonial masks, replica totem poles, and other items. It's open daily from 9:30am to 5pm; admission is $7 adults, $6.15 seniors and children.

Judy Hill Gallery and Gifts, 22 Station St. (☎ 604/746-6663), represents important Native Canadian artists such as Robert Davison, Danny Dennis, David Neel, and Roy Vickers.

Duncan is called the City of Totem Poles. Its Totem Poles Project, begun in 1985, consists of 41 outdoor poles that stand in front of the various businesses that commissioned them; they're striking works of art to commemorate the city's early heritage. Just follow the yellow footprints painted on the sidewalks to take a complete self-guided tour.

The **Cowichan River** in Duncan has a 19-mile-long fishing path from the Robertson Road clubhouse to Cowichan Lake where you'll find great year-round catches like brown, cutthroat, rainbow trout, and steelhead. Some sections of the river bank are designated as fly fishing only. To get there, drive west from Duncan along Highway 18 towards Cowichan Lake.

WHERE TO DINE NEARBY

⑨ Six Mile Pub

494 Island Hwy., View Royal. ☎ **604/478-3121.** Main courses $4.50–$7.50. ER, MC, V. Daily 11:30am–2pm and 6–9pm. Pub Mon–Sat 11am–1am, Sun 11am–midnight. PUB GRUB.

This 1855 heritage pub was named the Parson's Bridge Hotel when it first opened. The site's current 1898 building has a loyal local clientele who come for both the atmosphere and the classic British pub dinner specials—all seasoned with fresh herbs from the pub's own garden. You can enjoy the warm indoor ambience of the fireside room, which boasts an oak bar and other classically British touches or the beautiful scenery on the outdoor patio.

5 Nanaimo

Nanaimo is a good base from which to explore Vancouver Island's north and west coasts. Mount Sicker's coal and copper deposits originally attracted the Hudson Bay Company to Nanaimo, and you'll find some abandoned mines here, as well as a couple of museums documenting the company's history in town.

ESSENTIALS

VISITOR INFORMATION   The **Nanaimo Travel InfoCentre** is at 266 Bryden St. (☎ 604/754-8474 or 800/663-7337).

GETTING THERE   It's an easy drive from Victoria along the Island Highway.

Air BC (☎ 604/663-9826), **Canadian Air International** (☎ 800/426-7000 in the U.S. or 800/363-7530 in Canada), and **Horizon Air** (☎ 800/547-9308) all have regularly scheduled air service between Vancouver and Nanaimo, cutting travel time between the two to about 45 minutes including the drive into Nanaimo.

B.C. Ferries (☎ 604/386-3431 or 604/656-0757) operates a ferry that runs from Horseshoe Bay in West Vancouver to Nanaimo. The **Mid-Island Express** operates between Tsawwassen (south of Vancouver) to Namaimo.

The **VIA Rail/Esquimalt & Nanaimo Railway** stops once daily at Nanaimo on its route from Victoria to Courtenay in the central island area. The trip takes about two hours.

Maverick Coach Lines (☎ 604/380-1611) operates between the Victoria Depot and Nanaimo. They are located at 710 Douglas St. (☎ 604/385-4411) directly behind the Empress Hotel.

GETTING AROUND Since Nanaimo centers around its waterfront and the Departure Bay ferry terminal, you won't have trouble walking around the city itself. The city bus (☎ 604/390-4531) which maintains a hub at the Gordon Street Exchange, does offer you alternate transport to some areas around town. The fare is $1.25 and schedules are available at the Travel InfoCentre.

SPECIAL EVENTS The third weekend in July brings the **Nanaimo Marine Festival and Bathtub Race,** an annual 34-mile Bathtub Race from the beaches of Nanaimo to Vancouver's Kitsilano, with dozens of homemade craft gliding across the strait.

The Native Heritage Center (☎ 604/746-8119) offers **Feast and Legends,** a program of song, dance, and storytelling along with a full buffet dinner every Friday in July and August.

EXPLORING THE TOWN & ENVIRONS

The **Bastion City Wildlife Cruise,** 1000 Stewart Ave. (☎ 604/753-2852), takes you on a $2^1/2$ hour tour of the surrounding waters to view eagles, sea lions, and Gabriola Island's sandstone cliffs. Reservations are required. Cruises depart Wednesday through Sunday at 1:30pm, early February through early April (Thursday through Sunday mid-June through late September), for $20 adults, $18 seniors, and $11 children ages 5–15.

You can rent canoes or kayaks at **North Island Water Sports,** 2755 Departure Bay Rd. (☎ 604/758-2488). Single kayaks rent for approximately $40 per day ($75 for a double). **Kona Bud's Beach Rentals,** 2855 Departure Bay Rd. (☎ 604/758-2911), also rents canoes and kayaks for about $10 per hour.

You can plunge off a 140-foot trestle at **The Bungy Zone** (☎ 604/753-5867), North America's only legally sanctioned bridge jump. Leaping high over the Nanaimo River from a specially constructed steel trestle bridge, your first leap of the day will run you $95 (the second is $75). You can even choose how far into the icy mountain waters you will go. Open daily from 10am to 4:30pm, year round. For a small admission fee (around $2–$4), you can be a wide-eyed observer. Reservations are recommended June through August. The Bungy Zone is located 41 miles north of Victoria or 8 miles south of Nanaimo, off Highway 1. There's a free shuttle service from both Victoria and Nanaimo.

The Bastion

266 Bryden St. ☎ **604/754-1631.** Admission by donation. Mon–Fri 10am–6pm. Closed Sept 16–June 30.

The Hudsons Bay Company built this 1853 fort to protect early settlers who came to the area in search of coal and copper riches. A noontime ceremonial gun salute is conducted by staff dressed in period costume.

Nanaimo Centennial Museum

100 Cameron St. ☎ **604/753-1821.** Admission $2 adults; $1.50 seniors and students; 50¢ children under 12. May–Aug Mon–Fri 9am–6pm, Sat–Sun 10am–6pm; rest of the year Tues–Sat 9am–4pm.

The city's small museum has exhibits on local history: the heritage of the indigenous peoples, the arrival of the Spanish, and the discovery of the area's coal resources (there's a restored miner's cottage).

A SIDE TRIP TO NEWCASTLE ISLAND

Newcastle Island, just off Nanaimo, is an ideal place to hike, cycle, or camp. Trails around the island lead you to quiet beaches, caves, and caverns.

To get there, take the ferry (☎ 604/753-5141; off-season 604/387-4363) that leaves from the wharf behind Mafeo-Sutton Park's Civic Arena (just north of downtown) daily between May and October with almost hourly departures from 10am to 7:30pm. It even runs on pleasant weekends throughout the rest of the year. The 15-minute trip costs $4 round-trip.

You may want to take a bike over to the island and ride along the Shoreline Trail. You can rent a mountain bike at **Chain Reaction,** 4 Victoria Crescent, Nanaimo (☎ 604/754-3309), for about $12 per day, and it will cost an extra $1.50 to take it across on the ferry.

Newcastle Island Provincial Marine Park, 2930 Trans-Canada Hwy. (☎ 604/387-4363), was once a bustling island community. Two Salish villages were here before the 1840s, and the island was also a Japanese fishing settlement until 1941. The Canadian Pacific Steamship Company had a 1930s pleasure resort—dance pavilion, tea house, and picnic areas—on the island's southern tip. Now, people come to hike, cycle, and camp. Mallard Lake Trail leads through the forested interior toward a freshwater lake while the Shoreline Trail crosses steep sandstone cliffs, sandy gravel beaches, caves, caverns, and a great eagle-spotting perch—Giovando Lookout.

WHERE TO STAY

Carey House Bed & Breakfast

750 Arbutus Ave., Nanaimo, B.C. V9S 5E5. ☎ **604/753-3601.** 3 rms. $45 double; $50 basement suite. Rates include full breakfast. No credit cards. Take bus no. 3 two stops to Townsite Road, and take a right on Arbutus Avenue. Complimentary ferry pick up.

This centrally located inn in a residential area has an unfussy atmosphere that lets you quietly unwind. The single and double rooms share a bathroom, while the basement has its own. A TV room, garden, and library are also available for your use. A huge English breakfast gets you going.

WHERE TO DINE

Dinghy Dock Pub

Protection Island Dock. ☎ **604/753-2373.** Main courses $4.95–$11. MC, V. Sun–Thurs 5–10pm; Fri–Sat 5pm–midnight. Take the Protection Island ferry (☎ 604/753-8244). BURGERS/PIZZA.

Burgers, pizzas, or Cajun-style blackened halibut burgers are served up in this very casual local pub, which gently rocks on Protection Island's floating dock.

Index

*For more information, see specific regional indexes.